Me, My

I0161023

TORSK

And

GOD

The USS Torsk is a floating museum in the Inner Harbor of Baltimore, Md.

Author

Lynn Zack Wardlaw

For more about the author; www.lynnzwardlaw.com

Copyright 2014 - Lynn Z. Wardlaw – Savannah, Ga.

Published by: WARDLAW PUBLISHING - Savannah, Ga.

DEDICATION

This book is dedicated to the crew of the U.S.S.TORSK that served during 1957, 1958 and 1959. GOD and the U.S. Navy directed my passage into manhood.

The crew, as well as pictures that are pertinent to this time period, are available at the website; [www.usstorsk.org]

Thanks to: JAMES B. SICKEL, [PH.D. Emory 1976] Emeritus Professor Murray State University, for his detailed review and editorial suggestions. Thanks to: MAC MCCORMICK , Chief Data Processing Technician, U.S. Navy, retired, for his technical assistance. Thanks to: LARRY "SKI" SIBISKI, member of the Torsk Volunteer Association, for his support and encouragement.

CLAIMER – DISCLAIMER

The following book is true. The names may or may not be the actual names. It is not necessary to protect the innocent, no one is innocent, and then again, no one is guilty.

The dates are accurate, according to the deck logs of the U. S. S. Torsk SS423, obtained from the National Archives.

There is no fabrication of incidents or instances in this book. There is no need for any.

The rhetoric in this book may not be precise due to the passage of 54 years. Some phrases are exactly as quoted, some are formed to deliver the occurrence as I remember it.

The language in this book has been toned down to make for pleasant reading. The foul language that is in this book, is there because, that is what was said.

If you, as a reader, are offended by the reference of GOD, then don't read the book.

PREFACE

It's been over fifty-four years since I served on the U.S.S. Torsk SS 423, but she has never left my mind or my dreams. Friends, family and "Divine Inspiration" have encouraged me to write this book about my active duty tour that spanned over two years of my eight years of total Naval Reserve Service.

I wish we could go back to that time in our past, commonly called "The Glorious Fifties," when things were just plain good! Life was not nearly as complicated as now, and we all revered GOD and Country. Patriotism was the "in thing". Young men had to obligate themselves for service to their country and willingly did so. It was when I became a man. GOD and the U.S. Navy shaped me into the man I am today.

I received an invitation to return to my Torsk in October of 2012. I spent a long weekend on board the "Valiant Old Gal." I was blessed with working with "The Torsk Volunteer Association," a group of dedicated people from all over the country that devote time and money to loving and maintaining the Torsk, far above the tourist and Museums expectations. They are intent on keeping the Torsk's soul alive, as she lies in Baltimore's Inner Harbor.

I scheduled a visit to the National Archives in College Park, Maryland while in route to my Torsk. I obtained copies of the ship's logs.

The Torsk now rides much higher in the water and sports a set of garish shark's teeth under her brow. The Navy grey and black paint are separated by sharp lines. I noticed these things because I knew her in her prime. In her day, she sat low in the water, her saddle tanks well below the water line. The grey paint covered the boat as seen from the surface and the black paint covered the deck and structure visible from the air. The two paints faded into each other with much subtlety.

She was a picture of stealth and a wonderful old girl that took everything that came her way with dignity and ability that often made us look good, in spite of ourselves.

I spent my weekend working on the sound powered telephone system, under the supervision of Larry Sibiski, Ski, for short. When we finished we had all but two stations fully operational. It felt good to bring a little more of the Torsk soul back to life.

On a Saturday morning, I was sitting in the crews mess, working on the SPT. My back was to the corridor that ran through the boat. Groups of tourists were coming through at various intervals. I was engrossed in my work as Chuck Weaver came in with a group. Any group was lucky to have Chuck, a Torsk vet, as a guide.

As I worked, I became intensely aware of this group. I can't explain why, so I'll simply tell you as it happened. I glanced over my right shoulder and caught the eye of an attractive blonde. She was fiftyish, petite and dressed much too nice to be touring a submarine. Chuck reached a breathing point in his narration.

Now please don't misunderstand what happens next. I am a devout Christian and happily married man, but I felt an intense awareness of this woman. Fifty years fell away, that young brazen sailor of twenty was back.

I slammed my pliers on the table top with a loud crack and loudly stated. "It's not fair! I sit here all morning working and you guys get to see all the pretty women, I don't even get to see 'em walk by!" I quickly glanced at the lady and to my relief she smiled.

Everyone laughed and Chuck explained this was my first visit back in fifty years and I didn't know any better. We all had a good laugh and the group moved on.

As I returned to my work, I heard a meek "Pssst!" I looked down the corridor and there was the lady. She smiled ever so slightly, looked straight ahead and moved toward me with a nice, but not too nice, walk. It was a pleasure to watch. She stopped and timidly smiled.

I said. "Thanks - I needed that."

Her eyes welled with tears and she softly whispered, as she leaned to kiss my cheek. "No! – I needed it more!" She turned and was gone to rejoin her group.

I dared not look her way. "Man!" I gotta write this book!

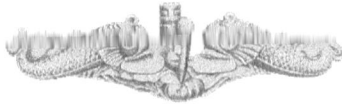

INDEX

CHAPTER I

HOME

"HUUP –TUU – TREEP – FO – TREEP -- FO – TREEP – FO!"   Renny's voice was loud and clear as he called cadence in the classic manner of a marine drill instructor.   He marched two strides ahead and one stride to the right of thirty-two reservists from Savannah, Georgia's Naval Reserve Training Center.

"HUUP –TUU – TREEP – FO –TREEP – FO!"   His lilting cadence gave clear proof of his ability and resolve.   Renny had requested permission to form a drill team at our reserve unit and Commander Lambright had given approval. Renny had asked me to help him.

Renny Painter and I were friends through high school. I was a year ahead of him, but we bonded, I suppose, because we rode the same school bus and had a rather lengthy trip each day. I lived on Wilmington Island and Renny was a "Tybee Island Bum." This was not an insult; every kid in Savannah wanted to live at "The Beach."

Chief McKutchen was our driver and also the Tybee Island Police Chief.   I finished high school in 1955, but joined the Naval Reserve in 1954 before my senior year. I would tell Renny, as we rode the bus home, about our weekly drills, boot camp and my cruise to St John N.B.   I liked to think I had some influence on his decision to join in 1955. We both were intensely devoted to high school R.O.T.C. and had done very well.

At the beginning of my senior year, I was appointed Battalion Commander over the Savannah High School unit. A church friend, Ed Beasley was Battalion Commander over Commercial High School. The two battalions made up a U.S. Army sponsored R.O.T.C. Regiment. There was an agreement that the two school units would swap years in the appointment of a regimental commander. Lady Luck played her hand; it was Savannah High's turn.

At the conclusion of the first semester in 1954, I was selected as the Regimental Commander, a Cadet Colonel rank, and got to wear the coveted three diamonds and dual school colors on the Regimental Citation Cord. Ruben Ware was promoted from Major to Lt. Colonel and Carl Showalter was made a Major. Renny was appointed Platoon Leader, 1st Platoon, "A company" in only his second year. Renny then joined our reserve unit in summer of 1955, did boot camp and a cruise to Miami all in one summer before his senior year. He was a natural leader and never let his peers get him down with their "gung ho" insults.

"DOWN – YO – LEFF!" Barked Renny, a resounding, ground shaking crack followed as thirty-four left heels, mine included, mounted with steel taps hit the pavement in unison, the precision timing was a result of months of dedicated practice. We had learned to march without our taps making a sharp impact on the ground, it's not easy and required special, and somewhat painful, muscle control, so when the resounding crack hit the ground it instantly snapped the observing crowd's attention to our group.

"Boy what a thrill" this was St. Patrick's Day, March, 1957 and quite a privilege to be included in the prestigious parade. We were approaching the reviewing stand and I could see the majesty of the old Desoto Hotel in the background. I scanned the area ahead and to my left, I needed a spot, out of the way, to freeze, as I was not a part of this drill. Renny and I had agreed we would do a show every block and would swap as commander. It was his turn and I needed to be out of the way. We would perform directly in front of the reviewing stand.

I had marched in five previous parades that included two for Armed Forces Day, but suddenly I realized, this was special. We were no longer just a part of the parade, we were in the spotlight. I could see all the city and county dignitaries, Mayor Mingledorf, his staff, military leaders from Hunter Air Field, Fort Stewart, Paris Island Marine Base, Charleston Naval Base and staff from "The Citadel" in Charleston, S.C. Miss Savannah and a multitude of green clad parade and Hibernian Society members were in the stands.

I caught a glimpse of Captain Caulder, my old P.M.S & T. from high school. At his side, were Sgt. Sponseller and 1st Sgt. Cannon, my R.O.T.C. mentors. Cannon was a paratrooper and highly polished; he was not a tall man but did not need to be. He was sharp, stern and stiff as a board in his starched khakis', and gleaming jump boots. He stood proud with his chest of medals and twin peak garrison cap with the paratrooper's insignia on it. Behind them were Commander Lambright and Lt. Blackburn from our Naval Reserve Center. It was not easy to get a spot in this prestigious parade and Commander Lambright had enlisted the help of Lt. Blackburn, who was an up-and-coming young lawyer in Savannah.

"DOWN – YO – RIGHT!" The next command came. There was another resounding crack of steel heels against pavement. I glanced at Renny and thought. "Man you sure are lucky." He caught my eye and flashed a sly smirk. Suddenly it hit me; he had planned it this way. The "son of a gun" had counted the blocks.

"DOWN – EM – BOTH!" This time, two sharp cracks. Renny stood about 6' 1", darkly tanned and was chiseled. I mean, really chiseled. He had hired on with the power company and his lineman job had definitely defined him. I was two years with the telephone company and my job as a repairman had me in shape, but not like Renny. Climbing poles and working aloft creates a special physique in a man, but where I would spend an hour up a pole with a minimum work load, Renny would be up all day with a work load that was much heavier.

"BOX – STEPPPP - ------ HARCH!" The command was dragged in the middle to give the emphases and timing to the command of execution. It's like flipping a switch on a fine tuned machine. On Renny's command, he and I leave our positions, mine is on the left front , one stride out, but even with the first line in the column, Renny's is on the right, even and one stride out. We both continue two strides forward, halt; I do left face, take two strides forward, about face and freeze at attention. Renny halts, takes a left face, takes two strides backward and freezes in command. The company is engaged in a planned movement that can take your breath away. The steel tapes are tapping out a staccato that is spellbinding. The drill is far too complicated to try to explain, but the crowd was ours.

I could see the hundreds of cheery faces fixed on a group of sailors in startling whites, black flowing neckerchiefs, gleaming white helmets, black web belts and leggings, rifles with white straps and black shoes that glistened with an ambitious spit shine. The rifles, at right shoulder arms, protruded into the sky as if on a rack, all at the same angle. No corners were rounded, all sharp and square, the steel heels played a rhythm that was hypnotic and broadcasted confidence.

The crowd pressed closer and I began to feel uneasy, I've always had a premonition when something dreadful was about to happen. "Man not now," I thought. I allowed my eyes to wander and sure enough, I caught a glimpse of BB Saxon making his way toward me through the crowd. BB was a tough guy and had always been at me in school, we never fought, but he was always out to provoke me. I don't know why, I guess it was the R.O.T.C. thing. Every boy was required to take two years of R.O.T.C. and those that chose to take the third year sometimes suffered in the popularity scheme. I said a quick prayer and suddenly the drill came to a climax. Renny and I moved back into position with perfect timing and right in step. A quick look at Commander Lambright revealed his pride. I knew Lt. Blackburn was pleased even if his professional face didn't show it. The crowd erupted in applause and cheers. I glanced at Renny. I could see the pride in his rugged face. I mumbled. "Hey man! - You done good! - Is that a tear I see?"

As we marched away and the crowd noise subsided, I heard a mocking voice call out. "Aaa – Kaaaay ------- Wardlaw!" I thought. "Yeah BB - I hear ya!"

The next block was mine and I knew all we would do for the remainder of the parade would be anti-climactic, but it was still fun. As we proceeded, there were friends taking our pictures, kids in the family would run out and walk proud-fully beside you, buddies would try to slip you a beer and we constantly eyed the crowds for any of our girls, believe me, if you missed one, their feelings would be hurt and you know what it's like to deal with a miffed female.

The down side, of course, is always the occasional hateful jeer. "Wipe yo nose – Wardlaw! - The brown's showing! - Hey Painter! - Why you walkin funny? - Bent over in the shower again - eh?" We let it slide; we knew we had nailed it.

We marched through downtown Savannah, surround by a profusion of blooming azaleas. As we traversed the magnificent squares, with statures honoring Savannah's historic past, it came to my mind, how beautiful this city was and it was finally my home.

---FLASHBACK---

My family came to Savannah in 1951 from the Cajun country south of Baton Rouge, Louisiana. We lived near Klienpeter Station on the Old Highland Road. I was supposed to attend school in Baton Rouge, but after only one semester, I threatened to run away and live on Bayou Manchac, unless I could get back to 7th Ward School on Tiger Bend Rd. Momma and Daddy got the Denhams to sign some papers saying I lived with them. Mr. Squire and Mrs. Essie Denham owned a general store on the Airline Highway at Hope Villa, Louisiana. Their motto was, "The store that sells everything" and I think they did. I went to work at Mr. Denham's in early 1947, I was eleven years old and by the time I was twelve, I could hoist a sack of feed on each shoulder, carry them out and dump them in the back of a wagon or truck with no sweat. They had a 1947 Mercury and at twelve, they let me start driving. My main job was to chauffeur Mrs. Denham's aged mother around. She lived across from the Singleton's Ranch on Antioch Road between Airline Highway and Tiger Bend Road.

Moving to Savannah in October of 1951 was a tremendous change for me. I had never been subject to much profanity, so, when boys, at Chatham Junior High, would insult me or my Momma, well, it was fist city, in a hurry. I had a fight my first day at Chatham. Joe Browning called me a "Big mouth son of a bitch." I popped him good and he pushed me off the stair landing between the first and second floor. The fall really didn't hurt and as I charged back up the stairs, someone grabbed me from behind. It was Mr. Ball, the school principle.

As I struggled to free myself, Mr. Gerkin, the shop teacher grabbed Joe from behind. Suddenly I broke free, and lunged for Joe. I swung a wide right, he twisted his head to the left and my fist landed square on Mr. Gerkin's Adam's apple. All fight left me. Joe, now free, saw the severity of the situation and backed off. Mr. Ball and some other teachers began to assist Mr. Gerkin. His Adams-apple had swollen shut instantly and his breathing was becoming difficult. Slowly he began to recover and I began to apologize profusely. Mr. Ball turned, he was a huge man, and without a word pointed toward his office, Joe knew the routine and was already on the way. I was about to learn about Mr. Ball's discipline.

I had two more fights before the first week was out, one on the cinder playground and one in the basement at the entrance to the boy's bathroom. The basement fight was not really my affair, but I felt like I had to step in. I was headed to the lunch room, also in the basement.

At the foot of the stairs was a circle of kids and a rather large boy was slapping a much smaller kid around. The smaller boy was Jimmy Deal, a fairly skinny kid that was always very quiet, he was in all my classes and never caused any problems. The big boy, I didn't know, and never found out who he was, but he was just slapping Jimmy's head and face as Jimmy did his best to cover up. I could hear Jimmy crying and his voice would shudder with each impact. Instinctively I knew this was plain bully crap.

I stepped forward and loudly shouted "Hey! - Leave the kid alone!" I guess He thought I was a teacher or something, because he stopped and spun around.

He saw I was nothing but a kid myself, and gave me a hard two hand push on each shoulder, and uttered, "Screw you!" I suppose his bullying had been effective in the past and he thought he had handled me, because he turned his attention back to Jimmy.

Wrong!   Before he even raised his hand to slap Jimmy again, I grabbed the back of his shirt at the collar with my left hand, and with all my strength pulled him to the left against the wall by the boy's bathroom. I stepped between him and Jimmy.

My body language clearly stated; it's me now, not Jimmy. He had a stunned look on his face, but the crowd of kids definitely sensed a change in the program. His eyes told me he was concerned but now, his resolve was, to teach me a lesson. I think he may have been a little older than me. He began a kind of strutting walk toward me. I really think he felt like he would pop me and that would be it.

I struck first, my left jab hit him square on the nose, the right cross didn't do much, because he was falling backwards, the blood just gushed from his nose. His hands went up to cover his nose immediately and the sight of the blood, running between his fingers, was too much for him. He just sat down on the floor and began to holler.

"That's done!" I thought, and turned my attention to Jimmy who stood in amazement. "Come on Jimmy - let's get a salad!"

He followed me quietly and we both got my favorite, a quarter head of fresh lettuce doused with that creamy thousand- island dressing. We had no more than sat down when a quiet hush fell over the usually noisy lunchroom. I looked up to see Mr. Ball at the door surveying the lunchroom. I knew why and raised my hand, it caught his eye and he made a disgruntled facial expression and a hand motion for me to head for the office. I pushed my salad aside and started to rise when he made a motion to bring my salad with me. I liked this man.

Mr. Ball gave me the usual lecture on why fighting was a waste of energy and never proved anything and seldom solved a problem. He then made me run and walk the Church across the street numerous times. He had a paddle he used on a lot of the boys, but he never even threatened me with it. He did call a meeting with Momma one day and said that if the fighting didn't stop, I would be put out of school.

I argued. "Momma - they cussin' me an' they calling you a witch - with a "B" an' they're beat'n up on little kids an' all kind'sa stuff!"

Momma shushed me and leaned over, smiled slightly, cupped her hand to my ear and whispered loud enough for Mr. Ball to hear. "Lynn - if it really bothers you that much - just catch em on the way home from school."

Mr. Ball smiled, and then with a straight face said. "That'll be all Mrs. Wardlaw! Thank you so much for coming in, it's been a delight." I found out later that Mr. Ball had been a "Golden Gloves Boxer." I suppose, kids fighting in school is like gun slinging in the "old west." It seemed like every day there was some kid waiting to try me on. I became pretty good at talking my way out of a lot of fights. I never showed fear, told the truth and tried to find something good to say about the challenger and a lot of times it worked.

-------------------------------- STILL FLASHING BACK --

One afternoon on the city bus going home, I saw James, a colored boy I worked with at the Handy Market sitting in the back of the bus. I simply went and sat by him because he was my friend. I proceeded to start a conversation with him and noticed how uneasy he was.

He softly said "Lynn! - I think you better move!"

I looked up to see the whole bus craning their necks to see this white boy sitting beside a colored boy. I had never thought a thing about it.

James whispered, "On the other hand - maybe you best stay on with me 'till we get to the sto and not get off at yo house first!"

"James!" I said. "If I don't get to the house on this bus - on time - my Momma will whup my tail and that's worse than anything these guys can do to me!"

Now, my Daddy was a kind, gentle man and never whipped me in my entire life. Momma did the whipping and I got my share, looking back I guess I could say I averaged at least one whipping a day, if I missed a day, then I probably got two the next day. Daddy, as gentle and kind as he was with us kids, took no fool from anyone; he was a natural fighter that took care of business in a hurry. Every finger on both hands was crooked from being broke and never properly set. Daddy had given me some instruction that had served me well many times. Daddy would say, "Son - when you see trouble coming - go meet it. Hit first - hit hard - hit a lot and don't stop 'till you see he's done. Don't shut your eyes - you can't hit something you can't see and don't quit - I never seen a man get whipped - long as he kept fightin!"

The bus made a right off Bay Street at Caroline Ave, and stopped at Bayview to let kids off at the first stop. We proceeded across Cunyun Creek and there was my stop at Clearview Homes, not the finest place in town, but all we could find at the time.

Normally there were six of us kids, living in Clearview, that made this stop, but two boys, one of them about sixteen and tall, got off also. I knew them as Hudson Hill boys, a stop on down the route, before The Handy Market back on Bay St.

Another one of the kids was a very pretty girl that lived across the lawn from me. I eyed the two boys and had a feeling that a fight was imminent. My books were under my right arm. We crossed the street from the bus stop and it was my custom to walk as close to the pretty girl as possible, you know, in case she wanted to talk, or something. She never did. Usually we would walk down the street to the first set of bungalows on the left and up the common lawn, I lived in the last house on the left and she lived in the last house on the right.

I asked the Lord for some guidance, and the thought came, to try a way out of this, I would go straight to my house's back door, as it faced the street where the bus stopped.

As I began to veer from the group the bigger of the two Hudson Hill boys pushed me on the right shoulder and as I spun around, he sneered "You're a nigga lover, ain'tcha?"

He never saw it coming; I simply released the books under my right arm and shot my left fist as straight to his nose as I could. Maybe it was his height that threw me off, I don't know, but I missed the mark. Now, I'm looking for a nose bleed, I had found that's the quickest way to end a fight. It's very painful and the blood flow takes a lot out of your opponent. My blow struck him full on the lower right side of his jaw and he instantly dropped to the ground. There wasn't any falling over, or staggering back, he simply dropped.

It kinda scared me, but I knew he was finished. I glared at the other boy and stepped his way, ready to give him a lickitty-bop, but I didn't need to. He lit out down Clearview Avenue like a stripped ass ape. "Man", Jim Thorpe couldn't have caught that kid. The other kids backed away and continued to walk home, the pretty girl, I don't think ever turned around. She never rode the bus to or from school, or even spoke to me again.

I was worried about the fallen boy and ran to my back door calling "Momma! Momma!" She met me at the door, "Quit screaming Lynn - you'll wake Poco!" That was little brother's nickname.

I quickly told Momma about the fight and we went out to check on the boy. There was no trace of him, he musta been faster than his buddy, because we had good vision for blocks in all directions and he was not in sight.

------------------------------------ BACK TO THE PARADE ------------------------------------

The parade came to an end and we loaded our special gear in the waiting Navy panel truck. It departed and we were free to enjoy the rest of Savannah's most celebrated holiday. The driver told us we had won some kind of parade award and Renny and I congratulated each other, we then relayed the news and our thanks to the company. Everyone agreed that it was a most wonderful experience. I walked down Broughton Street and stopped at a few shops to soak up some accolades from viewers that had seen our performance then proceeded to Tanner's for a couple of their world famous chili dogs and orange juice. There was quite a line, but it was worth it. There were no seats in the place, you had to stand at the counter or walk outside. I never enjoyed standing at the counter, but always did just for the thrill of giving my spot to a lady. It was fun.

I then began to make my way south down Bull Street back to Forsythe Park where the parade had formed. I had parked in the parking lot at Candler Hospital next to the Nursing School dorm. My buddies and I dated nurses in training at Candler or St Joseph's Hospitals. I dated Pat Stokes, my girl from Church. Pat was in her first year of training. She was a tall, good looking blond, moody, devilish, and a good dancer. We were close and I knew her family well. We never talked marriage, but often talked of "down the road stuff" that would only happen if we were married. Her brother, Bill Stokes, nicknamed, "Pee Wee," was a graduate of Georgia and had been prominent on the weight lifting team. He was a tall hunk, and dated Sue Stafford, Patty's best friend from Church. Sue was the daughter of Carson and Claudine Stafford. Carson was my barber, and one of our church's youth group counselors. We had some fine times at his home.

I walked through the park and took a left at the fountain to approach the parking lot entrance of the hospital when my blood ran cold. There standing on the sidewalk of Drayton Street was BB Saxon, directly in my path.

My mind raced, is he waiting on me, has he seen me? I had thoughts of turning around, I was in no hurry, it was early afternoon, my date, with Patty, was not 'till seven. I could walk on down to Sears. That little voice, called conscience, said "Remember what your daddy said, when you see trouble coming son, go meet it." The die is cast, I picked up my step and as I approached BB, he turned and slowly moved to block my path crossing the street. I planned my stop to put him in place for my left jab, but something made me hesitate. I noticed how much he had changed since high school. He wasn't nearly as tall as I remembered and looked a little heavier. His hair was thicker and his bushy eye-brows were almost grown together. I could see strands of course chest-hair peeking over the top of his tee-shirt. I was about to fight my first man, I thought.

BB spoke, "I met some buddies downtown and a couple of 'em work with you at the phone company." BB continued, as I eyed him warily. "Red Helmy says you gonna be a submarine sailor - that right?"

I looked him straight in the eye with my sternest look and answered. "Don't know BB - I'm leaving in a couple of weeks for sub school - I gotta make it through that first - then maybe I'll get a sub".

There was a tense pause, the slightest move and I felt all hell would break loose. A horn blew two quick beeps and I saw Ray Lewis's beautiful '57 Olds pull to the curb.

The car was full and a voice calls out. "Hey! BB, come-on we're going to the beach".

BB never flickered an eye, but they softened, and he softly said, "You'll make it – man - you got balls!" He turned, and in a flash, was in the car and gone. I stood there, dumbfounded, and as I gathered my thoughts, I began to feel like, maybe, I had just been knighted or something.

I proceeded to my car and as I slid under the wheel, I thought of that '57 Olds that just left. That was one fast car. I had a '54 Ford two door sedan. It lost an engine due to me asking it to try and out-drag a '55 Chevy. My Ford tried, but blew up in the process. Daddy ran the Traffic Circle Salvage Yard at the time and put a 55 T-Bird engine in my '54. Boy that engine brought that little Ford to life, but it was still not enough for that '57 Olds of Ray Lewis.

I looked up and caught a glimpse of Patty and a group of nurses, all in their whites, coming out of the hospital. I gave a quick beep on the horn and Claire, a nurse trainee from Brunswick, Ga. looked my way. I made a sly wave and she leaned toward Patty. Patty never looked. I watched until they entered their dorm. I cranked up and proceeded to back out. I looked up at Patty's window and saw her looking out at me. I waved again and imagined a little smile, but no wave. "Another mood." I mused, and drove away. I thought I'd go home and wash and wax my baby. I had polished it so much that the grey primer was showing through the deep metallic green on all the creases. "Oh Well!" I loved her anyway, the car and Patty.

-------------------------------------- BACK GROUND --

Daddy was now working as a mechanic at J.C. Lewis Ford in 1957; they were the local Ford, Lincoln and Mercury dealership in Savannah. I was out of school and working full-time.   My middle brother, Gray was thirteen and in Jr. High. James Elvis the younger was seven and went to school two blocks away at Penn Ave. Grammar School. Momma had decided she wanted a new career in her later life and had earned her papers as a L.P.N. Since everyone was gone all day, Momma would sleep until about 4pm, then get up, do a little house work, get supper and worked the night shift at St. Joseph's Hospital.

Momma had enjoyed quite an exciting career as a young woman. She managed the largest riding club and stable in Shreveport, La. The Broadmoor Riding Academy was an exclusive stable that boarded over one hundred privately owned horses as well as a string of rental steeds that numbered over fifty. Momma taught equestrian classes at Centenary College and Fairmont High School.

I was lucky as a little kid to travel all-over western Louisiana and Eastern Texas when Momma would do horse shows and Rodeos. In addition to showing horses, she was a trick rider. I remember one show she did at the Fat Stock Show in Ft Worth. Momma and Daddy took a napkin and pinned a number on my back like I was a bull rider. I was probably three or four and I really thought I was something. I did get my shot though. In 1948, Momma let me enter the Jr. Bull Riding Event at the rodeo in Gonzalez, La. I made it for about three bucks before the heifer dumped me in a pile of horse poop. "Man", that was embarrassing.

Daddy was a pistol and whip expert and occasionally would do exhibitions. Momma would hold cigarettes in her mouth for his whip act. Daddy taught me to use the bull-whip, but I never mastered it like him. Momma would toss silver dollars in the air for Daddy and he would shoot holes in them. All of us boys learned to shoot, but I have to say, Gray, the middle brother was probably the best shot, next to Daddy.

-------------------------------------- BACK TO PRESENT ---

I drove up to my home on Screven Ave. in East Savannah and parked. I went straight for the hose to wash my ride. I looked up the outside stairs that led to our home and saw Silly Willy asleep on the top step. We had to be real careful with Silly Willy. He was probably the most skittish cat ever. I couldn't count the times he had sailed off that top step when he was surprised. The hard landings had taken their toll on the old cat as his head was constantly cocked to one side, his eyes took time to focus and there was no way he could walk a straight line. He was a huge yellow tom and if he ever settled down in your lap, you could forget watching TV, because his purring motor had no muffler and never hit on all cylinders at the same time. If he started purring while in the house, Rex, our dog, would ask to go outside.

As I washed the car, I noticed a note pinned to the bottom stair post. Momma wanted me to pick up her clean uniforms at the laundry. The laundry was just around the corner at a little plaza on Pennsylvania Ave. next to the soda shop. I never missed a chance to drop in the soda shop and flirt with Jeanie; she was a few years younger than me so the flirting was like investing in the future. She was a very attractive girl in every way, if you know what I mean. I would ask her to come to my Church which was only two blocks from her home. She never came. I guess it was for the best, Patty was no dummy and I was probably just asking for trouble.

I finished cleaning up the car, picked up Momma's uniforms, bathed, had a helping of Daddy's warmed up chicken and dumplins, helped Gray with his math, did a load of clothes and hung them out. I guess I need to explain about the laundry, you see, Momma's uniforms were the only thing we didn't do ourselves. Those white things came back from the laundry so stiff you had to pull them apart to put them on. You could hear Momma coming a block away. I think the hospitals had some kind of deal with the laundry, because we were a pretty frugal family.

I treated myself to a long hot bath and shaved, for all the good it did, at twenty years old I had facial hair, but it wasn't that thick stubble most men had. I splashed on some crisp Aqua Velva and immediately wished I had used Old Spice, too late now, "OH! Well! What the hey!" I thought. Patty never mentioned a preference anyway. Momma was up, cleaning the house a bit. Daddy would be home shortly. Gray was watching Capt. Sandy on WTOC TV. James was playing with the Sharp brothers. Both boys suffered from muscular dystrophy. James was their constant playmate and confidant.

I was to pick Patty up at seven, so I drove up Goeble Ave. to President Street, hung a left and nailed my Ford. That solid lifter 292 would wind forever, but really got a work out trying to run with the new short stroke 265 Chevys. I had a reputation around town as a hot Ford, but I knew the truth.

Most of our "draggin" was on Victory Drive and I would maneuver my challenges to a traffic light near one of the three drive-in restaurants, all within about a half mile of each other. You know the routine, my opponents and I would tease each other up and down Victory Drive by pumping the gas and chirping the tires and finally catching the light just right. We would line up side by side, pump the gas and cut our eyes back and forth in anticipation. It drove the neighbors crazy. We all had glass packs and Smittys, hard street tires, and if you had a clutch like me you could chirp your tires with ease

When the light flashed yellow, the serious process began, left foot on the clutch, your right foot on the brake hard, but sideways so as to mash the gas as well. "Man," let me tell you, there is an art to this. Your engine must be at exactly the right RPM, if too high, you would light up those old hard, street tires. If your RPM was too low, your engine would die. There was always the possibility that some part between crankshaft and rear tires couldn't handle the impact and your opponent would blast off with a howl of laughter as you set there in a puddle of dust, steam and oil. To top it all off, you now had to fix the shattered night with your date, because she had spent ten minutes begging you not to drag race and warning you of the consequences. Many a romance was doomed by this very scenario.

If all went well, at the first flash of green, the clutch foot was lifted and the right foot side stepped the brake and floored the gas. Considering that everything was done with perfect timing, the long stroke with a big heavy flywheel and clutch on the Ford would launch the car with momentum that the short stroke Chevy engines couldn't match. My strategy was to max out that lead and as soon as I could see the short stroke power in the Chevys start coming on, I would wave, "Bye - Bye", out my window, slow down and turn into one of the drive-ins, usually the "Dixie Land". It most always worked; well anyway, it worked enough to build my reputation.

I reached East Broad, took a left to Liberty St. made a right over to Abercorn and headed south to Candler Hospital. As I pulled into the parking lot I saw Billy Miltiades' sleek '49 Mercury in the lot. It was a beautiful candy apple maroon with twin chrome pipes that sang sweetly through those wonderful glass packs. The car was chopped and lowered and was our favorite ride. Billy dated Hannah

Meeks, a petite beauty from Brunswick, Ga. Billy and I had been friends for more years than I had lived in Savannah. I didn't realize at the time that Billy was part of God's plan in my life.

-------------------------------------ANOTHER FLASHBACK -------------------------------------

When I was five years old the Japanese bombed Pearl Harbor and our lives in Shreveport, La. came to an abrupt end. Momma's riding Academy supported a division of a Club called the "Red River Rangers" Momma's group called themselves "Wardlaw's Dirty Dozens", and sported a number of notable people, like Ben Saur, Tommy Merrill, of the "Bar 100 Ranch" in the Seven Devil Hills of Oklahoma and Jimmy Davis, the country singer and future Governor of Louisiana. Davis was commissioner of public safety in Shreveport at the time. Daddy had his own automotive business and maintained a number of diesel truck fleets. One of his largest accounts was Schuster's Produce Company. Mr. Schuster had purchased the Broadmoor Riding Academy from Momma and hired her to continue running it.

When the war broke out, Daddy enlisted at age 42. He went to Fort Humbug south of Shreveport for enlistment and was told that the age cut-off was 39. However, they asked him to report to Camp Beauregard for further assessment. That's where the big change came, Momma said our life was never the same after that and she always longed for that long lost era at the "Broadmoor Riding Academy." The government found that Daddy had a degree in auto mechanics and diesel engines from Sweeny's Automotive College in Kansas City, as well as a Bachelor's Degree in Agriculture and Animal Husbandry from L.S.U. The government placed Daddy in Civil Service and moved our family to New Orleans in Feb, 1942. I started school there and did the 1st grade twice. The trucking companies of Couch and Herrin Motor Lines were combined under Daddy's maintenance care for the duration of the war. After the war we moved up to Baton Rouge and Daddy had a number of mechanical businesses, but none ever reached the magnitude of his W&W Service in Shreveport.

During the summers as a kid in New Orleans and Baton Rouge, I would visit my Mamaw and Papaw in Cedar Grove, La. They lived on 72nd St. two houses off Southern Ave. "Man!" Those were great summers, I played with my friend, Bicky Thatcher and believe it, Billy Miltiades, along with his kid brother "Butch." Billy's Momma had divorced Billy's Dad, Arthur Miltiades, and remarried a Mr. Banks, who then moved them to Cedar Grove.

When we moved to Savannah in 1951, I went to work at Mr. Miltiades' Handy Market on Bay St. never knowing the connection until one day, Billy and Butch walked into the store after moving back from Cedar Grove. Billy and I were buddies from then on. He was a year younger than me, but shared my interest in ROTC and was a second year Lieutenant over Third Platoon, Company A in high school.

Fred Robinson, son of the director of the local teamsters union, was one of our group. Fred lived in the loft of his parents' home on the bluff at Isle of Hope.

"Boy!" We spent many a fun night in that loft, as a matter of fact, that's where I saw my first and only fart burn. We were having a sleep over at Fred's when we started talking about burning farts. None of us had ever tried it and didn't know if it was true or not. We were all in underwear, in Fred's loft and just lounging around.

We all started to see if we could build some gas. We spent considerable time, drinking cokes and eating boiled eggs and pork and beans, I think Billy even sipped some beer from Fred's Dad's fridge. We had about given up and were talking about other things when Billy shouted, "I got one building – Boys!"

"Hold it!" said Fred. "Where's the lighter? - Don't lose it Billy! - Hold on!"

Steve Tankersly tossed me his "Ronson" and I flipped it open with one hand, snapped my fingers and the lighter sprung to life.

Billy said. "Easy now - it ain't quite ripe yet - but boy it's working!" I snapped the lighter shut and relaxed a bit, but I was set on ready.

Suddenly Billy shouted. "Here it comes boys!" He flipped over on his hands and knees, pulled his skivvies down and there was the hairiest behind I ever saw in my life. Now, I must admit that I was not experienced in looking at men's behinds and this was a shock.

Billy shouted. "Here it comes! – Lynn! - Hit the lighter!" I was a smoker for two years now and had the lighter bit down pat, the lighter flamed and as I moved it into position a sheet of green flame erupted. We all expected a little poof, at most, but a blast like this was a total surprise. A green blast reached the foot of the bed, singed the hair on my hand, rose to the ceiling and ignited the thick, black mass of hair on Billy's behind. Billy screamed and began to beat at the flames, calling for help, but how do you help a buddy when his ass is on fire. We could only watch. The flame was gone as quickly as it came and Billy was not really hurt, just singed and minus a lot of hair, however, he had some pain and complained all night. Billy made us all promise not to tell the girls. I never did, but I don't know about the other guys.

-------------------------------------BACK TO THE DATE---

The girls came out and we decided to go to the beach that night, the weather had warmed up considerably and we could build a fire, roast some wieners and lay in the dunes on our blankets. The folks at Ft. Screven really didn't like fires in the dunes, but we were pros at this. We brought our own wood, our blankets and a shovel. We would find a deep dune, build a small fire, huddle around it, cook our wieners, squirt condiments out of a homemade bottle, drink our cokes, listen to music, make out a little and just enjoy life.

None of us were given much to beer drinking and that was never a problem. The only problem was rival groups that did bring beer would often try to start trouble. We had that covered; one of the girls would go to a nearby house and complain about kids building a fire in the dunes.

We then would wait until we saw the lights of the approaching patrol, take the shovel, cover the fire with sand, and jump under our blankets. Here's the trick, we all had Navy issued sand colored blankets, and were virtually invisible under the search lights at night. The rowdy guys, who gave us trouble, usually got caught and were forced to leave.

We had a really good time this particular night and as we were cleaning up and preparing to leave, Patty missed my graduation ring she had worn. When you go steady, a guy gives his girl his high school ring and she either wears it on a chain or wraps it with tape and places it on her finger. Patty wore mine on her finger and it had come off. The guys made a futile effort to find it, but all that soft sand and one small ring, we knew it was hopeless.

We took the girls home by the only route available, heading west along the "Old Tybee Road," which was officially U.S. 80. There was a sign at the beginning of Butler Avenue that read, "My Other End Is in San Diego, California." This old road was a spectacular drive by day, but at night it took on a mystical air that could sooth any mood. Heading west our convoy would snake as slow as possible to enjoy the air and company of our dates. The broad expanse of stars gave witness to God's massive creation; our headlights would light up the staunch palm trees that lined the twenty mile ride. We crossed Lazaretto Creek and caught a glimpse of the ancient old light on the crumbling lighthouse at the tip of Cockspur Island. Fort Pulaski's hulking mass soon emerged, silhouetted in the darkness of the trees on the right.

The glow of the Coast Guard Station could be seen, beyond the Fort. A straight stretch of road, that tested the top end of many a hot car, and ended the life of many a bold driver laid ahead. Billy couldn't resist rapping his pipes a couple of times, but everyone stayed calm.

We caught sight of the lights on a massive freighter leaving by the main channel of the Savannah River. The main channel was the other side of Cockspur Island and a shallow south river flowed between us and the Island. The old train line was immediately to our right and the scrub growth gave the ship, which was ablaze with lights, the illusion it was sailing on land. On the darkened horizon was the glow of Savannah.

Downtown Savannah, like any big city, had a lot of lights, but this is not what made this scene so impressive. The numerous old oaks that populated all of Savannah shrouded most of Savannah's sky glow. On Savannah's east side at the river stood the National Gypsum Plant, from our view coming back from the beach it resembled a cluster of white Christmas lights dropped on the ground. Beyond was the brilliant glare of the Union Bag Plant. The scene presented was spectacular.

As Bull River approached we could see the low glow of the city with the bright lights of the industries casting a halo over the city that was spellbinding. On some nights there would be numerous cars lining the road just to view, at length, this marvelous site. To the left of this magnificent drive were the many hammocks that dotted the vast marsh, some were inhabited and the flickering lights resembled floating stars in a black sea.

We made our way through Wilmington Island, then Whitmarsh and Talahi Islands and past Isle of Armstrong, over the old swing bridge, one block, take a left on Mechanic's Ave., go maybe two blocks, then right onto old Victory Drive. That's when it started. The girls would start pleading for us not to race, and threatening us if we did. However, the one thing they would never say, if we were ever challenged was, "You know, you can't outrun him." That phrase always guaranteed a race and quite often ended a romance. "Man", don't insult my ride, even if it's true.

I pulled into the Candler parking lot and sought out my favorite spot under the huge old oak tree. I pulled in slowly and stopped perfectly to allow the bulk of the friendly old oak to block the light on the dorm.

Ahh! Blissful dark!   The girls had an 11:00 PM curfew, so we had a few minutes and I planned a nice long kiss before walking Patty to the door.

As was my custom, I remained behind the wheel, pushed the seat fully back and reached to turn Patty and pull her into my arms. I'm sure every boy and girl that ever dated in the front seat of a car instinctively knows the routine. Patty went stiff and resisted. "Crap!" I thought, another mood coming on, and me leaving in less than two weeks.

My mind raced. "I need some psychology here!" I thought. "Ping" I had it. I leaned close to Patty's ear and whispered with a heavy breath. Breathing in her ear usually had a positive effect.

"Patty - don't let that ring bother you - it's only a hunk o' metal and glass and I'll get you a much nicer one someday!" "Look!" I whispered. "I'm leaving soon and you're still my girl and I'll be back from time to time and you'll wait on me - right?"

She snapped her head around and looked me straight in the eye. "Uh Oh!" This didn't happen often, I thought.

She spoke with deliberation.   "You're leaving to go to some stupid submarine, wind up in some stupid foreign land, meet some stupid foreign girl and here I am in stupid Savannah, in stupid nurses training and stupid me is gonna wait on you!   I don't think so!"

My head was spinning. I wasn't prepared for this.

She continued, softer now. "Lynn! - Every time we had a fuss you found another date - I remember them all – Phyllis – Betty - Ann and that Betty Joyce and not to mention Hazel and Glenda - who are in our Church. I know you – Lynn - you'll be about as true as far as you can see!"

I had no defense, she was right, I always did the breaking up, I did go out with all these girls, but would always find a way to make up and go back to Patty.

This time she was the aggressor. I had completely lost control of this situation. I had not even thought of going off without a girl back home. The thought felt unnatural. "Man, what kinda' sailor didn't have a girl back home?"

Patty still had the floor, "We need to make a clean break, be free to date others without any guilt. We need to be ourselves, if you come home sometimes and I'm not busy, we can go out, but no promises and no strings, O.K.?"

I was at a total loss, I never saw this coming. I had always been in control. Whenever we would break up in the past, I had never known her to date anyone else. This was not the Patty I knew.

I tried to gain some composure and said, with as much dignity and casualness as possible. "I guess you're right kid, this might be best for us both, anyway we got next weekend." I leaned over and placed a sweet but light kiss on her unresponsive lips, and walked her to the dorm. She went in, never turning or speaking to me.

I left and almost forgot the guys were waiting at Porzios. There was only one pizza place in town, Porzios. An immigrant Italian Family with their first generation kids operated an authentic Italian Restaurant on the corner of 37th and Montgomery Street. There would usually be from four to six of us guys. We had all been friends through school. The one exception was Steve Tankersly from Brunswick. Steve's girl was in training at Candler and he would sometimes stay over with Fred, Billy, Angus Faust or me. You already know about the night in Fred's loft. We would all meet at Porzios, order a large ground beef and a large glass of milk, each. What a feast. The pizza was $1.50, the milk a quarter and a quarter tip killed a $2.00 bill.

Porzio's had two night waitresses that were classics. Tall blondes, hair rolled up on the top of their heads, long earrings, nice make-up, little petite hankies tied above the left breast pocket, starched white outfits with those tidy little aprons that accentuated their curves. They were a little older than us but knew just how to treat young men who still had a lot of boy in them. The pizzas were fantastic, and have set the scale by which all pizza lovers in Savannah have judged other pizzas by. I have never found any other to compare. We placed our order, and as always, there was a long wait.

I remembered I had Dad's bull whip in my car and worked up a bet with the guys, that I could pick six straight azaleas off a blooming bush located in the median of 37th Street. Outside under the street light the flowers did not stand out as brilliant as I hoped but "what the hey!" The bet was on, if I did it, they would chip in to pay my tab. There was no penalty for failure. I would just pay my own tab and they got a free show. I had recently braided a new popper on the end of the leather thong at the tip of the 10ft leather bull whip.

It had performed many a show under Daddy's skilled hand. It sported a leather bound, swivel handle that made the action much easier and added power to the snap. I swung the whip in wide sweeps that I would describe as a figure eight, first there were three cracks on the right side, then three cracks on the left. I was ready. The loud cracks occur when the end of the whip changes directions so quickly that it actually breaks the sound barrier, the larger the tip, the louder the crack. If the end of the whip is too heavy it can never achieve full velocity and usually will not even crack. The new popper was doing its stuff. The waitresses were at the door and a couple of customers were at the window.

Now remember, it's near midnight and the boys are split in support and ridicule. I picked my bush, stepped back the perfect distance, snaked the whip out in front of me, then gently snaked it straight out behind me, the guys were expecting a slow overhand pop and a flower to fly through the air. Not so. I brought the whip up from the ground and did the first pop underhanded. I never stopped, the whip swung into my windmill routine with resounding cracks in front, sides and rear. If you've ever seen an azalea bush in bloom, you know how profuse the blooms are. I concentrated my front cracks on about a square foot section right in the upper front of the bush. I probably cracked the whip a least a dozen times. The section on the bush went bare, the air was filled with azalea petals, the ground was covered with leaf debris and demolished azalea blooms.

I stopped and as I coiled my whip, gave my best "Lash Larue" impression, "Sorry, boys, it felt so good, I had to make it ten!". The laughter was genuine but the arguing started anyway.

"Pizzas ready!" called Flo. Yep, that's right; her name was "Flo". The other waitress's name was "Mert". The fussin subsided as we sat down and began to relish the treat we had before us.

Fred looked up and said. "Something bad must have happened - hear those sirens?" We piqued our ears and without a doubt, something was going down and nearby too. The sirens grew louder and we could see the flash of red reflections on the buildings far down Montgomery Street.

Billy rose up a bit and trained his gaze down 37th Street. "They're coming that way too!" He stated.

The sirens grew to a deafening pitch as probably six police cars squealed to broadside halts. Tire smoke filled the air as a well-coordinated four way roadblock formed right before our eyes. We thought that maybe a bank vault had been blown open downtown and the crooks were heading this way. We could see the officers deploying to stations and positions that training had prepared them for.

As we watched the tense situation developing outside, two officers with pistols drawn eased the restaurant door open and slowly stepped inside, "Everyone in here OK?" One asked cautiously.

No one spoke but all heads nodded "Yes", in unison. The pistols lowered. The other officer looked puzzled.

"Anyone in here report gunshots?" Again no sound, just heads nodding "No". The pistols were holstered and we could see the officers outside beginning to move about, much more relaxed. Still, there was not a word from anyone in the restaurant.

The officers slowly walked in, looking first at the older couple seating around the corner, but closer to 37th Street. We sat in the fourth booth from the door and facing Montgomery Street. They approached us with hands at the ready, close to their pistols. The taller of the two approached, while his partner went into a covering position at our rear.

"Any of you boys, been shooting a pistol outside?" He asked. Accusation was clearly in his voice.

No words, just heads, shaking the now familiar "No".

The officer leaned forward and as if he had suddenly solved a riddle, asked. "Firecrackers! - Been shooting firecrackers haven't ya?"

The first words now came, Steve had the clue. "Mr. Policeman, I swanee promise you - we ain't shot nary a farcracker nor anything like it and we sho ain't got no gun!" Steve used his best country boy persona.

The officer turned to Flo and Mert, standing behind the counter, "You girls didn't hear shots or firecrackers?"

Mert's eyes darted our way. "Jig's up!" I thought.

Flo, bless her heart, saved the day. She placed her left hip in park, then hooked her thumbs over her waist with her fingers flared out and in the most convincing "put out tone" we ever heard, smartly stated. "Sir! - Do you think that if there was some pistol shootin' going round here - we'd be standing here serving pizza to these fine young men!"

The officer looked perplexed." Y'all best not be lying to me!" He grumbled.

At this, there came an Italian outburst from behind the cash register. Mrs. Porzio had been there all the time, and in all her wisdom was enjoying a great show. She was not a large woman, and her command of English was not polished, not even a little, but she made it perfectly clear that every question asked had been answered truthfully and it was not our fault if the police didn't know how to ask the right questions. The officers had no idea a whip had made the noise. We were sweating that she would give us away, but she didn't.

As it turned out, the police did receive a report of a group of men engaged in gunfire at 37th Street and Montgomery. The police responded, thinking it was a gang war.

Flo and Mert got a fine tip that night. No one told a lie and I never cracked my whip in midtown Savannah at midnight again.

"Plink! ---- Plink-Plink", the sharp sounds woke me. I raised my head and saw the dim light, beginning to show, over the rooftops of Savannah Gardens. My two brothers and I shared a room that was on the back of the two- story home we lived in. The Sharps lived downstairs and my family lived upstairs.

I glanced at the alarm clock. 6:10 on Sunday morning, what was that noise? "Plink- Plink", again. I sat up on the side of the bed, and leaned forward to look out the window. Billy Miltiades, Angus Faust and Fred Robinson were on the ground below grinning like Cheshire Cats and motioning me to come down. I slipped on my clothes and eased out, careful not to wake the boys. Momma wasn't home from work yet and Daddy slept soundly, but if the boys woke up, they would want to be part of whatever was going down.

---------------------------------- FLASH BACK ON BROTHERS ----------------------------------

Gray was my middle brother, born December 8, 1943 in New Orleans. Being seven years younger than me was a distinct disadvantage for him. I picked on him unmercifully. As we grew older he began to retaliate and in some cases got the best of me.

We had moved from Clearview Homes, in early summer 1952. I had a disagreement with Mr. Miltiades's store manager, a Miss Bowen, and quit. Momma supported my decision and I had a summer off. This was my first free summer since I turned eleven.

We moved to a small concrete block house on the Old Augusta Road, about a half mile west of the Dean Forest Road. In 1952 this was the country. Our next door neighbors were the Carter family, a fine family of four. Presley was their oldest, at fourteen and his sister, Marie, at about twelve.

We would make our own arrows out of bamboo shoots, and would use acorns in our sling shots.

One day Gray and I were having a sling shot war. Now I'm fifteen and Gray is eight, but that doesn't matter with sling shots. Gray was a much better shot than I was. Gray had built a fort from firewood on the side of the house next to a freshly harrowed field. I made my attack from the front and was using some slender saplings for cover. Gray's cover was perfect; all that was visible was his head. The saplings were not very big and it seemed that my thigh, shoulder or butt cheek was always sticking out. Gray was picking me to pieces. I'll never understand how an acorn, being sort of round, always hits you with that little point.

I simply could not get a good shot at Gray. Now, we had a rule; you must not shoot your opponent in the face. This obviously was a good rule for self - preservation, but I'm getting blistered pretty good in this war. Gray had very good cover, all but his face. I needed some revenge, so I deliberately took my time and careful aim and shot Gray, in the forehead, right between the eyes.

"Bad move!" I had seen that look in Gray's face before, hell hath no fury like Gray betrayed. He slowly stood, stepped out from behind his cover, dropped his slingshot and began to look around on the ground.

I didn't need any advice to tell me to get as far away from Gray as possible, you see, Gray was looking for something much more deadly than an acorn. I struck out across that freshly harrowed field, outrunning Gray was no problem; I simply had to get out of his range. I glanced around and there was Gray with a piece of broken terra cotta drain pipe in his left hand. Oh! Did I mention! He was left handed?

Gray was lightly weighing the piece with his hand, getting the feel of it. It was much too large for the slingshot. It was about four inches across and slightly curved. Gray calmly looked up in an almost reverent manner. I thought, was he praying?

My brother drew back, in that awkward way a lefty does, and released that missile with all his might. I really was not concerned; I thought I was well out of range. I watched the crude saucer ark high in the air and began a slight turn my way. I moved a few feet, looked back and that reddish brown dish was still tracking my way.

In a flash, I knew I was doomed, no matter which way I turned, that piece of pipe had my name on it. Gray had prayed, and God heard him, and agreed with Gray. Lynn needed to answer for his betrayal.

Needless, to say, it took seven stitches to close the gaping hole in the top of my head. I learned about divine intervention that day.

It was a fine summer. Presley was a tough kid and even though I was a year older and twenty pounds heavier, he stuck with me, physically, on everything. Our friends, Raymond Croslyn and Bob Knight, lived on down the Louisville Road.

We all went "trick or treating" Halloween night in 1952. Houses were far apart out in the country. We had walked to Central Junction and on the way back, made a short stop at Ann Lax's house for a coke, she was my girlfriend at the time. We had done well, this night, our bags were brimming. We knew we were a little old for this, but "What the Hey", it would probably be our last Halloween and "Trick or Treat".

As we walked along, it became obvious, how quiet it was. We actually began to speak in subdued tones in respect for the silence.

Off in the distance we could hear the roar of a car as it accelerated and began to change gears. The car was probably back in Central Junction and headed our way.

Raymond excitedly outlined a plan he had heard of. Two boys would get low, one on each side of the road and as the car approached, they would spring up in a crouched position and pretend to hold a rope or wire across the road. It was supposed to have a hilarious effect on the driver of the car.

We positioned ourselves, Presley in the woods, out of sight. Bob was across the road laying low in a freshly harrowed field. Raymond and I were going to hold the imaginary rope. I was on the wood's side and Raymond on the field side. I made mental notes of my escape route. There was a hog wire fence between me and the woods. It was crushed down due to neglect and ground growth had covered it. The crushed fence probably stood only a foot or so above the ground. I made a mental note of this, so it would not interfere with my retreat into the woods. The night was very dark, no moon, just a broad expanse of stars.

The roar of the car decreased somewhat as it slowed for Dean Forest Rd, then it roared again as apparently there was no traffic. We could see the headlights rise as the acceleration caused the front end of the car to lift. The scream of the engine rose to a crescendo.

Raymond cried. "Now!" We rose, in unison, from our prone positions and in our best impersonation of holding a rope, stretched the invisible line taut across Old Louisville Rd.

The roaring car's reaction was immediate. The headlights dipped to the ground. The engine roar was replaced with the screech of brakes. The headlights swept to the right, as the car swerved, the screech changed to a deep scrunch as the tires slid sideways. Suddenly the lights darted to the left as the driver overcorrected. The driver regained a degree of control and the car came to scalding halt right on our imaginary rope.

I leaped up and dashed over the fallen fence to escape to the woods. I didn't clear the crumpled fence. It was as if the hog wire reached up and clasped my foot. Down I went, hard on the undergrowth.

I heard the drivers voice call out, "You lil bastards, - I'm gonna fill yo ass's with buckshot!"

If I got up now I would be a perfect target. All I could do was roll under that crushed down, overgrown fence. I turned my head and looked sideways through the undergrowth, as the tire smoke completely engulfed the car. From within the smoke we could hear the gruff voices of two men.

The driver, obviously was ticked off, big time. "Them lil sons o bitches nearly wrecked my ass!" The driver growled.

The passenger asked. "What da hell wuz they holding across da road?"

"Not a damn thing - it's an old kid trick - can't believe I fell for it!" the driver retorted, as he walked into the headlights.

By this time the smoke had cleared enough for me to make out the driver's image. He was a giant, wearing a fedora hat and leather jacket, the passenger was in the dark on the other side of the car.

"Hold on a minute." Grunted the driver. I saw him walk back into the dark beside the car. I could now see the trademark grill of a big Buick, the car was still idling. The back door of the Buick opened and closed, I heard the familiar sound of a shell being loaded into a breakdown single barrel shotgun. My blood ran cold!

The driver started my way, "I saw one of them assholes run this way"! He hissed, as he walked down the ditch, up the side and straight to the low spot in the fence where I lay. He stubbed his toe on the crushed down wire of the fence and I felt the impact in my right side. He regained his balance and stepped over the fence and me, with one foot. He stopped, straddling me. He had no idea I was directly under him.

"Dem lil bastards is long gone - Alec!" I heard the passenger say.

"Yeh - I reckon - but we need to scare hell out of em anyway! - I'm gonna fire a shot in the air! - That'll scare the shit outa em! - Whatta you think?" He said, in a subdued tone.

I had heard, when you get scared, that you mess your britches. Well that's not true. When you are terrified, you don't do anything that will attract attention to yourself.

The passenger said. "Alec! No! – No! - Don't shoot in the air - that shot'll come down on some farmhouse! Just fire down in the ground - there at your feet!"

I heard the familiar "click - click" of the hammer being cocked.

"Our Father - Who art In Heaven!" I began to pray.

"F _ _ k it" the driver hissed." This is my only shell and I ain't wasting it!"

The men started back to the car, but I dared not heave a sigh of relief.

The driver asked the passenger. "So - you gonna buy my Buick or what?"

The passenger answered. "I'll tell ya man - she'll fly and she' got damn good brakes too!"

That was, indeed, my last "Trick or Treat".

------------------------------------ BACK TO PRESENT ---

The ground was wet with dew and my keds were toe- soaked before I made it to the corner of the house and confronted my buddies. "Man!" It's 6 A.M. what's wrong?" I whispered.

Billy whispered. "Come look what Angus made!" We walked to the rear of that low, sleek '49 Merc and looked into the now open trunk.

There lay a two foot by two foot, open box with a screen wire bottom. Beside the box were three shovels.

I looked up and saw the smiling faces of three of God's greatest gifts to man, Friends. Billy placed his arm around my shoulder and said. "Let's go find that ring!"

We went in Billy's car. Early Sunday morning traffic in Savannah, Georgia is very light and the traffic lights seemed all green. There was no one on the beach and most of the summer houses were still vacant from the winter season. Finding the same dune took a little time but as soon as we found the sand covered fire site, the rest was easy. We simply reconstructed the layout from the night before.

"Hannah and I were here!" Billy stated. "Fred - you and Beth were there - right?" Fred nodded.

Angus spoke up, "Lynn - Joy and I were over between those two small dunes and you and Patty were here to start with - but remember how the smoke started bothering ya'll and you moved to the right - over there?"

He continued, addressing me, he said. "Remember when you and Steve went to take a leak?" I nodded. " Well - Patty went and sat by Claire - 'till she saw ya'll coming back - so looks like - we got three spots to search."

Our attention was drawn to Billy; it seemed as though he was talking to himself, and motioning with his arms, he was lost, deep in thought. We all were beginning to realize the magnitude of work involved in shoveling through all this sand to find a high school ring.

Billy's voice was emphatic. "Remember when Patty got up and put that piece of wood on the fire and every one fussed about all the sparks that it raised?" We all caught the wisdom of his idea. She threw that piece of wood underhanded into the fire - it hit in the left side of the fire - didn't it?" Billy asked

"Yeah!" We all shouted. "Let's start there!"

I held the box and as a shovel full of sand went in, I would shake it from side to side. The sand was damp from the morning dew and was a little slow in passing through the wire. I thought how hopeless this was. There were no more than three or four shovels placed in the shifter when a glimmer of blue caught the morning sun.

"Hold on!" I said, I placed the box on the ground and felt through the sand where the gleam had appeared.

"Woo Wee! - Here it is!" I cried. A cheer went up from the boys. We started patting each other on the back and bragging about how smart we were as I blew off the damp sand, wiped the ring on my jeans and held it up for all to see. The blue stone glistened against the gold as it caught the morning sun. It was a great feeling and I was already planning my make up with Patty.

I thanked my buddies profusely and started pleading to get back to town, so I could make it to Church. Me, the lost ring, and Patty, all in God's house, "Man! How could this plan fail!"

Well, it did fail; Patty didn't come to Church that Sunday. She would not answer my calls during the week. I was beginning to have a very lonely feeling. A much deeper feeling of loneliness than ever I had before.

The following weeks at work went fast. I had finished a trouble report at Wherry Housing, quarters for Air Force personnel at Hunter Air Force Base, and called the test board about 3:00PM from a terminal on a pole near White Bluff Road. As I pushed up on the terminal lid I was suddenly covered with black wasps. The terminal had not been disturbed in a while so the nest was quite large. Most telephone men who work outside are accustomed to encountering wasps nest and normally detect them long before being caught in this position.

Picture this now, here is a man, up an un-stepped pole, in hooks [climbing spurs] and safety'd off [snapped climbing belt around the pole] about twenty-five feet off the ground, and covered with angry wasps. Good ending of a chapter in an old movie serial, "Eh?"

-- FLASHBACK --

The Lord had blessed me with a past encounter with wasps at the old Sugar Refinery. It was at the rear of an old colored fellow's home that lived in the retired section of the Refinery's provided housing. I had seen the nest and had burned it down in order to get access to my terminal to finish my work. There was a momma cat with five kittens nearby. The old black fellow, sitting on his rear steps, and the momma cat watched as each of the kittens was drawn to the squirming wasps, as they crawled with burnt wings, in the grass. The poor little things would playfully stalk an insect, pounce upon it, then squeal in pain as the wasp would stab it's stinger in the kitten's nose or paw.

The momma cat would look up with each squeal, and the old man would chuckle. "Dat ol' momma cat is lettin dem babies catch a lesson in life - she is!"

I commented, "Well it's not funny to those kittens - look at those poor little swollen faces!"

The grizzled black fellow eased back on the steps, reached into his top shirt pocket and pulled out a plug of chewing tobacco. He held a small pocket knife in the same hand, he raised them both up slightly and asked. "Chaw?"

"No thanks." I replied. He cut a corner off the plug, popped it into his mouth, shut the knife, stowed the tobacco and knife all in the same skilled move that was honed with years of repetition.

He looked at me and asked. "Young fella - you looks like a rite smart white boy! – You ever been stung?"

"Whoo! Yes Sir! A heap a times and it hurts - especially when they get you more than once!" I replied.

"Well - maybe I'm wrong then!" He said and fell silent.

I started back to work and pondered what he said, then it struck me, he meant he was wrong about me being a "right smart white boy". I was up the pole by this time and had pulled the now vacant nest from its mooring and was about to toss it to the ground.

I looked down and called "Uncle! - Let's hear this wisdom you got about wasps!"

He look up and grinned, "Well fust off - I ain't yo uncle!" He paused to gauge my reaction, seeing none, he continued. "I's yo brother! - In Christ - that is! - You unnerstan dat?".

Relieved, that he wasn't implying anything racial, I replied, "Yes sir."

He continued: "You gots to have plenty o' inner self to be able to do this now - ya heah me".

I nodded.

"You ain't gots no time to think when dis happens - you gots to let it happen as iffen its sposed to happen - ya unnerstan?"

"I think so." Says I.

"Boy! - I tol ya - dey ain't no time to think - OK!"

"OK! - I got it!" I retorted.

"You betta git it - or you'll git stung so many times - deys'l hafta cut dat hat offen yo haid!" He laughed at his own gruffness, because he knew he had me going.

I sighed at the frustration of this game and gave in with these words. "OK - my Christian friend - I'm all ears now!" He looked up at me and in all sincerity gave me some of the wisest instructions I ever received and this wisdom has saved me numerous times from painful encounters with wasps.

------------------------------------- BACK TO THE PRESENT -------------------------------------

Now back to my present situation, the wasps have covered me. The words of the old black brother were now part of my inner self. No panic, no movement, my body went relaxed, not limp, just relaxed, eyes shut, a peaceful feeling enveloped me. I could feel the vengeance in the movement of the wasps as they combed my body, the body of their invader. Their tiny feet tickled the hair on my arm. I could feel them move feverishly, as they covered every inch of my exposed face and limbs. They searched in my ears and nostrils, the corners of my eyes and under the collar of my shirt. There were hundreds of them, armed and alarmed, but not the first sting occurred. The old timer's words had been true. He had shared with a total stranger, and a Christian brother, a secret that was as old as life. Wild creatures have a super sense and respond to things they sense.

When the wasps are disturbed they respond instantly and attack the invader, however they will not waste a sting. They attack the movement first, then the fear, anxiety and surprise they sense in you. When you train yourself to instantly suppress those feelings, the wasps do not sense you as a threat. It's an uncanny feeling and the encounter can sometimes last ten minutes or more as they crawl and measure you all over. Little by little, a few at a time, they will return to the nest and you can slowly and calmly make your retreat. Your real test is when you are stung before you realize your situation and you must endure the pain to avoid further attacks.

Let me draw a worst case scenario and this has happened numerous times to men that work aloft.

You are up a pole, it may be a stepped pole or you may have on hooks, you safety off, suddenly you disturb this gigantic nest and they swarm you. You panic; you cannot get down unless you undo your belt.

Oh! You can get down, by pulling your hooks out, or stepping off the steps and if the pole is un-stepped, down you go, with your shirt, chest hair, chest skin, jaw, face, groin, inside of your legs and arms being devoured by a splintered creosoted pole that your safety belt has kept you too close to. If the pole is stepped, your safety belt will hand you up and you are a flailing target for the enraged wasps. If you do manage to release your safety belt and climb down, the wasps will follow and viciously attack your every move. A wasp does not lose its stinger when they attack and they will sting repeatedly, hundreds of them.

Last alternative: Undo your safety belt and jump. Jump twenty-five feet, down, loaded with work gear, no control over where you land. It is a losing situation; you are looking at broken bones, multiple stings, considerable pain and possibly death. I've seen it happen, many times. That old black man did me a great favor. "Thank God!"

I tell you true, I have had wasps come at me with full intent to sting and upon lighting on my relaxed, calm body they will change their mind. In most cases, if possible, I will not destroy the nest. In the rare case when I must destroy the nest after an encounter, I have a terrible feeling of betrayal. This time, it was necessary to burn the nest in order to complete my work and it caused me some compassionate pain.

I have found this art is not effective on all types of wasps. The ground dwelling, yellow jacket, is a different beast and I think they are in league with the devil. They have a keen, conniving, vengeful attitude, and my advice is to stay clear of yellow jackets at all cost. Luckily they are not given to building aerial nests. Encounters with yellow jackets are generally on the ground, so the best advice is to run like hell!

I finished my work and while still up the pole, I called the test board to close out my trouble and get another assignment.

Apple Moore answered and took my report. "Hold on!" He said. "Craig wants to talk to ya".

"Hey! - Bubba!" This was Craig Neidlinger's greeting to all the guys. "Wardy, the district office called and needs you to sign some papers concerning your military leave. Listen! – Bubba - you check them papers good - I hear they say - you ain't coming back!"

"Whatta you mean, Craig?" I asked.

He replied, "Don't know Wardy - just check it good fo you sign it - boy! - See ya!" He clicked off.

I came down from the pole, packed up my gear and headed for 134 Whitaker Street, to the office of Mr. I. Degaris, our company's district manager.

The district clerk was a most proper lady by the name of Mrs. Goldstine. She handed me some forms under the title "Request for Formal Leave of Absence."

She said. "Mr. Wardlaw" - I strongly suggest you read these papers thoroughly before signing - once they are signed - they are contractually binding!" She ushered me into a massive conference room and shut the door.

I began to read. There seemed to be no changes in the pre-printed form of the agreement. I was very close to signing when I re-read the paragraph on the Company's position on re-hiring me when my service time was up. It indicated I would be re-hired if my position was still open or if there was a position of equal level open elsewhere.

At this time in 1957, practically every young man had some type of obligation to serve his country. Of course, there were exceptions, like college, hardship and any number of other reasons, but I had never considered anything but serving. I had enlisted in the Naval Reserve within a week after my 17th birthday. The requirement of my enlistment was six years reserve service and two years of active duty. I had completed boot camp, three cruises and had time in grade for being rated.

I was an E.T. striker. This meant I could take the test for Electronics Technician at any time and be rated third class. I really don't know why I never had. I was nearing three years in service and was a leading seaman. My reserve unit had informed me that my overall qualifications allowed me to take the test for any rate I desired. I just hadn't found a job I really liked. The Navy had any number of rates that my telephone experience would really have been a great asset. The Sea Bee's had offered me an automatic advancement of two rates to transfer and become a Telephone Technician.

--------------------------------FLASHBACK TO SUBMARINE CRUISE ------------------------

You know, I suppose the real reason was the effect a cruise on a submarine had on me. When I departed that boat after the cruise, I was hooked.

The attitude of most regular Navy personnel toward reservist is not good; in fact, they have a name they refer to us by. "F - - king Reservist!"   But that attitude was never visible on this boat. The crew would make room for us in the chow hall, gave up bunks so we could sleep comfortably, included us in their bull sessions and most importantly, showed us how to do the actual jobs on board the boat.

I fell in love with the helmsman position. The quartermaster stood behind me, showed me how to operate the wheel, anticipate the compass, meet the course, over-steer to correct, operate the enunciators, adjust for a pushing sea and how to respond to voice commands from the bridge. There is way too much to attempt to explain further.

As I stood at that wheel of one of our country's finest, I felt like a man at a man's job in a man's navy. There was a sense of reality. Simply put, I felt majestic. The voice of the deck officer rang down through the open conning tower hatch. "Come right to new course one six zero!"

I turned to my instructor, my senses went numb. He was gone! I was alone. There was no one in the conning tower but me, the helm and that command.

I answered, word for word, as instructed. "Come right to new course one six zero - Aye"!

The reply came from the deck officer "Very Well!"

I was hooked. I wasn't a "F - - king Reservist anymore.

---------------------------------- BACK TO CONFERENCE ROOM ----------------------------

The C.W.A Union contract had some clauses, based on federal law that addressed the obligation of the Company in regard to someone subject to the Military Service Act. It read In effect: If you are subject to the act and volunteer for the minimum required period of time, your job will be held for you. These papers didn't say that.

I called Mrs. Goldstine, she came into the room and as polite as I could, I stated. "Ma'am I don't think these are the right papers - you see - I'm going into the Navy and I think these papers should say Military Leave."

Her facial expressions never changed, she simply took the papers from me, never looking at them, and in a matter of fact tone replied. "I did as I was told!" She turned and as she left the room, she spoke over her shoulder. "I told you to read them carefully and you did - you may go - I'll get back to you!"

I returned to work, and the next morning the correct papers were ready and I signed. I never found out why this happened, but it was clearly no accident, once again God provided good friends. What a blessing!

There was just no reaching Patty, these past few weeks. I left messages, but no response. Saturday morning came. I tried one more time; Claire answered the phone. "Claire" I asked. "Is Patty getting my messages?"

Claire replied. "Yeah - I know she got some of em - but she says nothing - just goes on about her business."

"I guess it's a done deal then. "I sighed. "Man! - I leave Friday!"

There was a slight pause. "Listen Lynn- Steve's got to work this weekend and if you want to cruise and get a coke or sumthin- then I'm your gal!'

Claire had always been a pleasure to be around, an attractive dishwater blonde that did not lean toward a lot of makeup and also somewhat larger than the average girl. Her proportions were good, she was just large. I had never put much regard to her size, because Steve was a big man and they suited each other.

I was not keen on taking Claire out, but agreed. "OK!. How about five o'clock?"

"Super - I'll do capris - hear?"

"O.K. - Khakis for me!" I hung up and paused to reflect. It was not unusual for us to cross date on an informal basis. But I had never personalized with Claire.

The date went well. We got along and had fun. I guess it was due to the fact that we already knew each other and neither of us even considered making any intimate moves. We cruised; I even stirred up a drag race on near deserted Stephenson Avenue. Of course, I broke my rule, there was no drive - in to take an early departure and my opponent was a '56 Chevy with a "glide". He caught me half way through second gear. I'm sure he made the rounds that night to tell everyone how he dusted that little green Ford.

Claire never fussed or complained about the drag race and her only comment was. "That's a pretty fast Chevy!" You know, I think that may have been a compliment. I liked her.

We sat in the car that night under the oak and talked, I was tempted to ply her on information about Patty, but thought how unfair that would be. She was Patty's friend.

I told her how I felt about leaving without a girlfriend, and I didn't even have a decent picture of Patty, even if she was still my girl.

"Hold on – Lynn!" She was out of the car and gone in a flash, she stopped at the door and looked back, and raised the one finger, "Hold it," signal. The wait was uncomfortable, what was she up to? Was she looking up Patty? I didn't like situations when I wasn't in control.

My mind was going bonkers with scenarios. She flew out of the dorm clutching something to her breast, and ran back to the car. Once in the seat she heaved a deep sigh, took a breath and became very quiet, still clutching something to her breast.

"Claire - what is it"? I whispered. She placed her open hand over my mouth and said. "Shhh! - I gotta gather my nerve!"

"Man" if I thought my mind was going bonkers before, now I was really bent!

She let a long slow breath out and said "OK – Lynn - here goes! - You gotta promise you'll never show this to anyone around here – ever – ever - you understand?"

"What is it girl?" I'm really pumped by now!

"Promise - Lynn! - Please promise!" Claire was insistent.

"Sure – Claire - I promise." I said. She drew back a little and looked me square in the eye, "I really do promise – Claire - I swear to God!"

"No boy has ever seen this – Lynn - I mean no boy - not even Steve!" She spoke without looking away. "When you're away and all the guys are bragging about back home and their girls and stuff - you won't hafta feel bad or lonesome. You can show them this and tell them this is your girlfriend and it won't be a lie – cause - I am a girl and I am your friend!" She handed me a picture with a resolve that said OK! - It's done now.

I held the photo up to the light and there was Claire, in a classic pin-up pose, like the one Betty Grable made famous. She was posed in front of an open gym locker, in a skin tight one piece bathing suit. This picture brought out Claire's full female charm, and magnified it to the point that you had to look closely to see if she was not some movie star. There was nothing wrong about the picture, but there was something there that made you want to gaze at it.

"Claire- I don't know what to say!" I whispered.

"Don't say anything – Lynn - take care of yourself and come back safe - I think you are a swell guy and I think Patty's interested in a lab technician here at Candler!"

"What?!" came my startled reply.

"Don't say a word!" She uttered. She leaned over, gave me a very sweet but not lingering kiss.

"Bye - please don't walk me to the door!" She was gone. This was one of those moments that make you wonder if it really happened.

The gang didn't go for pizza that night and at the time it didn't occur to me, that I would never see Fred, Angus or Steve again. It would be over two years before Billy and I crossed paths once more.

God still had his plan.

I knew that Fred Robinson had a job lined up as a truck dispatcher at some big shipping hub near Washington, D.C. I knew nothing of Steve Tankersly or Angus Faust's plans for the future; however I was aware that Billy was going to be an agent for the F.B.I. He was scheduled to report for training shortly after I left for the Navy.

We had a great year, this bunch of Southern Gentlemen and no brag, we were just that! We had the pleasure of dating some of the nicest, smartest and most dedicated girls a guy could ever hope to find. I think these girls probably set the standard by which we measured all the women in our future. I don't know if the girls were so great because of Candler influence, or if Candler is so great because of the girl's influence.

The Church service at Clayton P. Miller Methodist Church was special on that April 8, 1957. It would be my last Sunday and everyone wished me well.

Brother Blackwell took me aside to warn me of the impending evils that lay ahead.

"Look Son - remember that sin loves company and your buddies are gonna reach up and grab a double handful of your innocent soul and if you aren't careful and don't stay close to the Lord - your soul will look like a rag full of axle grease!"

Brother Blackwell owned the salvage yard where my Daddy had worked for a while. He was a dynamic preacher, yet had no seminary training.

Clayton P. Miller was a small Methodist Church, a half block from my house and had one of the largest youth groups in the Savannah District. This was probably due to the support and interest of the Stafford family along with Layton Sheppard and his wife. This little Church had been a big part of my life.

In fact, before I started to Clayton P. Miller, there was Robert McIntyre Methodist and before that was Trinity Methodist, and they all had very active youth groups. There was always some church related activity going on. I never got involved in any shady activities and most of my girlfriends were met at

Church related activities. I suppose that's why I had that innocent soul that Brother Blackwell referred to.

I made all my good-byes as sincere as I could, but I'd be fibbing if I didn't admit that some affected me much more than others.

I walked the half block home with my two brothers and presently Momma and Daddy were ready for a rare Sunday dinner at Uncle C.F. and Aunt Nelva's.

We all piled into the green Ford and proceeded in almost a straight line across town to the traffic circle in Garden City, Georgia. Uncle C.F. managed the "Johnson and Coffee Trailer Sales", located on the west side of a paved circle, where U.S. Highways 80, 17, 21 and Bay Street all convened. This was an extremely busy location and was a choice business site. Next to the Trailer Sales was the Traffic Circle Drive-In Theater, also managed by Uncle C.F, Aunt Nelva and my cousins. "Man" what a set up.

Maurice was the oldest of my uncle's four kids. He was a few months younger than me and we had been raised together until the onset of WW II. My Daddy was sent by Civil Service to New Orleans. Uncle C.F. was a master welder and sent to Charleston Naval Yard as a welding inspector.

The three girls were Christine, Brenda and Patricia. Patricia was a two year old, and the other two girls were in their teens.

All Momma's kin were light skinned and mostly blondes like me. Aunt Nelva was an in-law and from an old Louisiana French family. The dark hair and smoky eyes dominated this side of the family. Uncle C.F. always wore a white Huey P. Long style, Stetson hat, white shirt and a red ribbon bow tie. He was a picture of the southern politician. He was always chewing gum. He was also quite a character. Uncle C.F. knew every politician in the state. He was acquainted with many movie stars and international dignitaries and proudly displayed their photographs on his office wall to prove it. A photograph of him and Dan Duryea, always fascinated me.

Uncle C. F. was the reason my family came to Savannah. In 1947, the returning troops and the rapid growth of the country's population had created a huge market for mobile homes. Johnson and Coffee, a company in Charleston, S.C., handled the major manufacturer at the time. The Spartan Mobile Home, or house trailer as we called them at the time, was a premium product. It was all aluminum, polished and very nice. It was high end. Johnson and Coffee had added a new line, another high end product, but more roomy and more affordable, it was the New Moon line and sales were sky rocketing.

The Korean Conflict was still going on in 1951. Hunter Air Force Base in Savannah and Fort Stewart Army Base in Hinesville were bursting at the seams with military personnel and the demand for housing was more than my Uncle could handle alone, so when he made Momma and Daddy an offer they could not refuse; it was "Georgia Ho!"

In a short time the conflict ended and suddenly there was not enough business to support two families. No problem, a good mechanic will never be out of work. Between early 1953 and early 1957, my Daddy worked at five different major auto mechanical businesses in Savannah. He finished his career as shop foreman at Bowyer Motors, the Packard, Jeep and MG Dealership.

---Flashback---

Upon Graduation from Savannah High School, Bill Kehoe, one of Savannah's old school patriarchs hired me, in sales, at his appliance and tire dealership.

In short order, things really began to open up for me. I received a Congressional Appointment to the Naval Academy and my application at Southern Bell Telephone Company was accepted. My friend and fellow ROTC officer, from high school, Charles Davis, received his appointment to the Military Academy. The telephone company wanted me to come to work immediately; however, there was a strike at the time. I felt it was wise to decline and take my chances at being hired again when the strike was settled.

God had a plan.

I was working steady at Kehoe's and doing well. I had taken the admittance test for the academy some weeks earlier, and had placed my application with Southern Bell before the strike had begun.

I received notification from the office of our Congressman, Prince Preston, of my appointment to the Naval Academy and my acceptance at Southern Bell on the same day. Of course, the decision was a "no-brainer."

Before I could even comprehend my good fortune, my Daddy, had a terrible accident. Daddy was working at Critz Buick at the time and suffered a massive lower hernia. The doctor said it was so massive that Daddy would require a complete lower net. The convalescence was eight months to a year and then light duty for a considerable time after. Momma was working but it was evident that they needed me. I made the decision to apply for a waiver of a year to the Academy.

Congressman Preston handled it for me and an agreement was reached. The only catch was I had to retake the admittance exam. I thought that was fair. I had been number three out of the four receiving appointments in 1955, so what's the sweat. How dumb can you get in a year? Well pretty dumb, I guess, I was not even ranked in the top ten when I retested in 1956.

Southern Bell came through two weeks after the strike ended and I began my career in September, 1955.

I remember my discussion with Mr. Kehoe concerning the new job. He leaned forward in his big chair behind his office desk, placed both hands together in a prayer fashion. In a most philosophical tone he informed me that he would be remiss if he did not make an effort to keep me in his employ. He then offered me a ten dollar a week raise and mentioned some other perks, then continued to advise me how foolish it would be for me to accept his offer. He told me that he could never offer me the long range security and opportunity that a productive career with Southern Bell could offer. "You'll go far – Son!" He smiled and shook my hand.

----------------------------------- Back to Sunday Dinner -----------------------------------

Fried chicken is a great southern tradition for Sunday dinner. Aunt Nelva's fried chicken was influenced by her heritage. She was from a fine French family with a couple of centuries of southern cooking in her genes and brought a meal to the table that was fit for the most notable of connoisseurs; collard greens, rice and Cajun gravy, potato salad, green beans and yeast rolls.

"OH Yeah! - Iced tea!" Daddy had made banana pudding and brought it along, the pudding was his specialty. "Wow", what a meal.

My cousin, Maurice, was in his second year at the University of Georgia. He had graduated from Benedictine, an exclusive boy's military school in Savannah. The school was staffed and sponsored by the Benedictine Order. It's heritage and history was a part of Savannah's mystique.

We were all gathered in Uncle C.F.'s front office. They really didn't have a formal living room, so even on Sunday, every one gathered in the fully glassed front office. There were constant hand waves and smiles as folks would drive by and honk their horns. If a potential customer dropped in, well, they were welcomed and generally were offered coffee and cake. You know! I bet they made a lot of sales that way. Aunt Nelva always had the lower shelf in her fridge full of cold Coca Colas. I always took my breaks there, morning for coffee, evening for cokes, if my trouble route was on the West Side.

We were all talking about me leaving for the Navy and my cousin Christine said. "I'll bet Mom and Dad will save a bundle on coffee and cokes with Lynn gone." Everyone laughed.

Uncle C.F. leaned over in his leather chair, opened the side drawer of his desk, took out a box, moved some papers, to clear a spot and set the box on his desk. He looked at me and smiled and with his head, motioned me to take the box.

The Watkins were benevolent with coffee and cake, but believe me, they were frugal in everything else. There were six members in that family, all the kids were in Catholic schools that required tuition and uniforms. The gift was not wrapped, but in a nice gift box. I pulled the lid off and there was a brand new, top of the line, Remington Rolectric Razor. The dual foil heads gleamed with the precision that accompanied the Remington Brand.

I felt like a rich man. I was a daily shaver by now, but being a blond, and blued eyed boy of nineteen, plus being of Scottish heritage mixed with one eighth Choctaw Indian, I really didn't have a lot of facial hair. I would never be accused of not being closely shaven.

Daddy stood up, as tall as he could, being handicapped by the lower hernia he had suffered. He had healed extremely fast and was back to work, this time at J.C. Lewis Ford, in only seven months, but he favored those abdominal muscles and walked slumped over.

Momma would scold him with a command. "Staighten up! - L.Z.!"

He would pull himself erect to his once six foot frame, but soon relax to that now familiar slump. Daddy would chuckle, and boldly say. "Why straighten up?" I'm a mechanic; everything I work on is under a hood - under a car or on the floor! If I straighten up - I'll just hafta bend over again - so it's just a waste of time!"

Daddy looked at me, a hint of a tear in his eye. There was no question that he was proud of his oldest boy. He raised himself to his full height and with his chest proudly thrust forward, pulled another box, smaller this time, from his tweed coat pocket.

He was beginning to slump. His voice cracked a little. "Son - You're gonna be under water quite a lot in that submarine and you may have trouble telling morning from night - or the time o'day - so here's something that won't ever let you down!"

This box was not wrapped either. It was maroon, and had a gold coiled spring embossed on the top. I opened the box and there was a prize that I did not even know existed. It was a "Ruxton self-winding wristwatch". Ruxton was the private label of Friedman's, one of Savannah's exclusive jewelers.

I really felt like a rich man now. Everyone cheered and laughed and I made a little speech. I told 'em how I loved 'em and would miss 'em and kissed the girls.

I guess the kisses set Aunt Nelva off, because nothing would do, but to tell that story again. It always embarrassed me and to tell the truth, I never remember it really happening. Aunt Nelva and the girls swear it did and my denying it only made me out a liar, so I simply had to endure it. No one, including Momma, ever condemned me in any way, so I guess it wasn't so bad.

It seems that Aunt Nelva caught me peeping through the keyhole as the girls were taking a bath one day. I was fifteen at the time and Christine was maybe twelve or thirteen. Brenda was maybe eleven, Patty was an infant. Aunt Nelva's story states she chastised me and then made me go in and watch as the girls finished their bath. My face would always turn red and they said my tears, pleas, and embarrassment cured me of peeping through keyholes forever.

I suppose they were right.

It was a wonderful Sunday. We made our goodbyes and drove home. After arriving, I slipped out and walked down to the Church. I didn't go in, I felt as if it would be anti-climactic.

I was really just looking to see if Patty was there.

She wasn't. I was leaving in five days.

CHAPTER II

SUB SCHOOL

Clickty- Clack! – Clickity – Clack! Yes, trains do make that noise, and yes, it will put you to sleep. I slept a lot on my second train ride. The train was a streamlined passenger run from Miami to New York. It could not really be called an express, because it did make stops along the way. But it was by no means a local, there were long stretches when the constant chatter of the steel wheels on steel rails would, indeed, lull you to sleep.

---Flashback ---

My first train trip had been almost three years prior, when at the age of seventeen, I made the trip on a local from Savannah to Valdosta for my Naval Reserve physical examination. The trip by car would take less than three hours, but was an all-day deal on this local. We seemed to be stopping before we even got up to any speed.

Luckily, Valdosta was a typical small southern city that had grown from a small southern town, by this, I mean everything was downtown. The train track ran right through the middle of town, the station was right in the middle of town and the doctor I was to see, at the clinic, was right across the street from the train station. I stepped off the train walked across the street, had a brief clerical wait, saw the doctor, breathed in and out a few times, said "Aaah!", read an eye chart, dropped my drawers, bent over, coughed, dressed and walked out. I was officially declared "A1" for military service, all in less than forty-five minutes, including the walk.

I returned to the station, sat around for a while, bought an egg salad sandwich and slowly washed it down with a Pepsi. I stretched the lunch deal so long that the Pepsi was warm when I took the last swallow.

The train back to Savannah was late departing, due to recollecting the hogs that escaped while being loaded at a nearby side track. The hogs were destined for Meddin Brothers Packing Plant on Louisville Road in Savannah.   It was near midnight before I arrived home.

This ride to New York was different. The coaches were much nicer and I think the seats were wider. I had no problem sleeping, often having both seats available to lounge in.

Things changed when we reached Baltimore. Luckily I was still in my seat when the passengers at Washington boarded. These folks were pros at this train travel. They would heave their luggage, either over or under a seat, sit down, remove their coats, open briefcases, bags or whatever, and be engaged in whatever they did to pass the time, before I could have decided which way to go.

Not a word was spoken or any indecision as to where to sit. I think if I had not been in a seat already, I probably would have had to go look for a seat, possibly in another car. I figured most of these people were just going up the road to Baltimore. I was right; there was a mass exodus in Baltimore. It was nearly 2 AM, so I thought there would be very few getting on the train in Baltimore for New York on a Saturday morning. Wrong! The Washington crowd was nothing compared to this group.

There was no pushing or crowding, just a wall of humanity, all moving at the same pace, fast. They were filling the coach quickly. The man who had sat next to me from Washington had departed, so the window seat was vacant. I looked up and saw an attractive lady eyeing the seat. She was, visibly older than me but, "What the Hey," I'm a sailor now, all decked out in my dress blues. All women are fair game, I'll make my move. As she approached, I stood up, moved out into the aisle and with a slight bow, made a motion for her to take the window seat.

She was carrying some magazines that suddenly spilled from under her arm and fell behind her onto the floor. I sprang quickly to pick them up, as I bent over, she passed, then stepped aside for the fellow behind her to slide into the window seat and she immediately sat beside him and hooked her arm in his.

I picked up the magazines and turned to the couple. Neither one looked at me or acknowledged my efforts in any way. I was dumbfounded. "Man!" Talk about not being in control. I glanced around the coach, realizing that absolutely no one had seen what occurred and probably didn't care if they had. My mind raced; how do I handle this situation? Clearly it was a devised routine to get two seats together. If I caused a ruckus, I would be the guilty party. A United States Sailor assailing a civilian couple over a seat on a train.

My mind raced. I took my time placing the magazines in some sort of order thinking all the time. I wasn't upset with the man; obviously the woman had engineered this plan. I didn't have a lot of experience being devious but somehow this women should pay for taking advantage of this poor innocent, young, sailor, who only wanted to sit by her and talk and stuff.

I leaned over and gently placed the magazines in her lap. I never looked at the man, and with my best impersonation of a Southern Gentleman, said; "Your magazines Ma'am, I sure do hope you and your son have a mighty pleasant trip to New York." I reached up for my duffle bag, turned, walked forward, shouldered my sea bag from the corner and exited the coach, feeling I had avenged myself.

The next coach up was the dining car. It too was full. But there was room to stand at the bar. I would have thought the bar would be closed, being after 2AM, but the bartender was pretty busy. He was a slender colored fellow and moved with the swift hands of a professional. There was a touch of grey at the temples. His thin moustache was tinged with grey as well. He wiped his way down the bar to where I stood, leaned forward a little, he spoke and there was no hiding his distinct Gullah accent. "I don't check ID on service men".

With a smile, I answered. "Can't think of anything to drink other than coffee, at this hour! - You from Charleston?"

"No my man – Daufuski - been gone seventeen years now - but gonna go home soon and rest these legs!" He sighed, glanced quickly at me. "Don't hear no Carolina in you - maybe Florida"?

"No – it's Georgia!" I replied. "Only been there five years though!" He stopped me.

"Don't tell me - my man - I got it! - Louisiana! - That's where you from - Yassuh! - Louisiana - for sure - I hear that Cajun way down deep." He smiled with that pride you feel when you pull off something big. He knew he had impressed me.

"Hold on Mr. Sailor man - I got something just for you!" He turned and went back into a small cubby room at the end of the bar. He soon emerged with a cup of coffee and placed it on the bar about four feet away and with that professional touch that comes with seventeen years of practice, slid it to a perfect stop, right in front of me, never spilling a drop. "Sip that young fella and take a trip to "New Orleans!"

I had to play the game; this man had gone to too much effort for me to shy away now.   I take my coffee black, with two heaping teaspoons of sugar, but two wheelbarrow loads of sugar wouldn't have soothed the bite of that cup.

I never liked chicory to begin with, but Momma, Daddy, Aunt Lola, Uncle Red, Mr. and Mrs. Denham and all the folks around New Orleans and Baton Rouge liked it. This cup of coffee would have made "Earl Long's" day a little brighter.

I swigged the coffee, snapped my head to the side, winked at my new friend, faked a sigh of satisfaction and sipped it down in a fine rendition of finishing a jigger of whiskey.

He grinned and pantomimed the gesture for "Want another?"

I gestured back. "NO!" I then whispered loudly. "I won't sleep for a week now!"

He roared with laughter and drew a cup from the urn on the wall. "This cup is the house brand - that first cup was on the house - this cup is fifty cents! - Suh!"

We continued to talk, off and on, as he went about his business and the remainder of the trip went quite quickly. It was day break when we began to slow for our arrival at Grand Central Station. All in all, it had been a pleasant trip and I really was well rested.

I stood there in shock. I had left the train and walked into the main part of the station. I felt as if I had gone back in time. The massive array of wrought iron, glass ceiling and stone was familiar, but didn't look anything like my expectations. I had seen pictures, photographs, and movies depicting Grand Central Station. --This was not it.

My mind was in a whirl. I stopped to collect my thoughts. I knew my train had been the right one. My government travel slip had the info on it. The ticket folks in Savannah had checked it. There were numerous times it was looked at in route. I had heard "New York City, last stop, Pennsylvania Station," called out by the conductor. "UH! - OH!"- Pennsylvania Station. Had I got off at the wrong stop? Something told me that a major passenger train that began its journey in Miami would not make multiple stops in the same city and the conductor had stated "Last stop!"

This place was huge and as I looked up, my eyes caught the name chiseled in the marble "Pennsylvania Station – 1910". I reached into my pocket for my travel chit, I knew it said Grand Central Station. I unfolded the authorization form and sure enough, on the second travel authorization line it stated; "Departing Grand Central Terminal for New London, Connecticut. These government travel authorizations forms were not the actual travel ticket, you simply showed the form to the appropriate ticket agent and they handled the route and ticket for you. Well at least I was in New York City.

As I walked around a bit I started reading the signs and information, and arrival and departure schedules. I soon realized there was no train going from Pennsylvania Station to New London, Connecticut, but I did see signs directing folks to a subway that went to Grand Central Terminal.

"Boy" I felt like the smartest guy in the world, I had figured this out all by myself. Now, I don't know if this is true in all cases, but it seems that most trains that travel from far off will arrive and depart from Pennsylvania Station. The trains that run to nearby cities are served by Grand Central Station or Terminal as they wrote it.

This was pretty early on Saturday morning and I was not due in New London officially until Monday morning when my classes convened. I had already learned how important it was to be ready in this man's Navy. My plan was to arrive at the base as early as possible, get checked in and then scope the layout. There is an old saying, "The early bird gets the worm." Well, it's true. There will be a huge number of candidates arriving and those that arrive early usually get their choice of bunks and lockers. Normally the PO's [petty officer in charge] do not go to the trouble of assigning bunks, they will simply tell you to pick a rack and get back to them. A great many times you can worm your way into a job assisting the POs. There is a lot of work involved in setting up for a new class and the POs normally can use the help. The bottom line is: the job you choose is generally much better than the job you are assigned and in "Uncle Sam's Navy," every man will have a job.

I shouldered my sea bag, picked up my duffle and walked outside. This was Saturday morning, I suppose close to 9AM. I had never seen so many people in one place in my life. I thought I'd see a little of New York, but site seeing was out of the question. Walking, well, maybe, I'd better check.

I saw my first New York City Policeman. He was well over six feet tall and dressed in dark blue. The coat was mid-thigh in length with a double row of brass buttons down the front and as he stood at the entrance door to the Station there was no doubt as to who was in charge. He would rock back, first on his heels then forward on his toes. His hands were clasped behind his back. His night stick was attached to his wrist; it would swing in an arc behind him and stop as he caught it, hands still clasped. It would rest for a second or two, then swing back the other way, only to be caught again. The man had a rhythm to his swinging that blended perfectly with his rocking.

"Officer!" I called. He turned to look at me, but his stance did not change.

"May I help you - Sir" was his answer.

"Yessir - how can I get to Grand Central Station?" I asked as I lowered my sea bag.

"Go right back inside and follow the signs to the Subway - can't miss it." I guess he thought I was stupid. I should have told him I wanted to walk, if it wasn't too far.

"Well Sir - I thought I'd walk - if it wasn't too far."

This time he moved his stance and faced me. "Where'r you from sailor?"

"Savannah, Georgia" was my answer.

"Lived out in the country"? He asked.

"I have lived in the country". I answered back.

"Can you read? This ticked me off. I suppose he could tell. He didn't wait for a reply.

He turned back to his stance "See that avenue there, directly in front of you?"

I nodded.

"That's West 32nd Street - go straight until you come to Park Avenue - turn left - can't be more than a dozen or so blocks." He glanced around at me. "Can't miss it." He went back to his rocking and swinging.

I hefted my sea bag over my right shoulder, picked up my duffle bag and started walking. I took a quick look at my Ruxton, April 13, 1957, 9:22AM. I felt a keen sense of freedom, a feeling of liberation. Lord! - I don't know why, nothing could be further from the truth. I was in the U.S. Navy, heading for Sub School, looking for Grand Central Station and walking in New York City, but still had an exhilarating sense of freedom.

I walked about six blocks, I mean six long blocks before I found Park Avenue. I became confused along the way when I looked at a street sign that told me I was now on East 32nd Street. "Man"! How did that happen? I hadn't made any turns and by the sun I knew I had been walking east. 32nd Street was much narrower than I expected a New York Street to be.

The buildings on each side were not skyscrapers but considerably taller than any I'd ever seen, however I could tell the early morning sun was definitely in front of me. Retracing my steps soon told me; Fifth Avenue was the dividing line between east and west streets in New York.

I made my left on Park Avenue. This was more like it. A wide avenue with a median in some blocks, and numerous stairways down to subways with destination names that perked memories of movies and songs. There were even streets that disappeared underground and streets that came up from underground. I passed giant grates on the sidewalk that shushed vast amounts of air from time to time. I was walking north now and the dozen or so blocks turned out to be about fourteen. I made frequent rest stops. A full sea bag is a load.

I began to see a structure looming ahead, Park Avenue was ending there, but I'm sure it picked up on the other side.

There it was; the familiar stone structure with the precision cut stones that fit so tightly it gave the building a semblance of unity. The huge columns and arched windows confirmed it, Grand Central Terminal. It was not as tall as the surrounding buildings, but, never the less, it was a grand sight.

As I started in, a sign caught my eye: "Oyster Bar". It was nearly 11AM, so I found a ticket window. The agent gave me a good selection of trains to New London. I picked one that left at 3PM and scouted around to find the correct departure gate. It was a level down and the route proved not too difficult to remember. That "Oyster Bar" was calling.

-- FLASHBACK ---

I was born in Shreveport, Louisiana on November 17, 1936 at the North Louisiana Sanitarium. My family moved to New Orleans in early 1942. We then moved on to Baton Rouge in 1946. I grew up eating catfish, goggleye, crabs and crawfish, but never oysters. In 1951 we came east to Savannah, Georgia and Daddy made friends with a family named Olstrom that lived in Richmond Hill, Georgia.

One Saturday, Mr. Olstrom invited our entire family down for an oyster roast. Daddy loaded us up in the car very early that morning, telling us that we had to make the tide, so hurry it up! I had no clue as to what lay ahead.

Momma took Gray and Poco straight into the house upon arrival. Daddy's friend lived just a few blocks from US Highway 17 South and faced a school. It was early November and already in the fifties, temperature wise. We traveled for about fifteen minutes to a salt water river where we got into a wooden flat bottom boat about 14 feet long and a wide porch built on the front. It was powered by a Gale outboard. I don't remember the H.P., but it wasn't very fast.

We loaded the boat and were on our way in short order. Mr. Olstrom began to instruct me on how to rake the oysters. I realized that at sixteen years old, I was gonna be the oyster boy.

The tools were a couple of rakes, some poles with heavy wide blades and about half a dozen scraggly burlap bags. The rakes only had three prongs each. I soon learned why.

As we proceeded along the river, we would come to mud banks with areas of oyster clusters. Mr. Olstrom would scan the clusters and determine which group of cluster was ready for harvest. The rakes would be used to pull the softball size clusters from the bed of old shells that were left for future oysters to attach to. If an oyster cluster was stubborn, the pole with the heavy wide blade would be jammed at the cluster base and with a skilled twist the cluster would be pried off. The rake would then be used to pull them to the boat. We stuffed them into the burlap bags. Mr. Olstrom called them coon oysters and began to relay the virtues of coon oysters over select oysters. Coon oysters were better in taste, texture, and vitamin content, besides, select oysters were a rarity in these waters.

"Lynn!" Mr. Olstrom called out. "Shed yo clothes boy - Ya'll gonna hafta get wet here directly!"

"Sir?" I asked, with a question. "Get Wet?"

"Right! - Son - look in that bag, there!" He gestured toward a bundle wrapped in oilcloth. "Get yo stuff off - cause you'll ruin 'em - them boots there will protect yo feet and them britches'l keep yo legs from gettin cut up!"

"Tides going out fast and the water is gonna be too far from the rakes - ya'll gonna hafta wade up to em!" He explained.

I shed my clothes, even my shirt, keeping my "Fruit of the Looms", though.

In the bundle was a pair of, almost too tight, rubber boots and a pair of, linseed oil dipped, canvas pants, that tied at the waste. The material was heavy. I was soon to find out why.

We approached another rake and the motor started churning mud. "OK – Lynn - over you go boy"! I realized the ya'll, that was to get wet, was me. It was chilly, I had removed my shirt and the slight wind was not a real comfort. However, the excitement had my adrenaline flowing and my macho wouldn't let me complain. This is the first time I was doing the "Man Thing" instead of my Daddy. I felt empowered.

As I stepped to the side of the boat, I realized why it was so wide and flat bottomed, there was scarcely a list. As I stepped over the side of the boat my foot went "Sploot" in the mud and sank almost to the top of the boot. I continued to tumble, so I extended both arms to catch myself. The arms also went "Sploot!"

Here I am, in a three pointed "Sploot", my free foot still inside the boat, my face only inches from the water. The water was actually less than a foot deep, but that mud was murder. I was surprised how warm the water and mud was.

Mr. Olstrom chuckled and said. "Here – Lynn - Let me help you!" He didn't move a muscle. Daddy came back and helped me get steadied.

Mr. Olstrom continued. "When you decide to get up - remember to move as if you are on a cloud - don't put all your weight on one foot until the other foot is already moving to a new spot!" I was beginning to think this outing was not going to be a picnic.

Daddy whispered low, "Don't worry – Son! - I'm right here!"

I decided to let nature take its course and go for it. I lifted my free foot and fell to my knees in the water, at the same time pulling my hands free and pulling the stuck foot up and moving it forward before the once free foot could get stuck. It worked. I managed a gangling, wobbling walk up to the oyster rake. In a moment I realized that I could not stand in any one spot without beginning to sink in the mud. I began a kind of slow moving dance to stay mobile. I found how the thick fabric of the pants kept the razor sharp oyster shells from cutting my legs as I would fall into them

Actually it began to feel kind of natural after a bit. I realized now that I was the only productive member of the crew. The oyster rakes were well out of reach of the boat. It was taking some time, but we were really getting some oysters.

Every once in a while I would come to the water's edge to wash the mud from my hands. Quite often this was a job; there were wide swaths of mud much darker than the rest, almost black. The regular mud would wash off with ease, but the black stuff would just smear around. I found that reaching down for a handful of regular mud and using it like soap would do a better job at removing the black goo.

We had moved up a little creek where Mr. Olstrom indicated the oyster rakes were a little closer and perhaps we could finish our last two bags a little quicker. The tide was well out by now and even though there was probably a foot of water under the boat, there was no room on either side. We raised the motor and proceeded to pole through with the oars. I got to rest a bit.

Mr.Olstrom told us this creek ran into a small salt water pond about 200 yards ahead and on occasions; bass or trout would get trapped at low tide. If you were lucky you could come out of there with a boat load of fish.

I was out of the boat raking oysters and Mr. Olstrom and Daddy were able to reach some from the boat. We were steady working on reaching our fill.

From up the creek there came a loud "Whissing" sound, then two short blasts, almost like steam escaping. There was a great disturbance in the water. We could see nothing as there was a bend in the creek right in front of us. It was a good ten or eleven feet from our boat to the top of the marsh grass.

"OH! Sweet Jesus!" Exclaimed Mr. Olstrom. "Out of the boat! - L.Z.- Out! - Now! – Lynn – Quick! – get the damn boat out of the water! – L.Z.- grab the damn boat! – Hurry! -Lynn- Grab the boat – Pull! - Now Pull!"

We grabbed the boat by the side and amid shouts of " Why? – What For? - What's wrong"? We slipped and slid and managed to pull the boat sideways up on the mud bank next to the oyster rake.

None too soon either. The water commotion was getting closer and the steam blasts were getting louder. My mind was racing as wild pictures of some futuristic machine or such was coming around that bend. Never did I expect what I saw.

The lead porpoise was a least six feet long and the two behind were smaller but just as determined not to get trapped in that pond with a boat between them and deep water. The water in the creek was a foot deep at the shallowest and maybe two feet at the deepest, but the giant beasts were really trucking when they passed us. They were keenly aware of our presence. You could see the focus in their eyes; it was the same as when you know a person has looked at you. They steamed by, having no problem moving their massive bodies over the shallow spots in the creek. They were gone and quiet reigned once again.

Mr. Olstrom explained that the porpoises were in the pond feeding on the captive fish and could have remained there safely until high tide, but had sensed our presence in the creek and felt trapped. He said they would damage the boat in their panic to get out and that was too much of a chance to take. We were a long way from the hill and he didn't feel like swimming it, besides, we had our oysters.

I ate my first roasted oyster, that evening, straight off the fire. Actually they are steamed. Mr. Olstrom had a pre-dug pit in his back yard. I had to square it up a bit. We built a big fire, let it burn down to coals, spread them out, covered them with a sheet of corrugated tin, loaded it with a layer of oysters and threw some wet burlap bags on top and in moments we had some of the most flavorful hot oysters any connoisseur could ask for.

The first thing we did was to turn a fresh water hose on the mass of oyster we had harvested and then we quickly previewed them for waste, chunks that were dead and big rocks.

There is an art, to shucking oysters, most people will use gloves, because the steamed shells are still hard and sharp. Some skilled folks will bare-hand the oysters. These coon oysters come in a cluster that will offer as many as three to four oysters of varying sizes, per cluster. Holding the cluster in one hand will aid in placing your knife in the now steamed open shell. Perhaps there is no opening, so you use the knife in a convenient seam. You will twist your oyster knife and the top shell will fall away, leaving that luscious mollusk lying on a half shell of pearl that is kept in place by a shred of tough tissue at the foot of the shell.

There may be a tiny soft red crab inside, a co-dweller, you may or may not choose to eat it. A quick flip of the knife and the shred is cut and you now hold the delicious morsel dangling between the knife blade and your thumb. If all went well the liquid bag is now temptingly hanging down and is first into the mouth. You will press the delicacy between the roof of your mouth and tongue. Hopefully the liquid has cooled enough as to not blister your mouth. "Ahhh"! The exhilarating surge of taste is a pure delight and not soon forgotten.

---------------- BACK TO THE OYSTER BAR IN GRAND CENTRAL STATION -------------

I decided that an oyster meal was out of the question. It was a little after noon now and "Dag-gummit!"-- Grand Central Station, once in a lifetime. The world famous -"Oyster Bar"- The thought of passing it by and not getting oysters was unthinkable. I rechecked the menu: "Oyster stew $3.50" – "Yep! I can handle that!"

I placed my order and was surprised at the length of time it took; it wasn't a really long wait, but somewhat longer than dipping a ladle in a pot and pouring it in a bowl.

When it did arrive, it was a picture that would have made any menu proud. The milk soup had traces of golden butter swirling across the top, as it made its way through tiny green specks of some exotic seasoning. The little oyster crackers bobbed about in anticipation of the coming feast. I brushed my spoon in a side motion to rouse the oysters from the bottom of the bowl. I had to brush my spoon again before the first of maybe six oysters revealed themselves.

In disappointment I hoisted my first sip of liquid. No oyster, just liquid, it was familiar, I don't know what I expected. I supposed the "Oyster Bar" hype made me think the taste would be something other than coon oyster stew. Further spoons did nothing to change my mind. This famous stew was no better than the oyster stew we had at home and the oysters definitely were not nearly as deeply flavored.

"Well! – Whatta you expect for $3.50 a bowl?" I thought.

The stew however was my only disappointment. New York City has a charisma that affects everyone. I was already wishing I had more time. I thought, perhaps, I could change my train to another that departed later the next day. "No - that wouldn't be wise!" I thought.   What good is a plan if you don't stick to it?

Another first, the train to New London was electric: it seemed faster and, indeed was much quieter than the one from Savannah and was not really crowded.   I suppose that being Saturday and 3PM was not a prime travel time for commuters.   The trip was uneventful.   I only had a couple of hours of daylight.   The countryside was not really countryside; there is an awful lot of habitation in New York and Connecticut.   I went to sleep, without dinner.

I didn't realize how close New York was to New London.   I awakened at the announcement for New London, checked my watch and couldn't believe it was right at 6:30PM.

I stepped off the train in New London and faced the Station.   On the left of the station, was a bus, the familiar school bus type, but painted that familiar and friendly Navy grey.   A white sign was over the passenger door, "U.S. Naval Base - Submarine School".   I boarded and found the driver relaxing on the seat behind the driver's position.   I was the only sailor there.

"Not a big crowd tonight, Huh?" I asked.

He looked up and motioned for me to stow my gear in a cage at rear of the bus.   He then rose and moved to the bottom step and leaned out.   Looking back over his shoulder he called to a train attendant.   "How long?"

The attendant answered back, "Ten minutes, max!"

"Thanks."   The driver, dressed in undress blues, climbed into the driver's seat and cranked the engine.   " Sit up here - Buddy, this little heater ain't much and we gotta wait till the train leaves before we can go."   I sat down in the front seat on the passenger side.   "S'posed to drop to 40 sumthin tonight - and next to the water - that's cold man!"

"We have to wait for more guys?" I questioned.

"Naw - there ain't another train for a couple of hours and it's coming from up north.   You assigned for training or duty?"

"Sub school", I replied.

"Ah! - A f--king reserve! – Eh?" His remark was crude.

"What? – You see a tatoo on my ass that says reserve?"   I was now playing this crude game of insult the stranger.

Hey! Don't mess yo skivvies sailor boy - I see you're a seaman and going to sub school - that means you ain't been in the fleet or you'd be rated by now.   If you were in the fleet and not rated, you would be too damn dumb to qualify for sub school.

His deduction amazed me, so I told him so.

"Naw!" He stuck out his tongue and made a "Pluuup" sound, then said. "The only school starting Monday is a two week reserve school - You said training – an there ain't no humpin in the shower school - So you must be a F--king reserve!"

A thought occurred to me, so I played it. "Flunked out, didn't you?"

"Yeah, two f--king weeks ago - now I'm driven this friggin bus 'till my transfer comes through."

A sailor's rate insignia is on his left arm, so I had not caught sight of this guy's rank.

 "What's your job, buddy?" I asked.

The pride rang in his voice, "IC Electrician Third Class and I don't have a hash mark yet. I thought Subs would be the thing man, all that money, dolphins [Submarine Designation Pin] but man - my temper got the best of me - I couldn't handle it."

His sarcasm was gone now and I felt a little sorry for him. "Did they offer you any kinda choice of duty?"

"Naw - I told em, send me to Timbuktu - I didn't give a shit!" The sarcasm was returning.

Luckily the train began to move and my unhappy friend crunched the transmission into low gear and lurched ahead, as he reached for the door lever, he called out "Bus to the base departing!" He shut the door.

"That's where you submariners have got it made. - There is a special table in the chow hall. - There's a buncha sandwich stuff on it for you guys. - Sometimes you keep some weird hours." His information was welcomed.

The bus stopped about a block inside the gate and I departed with thanks to the driver and I wished him luck. I understood his disappointment. He never told me how his temper had caused his wash out. I wanted my submarine so badly that I didn't want to even think of washing out.

The administration building was a two story complex that was straight from the good old days, big, roomy ceiling fans and steam heat registers around the walls. It was toasty warm. The P.O. on duty took my travel packet, made his check- in marks, shuffled my papers and grunted occasionally. I sat and waited patiently. He finally looked my way and held up a piece of paper. I rose and saw it was my barracks assignment chit.

"When you check into your barracks - they'll fill you in on the rest of the particulars. - Wait a bit and I'll have a driver take you up by jeep!" He pointed at a bench along the wall.

"Is it far?" I queried.

"Not really – look - check the base map - there on the wall." He motioned behind me by the entrance door. The map layout was pretty easy to read and surprised me as to how small the base was. It was impressive to see the removable silhouettes of subs with names and numbers as they were berthed along the Thames. I noticed that there were a couple of boats with notations by them, one, the U.S.S. Jack was noted "Greece" and the other, the U.S.S. Paddle with "Brazil" by it.

My eye caught one name that made my heart jump. "U.S.S. Nautilus. However my excitement quickly waned when I saw the notation "TDA Pacific." I found my barracks and saw that it was only three blocks down and three blocks to the right.

"How long before a driver will be available?" I inquired.

The second class yeoman looked up and sarcastically exclaimed. "When he gets back!" That's when I noticed the P.O. had no dolphins.

I was beginning to feel that those symbolic pins made a tremendous difference in a sailor's attitude toward life. "Is it OK if I walk?" I asked.

He never looked up. "Suit yourself - Buddy!" His reply was nonchalant, as he continued to shuffle through my papers.

"You'll pick up your papers after your trainings finished. Report back here on Friday afternoon April 12 - to check in for the eight week Sub school. ---- This is weird!" He murmured.

"Something's wrong?" I asked.

"Not really - just unusual - you're scheduled for a two week Reserve Sub School and then right into an eight week Basic Sub Training Course. - I've never seen that before.

HUMM!" He murmured. "I assume you're planning to do your two year obligation also - Right?"

"That's the plan - Boss." I answered.

"Well - I don't see the paper work authorizing you for further assignment after training - but don't worry - we gotcha for ten whole weeks - it'll sort itself out - Good night - Sailor!"

I shouldered my gear and made my way down the steps to street level and started walking. The lights from an approaching vehicle blazed across my back, a horn beeped two short beeps. I stopped and turned to see the bus that brought me slowing to a stop. The door swung open and the driver smiled.

"Avast there, ye guppy! -- Barracks A or B?" He called.

"Barracks B!" I shouted back.

"Come aboard there me laddie - Har! – Har! Aye'l give ye a lift!" Boy! Had his attitude improved.

I hauled my gear aboard and quickly found the cause of the jubilance. There were four other sailors on board that were returning from town and they were all, including the driver, sharing a bottle of "Three Feathers Whiskey."

The driver mumbled. "Don't worry – Buddy - I 'm finished for the night - I'll drop you guys off - take the bus to the barn and sleep 'till noon!"—"Here - have a snort!"

A cry of protest went up from the passengers. "Ain't your bottle - prick!" Shouted one.

"You done drank half of it - you son of a bitch!" Hissed another.

He handed me the bottle. I just stepped into the aisle and passed the bottle to the nearest drunk, problem solved. I didn't like whiskey anyway.

The wall map in the administration building didn't indicate that the base was actually built on the side of a hill. So believe me, the ride was welcome. I never saw my new driver buddy again; I reckon his transfer came through. In the days that followed I thought of him often and realized that his actions that night, allowing an open liquor bottle on the base and then taking a drink himself while still on duty was not a wise decision. I would not want someone that can dismiss his call to duty that easily, to have my back in a crisis, but then, I didn't report him, so where does that put me?

The steps to my barracks led to a corridor and the PO office was on the right. The light was on, but no one was in the room. The office had the customary counter that ran the width of the office with a swing up section on the left. On the counter was a log sheet, it read "Submarine Training", under that was "Basic Two Week Reserve Training, in the right corner was written "Class 41 - 1957". Listed alphabetically below were 32 names.

I found mine second to last, a fellow named Zowolski was last on the list. I checked and found I was senior on reserve time, however was outranked by an YN3. This is a Petty Officer Third Class Yeoman, a clerical rating, it however, indicated the guy was sharp, to be rated in the reserves in less than three years is an unusual feat.

A reservist normally selected a "cruise" every summer. The Navy offered planned cruises all during the year that would include some schools, like Sub School. There were times the entire reserve unit would go on a special cruise and actually be the majority of the crew on a ship. The Navy would provide some ships solely for the purpose of training reserves. Actually there are areas of the country that provide enough reserves to have a ship assigned to them. Normally cities that host naval bases will be blessed with a reserve ship, usually a destroyer escort. These crews, even though they are reserves, are able to join the fleet in an emergency and in short order is fully operational.

In looking again at the log, I noted there were no markings by any names; the "log in time" column was blank as was "bunk number" column. No notation on any column. It appeared I was the first one to arrive. I decided to take a look at the crew's quarters.

Leaving my gear by the front wall of the office, I stepped into the corridor. The corridor ran all the way across the front of the building. The office was on the right, and a matching door was on the far left. In the center was a double door with two small glass windows, one on each side. I peeped into one of the windows and could see a typical huge sleeping area equipped with rows of standard over and under bunks. There were no lights but from the large windows, there was ample street light to see by.

I heard a toilet flush. The sound came from the office area. I turned back and re-entered the office to find it still vacant. At this time I noticed a door at the rear of the office and figured that was where the office head was.

"Ahoy!" I loudly called out, a brief pause, the rear door opened and out stepped a man well into his thirty's.

"Ahoy? -- Ahoy?" He said. "What are ya -- a friggin pirate?" – "Hell - I ain't heard "Ahoy" since I saw Treasure Island!" – "Ahoy - my ass!" – "You checkin in?"

"Yeah - I'd like to - if I'm in the right place!'' -- I'd really wanted to call him "Sir", but PO's don't rate a sir, unless it's in boot camp, if you slip up, it brands you as a recruit.

"Ohh ! -- Man ya're early - matter of fact I was almost not here." – "Don't have to be here till 0700 tomorrow – Man - we hardly ever get a reservist before Sunday". He glanced at my left arm. "Hell - Ya ain't the "Pen" either!" Old timer's sometimes call a yeoman "The Pen". "When he gets here, thirty minutes and I'm gone". The yeoman on the list was the highest rank in the class of 32, so he was probably going to be the CPO, or the man in charge.

"Ya check in at the main office"? I answered with a nod.

"They give ya a chit"? I pulled it from my tunic pocket and handed it over.

"Let's see ya I.D." I lifted my tunic and pull my wallet from my trousers, flipped it open and held it in front of him. His quick eyes caught all he needed to know, he wrote 19:33 in the "log in" column.

"Done any cruises yet?" He asked. This time he was looking right at me.

"Three - one to St. John, N.B. - one to Miami and a long week-ender on a sub out of Charleston." I began to wonder if he was a submariner. He was in blues, but tee shirt only. " You been on the boats?" I asked.

"Two - now I'm stuck with this wimpy shore duty break! - I wish they'd deep six that rule - the only good thing about it is my wife and she's only two miles away."

"Ever been CPO - son?" He asked. CPO meant Chief Petty Officer and did not mean actual rank, simply meant the man in charge. It was Navy custom that whenever you had a group, some member of that group would be put in charge.

"Well yeah -- lemme see -- boot camp - D.I. for our reserve's drill team. - Deck hand section leader on one cruise and inventory chief on the other."

"What about the sub?" He questioned.

"Quartermaster stuff mostly, you know, the helm and topside watch."

"Alright son - listen up - gotta deal for ya! - You cover the office tonight - it's simple - just do what I just did for ya! - Make sure you check the ID cards! - They get the records and papers at the main office and leave the ID check to us - log everyone in-- let em pick a rack-- get the number-- put it on the sheet. - That's it - I'll be back at 0700." This is all legal - long as ya ain't been drinking!" He cocked his head, making that a question.

"Nope nothing to drink - but I'm really hungry!" I replied. I then asked; "Excuse me - but what's the deal you mentioned?"

"He laughed. Yar're sharp! Man! - I'll see ya don't pull any duty while you're here - how's that."

"Man that's great"! I exclaimed. "All ten weeks?"

He snapped his head back in shock. "Ten weeks!" He gasped.

"Yeah! -- This school and my eight week regular sub school."

"No way - man! That' a whole different deal - barracks and everything - ya gonna hafta kiss somebody else's ass for that!"

I had to laugh.

"Hey if ya don't want the deal - just say so - then every time I post duty - I'll think how this young seaman screwed me out of time with my wife and" ------

"Say no more - my man"! I blurted out.

"Listen - stay in the back room there." He motioned toward the door where he had entered the room. "Everything's clean - 'cept the towel I just used and ya may want to wait an hour or so before ya use the head!" He looked at me and grinned. "It's the meatloaf and baked beans man- surely ya've been there!"

Yeah! - But it's corned beef and cabbage for me!"

He laughed. "That too – look - the chow hall is next door - there's plenty to eat - just keep ya eye out for the office!   I don't expect anyone before noon tomorrow and I'll see ya at 0700."   He went into the back room and picked up his tunic and pea coat. I saw the red and white flash on the arm. He was a torpedoman first class, with two hash marks and yes, dolphins.

I wondered what his wife looked like and if she wanted him home as much as he wanted to be there.

He spoke again. "Name's Carol Hardy - number's by the phone if you can't handle it! - See ya!" -- He was gone.

The room behind the office had a single bunk, and bathroom with toilet, shower, sink and a mirror. There was a locker and a chair on the wall opposite the bunk. In the middle of the rear wall was a door leading to the main sleeping area.

I didn't unpack my entire bag. I was pretty sure the CPO would take this room when he arrived, I was pretty sure it was going to be the YN3. I did change my dress blues to my undress. I carefully rolled my blues, inside out, so they would be ready for the next occasion when needed. I took my blanket out and noticed the blanket on the bunk was grey, mine was that familiar sand tan. The pillow case was bright white clean and looked inviting. My stomach reminded me that I had no supper, so I made my way outside, turning left to the barracks next door. It looked exactly like all the other barracks, except for the sign by the walk between the buildings that read "Galley". The sign over the front door was in big black letters, "Mess Hall". There were lights on inside. As I opened the front door the smell of fresh bread greeted me with a nostalgic fragrance.

We lived three blocks from Frankenstein's Bakery in New Orleans during World War II. That fragrance was an everyday thing in my young life. Just inside the mess hall was a stainless steel table with loaves of fresh bread, various sandwich meats, cheeses, condiments and a refrigerator standing beside a drink dispenser. The dispenser had a stack of pea-green cups beside it with a tray for empty cups. I opened the fridge and there was that meatloaf Hardy had mentioned. It was already sliced and just the right size for a sandwich. Using the large knife left on the table, I cut two fairly thick slices of bread and placed a slab of meatloaf between. I took a cup and stepped to the drink dispenser, one lever said "Milk" and the other said "Grape". I figured it was cool-aid, so I opted for milk.

As I made my way back to my barracks, I made a mental note not to forget to return the cup in the morning. "Man!" Was I hungry and after the first bite, I immediately wished I had fixed two sandwiches. I thought back and realized all I had eaten since leaving home Friday morning was a boloney sandwich Momma had fixed, two cups of coffee and a bowl of oyster stew.

As I munched on the meatloaf I decided to look around the office. There was a base map here also, with building numbers on them. I tried to make a note as to the order of building numbers in relation to their location. I didn't have much success. Surveying the board gave some insight as to the daily and weekly routine of the base.

The chow hall, opened at 0600, most classes started at 0800. "Opps"! Chow on Sunday was a brunch from 1000 to 1400 hours. "OH! Well! -- I'll sleep late - No! –Wait! -- Hardy said 0700. --Poop" - I may get another sandwich after all!

A short trip this time, I got cold cuts and milk. It was close to 2200, I didn't unmake the bed, just removed my shoes, lay back on the top blanket and covered myself with my trusty reserve issue blanket. I could almost smell the beach as I thought of the times I had lay on it there.

If I dreamed I don't remember it, the squeal of brakes awoke me, accompanied by voices. Early morning light was coming through the side window of the room, no sunlight, just dawn light. I swung my feet to the floor, slipped on my shoes, picked up my blanket, quickly folded it and placed it on the chair. I splashed water on my face and dried it on the same towel that Hardy had done whatever with, didn't matter, I wanted to be in the office when he came in.

Luckily my hair was short and a quick hand brush would do, I stepped into the office and through the window could see Hardy talking to driver of the jeep that had squealed me awake. "By the way!" All jeep brakes squeal.

Hardy was a rugged guy and looked exactly like what you would expect a submariner to look like. I had not noticed any tattoos the night before. His two hashmarks denoted over eight but less than twelve years' service. I figured he was career bound and if he made chief soon, it would be definite. The jeep pulled away, but Hardy walked to the right, not left to the chow hall, but to the first building to the right.

"I bet he went for coffee. "A thought struck me. All sailors love coffee. I looked around and sure enough there was a percolator under the counter on the far left. Behind it was a nice looking wooden box about the size of a shoe box. In the box was everything but cream. So what, I don't use cream anyway, maybe Hardy doesn't either.

"What the Hey! – go for it Lynn." I picked up the pot and dashed to the sink in the back room, flipped the top back and pulled the strainer basket and tube out. "How much water"? I asked myself. I looked in the pot and saw the stained coffee line from past pots, "Works for me," I thought and filled the pot to the line. Back to the counter and in the box was a fairly new pound of Maxwell House. I looked at the bag and frantically searched for a clue as to how much coffee.

Back home we kinda went by a teaspoon per cup ratio, but this percolator was much nicer than any I had ever seen and I didn't know its cup capacity. The coffee bag was fairly full so I figured maybe one pot had been made with it. The bag had been meticulously opened, then folded down and wrapped with a rubber band to seal it. Hardy was a neat guy and probably a coffee connoisseur, maybe this was not a good idea.

I held the bag up and plumped it to appear full, then noted how much coffee was gone. I'll just duplicate that amount and see how it works. The grounds came to about half way the stain marks in the basket. "Nope - that's not right!" I thought.

"Wait a minute," I said to myself. "The coffee will swell when it gets wet and also splash up on the sides, so maybe that is the right amount." I shut the top and plugged the cord into the wall socket. "I'll impress him or tee him off - one or the other!"

I looked around the office and noticed the trash can was about half full. I picked it up and walked outside with it. Hardy was nowhere in sight, so I turned left to the sidewalk that read "Galley," I found the big trash cans at the rear of the chow hall. They were clearly marked as to what went in them. Mine was dry trash, so that's where it went.

Walking back to the office I could really see the hill we were on. It was not really steep but I could see over some roof tops . The far side of the Thames was visible but the near side is where the subs are tied up, was blocked by buildings.

Hardy was still not in the office, I glanced at my watch. In my haste, I had not checked it before and was surprised to see it was ten minutes 'till 0700. I busied myself around the office, found a rag and wiped the counter down. The percolator was really working and the smell was permeating the room. The sound it made was not anything like the sound on the television coffee ad, but you knew it was perking. I began to fear it was too strong.

I heard the footsteps on the stairs as they approached the door, then again as they neared the office door.

As the office door swung open, Hardy exclaimed. "Man! - Is that coffee I smell? Pirate - ya been busy - boy!"

The timing was perfect. The pot quit perking and went quiet. Hardy set a package down on the counter and went to the locker in the back room. I heard him open the locker and he returned with two cups.

"I got my cup - brought it over last night." I said.

"Make sure ya return it - and don't let em see ya - if they do - tell em ya found it outside and was just bringing it in - they are stingy with those cups - boy!"

He poured two cups of the freshly brewed fragrant coffee and said; "don't use the moo myself-- if you want-- run over to the chow hall and get some-- use one of our cups from the locker -- see they're white -- you can sneak the green cup back at the same time."

"Naw! – I'm fine! - Look! - I'm a Louisiana boy and like strong coffee - hope it's not too stiff for you!"

"Sure smells good!" He stirs in two spoons of sugar, hoists the steaming cup, blows slightly and sips. There was a brief second of contemplation then a decent swig.

He looked at me and lifted the cup in an approving salute. "I'm sure this ain't the best cup I ever had, but it's as good as any cup I ever had!" He paused. "I hope that Yeoman is a no show!" The comment made me feel good. He continued; "Geez, Man" – You're a pro at this sucking up!"

I had to laugh at his frankness and realized that he liked me. It was a good feeling, but the benefits I hoped to receive were a lost cause. The Yeoman was on the first bus load to arrive at near 0930. It was a bus from a reserve unit near Boston somewhere and had driven down with about eight reservists. The Yeoman was immediately put in charge.

Hardy told the other sailors. "Follow Wardlaw - he'll square you away in the dorm!" Man! This man knew how to flatter a guy and save time. The Yeoman remained with Hardy to receive the same instructions as I received the night before.

I had already moved my gear into the dorm, and noted that there were sixty bunks available. There were thirty-two neat stacks, of linen and such, on a table in the center of the room, each stack contained two sheets and a pillow case.

As you enter the double doors at the front of the dorm, there is a row of twenty double bunks down the left side of the room. Moving to the right there is a long table with chairs lined around it, then two more double bunk rows. The large bathroom was on the far right wall. Inside the bath was a large shower room that could accommodate at least a dozen men at a time. There were ample porcelains to accommodate our class. It was obvious; this dorm was built at a time when our country was training a lot more than thirty-two men.

Hardy had given the impression that I was his right hand man, so I used my common sense and did the obvious in the obvious way. The racks were all the same, a wire spring strung across a metal frame. A four inch cotton mattress was folded in half and lying at the head of the bunk, with a grey blanket and pillow on top. There were lockers lined along the wall between the windows and steam heat units under the windows. Each locker was matched to a bunk by number. The lockers continued across the rear wall and the right side of the room. In the middle of the rear wall was a double door with windows in each side.

"Pick a rack - note the number - find your locker - stow your gear! Go back to the office and log your bunk number by your name! Y'all use 0930 as your log in time."

"Yee! Haa!" Came a subdued cry from somewhere in the group. "Hey boys - we got us a Johnny Reb here!"

I really didn't expect any comments about my instructions, but instantly realized it was the "Ya'll" that prompted the obvious insult.

"Thaaat's right!" I stated firmly: "And don'tcha ferget in neither! - Ya heah!"

At this there was an outburst of cautious laughter. I don't think they had pegged me as just another reserve yet. I returned to the office and found Hardy still going over the routine with the new CPO.

He looked up and asked: "Everything Kosher?"

"Yassuh boss," I answered, still in my southern mode.

"Don't be a smart ass - Pirate!" "Just cover 'till I'm done here—OK?"

"OK" I answered. "Want me to check ID's?"

"Yeah - at least 'till Simpson here takes over." He almost grumbled.

I wondered if there was a problem. As I made myself seem busy checking the log, I could hear parts of the conversation between Hardy and Simpson. I think Simpson thought he would just come and go through the two week course and that was it. It was obvious, he was unaware that responsibility comes with rank and should be welcomed. I really don't think he wanted the job, but Hardy knew how to handle it.

Before any of the recruits came in, Simpson came over, heaved a sigh and said. "Alright - I'll take over now."

"Names Wardlaw - Savannah, Georgia!" I stuck out my hand, he instinctively reached out. His grip was not impressive.

"Simpson – Nantucket -- Man! -- I wish I hadn't took this cruise—Man! -- Everything else was out of my schedule - college and all - I don't care about subs and this is all they had to fit my schedule – Bummer - Man!"

The Navy offers two week programs that cover a broad range of training opportunities for reservist. The ultimate aim is to have a well-trained sailor, if he is ever needed. The two week Submarine Course is obviously not sufficient for preparing a sailor to serve in the "Silent Service". Therefore, many reservists are in the school out of curiosity, have never been on a boat and may not really have a desire for a boat. My case was unique for a reservist. I had fallen in love with subs when I took that reserve cruise and had a burning desire for my own boat; I was determined not to be denied. Simpson simply took the course to fulfill an annual obligation, being a college student accounted for his study ethics and his PO3 rating in such a short time. He obviously didn't want any responsibility. This attitude would not fare well if he ever choose to do his active duty on subs, but then maybe that's why the Navy offered this abbreviated two week course to reservist.

"Look – Simpson - this job's a piece o cake! - You won't stand any watches and you gotcha own bunk and head – Man - that's worth something and I'll be here if you need any help!"   I spoke as if I knew something he didn't know. I felt like maybe I was misleading him, but I hadn't lied, I was there and I would help him.

He shrugged his shoulders and sighed. "Oh Well! – What the hell! - I suppose there's not a lot of choice. Now! - What's this about ID cards?"

Relieved, I answered as if I was in the know. "We need to make sure that each guy has got one and the picture is him". I shot him some bull at this point. "Reservists are not used to the strict routine of regular Navy and may have borrowed a card - or forgotten to bring it." A thought struck me, I continued. "Better look at birthdates close too - a lot of these young guys will fudge it - so they can drink." I knew this to be a fact.

The other reservist began to trickle in and log their info on the log sheet. Questions as to chow times were asked, and I provided the answers. Now I know this makes me look like a show off, but I had looked at the bulletin board closely the night before and knew the answers, so I told them.

It was not my nature to be curt and abrupt with people, I could, I guess if it was necessary. I saw Hardy come out of the rear room and I added.   "We suggest y'all check this board good - so you can be on board with base procedures."

Hardy glanced at me as there came a weak "Yee! Haaw!" from just outside the door. Hardy grinned and loudly said: "Ya'll!" – that's southern for "Youse Guys!" The laughter was loud and genuine and immediately set a tone of good natured bantering. I felt a bond beginning to grow with these guys.

"How about liberty?" A baby faced recruit asked.

Simpson looked at Hardy. Hardy looked at me with a "Well - Mr. know it all" expression. I turned my back as if I hadn't heard the question. Hardy was a genuine gentleman. He handled the situation.

"Ya're on a submarine base and a submarine training facility - This is a different world than regular Navy - You men are a different cut or desire to be a cut above the ordinary or you would not be here – Honor - diligence and courage should be natural to ya - Your ID card is ya liberty card - ya're free to do as ya wish - All class times - meal times and appointments will be posted on the info board just inside your dorm door - Read it and note all the other info posted there - If ya screw up- ya're out o here-- ya can pass that on!"

There were only the nine of us there to hear this brief message but the silence that ensued was evidence of its impact.

Hardy, now with a firmer tone, added; "Simpson is senior rate and is in charge! - Wardlaw will be out in the dorm with you guys - any questions or problems; take it to them! - Try not to bother me! - Got It?"

Murmurs of "Yeah!—Gotcha! – OK Chief and Aye - Aye Sir!" indicated that all were on board. Simpson and I agreed to alternate for brunch and the group agreed to split up into two groups. That way if any new students should arrive there would be someone in the office and in the dorm to provide guidance. This indeed was a different world. We were being treated as responsible adults. There was no evidence of regimentation, or the enforcement of discipline. To those of us that had been around a bit, it was refreshing.

Brunch was great; a selection of breakfast and luncheon meats, along with baked beans, eggs prepared anyway you wanted them, a fresh garden salad with standard Navy Thousand Island dressing. There was a large tray of macaroni salad, loaves of bread that you sliced yourself and cornbread. I had no problem diminishing my hunger.

The rest of the day was a breeze. Most of the seaman recruits and a couple of apprentices went on liberty, that's one and two strippers. For most of them, aside from boot camp, this was their first trip away from home; they had not even had a sea cruise. Boot camp, even the two week reserve version did not allow off base liberty. Simpson was busy getting up to snuff on being boss. It was evident the other members of his reserve unit didn't see him as an authority figure, but we now had twenty-three others that depended on that eagle on his arm to be their leader, including me.

By 1800 the log sheet was full and Hardy bid Simpson goodnight. Simpson came into the dorm. "Lights out at 2000 hours - Chow down's at 0600 - Class at 0800 - Be late and you're out – Got that!"

"Yaah! – Yaah!" was the response and a couple of towels came flying his way.

He turned his back and motioned toward the info board: "Better read that sign again!" He commented as he exited the dorm. He was referring to a somewhat larger sign that read; "THIS BARRACKS IS NOT A HOTEL - YOU MESS IT UP –YOU CLEAN IT UP! – YES – THERE WILL BE INSPECTIONS!"

We quickly realized why the Basic Course was eight weeks and after your assignment to a boat you had an additional six months to study your particular boat in order to "Qualify". That's when you were awarded those coveted "Dolphins." Man, I couldn't wait. Whenever I saw a sailor wearing a set of "Dolphins," it was like I could see a halo around his head.

After classes we were always around the long table, workbooks open, asking questions. Some of the guys were having difficulty with understanding the way the electrical, hydraulic and air systems worked. I could see that if they didn't have a knack for understanding the abstracts or physics of things, they would never make it. Most of the trainees never did understand why a submarine could submerge and surface without changing its weight. Yep! That's right, whatever a submarine weighs, it always weighs the same, even as fuel is used, sea water replaces the used fuel to maintain that weight. Supplies, fresh water, as it is used and discarded waste all must be compensated for. This is critical to the operation of a submarine. It is called "trim."

Hardy was true to his word. I didn't see much of him during the two weeks, but never was assigned any watches. Simpson assigned two hour watches starting at 2200. It was not bad duty. You simply manned the office and checked anyone who came calling. He used a simple rule. The men with the most time in grade pulled the early watches. In some cases, some of the older guys wanted the 0400 to 0600 watch, so they could be up and ready for the day. It's always a bummer to transcend from that beautiful restful dream- world to the realities of a long mind grinding day, but, you know, it happens, in most cases, to us all, every morning. A couple of times when Simpson and I would be talking late, I would tell the first watch to hit the sack. I'd stand his watch till midnight.

Trying not to brag is a hard thing to do, but this is my book and what I write is true so if that's what it sounds like, I can't help it. If you don't like it put the book down and don't read anymore.

I'm sure my long weekend on that sub out of Charleston gave me a distinct advantage over the other guys, plus I had read some Navy literature on subs. I vividly remembered my short cruise and was familiar with the actual operation of a boat. So questions that seemed difficult I could generally answer. I described the feeling one gets the first dive they experience. Those two blast on the klaxon have a special sound all its own.

The feelings differ for some. Some sailors are faced with a foreboding feeling, some with a feeling of serenity. I just felt powerful, with a feeling of confidence. To cruise submerged was an awesome feeling. To be there, where no one could see or hear you. My words really can't describe the feeling. Some of the reservist had been on sea cruises and would tell of different operations and activities. I would point out how it differed on a boat, for example, when entering or leaving port on a surface craft, a "special sea detail is set." This means that special people are put in specials places to accomplish special tasks that require a great deal of expertise. On a submarine or boat as submariners lovingly call it, this detail is referred to as "The maneuvering watch". The steering wheel, or helm as surface craft call it, is referred to simply as the "wheel," on a boat.

On a surface craft the device that transmits engine instructions to the engine room is called an "Engine Order Telegraph". On a sub the same device relays instruction to the "Maneuvering room" via an "Enunciator." On a boat if it opens by a single handle it is called a door, as in crapper door, shower door, locker door and "Chow Hall door." The door exception is the outer doors, which refers to the doors that open for torpedoes to fire. Openings that are dogged or turned down by multiple handles or wheels are referred to as hatches. Often, on a boat, the decks in the various compartments are referred to as floors instead of decks. Deck was reserved for exterior stuff, like forward deck, and after deck. Quarter deck or bridge and we actually had sidewalks, the two narrow walk ways on each side of the sail. The sail was the streamlined structure that surrounded the conning tower. "Man," I need to stop here or we'll be doing a whole training course.

Friday afternoon came and some of the guys and I walked down to the Gedunk. This was the Navy name for a kind of base canteen. There were pin ball machines, pool and snooker tables, snack bar and a juke box. Not many girls, but a nice respite from our grinding days. All the guys had caught the fever that was part of something as intense as sub school. It was evident that some of the guys would never make it in the sub program, due to either their comprehensive abilities or their desire; however, no one displayed any visible signs of throwing in the towel. The experience was much too valuable to waste.

As we sat in a booth, we began to discuss the rumors we had heard about selling some subs to Greece and Brazil. I told the guys about seeing the notations on the administration buildings berthing chart.

Our attention was drawn to a new song being playing on the juke box. "Love Letters in the Sand" by Pat Boone. Zowolski exclaimed. "That's one pretty song Man! - It's gonna top the charts!"

Boone's new release was soon followed by Elvis's already top chart song, "All Shook Up." It made me want to dance. I asked the guys if there were any dances that they knew of. No one was familiar with the area so there was not much discussion. A couple of the guys were going into New London and bar hop a bit.

That didn't appeal to me much so I bowed out and walked down to the berths and walked along looking at the subs. There were about eight of the older Balao and I think Gato classes all tied up side by side. There were considerable work activities going on.

I asked a guy driving a supply truck. " What y'all doing on these old boats?"

"These are the boats we sold to Greece and Brazil - we're getting em ready for transfer here in a coupla months." He explained. Wow, so it was true.

"Hey - maybe you can help me here?" I pleaded.

"Hope you don't want money!' he quipped.

"Naw! I need some information if you can help." I tried to sound innocent.

"Wann'a know where the whore houses are don'tcha." He grinned."

"Hey man! - Do I look that hard up! - I'd like to dance a little and don't feel like competing with drunks!"

"Well la de da - Mr. keep it in ya britches!" He was taunting me. "If you don't want a little snatch - just go to the "Y" - there's plenty o girls there - but there ain't no hooch and there ain't no cooch - so as far as I'm concerned - it's just a waste of time!"

"Thanks a heap - buddy." I turned and started walking away.

"Hey Mac!" He called. "They gonna love ya southern accent!" He laughed and began to unload his truck.

I thought. "No wonder he was driving a truck - I'll bet he didn't have dolphins either!"

I went back to the dorm, did the four "s's" [figure that out], put on my dress blues, walked to the bus stop, outside the gate and waited for the base bus.

As I stood, I saw a group of sailors approaching from up the hill nearer the gate. They were in navy blue dress but different from ours. I began to hear voices and immediately knew the Brazilians had arrived. There were five or six of them and they were in good spirits. I studied Spanish in high school for three years and could get some sense out of the conversation. It was difficult to keep up. Brazilians speak Portuguese. Spanish and Portuguese are similar, but only a few words were clear and I could only get a vague idea of the drift.

It seems they were on a lark and in a dream land. They thought they were rich, I really mean it, they thought they were loaded. It seems that our government subsidized their pay while they were here in our country. It appeared they were attending a special course preparing them to take the subs home that our government had sold to their navy. Some of the guys talked about sending some of their pay home to their families and I thought how fortunate we Americans were.

These Brazilians were not aloof in the least. If you made eye contact, they instantly smiled and would say "Hello, HI , Bom Dia or OK." I didn't attempt to talk, just listened.

The bus ride was interesting; the driver watched every move the Brazilians made, either out of the corner of his eye on in the rear view mirror. We stopped at the same location as when I first boarded on my arrival night.

I lingered a bit as the Brazilians disembarked, and asked the driver if he was going further in town. He said, there was really no need; everything was within a decent walk from where we were parked.

"Look Man!" I spoke softly. "I noticed how you watched those guys - do they give you trouble or something?"

"No way- man!" He exclaimed. "They're sweethearts - but my chief told me if anything happened to one of them on my watch - he'd have my ass!" It's not bad coming in town but going back is rough - some of our boys get out of hand and try to start something! - It's really not fair - them getting that extra money and all!"

I guess he's right in a way, but if we didn't help a little they probably couldn't even buy a coke at the Gedunk. I asked him if he knew where the "Y" was. "Why ya want the "Y?" He asked.

"I like to dance and figured maybe something was going on." I answered.

He looked at me sideways and said. "I don't know if it's the "Y" or not, but that's Bank Street up ahead. Take a left an a coupla blocks down on the right is a building that's got them studio windows on the top floor. There's somethin going on there weekends - never been - but I don't think there's much action or I'd a heard about it."

"Thanks." I started walking. There was a stature on my right, I didn't look at it too closely, but the marker commemorated the "Nathan Hale School House". Bank Street pulled off to the left.

I liked this town. I didn't see anything new or modern, but it was neat and clean. There weren't many people out walking. I realized that 7pm on a Friday night in New London, Connecticut was not the source of the phrase, "Hot time in the old town tonight!"

The bus driver was "right on" with the distance, about two blocks down Banks was a white building, the first floor was glass store fronts, the second floor was regular windows, but were very low and a lot of them, I guess it was for storage. The top floor was big windows with curved tops, this met my idea of studio windows. There was a door on the far right of the building, and I could hear music. "Yep," it was coming from upstairs and it was the Mill's Brothers version of "Glow Worm."

The shag was the dance that ruled the teens in the fifties. I had learned to shag from Martha Coatsworth in 1952 at her studio on Oglethorpe Ave. in Savannah. She never charged me a dime. I was working every day after school at Mr. Miltiades Handy Market, but would run down to her studio during study hall and she would use me as her instruction partner. She was a good looking blonde that left Savannah when she landed a part in a TV detective show based in Miami, Florida. I think the show also co-starred Rocky Graziano.

Martha taught me about the rhythm of dance. She would say. "It's very important to be precise with your moves and steps in ballroom dancing - but when dancing for the joy of it - that precision doesn't mean a thing."

She would tell me. "Feel the beat, let the rhythm flow through your soul and express it somewhere - in your feet - in your hands - in your butt and in your head!" Sometimes she would dance with me for the sheer fun of it. I really think she played a great part in helping to develop my love for dancing.

As I walked into the studio I instantly felt out of place. The girls were all either high school students or not long graduated. There were about eight girls and three boys. The boys were maybe seventeen or possibly a little older, but no sailors. I immediately knew the guys did not want me there.

An older girl came over and asked me if I was Wade. I took my hat off. "No Ma'am" I answered. "I'm Wardlaw - Lynn Wardlaw."

The girl laughed and the very coyly said "My goodness - such a gentleman." The other girls laughed and the boys just acted like they were above it all.

I hadn't removed my hat out of politeness. It was Navy protocol to uncover when indoors. I realized this action along with the subconscious Ma'am had branded me a southerner. I hoped it would not create a problem. I decided to just be quiet and see where it led.

The girl spoke, "Oh - I'm so sorry - we were expecting a service man named Wade. One of our friends invited him and she's running late."

One of the other girls broke in. "Wade's a cadet at the Coast Guard Academy – Mildred - this guy's just a sailor!"

Now I felt awkward, but Mildred didn't miss a beat. She took my arm and led me across the floor to a row of chairs that ran the length of the wall under the windows. She sat and gently pulled me down to the seat next to her. She was not a raving beauty but still pleasant to look at. She was dressed in typical bobby sox attire right down to the little scarf tied around her neck.

"I'm Mildred and we get together every Friday and Saturday night to dance -- We don't get many visitors. Now - do you dance?" She asked as "Be Bop A Lula" started from the 45RPM record player on a table against the wall.

"I'm in submarine school over across the river, and I do like to dance. This is a good shag song!" I was referring to "Be Bop A Lula." "How about It?"

She jumped right up and in two steps was on the floor. She did the cutest thing I think I've ever seen. She turned to me, arms down, placed her hands together in front of her, slightly turned her toes in, cocked her head ever so slightly and said not a word. She didn't need to, her every action had said. "Here I am!"

She knew the shag and I didn't deviate too much from the basics. We went well together and the girls noticed.

As the evening progressed Mildred began to mix around as other girls and guys arrived. The Coast Guard cadet never showed and I never met the girl that invited him. I didn't have much opportunity to deviate from a basic shag dance. They did play "Glo Worm" again and Mildred and I did a fair job of a mild swing. She took queues for in and out swings with ease and she could roll into a side by side Charleston kick like we had done it for years. She was a fine dance partner.

I never found out what kind of group it was, sorority, church or "Y". At 10pm they called last dance and by this time I had danced with a goodly number of the girls and they all wanted to hear me say "Ya'll." Mildred asked me to come back and I said I'd try. I really had a good time, but I never did go back.

The last week of school passed in a flash. These were guys from reserve units all over the country. It's amazing how a man can arrive at a training facility, totally uncommitted to the subject matter and depart with such a keen sense of accomplishment. I mentioned before, there were some students, that were aware submarines would never play a part in their naval future; however these guys stuck with the training and departed the better for it. I often wondered if any of these fellows ever fell in love with subs like I did.

We got out around noon on Friday. There were no announcements concerning grades or standings in the class. This was probably due to it being a cruise objective as opposed to a true school. I was the only trainee designated for further training in subs.

All the other guys were catching busses, making arrangements for trains or calling relatives to pick them up. I went into the office and found Hardy arranging papers and squaring the office away. "Got another class coming in soon?" I questioned.

"Naw – Pirate - no more reserve classes till summer - when ya shipping out?"

"I ain't shipping out - remember I've got another school starting Monday." I retorted.

"Woah! -- Hold on a sec!" He looked pleased as he shuffled through some papers. He grabbed up a sheet and scrutinized it carefully.

He looked at me and smiled. "Ya ain't gonna hafta kiss ass again boy - ya're in my course - we'll see a lot of each other!"

"Hey! -That's great, Hardy - what will you teach?" I quizzed.

"Most everything- there'll be three of us- all good guys 'cept for Griffin- he's got no sense of humor- all business and dull- but ya'll make it. By-the-way- ya aced this course."

"Thanks Hardy, I appreciate that." I turned to leave.

"Hold on!" He sorted through another sheaf of papers and pulled out a sheet, placed it in a large manila envelope and handed it to me. "When ya report back to the administration office - give them this. They'll re-assign ya to the new barracks - it's just beyond the chow hall. - Same deal goes there as here - 'cept ya ain't gonna have any clout for the next eight weeks! - We got over two hundred in this class and sixteen are rated in ya'r section alone!"

"Wow- I suppose some of them have got a little time too - huh?" I retorted.

"OH yeah!" He looked at a roster and ran his finger down the columns. "There's six first class, just in ya'r section."

"OK! -- My friend - see you Monday!" Again I turned to leave.

"Hey! - Wardlaw!" He hesitated a bit. "Eh – listen – eh - if anyone gives ya any shit - ya know - about being a f—king reserve and all – well - let me know if ya can't handle it!"

"It's all right - Hardy." I made the "so what" gesture with my hands. "I guess that's really what I am." He laughed, and this time, I did leave.

I packed up my gear and walked by the chow hall to the next barracks. It was a brick building, considerably larger than my previous dorm. I opened the front door and found the PO office was on the left. There was a set of stairs just before the office that led to a second floor section. I could see that there were already some personnel occupying parts of the first floor.

I knocked on the PO office door and a voice called "ENTER!" Inside was a second class radioman, not a big fellow, and not much older than me. On his blue tunic was that set of "Dolphins". His mystique was immediately enhanced.

"OK if I leave my gear here 'till I get checked in?"

"Going to sub school?" He quizzed.

I nodded, as I removed my bag from my shoulder and set it by the wall.

"Let's have your barracks chit then." He extended his hand.

To his surprise I grabbed his hand in a shake and said. "Don't have it yet - I'd just like to leave my gear here 'till I run down to administration and check in."

Puzzled, he asked. "How hell did you get here and by-pass administration."

I don't know why I do things sometimes, I just see a chance to have a laugh and it sometimes gets me in trouble. I saw he had no clue that I had been here for two weeks. He probably never encountered a trainee that had not just arrived.

Here goes, I thought. "Oh! - I'm sorry man - you see I live here! - My uncle [meaning Uncle Sam] owns this place and I thought I'd save some time by just stopping here first!"

He didn't say a thing, he just stared at me. There was no expression on his face to help me out. I was beginning to think he believed me.

"You shittin me - right?" he stammered.

I wanted to laugh, but common sense told me not to press my luck. "Yeah – Man - I just finished a two week course and Hardy told me this was my new barracks. - I just want to leave my stuff and go check in. - Is it OK with you?"

He relaxed a bit. "Yeah - Hey! You ever been rated?"

"Eh no- not yet- why?" I asked.

"Just curious - cause pullin shit like you just did - can get you busted - Hurry back - you got first watch!"

I looked at him, and realized I had the same expression on my face that he just had.

As I opened the door to leave, he laughed and said. "You shit me- I shit you!" He was still laughing as I went down the steps.

Check- in went good and sure enough, I was assigned to the barracks I just left. When I got back, there were two other sailors checking in, one was a seaman apprentice. Boy, if you think my accent was southern, you shouda heard him. He was signing in and as he finished he turned and I looked him straight in the face and asked "Alabama?"

"Close, brother, Miss-sippi!" He said. That's the way a country boy from Mississippi says it, "Miss-sippi". I took an immediate liking to this boy.

"Louzi-anna ." I answered. That's the way a country boy from Louisianna says it, Louzi-anna". I extended my hand and he took it with a grip that would make a Preacher proud. He grinned, a good ol boy grin. I had a buddy!

I reached down and grabbed his duffle as he hoisted his seabag, we were located on the second deck. I was familiar with the proceedings and he followed suit. We chose an over and under. He was tickled with the top bunk and said that was the highest he ever slept and hoped he wouldn't get nose bleed.

I told him about the dance club in New London and maybe we could go. He said dancing wasn't his style, but he sure liked to roller skate. I told him I skated also and maybe we could find a rink and go sometimes. We went back to the PO office to check the duty roster. The PO's name was Billingsley, he informed us that duty would not start until Monday. Billingsley also told us that our floor adjoined another wing that housed a group of Greek sailors also in training. We basically received the same instructions as described by the bus driver. Leave em alone!

My new buddy was Darrell Caldwell from Meridian, Mississippi. He was nineteen and wanted subs as bad as I did. He was a pleasure to be with. Darryl was not at all what one would expect a young man from Meridian, Miss-sippi to be. He had a deep southern accent but was well spoken and sharp as a tack. Darrell stood close to 5'10" at about 160 pounds. His dark curls were cropped close to his head and he wore his white hat close over his eyes. His looks said "All Navy." His pug nose was accented by cupiedoll cheeks and dark piercing eyes. His ears were a bit pronounced but "Hey" you can't have everything.

We walked down to the Gedunk and stayed till closing at 2200 hours. We probably played twenty games of snooker. I won exactly none. Darryl made it look close, but I knew better. He was a master at this. We spent Saturday walking around the base and getting familiar with the facilities. We found Rock Pond and discussed how much fun it would be when warm weather allowed it to open.

Later Saturday afternoon we caught the bus into town and hit a few bars, no one checked ID and Darrell didn't care for beer any more than I did. We met a few women, but nothing gelled so we decided to head back to the base. While waiting for the base bus, by the train station, we noticed a policeman parked across the street. Darryl went and talked for a few minutes.

When he returned he was grinning. "Found a skating rink, Podner!" He was beaming. "It's over in Groton. - The cop says it's one of the nicest in the state. - Wanna go?"

"Sure - but it's getting late and we won't get to skate long!" I stated.

 Well not tonight - but we sure will go - right?"

"Yassuh Boss!" I quipped. The ride back to the base was pleasant as we swapped stories about our youth and homes. We were astounded to find we had fished the same spot in the Pearl River. Neither of us could remember any names or location along the river, but when I told of the wooden bridge with no rails on the side and how it was just a huge hump over the river, he recalled crossing it on foot as his Dad drove the car across. Mine did the exact same thing.

I was not the youngest in the class, by a long shot, but I was really surprised to see how many guys my age were already rated. My section was number 102 of Class 114, scheduled for completion on June 19, 1957. It was evident that this group of trainees was altogether different than my reserve class. All were a cut above the average and had been pre-approved for training. I'm sure the Navy simply won't let anyone just try out for subs. The Navy goes to great expense to provide the necessary training for a sailor to be a functional and dependable member of a crew. I'm sure no officer would recommend or approve a sailor's request for submarine service, unless he was sure that the individual could handle the job. I would think that one's signature on the request form would definitely reflect on their personal ability to judge an individual's potential. Our class started bright and early on that Monday.

Hardy proved as fine an instructor as I've seen. He took us through the basics, nomenclature, construction and then the hard part, where the brains are separated from the no-brains.

For a submarine to dive and then surface again is an adventure in physics. It's not as simple as make it a heavier or lighter situation. You find even in professional discussions and in factual statistics that the weights of a submarine are given when surfaced and then when submerged. This is for general information and is, in reality, not the case.

The weight of a submarine is what it is. As mentioned before, there is a word that describes the condition a submarine must be in to function while submerged, it's called trim. Trim simply means the overall balance of the boat, not just forward and aft, but starboard and port as well. Simply put, a submarine, while submerged, and not under any power or propulsion should be free to just hover in the water. Actually a good diving officer can make his boat do just that. Let's say the officer takes his sub to 200 feet, goes to all stop, zeros the planes [bow and stern planes make the boat go up and down] and brings the rudder amidship. Given the ocean has no current or turbulence, then the sub will hover, if perfectly trimmed.

I suppose a perfect trim is possible, but in the real world you have to continually massage it to achieve your goal. The officers from the war were pros at this. In the movies we would see a boat lie on the bottom and outlast a depth charge attack. This did indeed happen, but quite often the bottom was a bigger enemy than the attackers, you see, the bottom was maybe a thousand feet or more away and our boats couldn't take that kind of pressure, so these men of steel would hover at two hundred feet or so and use skill and guts to outlast their attackers

------------------------------- Important, but Boring Physics Stuff ----------------------------

This may be boring to you readers but there are some life threatening occurrences in this book that will make no sense to you if you don't understand a little of these physics.

Water is pretty heavy stuff; a gallon of salt water weights a little over eight and a half pounds. Let's say you have a square of something and it's solid. Now you have a square of water the exact same size. Now let's weigh them. This is simple; if the square of something solid is heavier than the square of water, it will sink. If it is lighter than the water, it will float. Now let's say our square was made of steel, that's why it was so heavy and it sank. OK, now suppose that our steel square is not solid, it is simply a six sided square steel box and hollow. Wow, it floats. We have a crude boat. Now let's say we can stretch this steel square and make it twice its size, not any heavier though. Hey! We notice that the square floats much higher in the water, that's because we have increased the area of steel exposed to the water and we still weigh the same. We are displacing the same amount of water but covering more area. That's the key to how a submarine works. The area of the hull exposed to water.

A submarine actually has two hulls; the inner hull is where the crew and everything that must stay dry is located. The outer hull is where the fuel and ballast tanks are located. These tanks are wrapped around the inner hull and conform to the streamline design of the boat to allow it to cut through the water with the least resistance. There is a forward trim tank and an after trim tank, each of these tanks play a major role in keeping the boat on a horizontal plane.

Now, here's the strange concept that helps a submarine operate efficiently; the ballast tanks have openings on the bottom that stay open to the sea. The fuel tanks also have openings on the bottom that stay open to the sea. This means that the ballast tanks are never subject to damaging sea pressure when submerged and can be constructed of lighter weight steel. The fuel tanks use the pressure of the sea to send the fuel into the boats fuel system. Fuel is lighter than water and they will not mix. The sea pressure forces the fuel up into the lines feeding the fuel system. It works extremely well. As the fuel is consumed, water takes its place so there is never any concern about the minor difference in the weight of fuel and water.

The ballast tanks have huge valves on their tops. When opened by controls in the control room, the air rushes out and water floods in through the openings in the bottom, it floods in a hurry. We are putting water inside the outer hull and in doing so we have decreased our area of flotation. We weigh no more than before, but we have shrunk our size to the point we do not displace as much water as before, therefore we sink. To surface; simply shut the valves on top, blow air in the tank, the air forces the water out the open holes in the bottom and we now have the outer hull back in the size equation and we float. It's simple, efficient and very quick. There is a physics rule that governs this phenomenon; an object will float until it displaces its own weight in water, if it exceeds its water displacement weight, it will sink. It works every time.

When a submarine is submerged, the craft is in a state, we call negative buoyancy. That means we weigh more than the water we displace. It is critical not to be too heavy; not a true term but we use it anyway.   It's easier than saying we have insufficient surface area to support buoyancy.   Now since you have mastered the physics of why a submarine will dive and surface we will begin using the layman terms of light and heavy. Remember light and heavy really means sufficient or insufficient surface area to support flotation.

When submerged and the boat is too heavy, the boat will use too much power to maintain a certain depth. When cruising beneath the waves the boat is using power to push through the water and if it must use the bow and stern planes to fight gravity, or sinking deeper, as well as trim, then the boat operation becomes very inefficient. When submerged and in that state where hovering is possible, then the boat has achieved neutral buoyancy. This is perfect for under water maneuvering.

The boat has a set of bow and stern planes. These are small wings located on each side of the boat, their locations speak for themselves. As the orders are giving the planes are controlled by large wheels located on the port side of the control room. The bow planes will tilt up or down as requested and the force of the water flowing over their surface will move the boat up or down. The stern planes do the same thing. When a depth change is ordered, the dive officer will issue orders to the planesmen to achieve the new depth. He may do so with a certain up or down degree command. It is actually quite common to change depth without any up or down angle at all. A good dive officer with well-trained helmsman and plainsmen can maneuver the boat and the cook will never notice the movement.

A ships greatest worry is sinking; there is no return from this catastrophe. A submarine dives. We fear the term, sink, as much as any ship. We call it diving or submerging. You will hear terms like "Take her down! -- Pull the plug! – "Let's get wet!" or simply, "Dive the boat!" This sets up a chain of action commands and precision movements that have been portrayed in many a submarine movie. It is even more dramatic and exciting to be there and be a part of it. Mere words cannot describe the exhilaration and awe of "diving the boat!" We will read of this actually happening many times in this book.

The classes were intense. Most of the students had never been on a boat. Some had visited, when a sub would tie up next to their ship. The visit may have been a result of curiosity, or an invite from a buddy you met in a bar, but for whatever reason there was an inner desire to be part of something that was different.

Our instructors continually stressed the importance of understanding the pulse of a boat. There were spare parts and components stored on a boat for emergency repairs, but a boat carried no spare personnel. If something should happen to a crew member, the workload of that person would have to be absorbed by someone else. Everyone had a job and we soon learned that we were going to learn our job and the job of every other man on the boat. You read me right. This intense training and the qualifying time once onboard the boat required a submariner to learn every switch, knob, handle, wheel, button, valve, light, airline, pipe, hydraulic line, electric wire, system and circuit on the boat. He must learn how they operate, what they do and what they control. Now, it's not enough to just know these things, a submariner must understand them as if they are his second nature. Sounds impossible, doesn't it? We'll it's not, when you see a sailor with a set of "Dolphins" on his chest, you've seen a man that's done just that!

"Hey - Podna!" came the call from across the chow hall. Darrell was making his way to where I was in line. "Man - got some good news!" He was cut short with complaints from back in the line.

"Hey! Miss-sipp - No line jumping!" Another barked. "Back to de end o de line, pecker head!"

Darrell turned and flashed that magnificent grin. "Done et - puke face!" Just talking to my buddy here - now hush up - fo I spit in yor grits!". Laughter resounded through the chow hall. Everyone was happy, and we would always let a guy in line, especially if he was rushing to go on duty.

"What's going on Darrell?" I asked. "You gonna be a daddy or sumpin?"

"Not yet - but maybe tonight!" He retorted. "You know that third class – Brown - that bunks up front by the door?"

"Don't know him good - but what about him – Darrell?" I asked.

"Well - seems his girl's in nurses training up in Norwich and there's a little party going on tonight. - He can take three of us as guest - if we fill up his tank! How's that sound? - Eh!"

"That'll work – Man! - I hope he ain't got a big Buick though!" I groaned.

Darrell cocked his eye in thought. "I think he's got a '53 or '54 Plymouth. One of them little four door sedans - you know - two tone - yellow and green."

"Know em well – Darrell - I gotta Uncle that has one just like it-- good cars too!" I replied.

"I'm gone Podna - gotta load in the washer and they'll be scattered everywhere if I'm not there when it stops." He dashed away.

He was right about the laundry too, if you weren't there when the machine stopped, whoever was next in line would remove your stuff and pack in his own, and it was your loss. There were even signs to back this up. The machines were all good heavy duty machines and the dryers were very thorough as well. If you were careful during the week, one washer load would handle your stuff and you could buddy up with another sailor with a dryer.

The laundry room was always crowded, but we all worked pretty well together, so it wasn't too much of a hassle. The PO's rated second class and higher could normally afford to have their laundry done by the pros. I guess that comes with the big bucks.

Speaking of big bucks, there were some super poker games at times. Man, I couldn't even afford the "anti" in most of those games. I witnessed a Chief's game once. I was astounded at the amount of money that was won in that game. Later in this book I'll tell you about my big "Black Jack" game in San Juan.

I'll never understand why time drags when you're waiting for something big to happen, it seems like forever before Brown called everyone together and we set off for Norwich. It was a pleasant trip and we talked of home, girlfriends and cars. I painted a mean picture of my '54 Ford, and caught all kinda crap, --seems like everyone was a Chevy lover.

Man, I heard it all." F-O-R-D, Fix- Or-Repair-Daily, --"Laughter!"

"Ford saved the war!" – "Yeh! There were so many junked that we had no scrap metal problems!" –"Louder laughter!"

"A Chevy can be missing on two cylinders, and still outrun a Ford!" – Guffaws!"

It quieted a bit and I nobly stated; "F-O-R-D – First-On-Race-Day!"

They never missed a beat "Yeh! - At the tricycle races!" Pandemonium broke out.

Brown had to slow down and wipe his eyes. I just made up my mind to be quiet and enjoy the ride. I thought how nice it would be if we were in a Chevrolet and it would break down. I kinda smirked in my imaginary satisfaction.

Darrell smacked me backhanded on the arm, gave me an impish look and said. -- "Don't be dreamin up no ill will now - Podna!"

"How the Sam Hill did you know what I was thinking?" I stammered.

He chuckled. "Cause I know what I'd a been thinking - you duffus!"

The trip up to Norwich was not long, and the nurse's dorm was a two story brick building with a large reception room. The room however was not nearly large enough for the number of guys that showed for the party. It seems that the nursing school was connected to a community college in town and there were a large number of male students in attendance.

I don't suppose I need to tell you the tension in the air that night. I could feel the resentment of the college guys. I suppose they felt that the nurses were their private stock and they should not be expected to share with a "sailor" and enlisted men at that. "Humph! - The very nerve!"

Darrell and I didn't even attempt to fraternize with the girls. I was disappointed, because I had dated nurses for two years and felt a kinship. In reality I knew there was no purpose in doing anything but stay out of the way. We would not be back, the possibility of a night of delight was nil. Darrell located a couple of beers and we nursed them along and poked subdued fun at the college guys. This was unfair, I know, but gave us a little satisfaction. We all finally wound up outside, sipping beer and mulling over our poor luck. Brown, however, had a girl here and we had not seen much of him.

One, in our group, offered a note of concern. What if Brown decided to stay over, we would be in a quandary. No place to stay, strange town, definitely no friends and not to mention money. A nonrated sailor is not financially rewarded to the extent he can do as he pleases without careful budgeting.

The front door flew open and Brown emerged, clearly ticked off. He walked out a few steps, turned on his heel and started back in, stopped, turned back, pounded his fist into the palm of his hand, turned back as if to re-enter, stopped and cursed under his breath.

He turned and started toward us and growled. -- "The bastard's not comin out - I know it - he's not coming out!"

It seems that some guy in college had been hitting on his girl and Brown had invited him outside to discuss the situation.

"He's not coming! - I'm gonna hafta go back inside and embarrass myself and probably lose Gail! - OH! God! – What am I gonna do?" I could hear the frustration in his voice, his heart was breaking and I felt as If he was near tears. My heart went out to him.

The front door opened and four guys came out. We could immediately tell that they were on a mission.

"You Dale Brown?" asked the largest of the four. He was slender, but probably around 6'1", the other three were not really big guys. I thought how lucky we were that the football team didn't show up.

Brown answered. "Yeh! - I'm Brown! - Derrick thinks he needs an army, does he?"

"No!" The big guy answered.   We're just here to make sure no trouble starts!"

With that Darrell and I moved as one. We placed ourselves between the four and Brown and just looked at them. Shuman our other pal moved to the side and no one said a word.

"I just want to talk with Derrick- no trouble - less he starts it - now tell him to get his pansy ass out here!" Hissed Brown.

Darrell spoke in pure Miss-sippi country. "Gentlemen - there won't be nary a bit o trouble if'n ya'll don't start it! - Ya heah! - An by the way - if'n ya'll do start sumpin! - Ya'll ain't brung near nuf folk to finish it!"

Derrick showed at the door, but he wouldn't come any closer. Brown was now cool and determined. He motioned to the fearsome foursome and asked them to move aside enough for him to speak directly to Derrick.   They did so with no objection. Darrell and I relaxed a bit.

Brown looked at the ground for a second, then placed his hands behind his back and slowly lifted his head; he suddenly looked much older than before.

"Derrick! - I'll make this brief - Gail and I have gone steady since High school - she's the only girl I've ever loved - I have an obligation to my country that I must fulfill - I can't be here for her - I know she likes to enjoy life and this arrangement isn't fair to her - but Derrick! - Hear this now - if you take Gail away from me-- I'll come back and whip you preppy ass from here to Long Island Sound!"

You couldn't hear a breath, even the wind had stopped.   Brown really wrapped it up now.   "Derrick - if our roles were reversed - I'd go ahead and take her-- cause she's well worth an ass whipping!"

Brown turned to us a said. "Let's go fellas - I gotta headache!"   He tossed the keys to Shuman. "Sober?" He asked.

"Cold sober - Man." Shuman answered.

The drive back was quiet until we reached a small town that had a lake or pond right next to the road. The moon was shining across the water and it looked like a black mirror.   I don't remember the town, maybe Uncasville or something, but no street lights and the water was inviting.   Now it's near the end of April. The weather was not really cold but still way too chilly for a swim.

"Skinny dip!" Cried Darrell and four crazy sailors shed their blues, shoes, skivvies and socks and made a mad dash for the water. It was a crazy thing to do, water that close to the highway holds everything that anybody doesn't want in their car, broken bottles, barbed wire, jagged metal, all kinds of dangerous stuff.   None of this crossed our minds; it had been a disappointing night, so anything to brighten it up a bit was the thing to do.

We did have the presence of mind not to jump right in; common sense told us the water would be bitter cold, so we stopped at the edge and dipped our toes and feet, steeled for the cold impact. To our surprise the water was chilly but not bitter cold. I made mention of this, and Simpson said it probably wasn't deep water and the day's sunshine warmed it up. Sounded logical to me and in we went, we had a nice swim and I noticed the bottom was a little soft but felt very solid.   I had swum in rivers, lakes, swamps, oceans, creeks, bayous and swimming pools. This felt like none of these.

"Oh! Well! I'm already wet so why sweat!" I thought.

The rest of the ride back to the base was uneventful, and the walk from the parking area was exhilarating. The noise we made was probably what brought out some of our buddies that knew of our venture to the nurse's party. We had a grand time telling lies about our conquest and scoring with the girls.

My tale was; they were just too young and immature.

We really put it on in telling of Brown's stand against Derrick. In a few days the story had Brown whipping a half dozen college football players.

Shuman was relating our late night skinny dip to a couple of guys that were from up in that area and they were discussing the pond we swam in. Questions were asked like; were there a bunch of rocks, how about a bridge, were there some lights off to one side, did you see a water tower. No, none of that. I related about the strange feel I had noticed on the lake bottom, and one of the guys started to laugh.

"What's so Dad Gum funny? I queried.

He was really about to roll when he turned and half whispered to his buddy.-- "I bet they swam in some sewage retention pond, they're all over the place up there!" The laughter really peeled out now.

There was a mad dash for the showers, I led the way, falling as I shed my trousers, Darrell fell over me. No one thought to go for soap, there were always scraps of soap bars laying on the showers shelves, but no wash clothes.

This night only one little scrap of Ivory could be found. A wet Ivory bar is slippery enough, but a scrap is impossible to hold. The coveted piece would scoot across the shower floor and four wet naked sailors would dive for it. The noise had roused everyone within ear shot and a crowd was gathering.

Someone pleaded, "No washing your balls till everybody's face gets washed!"

Another cried, "Hey! – Man! – There's crap in my ears!"

Still another called --"Wardlaw, that wasn't sand you felt between your toes, was it?"

The laughter from the viewing crowd began to grow louder as the word of our swim began to spread. The fight for the diminishing soap was getting useless. We found it hard to stand.

The shower had a slight incline in the floor to allow water to flow to the center and as we struggled for the soap we inevitably found ourselves in a tangled heap in the center of the shower floor.

It was slippery as s--t, "Oh-- you know what I mean!"

No man likes to touch another naked man, much less one that is soapy and covered in real or imaginary crap. So chaos reigned as men tried to get up and not touch another man at the same time.

The laughter continued, in ever increasing volume.

Someone would be on all fours attempting to rise and a taunt would be heard. "Hold that pose darling, I'm coming in! – Somebody hand me the soap!"

The laughter would roar. Another cried. – "Woowee!--I've never seen so many swinging peckers in my life!" Howls would follow.

"That's not a pecker, Man, --that's a Pee-Wee!" This brought the house down.

Someone shouted, "Yowee! – I'm in love!"

Still another cried, "What's that crappy smell?"

Suddenly it grew quiet and someone said. "Hey the flippin SP's are here!" Sure enough, two SP's pushed their way through the crowd and entered the shower. The stunned look on their faces was priceless.

The first to speak was a second class boson [boatswain] mate. I knew he was permanent base police, because there was no required rate for Boson Mates on Submarines.

"Hot Dam! A real live genuine cluster f—k! -- I've heard of em - ain't never seen one 'till now! -- Hot Dam!"

The other SP spoke up. "Hell - we heard there was a brawl going on up here, figured them Greeks was whupping your whimpy ass's!—Damn! --wait 'till this gets out! --The 'Ol Man's gonna shit when he hears about this!"

They turned to leave and everyone started explaining, not us though, we were wet, soapy, naked and embarrassed.

Man! There is no need to tell how this story got twisted in the BS mill around the base. We even heard rumors about raising money to get us to put on another show.

Brown received a call from Gail on Sunday and all seemed to be well. I was happy for him. It took a great deal of courage to do what he did.

Week two was as intense as the first week. Actually the pace picked up a bit. I suppose we were becoming more familiar with the nomenclature and the dialog of the boat so we could perceive the new knowledge a little quicker. I had an edge for a while, having had a two week school and a cruise under my belt. That edge was dwindling fast as the other men became more familiar with the world of submarines.

It was interesting to see how many hydraulic motors were used to drive machinery and equipment on a submarine. A number of reasons contributed to this hydraulic motor use. Simply put, a hydraulic motor uses hydraulic fluid [usually oil] to turn a shaft and in turn the shaft does the work. Sometimes the fluid will push a piston and the piston shaft will perform the work. Hydraulic power is quick [liquid won't compress], quiet and low heat. The hydraulic fluid will respond to any source of attempted compression. That's the simple trick. You try to compress the fluid, you can't, so the power you put on the fluid will travel to wherever the fluid line goes and provide power at that far away point. All of these attributes go well in the close confines of a submarine.

We studied the electrical systems, low voltage and high voltage. We learned the AC and DC systems, and the low and high pressure air systems. The school offered mock ups and cutaways so we could better understand how the systems functioned. It was fascinating. Sadly though, we had lost a few of our guys. They simply couldn't grasp the abstracts of physics.

I guess the average person would wonder why, say, a cook would need to know about the physics of air pressure, hydraulics or electricity. Well if you remember, there are no spare sailors on a submarine.

There are nine basic compartments on a fleet type boat. All of these compartments have personnel in them at all times. Should a catastrophe occur, all the personnel in that compartment are normally lost. All of the personnel that perform a certain task are never put in the same compartment at the same time. With these safeguards in mind, we find if an electrical fire in the maneuvering room takes out two IC electricians, our cook, if necessary, knows enough about the systems in maneuvering to handle one of the jobs. This applies to every man that serves on a sub. There is a lot of pressure on the students to absorb this information and the pressures grow as the weeks progress.

Friday night came and I pulled the 2000 watch. Darrell went into Groton to check out the skating rink. I was watching TV when he came in a little after midnight.

He was obviously pleased. I saw him swagger around the corner from the stairs and look toward our bunks; his cap had that low brow cock on it. He could not see me in the dimness of the TV room. I watched him scan around and I knew he was looking for me. He stuck his head in the door and squinted his eyes to penetrate the darkness.

"You must not a done any skatin - Miss-sipp!" I teased.

"Why's that - Cracker!" He insulted back.

"Shoot! – Man! - You ain't in no cast - a fella who can't walk without trippin would surely break his leg if'n he'd been skatin!"

"Wait till I get you in the shower - smart ass!" Darrell had picked up on the newest insulting jab in the Navy. It all started with that bathing fiasco from the previous weekend.

"Quiet! - Knothead!" Came a curt request from the dark. Darrell asked me outside to hear the news.

"Well did you find it - Darrell?" I asked.

"Sure did - Lynn and it's really nice! - It's got a big floor - with carpet around the outside - there's booths all around and some kinda special floor - ain't a seam anywhere in it - Man - it's smooth and super quiet!"

"Girls – Caldwell - girls! – How bout the girls?" I pleaded.

"Plenty girls – boy - but plenty sailors too! - They tell me tomorrow night is even worse." Darrell was still pumped.

"Look Darrell - that should be bad news - but you're confusing me - cause you don't make it sound bad!"

"Lynn - her names Carol and man is she ever cute! We're gonna meet again tomorrow night - Man! - She's cuter than a new born hound dog and Man - can we skate together!" He was still pumped.

"Hey that's great – Darrell - is she grown up?"

"She's just out of High School - going to Community College up in Norwich - I told her I had a buddy that looked like Roy Rogers - she said she had a girlfriend that looked like Margaret O'Brien - so you wanna come tomorrow night?"

My mind went blank in trying to remember what Margaret O'Brien looked like, as a women. I guess I had never seen her as a woman, as all I could picture was pigtails and freckles. "I'll give it a try – Darrell - sure hope she ain't no pig in a poke!"

I pulled the 1400 watch Saturday. It was a piece of cake. Just man the PO office, answer the phone and handle any emergencies that should occur.

I did some washing and counted my money. We were paid on Friday and I needed to budget myself for two weeks. I never took all my money when I went ashore. I had a special hiding place for my stash. I always kept a pair of very dirty skivvies in my laundry bag, my cash was rolled up in these dirty skivvies, and I always felt safe.

Darrell and I caught the base bus to Groton. Darrell knew the stop. We only had to walk about three blocks and there it was, a big place, with neon lights everywhere. A neon figure of a gal in a skating skirt, blazed away over the entrance, her neon legs flicking back and forth in time with the flicking arms. No doubt, this was a classy rink.

It was only about 1830 when we arrived; Darrell said the girls would not be there until about 1930. We had about an hour or so to loosen up. I hadn't skated in maybe three years, but really didn't expect any problems. I considered myself a good skater, and could turn around backwards. I had never mastered skating backwards in a smooth fashion; I just couldn't seem to propel myself in a graceful manner.

We hit the floor and I instantly realized that this Mississippi country boy was as much at home on skates as he was on a pool table. "Dag gummit" I couldn't do anything as good as this kid. -- I still liked him! As I stumbled around as graceful as I could, he went sailing by, backwards, with his hands behind his back, looking every bit the mischievous imp that he truly was. I still liked him. The next time he came by, he flipped me a sly underhanded finger, turned, did a layout, then straight into a figure eight. I couldn't help but wish he'd bust his ass! – I still liked him.

The next forty-five minutes or so was spent with me just getting my skating legs back and Darrell being warned to slow it down or cool it. As I was moderately moving around the rink, moving my body and legs with the rhythm of the music, Darrel swished by and motioned for me to follow.

We reached the raised perimeter of the rink and stepped up on the carpet, this was a great idea; you could skate, but slowly, or you could walk on your skates. The carpet provided excellent control.

"The girls are here - come on!" He grinned.

"Darrell - don't show me up now - ya heah!" I pleaded.

"Don't worry. - Carol won't let me show off!" He was beaming. This guy was really excited.

We approached two girls, one tall and one, a little shorter, they were trim, and cute. The shorter girl was blonde and fair. The taller girl was a brunette and a beautiful smile. I knew immediately, this was "Margaret O'Brien."

They were dressed in short sleeve sweaters and capris, complete with little neck scarfs. As they stood and watched, I knew I was being "checked out". Their skates were at their feet.

Darrell skated to the shorter one and stopped. She gave a little flat footed hop and Darrell bent over and kissed her cheek. "Wow!" – This gal was as glad to see Darrell as he was to see her. There was definitely some chemistry there.

The taller girl watched me intently. She probably felt as I did. This was a blind date and we were stuck with each other, like it or not.

"Podna!" Darrell beamed. "This here is Carol, and her friend--Yvonne!"

"Hi! –I'm Lynn – Nice to meet y'all!" The girls looked at each other quickly and did a little silent shoulder hunch that definitely denoted approval, I instantly felt honored to have passed the "Eye Ball Test", and I know girls do it just like guys do. "Don'tcha?"

"Hello –Lynn!" Yvonne said. She extended her hand, which I took and guided her to the nearest seat.

"Let me help you with your skates." I reached over and pulled her skates over to where she sat. These skates were nice and definitely not a pair of rentals. She crossed her legs and placed her free foot in front of me. My mind was racing with "shouda –woulda –coulda –stuff, but I kept control. I felt obligated to Darrell not to ruin his night. My Buddy was definitely "moon struck!"

As I placed her skates on her feet I noticed her legs were very nice and long. Yvonne stood about 5'6" which is perfect for a fellow that is 5'11". I paid close attention to lacing her skates and noticed the laces were marked black where they had been positioned in the lace holes before. I made sure that they went back in the same spots, hoping they would be comfortable.

"How's that feel - Yvonne?" I smiled and patted her leg.

She stood and kinda bounced a little, turned her ankle, glanced down and said. "It's just as if I tied em myself!" That smile flashed.

I thought. "Hey thanks Darrell!" I wondered if Darrell had asked Carol if she had a friend for his Buddy or was it vice – versa. I never asked.

Darrell and Carol were still "gah-gah –ing" each other, so I said. "Come on Yvonne- we're cramping their style! - Let's skate!"

Yvonne looked at the couple and asked. "That's style? – Looks downright embarrassing to me!" We both laughed as we skated out onto the floor.

I should have known that a young woman with a pair of nice personnel roller skates, that already had black wear marks on the laces, would be at home in the rink. It was a pleasure to skate with her. Never once did she show out. Not once did she ever take off on her own, she was with me every minute.

As we skated she would hold my hand, if I pulled her to me she would extend her hand in front of me to take my far hand and position herself for me to reach around to her waist. It was as if we had skated together for years. Now, remember the problem I had with propelling myself backwards, well not to worry! Yvonne would do the propelling and never mentioned it the first time. I was beginning to like this girl.

We had a fine time, this first Saturday in May, 1957. We didn't drink anything stronger than coke, met two nice gals, and skated our butts off. I was sore before we left the rink, but Darrell wouldn't admit he felt anything but good.

Hey! Did I mention they had a car, or Yvonne's Dad's car? We made plans for the next weekend. I got a kiss goodnight as the girls dropped us off at the base gate, it was only a respectable lip peck and could not compare to the lip lock Darrell had on Carol, but it was a start. There's always next weekend.

The girls were from Jewett City, Connecticut, just up the road, twenty or so miles. Darrell and I were going to come up Friday afternoon and get a hotel room in town. That would put us much closer to the girls. The girls said that was fine, but don't expect them to come up to the room. We laughed, but we dared not discuss the thoughts that we all know dwell deep in a man's libido.

Back in the real world, we were engrossed in fire control, compartment security, damage control, and under deck nomenclature. We were learning how important it was to learn the proper names of components. Very few things on a boat have just one name; it is important to specifically identify the item. Take the term, hatch; hatch will not suffice unless you are standing by the one you are referring to and pointing at it." Shoot! – man!"—There are fourteen hatches I can think of without any effort, and then there is the term, line, "Good Lord!" There are so many lines that sometimes it takes three adjectives to identify it. Let's see; "Forward torpedo room low pressure supply line!" I hope you get my point.

We got the word concerning the escape tank; seems that it had been under repair and some arrangements were going to be made concerning our mandatory escape training. The tank had been repaired, it is a three hundred foot tower that a submariner must make a series of ascending escapes from to qualify and continue in the training program. We must make a 30' and then a 50' free ascent escape to proceed in the course. A voluntary 100' escape is offered to those that wish it. There are not many takers, I don't know why any man in his right mind would get in a compression chamber and allow himself to be acclimated to a depth of 100'. The man must strap on a life vest and then step out into a tower, with 100 feet of water above him and plummet to the surface. 30' was gruesome, 50' was brutal, but 100', that takes a total idiot.

"What the HELL am I doing in here!!!!"-- My mind raced as I remembered the panic I felt in the 50' escape. My lungs screamed for oxygen as I continued to blow out, I could see the bubbles from my lungs following me up to the surface. I wanted to suck that air back in, but training said you must continue to blow, or your lungs will explode.

Free escape from 100', I didn't have to do this, the other nine guys in the chamber didn't have to do it either, but here we were. Were we ten idiots, or did we value our lives enough to make sure we had that little extra, in case this scenario ever presented itself in real life.

The compression chamber is at the 100' level in the escape tower. The men sit on benches on either side as the chamber begins to exert pressure until it equals the water depth at 100'. A hatch is then opened and each man goes out the hatch, places his hands around a line that stretches to the surface and lets his natural buoyancy and the buoyancy of his life jacket, lift him to the surface. There is no threat of the bends because the trainees are not under pressure long enough for much nitrogen to be forced into their blood stream.

The Navy has trained personnel stationed along the way to aid if a sailor has a problem. These men are trained in observing the trainers as they rise and will react immediately to stop a man and render whatever need is necessary, however it is not good to be stopped. If you are stopped it usually involves another shot at getting it right, or dismissal from the program. This includes the voluntary 100' ascent if you choose it.

"RUN! – SCREAM! -- Get out of here!" Every fiber of my consciousness made these demands. I thought I was gonna die at fifty feet! Now, at twice that depth, "what was I thinking?"

Apparently the guy running the show couldn't see the turmoil I was in, as he opened the hatch and put his hand on the shoulder of the first man and cheerfully said. "Out de hatch, an meet yo maker, ya buncha candy ass pussys!" This would be my third escape, it should be a piece of cake, all the instructions came flooding back and this voice kept saying. "Blow! --No matter what! --Keep blowing! – Blow! –Blow! –Blow! --Don't stop! --You won't die; you just think you will die! – Blow! – Don't stop - if you do stop - you will die!"

I bent over and was out, I reached for the hand line, and released my grip. I felt like I was shot from a cannon. I turned my eyes upward and realized I couldn't see the tank top. Hey! I could always see the tank top!

Something's wrong! Am I going the right way. I was already feeling starved for oxygen, but the bubbles were going with me. The panic eased up but the urge to suck that air back in was overwhelming.

That voice again, "Blow you knucklehead - Blow!" Suddenly a feeling of confidence flooded over me. I was not the first to do this, nor would I be the last, it was not necessary to do it, so why offer it to us. The Navy does not do stupid stuff, they had a reason for this volunteer escape and I had walked right into it. Failure for me, was not an option.

I relaxed my entire body. I figured a relaxed system would not demand as much oxygen as a tense system and I could go nowhere but up. I concentrated on blowing and shut my eyes and decided not to worry about not seeing the top of the tank.

Suddenly I realized I wasn't rising anymore. I opened my eyes to find one of the attendants holding me by my life vest. You can't talk under water and blow out at the same time, but my eyes definitely asked; "What the hell are you doing?"

He looked through his mask with a quizzing expression and flipped me the finger. I flipped him back and swiped his hand away from my life vest.

I zoomed away. "Dag Gummit" I never had been one for bad language. Momma would say; "An intelligent man can communicate effectively without resorting to vulgarity, " but this smart ass, bastard that stopped me was causing me grief.   A 100' free escape ain't no picnic, if it was, everyone would do it. This guy had stopped me; I was already near panic and now had at least 5 or 6 more seconds added to my trip. Man was I mad.

I came out of the water to my knees and you could have heard my first gasp for air across the river at the Coast Guard Academy.

"You all right - boy?" questioned one of the men posted at the top.

"Don't worry! - GASP - bout me! – GASP! - You best worry bout that –WHEEZ! --dummy that grabbed me down there!"

"Well - believe me – boy - we'll talk to him - but it ain't him that's in trouble - now sit over there and relax!" He motioned to a bench along the wall.

I felt angry and was now concerned as to what I did wrong. There were four more guys to follow me and they all made it OK.

One asked me what was up, and I just shrugged.

Soon the sailors that had manned the tower arrived and shed their gear. I scanned the faces of the group, but with me looking through water into a guy's face in a mask, there was no way I could recognize him.

The boss man was apparently the one that spoke to me as I exited the tank. He tapped one of the divers on the arm, pointed at me and half-laughingly said; "That kids waiting to whip your ass, but first, what's his story?"

I gave him my best "evil eye."

He looked at me intently, then flashed a smiled. "Hell! He was so bored with the whole thing, he was taking a damn nap!-- I ain't never seen a man sleep through a hunert footer -- Shit he's fine!"

There was a pause then he said. "Hey boy - still wanna whip my ass?" He flipped me another finger.

"Naw! – It's OK!" I said, and tossed my life vest to him. "But you can stick this up your ass!"

The laughter fairly shook the tower as I hastily departed. I think his laughter was loudest. You know what - I'll bet he wore "Dolphins" too.

CHAPTER III

JEWETT CITY

Brown was going to Norwich to see Gail on Saturday and gave us a ride that far. Jewett City was just a little further up the road so we thumbed from Norwich. The Navy really doesn't care if you hitch a ride, but if you are near the base, they must make an effort to control situations, therefore we don't thumb near a base.

We caught a ride from Norwich in no time, straight to Jewett City and right to the hotel.

The hotel was on Main Street and Ashland. Our room was on the second floor. There was a magnificent veranda that stretched across the front of the second and third floors. It was old school and we loved it. There were no frills, but clean and convenient.

We lounged around the room for a bit then walked around town for a while. It was a nice place. I don't know if there was even a traffic light in town. Main Street forked about a block up from the hotel; in the fork was a nice grassy plot with a stature dedicated to a soldier or something and a big brick Church. The people in town would smile and everyone seemed to acknowledge our presence. I think we may have been the only guest in the hotel. It was obvious that service men didn't come to Jewett City a lot, which suited us, just fine.

Darrell nor I favored the bar hopping scene much and neither of us gave in, to much drink. This drinking attitude would quite often bring us grief. If we were with a group of guys, there was always one or two that took offence if you wouldn't drink with them. It's sad to go ashore with a bunch of buddies then have to split up with hard feelings. The bitter feelings seldom carried over but little by little your liberty buddies would dwindle to the point where you would become a loner.

But not to worry! Darrell and I had our girls and they had a car! "Sweet!"

We had gone back to the room and were on the veranda when we saw the green Mercury approaching from north on Main Street. "Here they come - Lynn!" Darrell fairly vaulted from his rocker.

"Slow down Miss-sipp!" I called. "You'll break a leg on them stairs and I'll have to carry you around with Carol hanging on your neck!"

Darrell laughed and as we stumbled our ways down the stairs, the impish 'lil devil quickly outlined a plan to have some fun with the girls.

As we stepped out onto the sidewalk we stopped and without acknowledging the girls, began to primp. I straightened Darrell's cap and he gently tugged my tie in mock manner. We brushed each other's shoulders as if to remove fluff or such, then turned to walk up the street.

The '54 green Mercury was at the curb with Yvonne at the wheel and Carol in the front passenger seat. As we were walking away the horn beeped. We stopped and timidly looked back to see Carol leaning from the window and calling ever so softly, "We're here - Darrell - In the car - Here!"

We looked at each other and made signs as if to ask: "Are they talking to us?"

"Yes - you dummy - are you blind?" scolded Carol.   Yvonne sat expressionless at the wheel with her fingers pressed pensively to her lips.

With feigned shyness, Darrell and I walked back to the car. Darrel looked around as if to make sure no one saw. "Are you addressing us - Ma'am?"

"Carol grimaced and said. "Get in the car boys and quit trying to be cute!"

I thought. "Darrell - maybe we ought not press our luck!"

Darrell struck a pose with his hand on his hip and stated. "Well! - I never! -- A couple of nice gentlemen sailors can't even take an afternoon stroll without some brash females trying to pick them up! - Huumph!"

I chimed in. "They must think we're easy!"

We heard the gears crunch as Yvonne angrily engaged low gear and began to pull away.

"WE'RE EASY! – WE'RE EASY!" We both shouted, as we reached for the back door handle.

The Mercury screeched to a halt and as we tumbled in Yvonne said, "You sailors are all alike - pushovers." We all laughed and Yvonne drove away.

Carol asked Yvonne to pull in at the Church. "We need to swap seats before Darrell and Lynn start holding hands!" Both girls laughed.

Darrell and I moved our hands to our laps and looked at each other in mocked suspicion.

Carol slide into the back seat and immediately Darrell pulled her into his arms and placed a kiss gently but squarely on her lips. I glanced at Yvonne and she smiled as she rolled her eyes.

"Darrell quit- not here!" Carol chided. "It doesn't look good - Now stop it!" She now was curt, as Darrell continued to nuzzle her. She pushed away.

"My word - Ma'am - such a fuss - I thought that was what a fellow was supposed to do when he got picked up!" Darrell acted indignant.

"Well that's what people will think if they see us acting this way – Darrell - this is a small town and everyone knows us and our parents!" She lowered her voice and with a giggle, shyly said. "It'll be dark in a little while anyway!"

Yvonne glanced at Darrell and Carol in the rear view mirror and laughingly said. "So much for being coy - Carol."

The '54 Merc was a great deal like my Ford at home. Same color green but the upholstery was much plusher and was a four door. I wanted to offer to drive, but thought it best not to say anything, at least not yet.

We drove around the country side and it was truly beautiful. I thought how this was the land of the Mohicans and gazed into the forest and imagined Hawkeye, Chingachgook and Uncas hiding behind the boulders as they spied upon the French, or searched for that villain, Magua.

James Fennimore Cooper did a fine job on my imagination when I was a youth. There were crystal clear lakes, lined with colorful rocks and stone cliffs with waterfalls gushing over their brinks.

The trees were tall and the woods were very open compared to Georgia and Louisiana. Our woods are flat and thick with giant old, mossy oak trees and profuse undergrowth, laced with shallow swamps and bugs. I don't think I saw a bug the whole time I was in Connecticut.

We stopped and met Carol's parents; they were very proper and courteous. Darrell was on his best behavior and did none of his southern hicky stuff. I could tell that Darrell really liked this girl and was not going to be the least bit hypocritical with this family. I respected that and realized that my buddy, Darrell, truly, was a southern gentleman.

It was close to 1600 hours when Yvonne suggested we head for her house. We drove up the same road that was Main Street in Jewett City. I suppose we went, maybe five or six miles from town and turned left into a drive leading up to a neat two story home, close to a hundred yards back from the road.

We were in the Connecticut countryside. The home sat up on a slight rise and we could look out across the road and see the grassy fields. Across the fields we could see the sharp contrasting rock and forest outcroppings. This was April and the snow was all gone and the green of spring was on the way. It truly was a gorgeous view and with snow, would make the perfect Christmas card scene.

The home was comfortable. We meet Yvonne's Mom, Dad and Brother. Her brother was a high school senior; his physique was not just the result of playing sports but indicated extensive weight room time.

I never had the time to play organized sports, but managed to play a lot of "sand lot ball", however, I knew sports well.

This young man was a classic example of a high school football player and I assumed he was a good one too.

Yvonne's Dad talked in length with Darrell and me. It was natural, I guess for him to address most of his questions to me, since it was obvious I was Yvonne's date. I felt comfortable but was terribly self- conscious about my accent.

Yvonne's Mom scolded her Dad for funning me on my "o" pronunciations. He said he couldn't see where I got "dawg" out of dog and "hawg" out of hog.

I thought for a moment and said," Well - it made as much sense as dahg and hahg, cause there wasn't an "a" in either one of them.

He thought for a second, looked at me, grinned and asked, "Youse guys want a beer?" We declined.

I told him I wouldn't be twenty-one until November, he said he wouldn't tell, but I said. "No thanks - just the same."

Yvonne and her folks disappeared into the kitchen for a short time and Darrell and I talked to the brother about football. Darrell had played in high school and they hit it off good. It was interesting to hear the inside terminology that only guys that played could know. It was a bonding agent. I kinda felt left out.

Yvonne came back into the room with a smile that told me something was up.

Presently her Dad came in, looked at us and spoke. "Boys it's Saturday night and if youse are taking these girls out, then you better get started, because Yvonne needs to be home by midnight." She wore a full smile by now.

Darrell jumped to his feet, he had been sitting by Carol for an hour and she had slapped his hand a dozen times. "Sounds good to me - how bout it Georgia Boy"

"OK by me!" I looked at Yvonne and she winked. Her Dad moved my way, and stuck his hand out.

"I don't like Yvonne to drive after dark if she goes far - so I'd appreciate it - if you'd drive - Lynn."

He handed me the car keys. As I took the keys he grabbed my wrist, pulled me close and said. "I'm trustin you - son."

He paused. I nodded yes. "Need any money?" He asked. I nodded no. I liked this man!

The girls were delirious; it was as if this was the greatest night of their lives. I will never understand why this night was so special, but we were a part of it, and also, we were willing participants.

We checked the movies and decided the drive – in, back down Norwich way, was our goal. It was a science fiction flick and all agreed it was the best deal going.

Man! What could be better, burgers, fries, cokes, your girl and the drive-in. somebody ought to write a book about that! I don't remember much about the movie, but I do recall something about giant water lilies that would eat people. What do you expect, I mean the windshield kept fogging up and Yvonne demanded a lot of attention.

Now don't get me wrong, because if you expect a lot of graphic words to describe a very private situation, then you expect wrong.   Now I can't speak for the back seat, but the front seat activity was very appropriate. Yvonne was every bit a lady, and quite a lady at that.

The girls dropped us off at the hotel and made it home by their curfew. Darrell and I sat on the veranda rockers and smoked cigarettes 'till well past 0100 hours. I slept like a baby, Darrell said Carol kept him awake all night, I looked quizzically at him and he grinned.

Darrell went to Carols for dinner on Sunday. Yvonne came by and we went to a local restaurant for lunch. We talked and got to know more about each other's early lives. I began to realize that Yvonne was refreshingly naïve and very trusting. She never gave any indication she had any serious relationships before now.

She let me drive back to the base that afternoon and as we got out of the car, she walked me to the gate and gave me a lingering kiss well in view of the gate guards.

Wow! What a feeling. When I flashed my card and walked through the gate the guard on my side flashed me a thumbs up. I grinned and gave him a "weren't nothing shrug!"   I worried about Darrell.   Yvonne said she had not discussed anything about Sunday with Carol.   I never saw Darrell come in, but he was bright and cheery at breakfast.

"I was worried bout you 'ol buddy!" I said, as I placed my eggs and hash on the table across from him. "I didn't see you at all last night - what time did you get in?"

"No need to worry about me – Podna - I was in heaven. - Can't nothing bad happen in heaven." He looked at me and asked. "How bout you and Yvonne - still getting along?"

"Sure Darrell - she's a great gal - we had dinner yesterday and she brought me back yesterday afternoon - how'd you get back?" I asked.

"A friend of the family works here at the Naval Yard and I rode in with him." He explained.

"Man - I couldn't afford another night at the hotel – Darrell. - How'd you swing that?" I queried.

"Didn't have to – Lynn - Carols family put me up! - Know what – Buddy - I think I'm gonna marry that gal!" He picked up his tray and left.

I sat there in a state of shock. I suddenly realized that Darrell and I weren't playing the same kind of game. I was dating, my Mississippi buddy was in love. I was gonna lose him.

We had discussed the possibility of being assigned to the same boat and sailing under the seven seas together and seeing the world through the eyes of two southern gentlemen that had each other's backs. Marriage put an entirely different concept on everything. I felt a loss but at the same time felt good for him. I thought, perhaps, in time maybe I would feel that way about Yvonne. I thought about it for a moment, but then my attention turned to those eggs and hash, there weren't any grits, but that hash wasn't bad. I wondered if there was some more. Class was in ten minutes.

I couldn't believe it, I was about a month away from my own boat. I would walk down to the piers at the foot of the base and look longingly at the boats tied up along the Thames. The Nautilus was still out in the Pacific; rumor had it that she was on a good will tour, hitting most of the major west coast cities to give them a view of a nuclear boat. Boy did that crew have the luck. When a Navy ship would visit a coastal city or town there was always some type of special welcome planned for them. Should it be a non- Naval base town or a special ship like the Nautilus, then you could only speculate as to the extent of the welcome.

Yvonne and I had become very close in the next few weeks, sharing past histories, aspirations for the future and hopes that we shared. We didn't talk of marriage, but I had difficulty steering away from it when the subject of my naval career came up. After graduating from sub school each sailor would request his assignment. It was rumored that if you scored high enough in the overall grading average, that you could have your choice of available assignments. This helped in keeping Yvonne and I from making any kind of definite plans. It had no effect on Darrell and Carol; they were headed down that primrose path of matrimony.

We went from our wool blues to whites the first of May, 1957. The base opened Rock Pond on Saturday, May 4th. Darrell and I were there for the opening. I was terribly disappointed, the water was still very cold and not nearly as clear as I expected. Yvonne and I had seen a lot of countryside ponds that were crystal clear, but Rock Pond was like our dark waters down Georgia Way. I didn't spend a lot of time there that day. I needed to catch up on laundry and we were meeting the girls at six to go skating.

I began to feel a sore throat coming on at the rink that night and told Yvonne that I hoped it was not going to be another tonsillitis flare-up. I had been plagued for years with one or two yearly cases of this painful ordeal. Well as luck would have it, I woke up Sunday morning with a throat so sore and swollen that it was impossible to swallow solid food. Luckily the cook had some oatmeal in the cooler and with a little heat, cream and sugar, I got it down, but now my ears were beginning to ache. I took some salt and warm water, gargled and went back to bed. By 1100 hours I could hardly swallow water, and the fever began.

I roused up near noon and looked in the mirror, my jowls were visibly swollen. I went to the payphone and called Yvonne to cancel our Sunday afternoon ride. She told me how badly she felt about my throat and asked if the Navy would release me so she could nurse me. I laughed, it hurt, but it was a sweet thought.

I dressed and made my way to sick bay. I could not believe the number of people waiting in the reception area. I checked in, and gave my symptoms to the nurse.

She said, "Hold on a sec! – Come over here! – Sit!" She led me to a stainless steel table and motioned to a chair, she turned a standing spot light on me. "Tilt your head - open up and say AHHHH!" I complied. "Good Lord! - Boy! -- Sit right here - I'm going to get a doctor!"

She hastily exited the room and returned shortly with a colored doctor, this was a first for me.

A doctor in the military is always an officer. Sometimes there will be civilian doctors that will work for the military, but there was no mistaking the kaki shirt with a lieutenant bar and the medical emblem on the collar.

Let's have a look sailor. "Geesh! Boy! That's text book stuff there. "Hold On" He exited the room.

The nurse approached me with a thermometer flipping it as she walked. "Open up! – Under the tongue! –Don't bite!" Why do they always say that, do grown men really bite a thermometer?

"Hey Madge, did you wipe this thermometer after the last user?" She called out.

Madge answered back. "I think so - Heck I don't remember - we've got so much going on - why?"

My nurse called back. " Well I'm using it and was just wondering!"

She pulled the instrument from my mouth and held it to the light. "Wow! – 104 - that's some infection sailor!

"Guess it don't matter if it wasn't wiped then does it?" I quipped. "Couldn't get much sicker - could I?"

"Oh - that's not it!" She answered. "You see this is one of those new thermometers - you can use it in either the mouth or the butthole!"

She looked directly at my face to see my reaction. I didn't disappoint her.

She cracked up and laughingly called out. "Got another one Madge!"

I could hear Madge laugh from the other room.

The doctor returned with a group of nurses and interns, I guess, and each took a turn down my throat to see a text book case of tonsillitis. The doctor then ordered some more test and told me I needed to be hospitalized, for a few days to reduce the infection.

"Those tonsils need to come out, young fella, or you'll be plagued with this situation all your life." The Doctor said.

My heart sank, if I missed too much school, I'd be dropped from the class and do shore duty on base until another class got to the point where I could join them. I had worked hard and didn't want to lose my boat assignment.

"Doc - Please Sir!" I pleaded. "What if I stay out of the weather - get plenty of rest and take my medicine - please Doc don't take me outa my class - I've had this plenty o times before and I always made it! – Doc – please - help me out here!"

"Listen sailor!" He looked at me intently. "Your wellbeing is my prime responsibility and I would be remiss if I didn't have some guarantee that you would receive your treatment!"

I thought of Hardy. "Would my instructor's word be good enough for you - Sir? I'll try to get him on the phone if that'll work - He's Hardy - Carol Hardy - torpedoman first class - Sir!"

"Alright now - take it easy - give me a minute." He said as he turned. "Hey! – Nurse! -- Put him in the waiting room and I'll do some checking, and get me a bed availability count from the hospital!"

I went back outside and could feel the burn around my ears. There was pressure from the swollen flesh under my ears and yes, my ears still hurt. The nurses were doing a good job of preliminary examination as personnel continued to come in. There were close to a dozen when I first arrived, but by now there was almost twenty.

Some of the arriving personnel were seated in the waiting area as soon as their check- in was completed; a few were examined immediately after check in, the same as I was.   I'm sure the nurses were screening those that needed prompt treatment from those that could wait. I was about to resign myself to an all-night wait, when my nurse came to the door and beckoned to me. There were two bottles on the little table close to where I had sat and a needle. I thought this was a good sign, if they were going to put me in the hospital they wouldn't be going to treat me now.

"The Doctor says your PO doesn't want to lose you either - so I've got a shot of antibiotic and these tablets. - Pull your tunic off so I can get to your arm."

I did as she requested and took my shot like a man, it stung, and I wanted to ask what an antibiotic was.

She picked up a bottle of tablets. "OK - take one of these as soon as you get to your barracks and one tomorrow morning and then repeat that 'till they're all gone."

Taking the other bottle, she said. "This bottle is for gargling - put about a tablespoon in a glass of warm water and gargle 'till the glass is empty.- If you get sick or your fever does not come down by morning - then come straight back here.- Sailor Boy - don't mess this up - or you'll be in trouble and your PO will be in Dutch also - do you hear me?"

"Yassum!" I answered. She smacked my shot arm and then tossed me my tunic as she picked up a clipboard.

"If all goes well!" She stated. "We will see you Wednesday afternoon." She glanced at the clipboard. "Good luck -- Lynn!" She gently pushed me out of the room, glanced at the clipboard again and called the next name.

I made my way back to the barracks, wondering if I had done the right thing.

My sleep was fitful and delusional. Little things would manifest themselves and repeat over and over. Around 0400 hours my fever broke and the sweats started. By reveille I felt better and luckily oatmeal was on the menu. Hardy caught me in the chow hall. He walked over and placed his hand on my forehead, the guys at the table looked at us rather funny.

Hardy spoke. "First one of you wise-guys that makes a crack is gonna get knocked to Chinatown and that's in New York City. - Wardlaw - go straight to class - don't go outside on break and don't make the sub tour this afternoon." He turned and left.

Man, did I have some explaining to do to the guys, and they made the most of it too.

"Oooh! - Teacher's pet! – Sucking up ain'tcha!" Well that's the price you have to pay sometimes, so I just bit the bullet.

I was disappointed at missing the tour; it was the U.S.S. Albacore AGSS 569, a newer fast attack boat that sported a new cigar shape design. She was operating out of Boston, but was stopping by, just for our tour.

We had seen a training film that pictured a speeding PT boat. In the film we could see the periscope of the Albacore as she passed the PT boat. That was most impressive. Missing the tour wouldn't hurt my schooling in any way, but I was disappointed just the same.

I continued to feel better and by Wednesday afternoon, I felt as if nothing had been wrong at all. I had never been to the doctor with my previous bouts of tonsillitis, I would simply nurse them myself or Momma would care for me. I think this was probably the first antibiotic shot I had ever had. I'm sure it was penicillin.

The waiting room was full this time, but I didn't wait long before a nurse called my name.

A first class PO complained about being there over an hour and I had just walked in. The nurse very calmly told him I wasn't going ahead of him; in fact I wasn't even staying.

This confused me and as she took me into the room, I questioned her about it. She told me her orders were, if I had no fever and the swelling had gone down to give me another shot and dismiss me. It seems that a flu epidemic was in full rage and the hospital was packed. I got my shot and was free. I said a little prayer of thanks and felt truly blessed. I'll mention here; I've never had another attack of tonsillitis.

I called Yvonne and made plans for the weekend. The rest of the week was as intense as ever. We had lost about eight of our guys along the way. If we asked about someone, we were told simply that they were not a part of the program any longer. I asked one fellow I saw packing his gear and he said his ears could not handle the pressure in the escape tank. His eyes teared up when he told me the 30' escape hurt him and the Doc said, the 50' escape would be too much for him, he had to go. He said he was going to be an Airdale [Naval Aviation] and drop rocks on us. I laughed and wished him luck. I knew how he felt. I felt heart sick just thinking about losing my boat.

Our class was set to graduate on June 19, 1957 and there was a big graduation dance planned for Friday, June 21, at the base assembly hall.

Yvonne was more excited about the dance than I was. Her eyes simply danced when I asked her to go. She began to talk about how it was just perfect, a big dance, evening dress, live band, just like high school and college. From then on, nothing would do but practice every time we got the chance. I enjoyed that, it saved me money and gave us some together time.

Yvonne was really a nice person and a true Yankee Lady. Imagine that; a Yankee Lady and a Southern Gentleman. -- Wow!—What a match up. We had a lot of fun together.

The only spat we ever had was because I made a comment about the amount of beer her Dad drank. I was not used to anyone drinking alcohol around the house. Beer was an everyday beverage for Yvonne's Dad. It would take some adjustment on my part to get used to having it in the fridge anytime you wanted it. I supposed I should never have mentioned it, I was out of line.

Graduation Day, Wednesday June 19, 1957. 1000 hours in the Main Base Assembly Hall, New London, Connecticut Submarine Base. The Base Commander was seated on the stage as well as the staff and dignitaries.

I noticed a Chief coming in the large doors on the east end of the building, the early sun was quite bright and was brilliantly shining, making it difficult to make out who it was. The silhouette and walk was definitely familiar. He drew nearer and then it was evident the gleaming dress white chief's uniform was new. Suddenly I knew it was Hardy, he had made Chief, and had a third hash mark on his sleeve. His left chest sported a proud three line array of campaign ribbons topped with those gleaming silver "Dolphins". His stride indicated his pride as he carried his hat under his left arm. Man! Forrest Tucker could not have presented a more perfect U.S. Navy Chief.

We had formed up at the barracks and marched down to the hall by classes. We then were instructed to take our seats in the arrangement of chairs set up in the center of the hall. We sat by classes and the entire front row was left vacant. The hall had bleachers that folded into the walls and the sections behind us were set up for visitor viewing.

I soon caught sight of Yvonne and Carol, both waved and I jerked my head at Darrell to show him where they were. That Mississippi boy could sure grin. All the guys around him were ribbing him about being a Cheshire Cat.

The base Executive Officer welcomed the brass. He then introduced the mayors of New London, Groton and a couple of other nearby towns, along with other members of the elite. He then thanked the instructors for their hard work.

The Base Commander was introduced. The Commander gave a short speech that expounded on the intensity and extent of our training. I noticed he wore gold "Dolphins". The man knew of that which he spoke. I was trying to be inconspicuous in looking at Yvonne, when I heard the Commander say. "As your name is called, come forward and stand in front of these vacant chairs starting here." He motioned to the first chair on the vacant row up front. He began to call names of men in the class; the first name called was a first class in our section that had a degree in engineering. I noticed the names were not being called in alphabetical order, some names were in our section, some in another section and then to my shock, the Commander called "Wardlaw, L.Z. --Seaman."

I rose and took my place up front, still wondering what it was all about, Darrell was the last name called and as he took his place, the Commander resumed speaking to the students and guest. He again spoke of the training and how important our training was, how we were the front line of our nation's defense and the sacrifices that we made and how special we were. I was then shocked to hear him refer to a young man that became gravely ill and refused hospitalization so he would not miss his training. "That's what makes a Submariner special." He never called a name so maybe it wasn't me. Hardy looked at me and smiled, I felt warm all over.

The Commander stated; "My fellow Americans, you've heard me tell you how the United States Navy feels about these men gathered here today, and you've heard the names of twenty-two of these men." He directed his attention to those of us in the front row. "Will the front row please rise!" He motioned to us and as we rose he spoke again; "Ladies and Gentlemen, may I present the top ten percent of this 144th class of the Enlisted Basic Submarine Course!"

I think I could have cried, because my throat became very tight. The Commander continued as he motioned for us to sit. "Now let me explain. It is not the policy of the U.S.Navy to pay anyone more money for doing good in anything, much less school." The crowd laughed heartily. But these guys will receive a reward; that reward is their choice of available duty assignments." Another round of applause. He motioned for the entire class to stand and placed his hat upon his head and said, "Congratulations Gentlemen!' Snapped a smart salute and exclaimed, " See ya at the ball!"

The Exec loudly shouted, "CLASS DISMISSED!"

Yvonne was all smiles as I approached her, Darrell had run ahead and was already embracing Carol. Both girls knew that we now had our choice of duty and would request to remain in New London, either assigned to a boat or sub related shore duty. It was official; we were both in the top ten percent and could have our choice of available duty. That was the catch, available duty.

Darrell and I were lucky in one respect, we were not rated yet, which meant we would be deck crew. There always seemed to be openings in the deck crew.

We spent the rest of the day showing our girls around the base and went down to the subs. The girls seemed interested. I suppose it was natural for them to want to become familiar with what would become our second love. We went off base for an early dinner and the girls went home. My Miss-sippi pal and I played a couple of games of pool and hit the sack. Thursday would be a big day. We would be profiled, given the duties that were available and make our choices.

It was a beautiful morning. I rolled out early and was one of the first to the chow hall. On the chow line I could see the grill set up, this meant we could choose fried eggs if we preferred. I always did and as the cook looked up I gave him two fingers with a flipping motion. I loaded a pile of hash brown potatoes and the cook gently laid the two perfectly fried eggs on top.

"Hey! You ain't covered them taters boy - want this un too?" he motioned to an overly fried egg he had moved to one side of the grill.

I nodded and grinned. "Good - the chief would have a fit if he knew I over cooked one! - The Chief don't believe in frying any egg done! - He says! - If'n a sailor asks for over well - just tell him to eat scrambled - same difference!"

I guess he's right. It made me happy anyway.

Darrell showed as I was getting my second cup. "Georgia Boy! I hear they got the grades posted and time slots for our assignment sessions! - Can you wait on me?'

"Can do - Miss-sip! – Got some news for you too! - Talked to a fellow a while ago that knows a florist in town and if we want he can get some corsages for us for tomorrow night! -- The girls will flip if we give em flowers and only three bucks!" I relayed a conversation I had with one of the PO's stationed at the base on the way to the chow hall.

"Man! -Three bucks!" gasped Darrell. "What kinda corsage is it - an orchid or something!"

"Hey! Miss-sip -- I don't know man! - By the time we went to town and got one and came back and all- we'd be all tuckered out and might get our whites dirty or get hit by a bus or get arrested for being ugly in public or something- besides- the guy might want to make a buck or two!" I suppose I was trying to justify my desire to get a flower for Yvonne. Darrell sighed and agreed.

We found the PO and placed our orders. He told us the flowers would be delivered to the barracks PO office on Friday about 3PM, he said he had fourteen orders; the florists would not deliver unless they had at least ten, so things looked pretty good.

There were a slew of fellows at the bulletin board in the PO office. We finally made our way close enough to the front to read the bulletins. I found my name in the fifteenth spot out of a class that graduated two hundred fifteen men. My score average was ninety-one percent and my grade was 3.6, I was very pleased. Darrell's grade was good too, but I had beaten him, I finally beat him at something, but I didn't mention it. It would not have mattered to Darrell in the least; he was in hog heaven because he could stay in New London. I made note of my assignment time and it was late in the day. I think they were assigned alphabetically and "W" is way down the list.

I spent the day doing laundry and pressing my whites for the big dance. Late in the day we walked down to the Gedunk and could hear the base orchestra practicing in the big assembly hall. They were playing "In the Mood", Boy! - They sure could swing.

Darrel beat me in a couple of snooker games. We sipped cokes as we sat in the booth and listened to LiL Richard blast out "Long Tall Sally", then Bill Haley cut loose with "See Ya Later Alligator". We must have heard Pat Boone do "Love Letters" at least three times, before I had to leave. Darrell had already had his evaluation and he got New London, but would not know which boat he was assigned to until Friday or Saturday.

I reported to the administration building and according to the signs I sat and waited for my name to be called. I waited a considerable time and noticed that names being called were In the Y's and Z's.

I walked to the PO desk to question why I was missed. "Were you here at the beginning of your time slot?" asked the PO.

"Sho was Boss - probably ten minutes early - matter of fact - they were still calling T's when I arrived."

I waited probably ten minutes before I heard him call from the door. "Hey! – Wardlaw come on back!"

I made my way down the hall and he motioned me to a desk were another PO was waiting. "Sorry for the wait – Wardlaw - but we don't know how to handle this - you see we do not have the proper paper work for you to begin your two years active duty! - We should not have even let you do the eight week basic course."

My heart sank, I thought; there goes my boat. "What does this mean - Man? – Will I have to do the course over again - or what?" I was getting a little concerned. "Maybe you better get your Lieutenant in here to straighten this out!"

"Look Wardlaw!" The PO was curt. "This ain't my fault and what I'm tellin you is from the Lieutenant. - He said – "Send the f—ker home! - Let his reserve unit straighten it out - they're the ones that screwed it up - so I'm cutting your travel chits now - that's my orders and that's all I can do."

I felt like my world was hurtling through space, I was numb with confusion and getting very angry. "What about my school – Man? - I was in the top ten percent - doesn't that mean something and I'm supposed to get my choice of duty."

I remembered the Base Commanders words and thought they might lend some leverage. "The Base Commander said so - in front of hundreds of witnesses!" I thought this might just do it. I was wrong.

"Sorry Sailor! – Look we've been hashing this around since we got the final grades and certificates of graduation."

He heaved a sigh of exasperation. "I've been authorized one alternative. - If you ship over right now [changing status from reserve to regular navy], we will credit you with eight weeks and you serve only three years and ten months - plus there may be a little ship over pay. "How's that sound to ya?"

My head was really in a swirl now. "Don't know man - I have a military leave from the Telephone Company for two years and that's all - if I'm gone four years – well - they won't hold my job. -- Man! – I can't do that - just send me home!"

I could feel the tears welling in my eyes. How could life be that cruel? Ten minutes ago I was on top of the world, only a few days from getting my own boat, staying in New London with a swell girl and now it's all trashed. How was I going to tell Yvonne that I was going home? The big dance was now a dreaded thing.

"Look – Boss - how about my school - won't it count?" I'm sure he could see the bitter disappointment in my face.

"Sit down - Wardlaw." We had been standing the whole time. "Look I'm gonna level with you - I think this whole thing is a conspiracy - and that doesn't mean it's a bad thing - it's just one of those things the Navy does to get the most for their money."

"What the Sam Hill you talkin about Man? The Navy conspiring against me - a lowly seaman!" I growled. I was getting hot.

"Hear me out now!" He lowered his voice. "The Navy spends a great deal of money on the training of you guys - the boats put in request for men to fill specific positions - they want a man to come and serve as long as they can on that boat.- The longer you serve - the more you learn - the more valuable you become. - We really don't think the boats are interested in a reserve that they spend the same money on as a regular and have less than two years to get some return on that investment .- We don't get many reserves through here in the regular program - but this very thing has happened before - so go home - your reserve unit will process you and your two year active duty requirement has not started yet. - You are still on reserve status. - You must report back to your unit by July first - by the way - you travel chits are open dated - so take a little vacation.

"What about the school man?   Listen it must have been legit - cause I got paid – doesn't that tell you something!" I was pleading.

"Tell you what I'm gonna do - Lieutenant Harris hasn't been in on this school deal - so I'm gonna post your grades to your 82-76 form and if he signs it - then it should be no problem." The PO seemed to be genuinely concerned about my plight.

The circumstances were completely out of his control, as a matter of fact I think the whole thing simply would not work unless I went home and got it straightened out.

He left the room and was back in less than two minutes, with a grin. "Done deal – Wardlaw - the school and your grade are yours now. "

I looked at my training form and, indeed, it was signed by L.L.Harris, Asst. Pers. Officer by direction of the Commanding Officer. The PO took the papers back and sealed them up in the usual Navy fashion. Sailor's records went with him as he transferred and traveled; they are sealed in a heavy manila envelope and best not be opened when a sailor gets to his new duty station.

As I picked up my gear, the PO said. "Look, you know you can spend the night on any military base on your way home. Your travel chits are your authority and you simply check into the overnight barracks. -- Good Luck - maybe we'll cross up again sometimes."

"On a boat?" I asked. I had not seen any Dolphins on him.

"Not a chance - there is only one billet per sub for a yeoman and that yeoman's office ain't big enough to even fart in!—Nope! -- Not this sailor. Maybe I'll see ya in Paris!"

I laughed, picked up my papers and left. Daylight was waning as I walked back to the barracks. I put my papers in my locker and sought out Darrel. He was in the chow hall; he could see the gloom in my face.

"Dag gum – son - you didn't get New London?" He questioned.

"I didn't get dippy doo – Darrell - I've got to go home." I relayed the whole story to him and he listened in silence.

"This is really going to upset Yvonne - you know that - don't you?" I nodded in agreement. "She and Carol have talked a little about a double wedding you know." I stood up in shock.

"'Miss-sipp - I promise you - I never talked marriage with Yvonne! I mean – well - maybe we talked around it - but nothing serious!" I suddenly felt very defensive. I was also beginning to feel sorry for myself, I didn't like it either, and a feeling of self-pity meant I wasn't in charge.

Now, don't get me wrong, I know that a person must deal with what-ever environment they are placed in, but I didn't realize this environment was partially my fault and I wasn't prepared for it.

"Thanks for the heads up – Darrell! - I didn't realize that Yvonne was this serious!"

"Where the dickens you been – boy - you're the only guy she has talked with - held hands with or kissed for the last two months! -- She's here every time your off-- you spend time with her family -- y'all ride around the countryside looking at stuff - Man - neither one of us has gone juking since we met the girls! -- Where do you think this is going?"

"Your right Buddy! - I'm just confused and Yvonne doesn't need to be hurt." I paused and looked at Darrell, I needed a favor. "Darrell, please don't mention this to Yvonne, I need to tell her in my own way."

Darrell squinted and his kewpie doll cheeks became quite prominent. "I'll try - but I don't like to lie and if Carol asks me how your assignment went – well - what'll I say?"

"Tell her I don't know yet and that's no lie - OK?"

"I'll do my best - Lynn." We best eat or they're gonna run us out of here!"

The food was the best thing about this day. The night didn't get any better. I fought scores of PO's trying to get me to ship over and making all kinds of promises.   Then some big guy would reach out and hold me from rising in an escape tank, then, everyone would laugh and the nightmares would start over. I could hear laughter and voices saying, "Hey –Man! –Can't you take a joke?" It was not a good night. I woke up at 0400 and found I was out of cigarettes. I walked to the lounge and found the ash tray from the night before. I searched for a long Viceroy stub and figured it was mine, it really didn't matter. I was really down and the tobacco had a soothing effect, or so it seemed.

"Alright!" I thought.   " I'll look at what has to be and then I'll look at my options that stay within those restrictions."

I had to go home to be re-assigned. I was still fifteenth in my class, so I still had my choice of available duty. I would request New London. My assignment should come before a new class would graduate, so there should be ample vacancies on New London based boats. I speculated that the time between reporting back to my reserve unit and re-assignment should not be over two weeks at most. That's not too bad, I felt I needed to broach this plan to Yvonne before she feels the disappointment. No one needs to experience disappointment if it can be avoided, especially a sweet girl like Yvonne.

The corsages were beautiful. Darrell and I were the first to get our pick. The flat box was on the counter in the PO office with a list attached. The flowers were basically all the same, with some slight variation in ribbon work.

Darrell picked an all-white arrangement and was a little bigger than the rest. I feigned anger and threatened him with "me shillelagh."

He said he didn't know I had one. I said I didn't, but if I did, I'd whack him with it. We both laughed.

There was one corsage trimmed with red ribbon and I chose it. Darrel asked what if it didn't match what Yvonne wore. I told him red would match anything a rose would wear, and Yvonne was my rose. We checked our names and went for chow.

Darrell and I walked out to the parking lot to meet the girls. Darrell had managed to get a temporary permit and our plans were for the girls to park in the lot behind the assembly hall. It was already getting dark and the lot was beginning to fill up before we saw the girls pull into the drive. My dread began to build.

Darrell made a mad dash to get their attention; he didn't want to cause any kind of traffic jam. It all worked out as Yvonne pulled down the lane where I waited and I popped into the passenger seat beside her. The dim light didn't do much to tell me how she looked, but she sure smelled good. I leaned over to kiss her and caught a glimpse of the red bodice on the party gown she wore. The gown was white with roses on it; the flower was going to be perfect. The gown filled the entire driver's area with the puff of crinolines. I prayed the dread would pass and this would be a great night.

We pulled through the main gate, the pass was on the dash and we were admitted with no problem. Finding a spot was more difficult; it seemed everyone had the same pass we had. When we finally did park, it probably wasn't much closer than outside the gate. I really didn't care. I made up my mind to be positive and make the best of this night.

Yvonne placed the gear shift in reverse and turned off the ignition. She passed the keys to me and closed her hand over mine. Pulling me close she whispered. "Stay a minute! - Please?"

"Hey! – Miss-sipp! - See if you can get us a table! – Please! - We'll be along shortly!"

"OK! – But if you get locked up for public spooning - I ain't bailin you out!"

"Shame on you - Darrell!" Carol chided, as they dashed off holding hands.

I could hear him teasing her as he nuzzled her cheek. "What's that you're wearing - it smells wonderful - is it chitlin grease?"

"Is it what? Are you talking dirty southern talk again – Darrell - You know I asked you not to do that!" Their voices trailed off in the distance.

"Yvonne! - I need to talk with you." I knew she was aware of my assignment failure. I wasn't upset with Darrell for telling. I suppose Carol asked him and he simply couldn't get out of it.

"Honey - the Navy can't assign me because my reserve unit at home did not provide the proper paperwork for me to go on active duty."

Her eyes grew wet, she looked away from me and I could feel her fight a desire to blame me. I didn't want her to be upset.

"Yvonne! – Look! - I'll go home - get the paperwork straightened out and get assigned back to New London - you heard the Commander say I could have my choice of available duty and this is where I want to be - it shouldn't take over a couple of weeks." I paused to see if she understood any of this.

She slowly turned her face and I could see the tears running down her cheeks. My heart broke, she was crying, crying over me, she had done nothing, but be sweet, kind, considerate and loving. It was more unfair to her than to me.

"Listen! – Yvonne! - You know I love you an------!"

"What did you say?" She exclaimed.

"I said - you know I love you!" I had said it twice now and it didn't bother me, it seemed natural and I guess it was true.

She pulled a hankie from her purse and began to wipe the tears away. "Now - explain how I was supposed to know that - Sailor Boy?"

"Well - you know - we kiss and talk and all an---!"

She grabbed my face and looked me straight in the eye. "I love you - Lynn!" She continued to hold my face and I knew it was time to commit.

I still couldn't help but put a little BS in it though. "Yvonne, I've loved you since I first tied your skates!"

She looked stunned. She released my face, popped me on the chest and cried out. "Then kiss me - you wild man!" I did. She had never kissed me like that before; our relationship had definitely turned a corner.

We continued to talk and it became evident that she and her parents had been discussing our relationship. She asked when I was being released to go home. I told her I had been free since yesterday at 1600 hours. I was still here for the dance and to see her before I left. When I told her it was over a week before I had to report to my unit she beamed that smile that would melt any heart.

"Mom and Dad would like you to stay with us until you must leave. - We'll take you to the train station when you're ready. - How's that sound?" She was still beamimg.

"Sounds great - but do you have room?" I was totally surprised at this invitation. "You'll have to sleep with my younger brother! - Is that OK?"

"That's perfectly alright." I smiled and she leaned my way.

"Sounds like a traveling salesman joke - doesn't it?" She giggled.

"I didn't know you knew any jokes like that." I answered.

"I know you didn't! -- There's a lot you don't know about me-- but that'll change-- Now let's go dancing!" She turned on the interior light and began to repair her face.

"Yeh - if we stay here we're gonna get a ticket for fogging windows without a license!"

"Can't you ever get serious?" She snapped.

"I thought I was being serious!" I said, as I slid close to her.

"She slapped my hand and snapped. "After the dance - Sailor Boy!"

The dance was wonderful. I finally found something I could do better than Darrell. He could get by on the dance floor, but that floor belonged to Yvonne and me that night. We helped close it up. The corsage I gave to Yvonne was perfect; it matched her party dress to perfection. She wore a knee length satin white dress with a red bodice and from the waist down was covered in tiny red embroidered roses. She had red patent leather pumps with a matching handbag. Her dark hair and eyes accompanied by that flashing smile topped off the best looking gal in Connecticut that Friday night, June 21st, 1957.

The girls waited for Darrell and me to pack up our gear and check out at administration. Yvonne handed me the keys and I drove us to Jewett City. I drove very slowly, so we could savor every minute of that magical night. It was hard to believe how an event I had dreaded so much had turned out with such promise.

We saw nothing of Darrell or Carol during my stay at Yvonne's home. We were together every day. I helped Jimmy, Yvonne's brother, with his chores, which were mostly yard work and fix up stuff around the house. Yvonne's Dad was at work each day, but left the car a couple of times for us to ride around and see the country side. I see now why Connecticut is so popular with New Yorkers. The country is magnificent. I didn't feel a single biting bug. No chiggers, ticks, mosquitoes, horse flies or gnats. The lakes and ponds were rock lined and crystal clear.

On the first Sunday, Yvonne's Mom and Dad called a small family and friend gathering near a beautiful lake. It was a covered dish affair and the food was almost as good as our southern fare. There was a noticeable lack of fried stuff, all the meat dishes were broiled or roasted, but there were a lot of potato dishes and cheeses. I also missed the sweet tea. Beverages were sodas, water and beer. I drank a coke with my meal and answered a lot of questions about submarines.

I supposed I talked a lot like an old salt, and my short cruise on a sub gave me an insight that proved very valuable. Yvonne was at my side the whole time. I think, maybe the gathering was to expose me to their family and friends. I really didn't mind and felt flattered. Her uncle told me; Yvonne had never been serious about any guy, even in high school. He said she thought they were all too juvenile and silly. When I would look at her, she would smile shyly, and her eyes would actually glisten. I felt very warm inside and a little frightened.

As the sun reached its afternoon peak, I suggested a swim, but Yvonne declined. She was wearing a pair of red shorts and sandals. Her halter top was white with a single strap that encircled her neck and met back at the center front. There was nothing provocative about her outfit at all, but never the less, her charms were evident and I was in total approval.

She watched as I dove bravely into the crystal clear, pristine lake. I had tested the water with my foot and remarked on the brisk feel of the cold water. A foot test will not prepare the body for the total shock of frigid water.

"My - God!" My mind instantly sought divine help, the water was so cold I couldn't come out of my dive form, my mind was numb, but deep inside that male libido spoke. "Your girl's watching, Mr. Smart Ass, what'cha gonna do now, come up all blue and gasping so she can see you for the wimp you really are!"

"No way - Jose!" I somehow squeezed that thought through the ice water in my brain. I remembered my resolve in the 100' free ascent and put my frigid fear aside. My diving form had taken me down deep, so I put on my best frog man imitation and pulled myself down with what I hoped were graceful arm strokes. I relaxed completely and began to pull myself along the bottom by grasping stones. There were stones everywhere, I saw no earth and I began to inquisitively pull stones from their positions and examine the ground under them. I found some earth but mostly it was simply more rocks. I was completely relaxed and not exerting myself in the least.

From the corner of my eye I saw Yvonne rise from the rocky point where I dove and began to walk along the bank. The water was so clear I could see her place her hands to her mouth, it was clearly a gesture of concern. I didn't feel I had been in too long and felt no desire for oxygen. I rolled over on my back and pulled a mighty back stroke as I kick a scissor stroke. As I glided backwards, I gave her a come on in sign and pretended to hug and kiss her underwater.

I saw her stop, place her hands on her hips and began stomping the ground, of course, there was no way to hear her voice, but I knew she was upset. I began to feel that panic that comes with oxygen starvation so I nonchalantly started making my way up the rocky wall to where Yvonne waited. I very gently broke the surface, careful not to show any urgency to take a breath. It took immense self-control not to suck in that first breath, but somehow I managed.

She was really miffed. "You looked like the "Creature from the Black Lagoon" down there! Were you trying to scare me?"

"Yvonne you could see me moving the whole time - I was fine - just a little cold." I satisfied my oxygen urge with a deep breath of feigned exasperation.

"She squatted in front of me and placed her hands on either side of my face. She studied my face intently for a second, laughed and said. "Well Mr. Macho - I think you better get out of there before you freeze cause your lips are turning blue!"

I agreed with her, but believe this; Mr. Macho had problems getting out of that lake. The sides went straight down with no slope at all. Every time I would grab a stone to pull up, it would break free and sink to the bottom. I finally found a boulder large enough to hold my weight and managed to get out. I immediately went and changed back into uniform, but I don't think I really got warm until Yvonne and I were alone that evening.

After Ed Sullivan's show that night, Yvonne's folks retired and left us alone in a little anti-room between the living room and a hall that led to the kitchen. We reclined on a sofa and as she lay in my arms we talked of the day. I learned that the lake I swam in earlier was really an old rock quarry and had closed years before. It seems a dynamite blast had breached an underground spring and the quarry had flooded. The water was artesian which accounted for the extreme cold. Yvonne told me most of the lakes and ponds around were fed by streams and brooks and the sun would warm them up to a comfortable level, but this lake was cold year round. She also said that it never froze. I'm sure the artesian source along with the depth of the lake was the reason.

I gave Yvonne my high school ring that night, and we talked of what all we could do when I got back. Little did I know that when you are assigned a boat, even though you have a home port, you are seldom there. I suppose that's why divorces are so high for sailor's that have sea duty.

It was a wonderful week, and I really had a lot of respect for Yvonne's Mom. She was in her late thirties and still very trim. I never got used to drinking beer on a regular basis. It was a natural thing for her family. I didn't feel that it was a problem that I needed to run away from, so I never mentioned it again.

Yvonne and I never seriously discussed marriage, even though it was almost a given at this point. I really thought I was in love with her and there was no doubt about how she felt about me.

She was going to drive me to the station in New London on Saturday morning. That would put me in New York by noon and I could make arrangements at LaGuardia to fly home. Yep! That's right, the PO gave me a deal. I was going to make my third air trip. The first was a short round trip from Savannah to Atlanta and return, to attend a A.T.&T. Basic Electricity School. I was hoping I would get one of those new jet jobs.

Please understand, Yvonne was every bit a lady and with my upbringing, there were certain areas of love making that responsible young adults simply did not venture into, until, well, I'm sure if you were a young adult in the 50'S, you know what I mean.

It was late afternoon Friday and Yvonne's Mom had offered to do my laundry, for me, before I left. She was a wonderful Mom and host. Yvonne and I were on the sofa in the anti-room. Her Mom was outside hanging up my laundry. It was a sad time for us both and I took her in my arms and lay back resting my head on the armrest. She rolled next to me, placed her head on my shoulder and turned her lips to mine. The kiss was gentle but different.

I felt the heat of my body rising as we entered that world where only people in love can go. It was familiar to me; I had made the journey before, but never casually. I had no intention of taking advantage of Yvonne and I don't think she would have allowed it.

The world ceased to spin; the whole universe held its breath as two young innocent hearts became engulfed in the sweetness of love's embrace. We were oblivious of all else in the world. These words cannot express the emotions that accompany the caresses and kisses and words that come so natural when enveloped in the smoke of innocent love.

I was shocked back to reality when Yvonne uttered a gasp. I pulled my face away and looked at her. Hers eyes were shut tight and her mouth was pursed in what I took for agony.

"Yvonne! – Are you OK?" What is it?" Her head arched back, a moan passed her lips and she went into a series of short convulsions. There were gasps as if she couldn't breathe. I was in a panic.

"Yvonne! – Please! -- Talk to me! – What's wrong?" She made no response, only doubled up, as if in pain. I ran to the back door, threw it open and called to her Mom, "Somethings wrong with Yvonne! - Hurry! – Please hurry!"

Her Mom dropped everything and was in the house in a flash, I led the way and her Mom knelt over Yvonne. There were tears on her face and she buried her face in her Mom's bosom crying.

"I couldn't make it stop – I tried – buy it wouldn't stop!" She began to sob.

Her Mom motioned me to leave. I started to speak, but was cut short. "Leave us! – Lynn - Please go out!"

I went outside and picked up the laundry that her Mom had dropped. Luckily I found everything was OK. I hung everything on the line and carried the hamper back but I didn't re-enter the house. I sat on the back steps and tried to make sense of the occurrence.

Maybe Yvonne had an illness and they thought it was under control. Perhaps she forgot her medication. I made my mind up, it didn't matter, I cared for her and if she could live with it, so could I.

It was quite some time before Yvonne's Mom appeared at the door. She opened the door and as if nothing had happened she exclaimed. "How sweet! – You finished hanging the wash out! – Thank you - Lynn!" Her Mom had yet to look at me. I felt estranged.

"Mrs.-------!" I started. Her hand went up in a halt motion.

"Please - Lynn - Don't!" She was polite but curt. "Yvonne's alright now - you can go in - but please don't upset her - Please don't!"

"Yes Ma'am." I answered and pushed my luck no further. I turned and went inside, Yvonne was nowhere in sight, I found her sitting on the front steps. I sat down beside her, she turned to me and placed a kiss on my cheek and took my arm.

"Sorry if I upset you - but I think the thought of you leaving was too much for me. She whispered. "I'm just a pill - I guess."

I couldn't believe she was apologizing to me for something she obviously couldn't control. "You're sorry - Yvonne that was-----------!

"Lynn if you really love me - then please - I beg you - let's never speak of it again!" She gave me that heartwarming smile and deep down I committed myself to find out about this problem and be prepared to handle it if ever it occurred again.

We spent the rest of the evening talking and dancing close in her living room. I really did not want to leave.

Saturday morning and we had a nice breakfast and I went to my room to pack my seabag. My washing was neatly pressed and stacked on the chest at the foot of Jimmy's bed.

Jimmy said I would never get all that in that bag.

I laughed. "Watch me!" I said, as I began to turn everything inside out and rolled them up tightly. When you take your time and do it right, you can dress straight from the bag and pass inspection without a hitch. Every sailor knows how to do this and it works.

"Can a girl learn something here?" I turned and saw Yvonne at the door.

"OH! – Please let me help!" She gleefully hopped into the room.

"Sure - I'll show you how - now watch!" As we proceeded to pack , Yvonne ran across Claire's picture, I didn't try to keep it from her and really didn't expect a problem.

From the look on Yvonne's face, I knew, there was a problem.

"Is this what you're going home to?" She hissed.

Thinking quickly, I hissed back. "Tell you what, put that picture in your pocket and I'll tell you the story on the way to the station - then you may do with it as you please - OK?"

"Not OK! – I'll not give you time to make up some story - you'll tell me now!"

I guess I should have been mentally searching for a plausible reason, but honesty is the best policy, so I began to tell Yvonne of my date with Claire.

Yvonne already knew of Patty, but Claire, I had not mentioned. I saw no reason to mention the date or photograph before, it was a single date and I had never even shown the photo to anyone. It was not out of any respect for Claire or anything, the occasion just never arose. Believe me; if the occasion had ever arose I would gladly have displayed it. I could see Yvonne was clearly impressed and concerned.

I finished recalling my date and emphasized how sweet I thought the gesture was, but assured Yvonne that Claire was nothing more than a friend.

"Lynn - you've got to be the most naive boy I ever met! - I know this girl dated one of your friends and you only went out with her the one time - but you told the story and even I can tell; this girl really cared for you."

"I don't know about that – Yvonne - but I assure you - she is nothing more than a friend. - I hope----------." She cut me off.

"Is! – Is a friend! – Shouldn't that be "was! - Was a friend! -- - Lynn! - promise me you won't call her when you get home!"

Her eyes began to well with tears. My heart sank. This was something new, a girl crying over me. It's a sobering moment to realize you did something so intense that it brought tears to someone you cared for. The reality hit me; I knew nothing about women, I was, indeed, naive.

I pulled Yvonne into my arms. "I love you girl and I'll be back as soon as I can! - Now - take that picture and tear it up for all I care!" I held her close and we swayed in that natural manner of condolence.

Yvonne gently pushed me away and placed the photo neatly in my seabag. "Claire seems to be a sweet girl and I'm not going to insult her - but you better behave - do you understand me?"

"Yassum! I fully understand!" I smiled at her and gave her a peck on the cheek.

"Don't give me any of that phony -Yassum talk! - Be serious Lynn." She scolded.

"Yvonne - I am serious - every word I told you is true and I promise to be good. Don't you believe me?"

"I do believe you Lynn - I don't think any guy could dream up a story like that in such a short time - now let's go or you'll miss the morning train!" She grabbed my duffel.

I realized I had just been insulted, but what could I do, say, "Oh yeah! - I can make up a story in a short time!" I thanked Jimmy and told him what a nice bed partner he was. He threatened to kick my ass as I hoisted my gear and fled the room in mock terror.

The whole family was on the porch as I threw my gear in the back seat and turned to wave. Everyone was smiles except Yvonne's Mom. She stood silent and expressionless as Yvonne's Dad raised his beer and shouted "Want one for the road - Son?"

She placed her hand on his arm in disapproval and he lowered the beer, but kept the smile. I wondered if she resented me knowing of Yvonne's episode. I also wondered if, somehow, I was the cause.

The ride to the station was quiet. Yvonne kept her eyes on the road in an attempt not to make eye contact. I would rub her arm and she would smile. I touched her cheek and she responded by pressing her face gently against my hand. The conversation was generic. I tried not to be sentimental for fear she would cry. Crying and driving don't go well together. We arrived at the station and a train heading west was being boarded. Yvonne helped me with my gear as I raced to the ticket master. The ticket lady was very familiar with a government travel chit and in no time she handed me my ticket. She looked at me and smiled.

"Going home - sailor?" She asked as she glanced over my shoulder at Yvonne. "Oh! - Dear! She whispered, "How sad!"

I turned to look at Yvonne. The tears were pouring down her cheeks and her lower lip trembled uncontrollably. My heart went out to her. I didn't want to go, I had to go, I had to go to arrange my return and I didn't think she believed I would come back.

I took my duffle bag from her and swung my seabag to my shoulder. She clung to my arm and sobbed as I walked briskly to the train.

I didn't want to cry, "Big boys don't cry," you know.

She never said a word. I set my bags down and embraced her. She buried her face in my shoulder and sobbed. I attempted to kiss her, but she gently placed her hands on my chest and then motioned me to get on the train.

I boarded and found a seat next to a window. There were plenty of vacant seats on this early train to New York. I threw my gear down and looked out at Yvonne.

She stood, dressed in that modest sundress, her dark locks pillowed around her face, her hands clutched over her heart. The tears were still pouring. I wanted to run back and reassure her, but the train lurched forward. I blew her a kiss and she simply nodded. She was still in that pose as the train moved me away from New London, Connecticut and Yvonne. I found it difficult to see through the tears.

Little did I know, that would be the last time I ever saw or spoke to Yvonne.

Cruel as it was, "God had a plan!"

"Aha!" – New York City again. It was lunchtime as I arrived at Grand Central Station. I found an airline ticket booth and presented my travel chit. The guy that served me was dressed like a pilot, but I don't think he was. He began to look through schedules.

He looked up and said. "Sailor - there is nothing going to Savannah until tomorrow morning - actually there are no flights directly to Savannah except on Sunday morning. - I can book you with connections at multiple cities but with layovers and all - you really won't save much time and your bags may be delayed.

"Tomorrow morning? - goodness!" I exclaimed. "Are there any kind of accommodations at the airport?"

"Of course - but they are obviously very expensive - your best bet - my friend - is to stay in town at one of the cut rate hotels and catch a taxi out to LaGuardia early tomorrow. - The taxies are plentiful on Sunday morning. - Your flight is on Eastern Airlines and departs at 10AM. - How's that sound?"

"Write it up Sir! I'll do some more sightseeing! - This will be my second Saturday in New York." I sighed. At least I had succeeded in getting my ticket home.

The ticket agent burst that bubble. "This is not your ticket - you must check in at LaGuardia at least an hour before flight time and then they will assign your ticket. - Don't be late. - Military personnel traveling under orders cannot be bumped but you must have your ticket first. - This reserves your ticket but you must claim it early enough or they will assign it to a standby - if there are any."

"Is there a subway to LaGuardia?" I inquired.

He lowered his head and looked at me intently. "Take a taxi - my boy - take a Taxi!"

I didn't press the matter. I thanked the gentleman and proceeded to find my way to a locker for my gear. I needed to scout around for a place to stay, eat lunch and see some sites. If all went well, I would retrieve my gear when I got settled.

It was a warm summer day. As the saying goes there was "a passel o people" in New York City and a great portion were at Park Ave and 42nd Street this early Saturday afternoon June 29th, 1957. I felt unusually light. I guess it was being out in the big city without lugging my gear. I took a right and started walking west on East 42nd Street. There were shops and restaurants and everything was exceptionally tall. At home we had a few, ten or so floor, buildings and a couple of twenty floor hotels and office buildings downtown, but nothing like this.

"Man!" Everything was tall here; I was getting a crick in my neck just from gawking.

I crossed Fifth Ave and remembered that East 42nd Street was now West 42nd Street. I felt pretty good and flattered myself with the idea that I knew my way around New York City. I walked about a half block and a park came up on the left side of the street. There were some stone stepped entrances and low and behold right by the nearest entrance was one of those "Hot Dog Carts" that were so popular in New York. It was the genuine deal, yellow in color with a painting of a steaming hot dog on the side and a cup with little bubbles coming out the top. It sported an umbrella to shade the operator, and sure enough he wore one of those little paper soda jerk hats. I noted as I crossed the street that his business was brisk, there was really no line but he was steady swiping that mustard stick down another dog.

As I stood and waited for a break, he glanced up and I knew he saw me. I still didn't say anything and people would breeze up to him and with little to no conversation he would slap together a dog, pour a cup of soda, take the money and if there was change, he just thumbed it from a coin devise that hung at his waist.

"Hey! - Mac! He called, as he looked at me. "Youse ever had one'a dees puppies?"

"Naw Sir! – Not one of those anyway."

He drew his head back in disbelief and said, "Naw Sir! – Naw Sir!

I thought. "Uh Oh! - He's gonna make fun of my accent!"

To my surprise, he said. "Geess! – Come here Mac - Damn I ain't been called Sir in twenty years. - Tell 'ya what - I'm gonna fix youse one'a dees puppies and load it for no extra charge - how's dat - Mac?

Caught by surprise I eagerly replied, "Yassuh! That'll be just fine.

"Damn! --Two Sirs in a row. Geess! – Mac! I ain't givin youse nuttin else free - so's knock it off - Ka Peesh?"

I almost said Yassuh again and tried to change it to Yep, it ended up something like, "Yasp."

He got tickled and spattered mustard on his cart. I won't attempt to write down the torrent of cussin that followed. To my astonishment, no one seemed to notice. Back home some man would have an issue with him about the barrage, especially if children were nearby.

The outburst was over in short order and he was back to his business self again. "Youse wanna soda wit dat - Mac? I nodded. He reached in a compartment, came up with a cup of ice, poured Coke from an open bottle and handed me my order. "Dat'll be sixty cents – Mac - youse saved a nickel wit da Sirs.

"Thank you." I responded.

"Damn - der youse go again Mac! - I wished I had a daughter - I'd take youse home!" The small crowd that had gathered burst out in laughter.

"Hell - Mac if youse keep up this politeness crap - youse'll end up wit da keys to da city!" More laughter.

I gave him a dollar and with a ching-ching flick of his hand he handed me my change.

As I reached for it, he closed his hand and pulled back a little. It was a clear request for the change to be a tip. I looked at him and nodded, but he opened his hand and gave the coins to me anyway. "Forget it – Mac - wouldn't be kosher - I've had a fins wortha fun outa youse today!"

He turned back to business, directing his attention to a lady with two kids, "One loaded - two lean - dat right?" She nodded.

"Coke and two oranges - Ok?" Again she nodded.

"Buck seventy" he said.

I moved away to find a bench in the park.

The hot dog was not a disappointment; the load was mustard, ketchup and my first encounter with sour kraut. The wiener was fat and juicy, the bun was warm and soft. I had never been a fan of hotdogs before, but I knew that these juicy jewels would be enjoyed many times over in my future. I had to be very careful in eating the hot dog; I was in whites and didn't want to walk around in New York looking like last night drunk.

I sat for some time in the little park and watched the variety of people that made up New York as they paraded by. It was interesting to watch them walk. It seemed as if their mission determined their walk. Some walks were determined, some seemed aimless and others were almost like a little jog. There were short steppers, long steppers and in between steppers. I became fascinated with how a ladies skirt would sway and move in rhythm with her walk. I don't think any of them responded the same way. I thought of "The Four Lads" and their recent hit "Standing on the corner, watching all the girls go by." I'll bet Frank Loesser, the author of that song, had been right here when he got that inspiration.

I thought of Yvonne, it seemed a lot longer than five or six hours since she stood crying as the train pulled away.

A group of young teens came by, maybe ten or so, boys and girls, some were holding hands. They were chatting away and there was no doubt in my mind, they were from the south. The ya'lls, sho nuffs and gosh awfuls were obvious. One particular girl, somewhat younger than the rest was holding an object and was excited about how she knew her Granny would love it.

I heard her say, "Granny's got one of them halfmoon things hanging on the wall and it's got little shelves on it, and this will fit perfect on it!"

As she passed me, I saw she held a miniature replica of the Empire State Building.

"Son of a Gun!" – I hadn't given the first thought to the Empire State Building. "Man - who would go to New York City and not see that world famous sight?"

I immediately stood up and called to the group of teens that had passed. Their eyes grew wide as they turned. I suppose they had good reason to be wary, this definitely wasn't down south. I took notice that two of the boys instinctively moved to be between me and the group, their eyes clearly told me that they weren't bent on being heroes, but they had something inside that branded them as true gentleman.

"I'm from Georgia and heard y'all talkin - it's been a month o Sundays since I heard good English! – Where y'all from, anyhow?" I gave em a big smile.

They quickly relaxed and told me they were from Wilkesboro, North Carolina and it was a Baptist Church trip.

I mentioned the Empire State Building souvenir and asked them if the building was near. Seems they didn't know, they were on a bus and the driver just took them to a spot and told them what was there and what to see.

One of the guys in the group said, "I know it's on 34th Street!"

I remembered walking from 32nd Street on my first trip. "East or West 34th, buddy?" I asked.

He turned the corners of his mouth down, cocked his head to the side, shrugged his shoulders with palms up and said. "I don't even know which way is up in this town!"

The whole group laughed as they moved away. A couple of the girls looked back, waved coyly and mouthed a "Bye- Bye!"

I gave a casual salute and they giggled. They were way too young, but I felt flattered just the same.

The young fella had said 34th Street, that was south from here. I started walking out of the park, back to 42nd Street; I knew where I was, on that street.

"Son of a gun!" there was a big sign on the side of this bus, about some business located in "The Empire State Building." 8 West 34th Street.

My years with the telephone company had taught me how to reason addresses. The number 8 would be in the first block of when 34th Street changed from East to West, and I recalled, that was at 5th Avenue. 5th Avenue was staring me in the face. How hard could it be? I took a right on 5th Avenue and soon I began to catch glimpses of that familiar spire between buildings. It was on the right side of 5th Avenue and appeared to be the first building.

As I drew nearer, I could visualize King Kong as he flayed his arms in defiance at the buzzing bi-wing planes. He would precariously hold the spire and lash out at the planes as they sprayed him with gunfire. I wondered if there were markers to immortalize where he fell. I suddenly remembered that was Hollywood fiction and I put it out of my mind.

As the magnificent example of American engineering loomed ahead I began to realize that the only vision I had of this skyscraper was from that movie. As I drew closer, I began to feel that bitter disappointment that comes when something not being as you expected or wished for. Oh, now the building was remarkable and huge and actually the main entrance was on 5th Avenue, but I had always pictured the building as being surrounded by a vast open space and set aside like a place to be admired, you know, like on a pedestal. If you were not specifically looking for it, you could just pass it by.

The entrances on 5th Avenue and West 34th Street were ground level and not really grand. The 5th Avenue door was a little taller and had the logo engraved in stone over the door.

As I walked completely around the structure I realized it covered the entire city block and was truly magnificent. I supposed my original intent was to go up to the top and view the city, but somehow, this thought had lost its luster. I found a souvenir shop and there were numerous rows of post cards on those spinning stands. I found a card with a picture of the observation deck on the building. It featured the telescopes that were available. The card was pre-stamped. I paid for the card and asked the saleslady if she had a pencil or something I could write with.

She replied curtly, "I'm not a secretary!" She looked up at me, I think this was the first time she had really looked at me. She saw I was in uniform.

I poured it on. "Ma'am - I'm so sorry – see - I just wanted to write a note to my girl and there ain't a lotta room in these uniforms to carry stuff."

She never smiled, frowned or blinked an eye. Her left hand went out and retrieved a pen by the register; she slapped it down in front of me and said. "Stay right here with it!"

"Yassum," I replied. She rolled her eyes. I thought how miserable she must be and felt sorry for her. I penned a little stick man looking in one of the telescopes on the picture side of the card, turned it over and wrote to Yvonne.

"This is me – looking for you in Jewett City. Love, Lynn." I handed the pen back to the lady. She never looked at me, but took the pen and placed it back by the register in the same spot, I'm sure, it seldom ever left.

I found a mail box then walked around some more and decided I would find "Times Square". I located a policeman and asked directions.

"Any taxi can take you there! He continued his scanning of the moving crowd.

"Well sir! -- I'm hankering to walk - if it ain't too fer!" I knew that would get him.

He looked at me in disbelief. "Kid you gotta be from Texas!"

I laughed and said, "Naw! -- I'm just putting you on - I'm from Georgia and to be honest - I'm not loaded and I've got plenty of time."

"Sure - Mac!" He smiled and pointed with his billy stick. "Next street over is Broadway. - Take a right - that'll be north and keep walking - you can't miss it - I'd say about ten blocks or so."

"Thank you - sir – eh -- I mean Mac!"

He half smiled and said. "You're learning Mac! - Now listen! - if any one tries to start up with you - just leave em be - ya unnerstan?"

"Yessuh! - Thanks a million." He saluted with his billy and I was on my way. Broadway was much wider than most of the streets I had crossed. I don't see how there can be enough people to support all the shops and businesses that were in this city. Sure enough, at West 44th the street opened with a median in the middle.

There it was! 7th Avenue merged with Broadway at this point and the scene that lay before me was the classic portrait of "Times Square." Some distance ahead I could see the familiar triangular building that seemed to split the street and after walking a few blocks I looked back and saw the same type triangular building where Broadway and 7th Avenue merged. "Boy!" I thought. I'm really going to have to keep my head straight. At first glance the view seemed the same either way.

I passed a pizza shop. The shop was open on the front and behind the counter was this fellow twirling dough. I watched him in amazement as he mashed the ball, pumped it with his fist and began a circular motion as the dough began to form a disk. There was flour on the table in front of him and he would slap the disk down with a puff, pick it up, and toss it in the air again. The dough disk began to get larger and larger, at the same time getting thinner. He would spin the dough disk and it would run up his arm, with his free hand he would reach behind his head and catch it before it spun away.

Suddenly he shouted some Italian phrase and without looking the now perfect pie disk sailed through the air to another man down the line. This new guy caught the disk and swirled it to a pan with one hand while grasping a ladle of sauce and pouring it on the now waiting crust. This guy now shouted some more Italian stuff and another fellow, down the line, held up a waiting finger, leaned over and scanned the long glassed door of a huge oven. He shouted back yet another Italian something and the second guy began to add, I suppose the requested, ingredients to the now forming pizza. It was huge.

I was a fan of pizza, having met with my buddies many times for late night pizza at Porzio's in Savannah. My mouth began to water. In a couple of hours, this would be my dinner. I was pretty sure of that.

Just off Broadway on West 44th Street stood the Majestic Theater were "South Pacific" had made such a long run. The theater was emblazoned with signs about the Broadway hit "Good Hunting" starring Ethel Merman and Fernando Lamas. I thought about maybe seeing it, but decided not to even try.

It was getting late afternoon and I thought maybe I would visit Central park. Looking around, I soon found another police officer standing on a corner. I thought I'd try my hand at not sounding southern.

"Hey Mac!" I called. "Can ya direct me to Central Pahk?" I tried to soften the "R" in park. It didn't work.

"I'm not Mac- and it's that way!" He jerked his thumb northward. "Take a hike!" He turned back to standing on the corner.

I was on Avenue of the Americas, that's just a block east of Times Square, so I started walking north.

I probably didn't walk more than a couple of blocks when I felt a soft hand slip in mine. The softness didn't alarm me, so I didn't jerk my hand away, but I did turn to look at who offered such a gesture. There was a very slender colored guy, dressed very preppy. He smiled and gently tugged my hand in an attempt to pull me from the sidewalk into a store front. That's when I jerked my hand away.

He made a little pouty face and said, "I was only trying to be friendly - I've been watching you and you are so alone." His voice was melodious and effeminate.

I was at a complete loss as to what to do. Men, especially sailors, make big talk of how they handle situations like this. I simply wanted to get away.

My only experience had been eluding one guy in Savannah that appeared to be a Major in the Air Force and would cruise Victory Drive at night looking for guys thumbing home from work. That's the only route I could take and thumbed home almost every night while still in school. He picked me up twice when he wore civies and drove a different car each time. It was a most uncomfortable situation and I always exited at the first light. My understanding of that nature was nil, and I was not the least interested in learning anything this guy had to offer.

He took a half step my way; I raised my hand in a stop motion and looking him very straight in the eye, growled. "Don't put your hands on me again!"

I felt no threat from this guy, but this scenario was putting a shadow on my day in New York City.

He gave a sigh of exasperation and dropping his shoulders in apparent disappointment, he softly said. "I guess that means - coming to my place for a party is out of the question?"

I felt insulted, I don't know why, but I was suddenly very angry. He's a stranger and he's colored and he was making a pass at me.

I gave my best tough guy impression as I answered. "Fraid so Rastus - completely out of the question!" The racial slur shocked him, but I didn't care. He simply turned and walked away.

I watched him walk for a few seconds. Yep! No doubt about it, iIf I had seen him coming, experienced or not, I would have been prepared.

Central Park did not seem near as inviting as before, so I decided to cross back over to Broadway and find that pizza place, it was fast approaching 1700 hours and pizza cures a lot of ills, especially a bad attitude. I had no idea that this little episode was an "omen" of what the rest of my night would be.

"Whatta you wanna ona it - Sailor Boy?" The brash counter man asked.

"Ground beef – please!" He shoveled a slice from a pie in the case onto a sheet of serving paper. It was a generous slice, but I was used to eating a whole large pizza by myself, so I felt cheated.

It was expensive too. I ordered a beer.

I would have really liked a glass of milk but didn't want to appear wimpy.

The pizza slice was nothing like what I expected. It was a thick crust and soft with a huge roll of dough at the end. I was used to a thin crust and a small crisp roll at the end.

The slices at Porzio's could be picked up with one hand, held between the thumb and second finger. The pointed end of the slice never sagged or fell down. Holding the slice, you could take the index finger and with a little pressure mash down on the rolled crust and the slice would fold ever so gently in the middle providing a perfect curved delicacy that never spilled a drop of topping.

The toppings on this slice were not nearly in proportion to the amount of dough. One slice was ample.

"Dag Gummit!" Why did I get a beer? I didn't care much for beer and here I was washing down pizza with it. The pizza was a disappointment.

I suddenly realized night was coming on and I had not even thought of where to sleep. I quickly made my way out to Broadway and started walking south. As I crossed the streets I looked left and right to see if any hotel signs were visible.

"Uh! Oh! – What's this"?" Down a side street there was a theater marque and I could see "Tarzan" in big letters. I drew nearer and began to read "Continuous Tarzan Movies – All night long." Man, what kid could resist Tarzan and just think, Tarzan all night long.

My mind went to work. From this theater, it was scarcely a twenty minute walk to Grand Central Station and there were restrooms and cushioned chairs and it was only a buck for all night. Seemed like a no brainer.

My night was planned. "AHHH! New York – New York!" I checked the show times so I wouldn't come in and see only half a show. 8PM would be just fine.

I rambled around and marveled at the variety of ethnic groups that traversed along these streets. The sound of car horns are constant, you can shut your eyes and almost hear a language in the sounds they make. You can hear anger, or a polite "hurry up" chirp, or maybe a long "look out" blast. I think I even heard a "hey good looking" honk. Taxies were everywhere.

The familiar "Yellow Cab" and the black and white of the "Checker Cab" were predominant.

I was beginning to feel the all-day walk fatigue, so I made my way back to the "Tarzan" theater. There was a pretty good crowd making their way in, so I paid my buck and made my way inside. It was a nice theater and every bit as fancy as anything we had at home.

I looked around for some girls. You know how frightened girls get when lions and tigers and such start prowling. Perhaps they would need some reassurance. No luck! Most of the folks were guys; quite a few men had kids in tow. I couldn't see a Dad sitting all night with his kids in a movie though, but this is New York. "Who knows?"

I bought some popcorn and a coke. "Hold on!" I guess I need to tell you about this term, Coke. As I grew up, we kids called all sodas, Coke, I know it sounds funny but when you read me writing Coke, it sometimes simply means soda. As a kid, it was quite common to hear, "You wanna Coke?' – "Yeh!" – "What kind?" – "Oh – I don'no- gimme an orange!"

The popcorn was good and hot and the soda was indeed, some kind of cola. I settled in my favorite spot for theater viewing, right in the middle. I was blessed with good kidneys and bladder so frequent up and downs were of no concern.

As a kid, living in the country kept me from being an every Saturday movie buff, so I don't think I had seen any of the movies I saw that night. Most of them were Johnny Weissmuller. One was Buster Crabbe and another starred a fellow named Bruce Bennett. I noticed that the different movies often used the same scene, especially the wild animal shots when there was a stampede or a lion chasing an antelope. Sometimes the scene would be reversed. One movie the elephants would charge from the left of the screen and in another movie the same elephants would charge from the right of the screen. You would see a lion on the run and realize the beast was really just walking along, the camera was speeded up. It gave the animal a quick stiff legged walk. It was kinda funny.

After 10:00PM the movie crowd really thinned out. By midnight there were less than a dozen left in the theater, mostly men. That's when it started. I was engrossed with Tarzan, in South America, searching for an explorer friend that had disappeared.

I was chuckling at the scenes of hippos on the Amazon River when this guy sat down beside me, placed his hand on my leg and with a slight caress, whispered, "Lonely isn't it".

"Damn! – caught by surprise again!" This guy had no sissy sound in his voice, and as I turned to look at him, I was astonished to see he looked like a late thirty something Dad or Uncle.

I wasn't going to let this thing get the best of me, but I didn't want to cause a scene. I sure didn't want to get arrested. "Hell" he might be a damn judge. [Excuse me, I was upset].

I answered, but not in a whisper. "Lonely? – No! – Hell man! - I'm in a boat with Tarzan and a dozen natives up the Amazon River!"

I rose and moved about four rows back and sat down behind him. I don't know what he thought, as a matter of fact, I didn't care or understand why I was the object of another man's affection, they must think I'm cute or something

Luckily, after a few minutes, he left the theater, but this movie was not going to capture me. I was uneasy and kept glancing around to scout what was left. This was the first time I even thought about checking things out thoroughly.

I noticed a couple of fellows in the back were hunkering down for the night. They weren't interested in Tarzan, just a soft seat and the cool air for a nights rest.

The half dozen or so left seemed interested in Tarzan wrestling a crocodile, and Cheeta doing backflips, so I relaxed a little.

It was close to 3:00AM and Tarzan was about to dive from the Brooklyn Bridge, when this guy walked into the theater and stopped to adjust his eyes.

By this time I knew how to tell when someone entered or left. The light from the lobby would glare across the lower right of the screen as the door opened. I felt secure with the few that had been with me this long, but now here's a guy coming into a movie at 3:00AM.

I observed him as his eyes became acclimated to the darkness. He never once looked at the screen; he began to scan the seats. Perhaps he was a cop looking for John Dillinger or some other crook on the lam.

Nope, not a chance! The guy spotted me and walked down to the row behind me, proceeded in and sat a couple of seats to my right.

I could feel his eyes on me. [Excuse me, again} "Damn, is there a sign on my back that says; "Lonely or easy piece?" I planned it out, this guy deserves a fair chance, but I was nervous and determined not to be at a disadvantage.

I turned to look at him. His eyes were not on the screen, they were on me. He smiled sweetly, rose and started for the seat behind me. He sat and leaned forward to speak. He never got the chance.

I rose to my full height, turned around, looked at him and growled. "Not tonight - I have a headache - don't press your luck!"

I exited my row the opposite way, went to the rear of the theater and sat in the farthest seat in the corner. He didn't even wait a few minutes, he left immediately. I felt the partition behind me shake as the door swung shut. There seemed to be no threats left in the theater now and if someone came in I would probably feel the wall shake. I hoped this was the last of the attempted invasions of my young manhood. I cautiously slept my last two hours in New York City.

I roused up and caught a glimpse of Tarzan diving into a jungle river. The scene flashed to a hungry shark making an apparent approach when he was attacked by an octopus. The octopus and shark battled as Tarzan swam safely to the far bank. As I exited the theater I realized, I had seen that scene in numerous other Tarzan flicks. I glanced at my Ruxton and saw it was 5:05AM.

It was still dark outside, and not a soul on the street. I walked the half block to Avenue of the Americas and headed south. There was some traffic, but the scene was remarkably different than yesterday. I passed some derelicts asleep in doorways and a few folks would exit doorways, from apartments, they would all cast a quick glance at me and then scurry away to catch a bus or subway. I figured that the whooshing sound I heard escaping the huge grates in the sidewalk was air being forced out of a subway tunnel somewhere under the street as a train streaked through.

I turned left at West 43rd Street and in the distance I made out the lights that illuminated Grand Central Station. I entered the great hall from a different door than I had left and it took a few moments to get orientated. I saw the familiar stairs and moved on to my locker, retrieved my gear and went to find the restroom.

My trusty Remington easily took care of what little stubble I had. I then performed a lengthy workout with the Johnson and Johnson tooth brush. I laced it generously with some new tooth paste called "Crest with Fluoride". I pulled my jumper over my head and applied a fresh smear of Mitchum under each arm.

I unrolled a fresh section of roller towel and proceeded to wash my face and arms as best I could. I couldn't believe how dirty the towel became. I was alarmed and began to check my uniform, I had clean clothes in my bag, but to my surprise the uniform was quite presentable, I guess the grime was just body oil from a day of walking the streets of New York.

I put my jumper back on, evened up my kerchief, wiped off my shoes, splashed on some "Old Spice" and stepped back to admire an example of Americas finest. He wasn't a bad looking chap and had a nice smile that made his high cheek bones force his blue eyes into a squint. The chipped front tooth was hardly noticeable when he smiled. I was ready for my ride to LaGuardia.

There are always taxis at Grand Central Terminal so when I walked up to one and stated my request, the driver told me he couldn't take me and directed me to a different group of Taxis a short distance away. I went to the last taxi in a line of maybe four and was directed to the first in line. The driver was asleep behind his wheel.

"Do you go to LaGuardia?" I asked.

He pushed his cap up with his thumb and said. "What time's youse flight - Mac?" Everybody but cops must be named "Mac" in New York.

"It leaves at 10:00AM - but I need to be early - because you see ---------."

He cut me off with a hand wave. "Yeh – Yeh! – I know! - Dis ain't my first day- Mac. - I need'ta wait for at least one more fare.- Have a seat in the back and catch a nap.- I have youse dere in plenty o time!"

My gear went in the trunk, and I slide into the rear seat. My Dad had a 1939 Packard touring car that was quite roomy, but nothing compares to the rear seat of a genuine Checker Cab. The seat was brown leather like material and very smooth. In a few minutes I was dozing.

I woke as a man in a grey suit slide in besides me. I heard the cabbie, almost pleading. "Mr. Shaw! – Geez – Sir - I didn't know youse wuz in town. - We haven't seen or heard from youse in quite a while. - Look I'll get the sailor out and I'll just take youse - OK?"

"No way! - Driver - we'll split this one." He looked at me. "How's that sound, sailor?"

"Fine with me - Sir!" He was distinguished looking with dark, slick hair parted high on the left side. He appeared to be in his late forties or maybe fifty. I knew he was some kind of professional.

The cabbie slide behind the wheel, turned and said to the man. "How youse want it Mr. Shaw - flat rate or meter?"

Mr. Shaw answered bluntly. "Look - I haven't been gone that long and I definitely know the way - so drop the flag and the chatter and let's go!"

"Righto - Mr. Shaw!" The driver pulled away.

"We are going to LaGuardia aren't we?" I inquired. I directed the question to Mr. Shaw. Maybe he was a Mafia guy or something and I didn't want to take a ride I wouldn't return from.

"Sure sailor – say - where you from?" He half turned in his seat to address me.

"Savannah, Georgia!" I answered. I couldn't help it if a little pride showed in my voice. I really thought Savannah was a classy place now.

"Thought you were from the south - did some business down there one time - didn't work out. - Cost me a bundle too." He furrowed his brow and for a moment was lost somewhere in his past.

"Served in the Navy myself - during the big one!" Again he paused as if reflecting.

"I just finished submarine school and going home on leave 'till I get assigned to a boat." I figured that was an easy explanation, even if not entirely true. He still appeared far away. I grew quiet. I didn't want to be pushy.

"Did you go to the school in Groton?" He inquired.

"Yessuh - sure did! - That's some pretty country up there.

His voice grew wistful, "Yeh - I know – I grew up in New Haven." Again he paused. "Wasn't my kinda town though - I got outa there - soon as I could. I live in Europe now.

The cabbie spoke up. "So's dats where youse been these past few years, eh! - Mr. Shaw?" He paused, waiting for an answer. None came. "Youse got one of dem European beauties yet – Mr. Shaw?" I thought how crude this cabbie was.

Mr. Shaw laughed and answered. "No driver - I'm still free but you never know - Number eight may be on the way!" My jaw must have dropped. Mr. Shaw looked at me and winked. He placed his finger to his lips and said. "Shhhh - don't let that get around - I don't think Evelyn wants it out yet.

"Somebody I know Mr. Shaw?" Queried the cabbie.

"Hey driver - drop it and drive - got it!" He was obviously tired of the way this conversation was going. He grew silent and once again seemed to retreat into melancholy.

"What type of ship were you assigned to in the war - Sir?" I thought maybe he would talk a little about his experience.

He looked at me and answered. "No ships – Son - just islands - the only ships I was on were the ones getting me to the islands- but planes - now there were a lot of planes."

I figured he was an airdale or something. I started to ask him what he did, but decided to let it rest. There was little conversation for the rest of the ride.

Arriving at the airport was an experience in itself. Cars and taxis pulled up to the sidewalk at angles. It was helter-skelter with disembarking and new passengers vying for passage and the porters hawking for the airlines. I received no attention at all from the porters; I guess service men were not known to be big tippers so we had to tote our own. It was no problem for me. "Shoot!" I had lugged the stuff over half of New York, so a little walk through an airport would be no problem.

"Hey sailor - we're going to split this fare - right?" Mr. Shaw reminded me of the deal.

"Yessuhree!" I stated, reaching for my wallet.

"OK! The fare is the meter plus a buck for the second rider - it was my taxi - so I pay the meter and you pay the extra buck and that's a fair split - as I see it!" He looked at me with a faraway look of nostalgia, raised his hand to his brow in a casual salute, spun on his heel and followed his porter into the terminal.

"That's sure a nice fellow!" I said as I handed the cabbie three dollar bills.

"Yeah - but some people wouldn't jive wit youse on dat - Mac!" He lifted the three ones in a "thank you" gesture and turned his attention to a group of turban headed men in robes. He had set my gear on the sidewalk and was dickering with the group in an effort to clearly understand their destination. I left him to his new fares and made my way inside looking for Eastern Airlines. I never did find out if Mr. Shaw was famous or just someone the cabbie knew. I thought he was a nice guy even if some folk didn't agree, according to the cabbie.

CHAPTER IV

HOME & LOUISIANNA

Eastern Airlines took good care of me and the four engines on the DC-7 were very comforting. I sat close to the right wing and had a pretty good view of the expanse of New York as we became airborne. It was mind boggling to see the man-made buildings stretched as far as the eye can see. I had a good view of Long Island Sound. It was impressive. I was really engrossed as I drifted off to a peaceful and secure sleep, it was nice, not to worry about a hand on my leg or some dude breathing on my neck. I didn't have to be concerned about parties, cabbies, cops or pizzas. I wondered what Yvonne was doing. "Zzzzzzzzzz."

Landing at Travis Field felt strange to me. I had not contacted my folks about coming home. I'm a grown man now, but Momma would have had to know all the details on everything I did and would have pitched a fit if she knew I spent almost a week at a girl's home, so reliving that experience with my family was out of the question.

I retrieved my sea bag at the baggage station and walked out of the terminal, took a right and in about two hundred yards was on Dean Forest Road. I was fairly rested after my long sleep on the plane. I hadn't even stopped and stuck out my thumb before a National Guardsman stopped in a jeep and offered me a ride to Highway 80. He was going for gasoline in the jeep. He was fussing about spending his own money on gas, because the National Guard pump was broken.

The gas station was at the crossroads of Highway 80 and Dean Forest Road. He pulled to the pump and I gathered my bags from the rear of the jeep, shook his hand and started for the Highway. Hitching home would not be a problem, it was late Sunday afternoon, traffic was light and that was a good thing. Weekend traffic is not as mission orientated as workweek traffic. Folks generally don't have deadlines to meet and are relaxed and flexible. I was a pro at hitching. I knew all the signs that attracted drivers and knew where to stand and where not to. It's always worthwhile to stand around gas stations and roadside restaurants.

As I walked past the gas island, I heard a voice call. "Lynn - is that you?"

I turned and caught a glimpse of a tall young man pumping gas into a two tone green Chevy pickup. "Hey! - Man! – That is you! - It's me – Neal - Neal Lax!"

Neal had grown; I had dated his sister, Ann, back when I was about fifteen or sixteen. Neal was probably seventeen now, and was every bit of six feet two inches tall. "What are you doing in a sailor suit?" He called.

"I'm in the Navy now and just flew in on leave." I answered back.

"Hey! - Man! - Come on - I'll give ya a lift home -- Where you living now?" He asked.

"Off President Street in Twickingham - do you know it?" I walked back to the pickup and stopped by the passenger door.

He put the gas cap back on, stuck out his hand and as we shook, I immediately knew he was working in the construction business with his Dad.

"Throw your stuff in the back and I'll be right back." He turned to go pay for the fuel.

We talked of the good old times and he remembered the Halloween Night we stopped for cokes at his house. I told him of the rope joke we had pulled, after we left that night. He cracked up and said he never knew I'd pull such a stunt. I assured him I never did again. It was a nice ride just across town and probably only took about fifteen minutes. I offered to pay for some gas, but Neal said I was crazy and Ann would skin him if he took any money. He told me Ann was off in Nurses training and doing well. I thanked him and was home.

As Neal pulled away I looked up the stairs and there was Silly Willy at the top of the stairs, asleep as usual. We lived upstairs in a two story rental that had the inside stairs blocked off for more room downstairs. The outside stairs had been added and gave us entry to the left side of the house between the bathroom and the foyer to the kitchen. I put my bags down for fear of alarming the cat. He was so skittish that the least fright would send him sailing off the top step. The repeated impacts had taken its toll.

"Hey! -- Silly Willy! – Look! – Bubba's home!" Don't laugh, everyone who loves animals talks to them as if they are kin. The wretched creature lifted his head and moved it from side to side as if to locate the source of the voice. "Here! – Buddy! -- Down Here! - It's Bubba - come on." He focused as best he could, with his crossed eyes and flopped ear. I noticed his tongue stuck out a bit, which was something new. I suppose the damaged lip suffered was still taking its toll. Silly Willy rose and looking my way gave a raspy mew that signified recognition.

I left my bags so as not to alarm him, climbed the remaining steps and reached down and picked up my little buddy

I heard a little "gruff" from inside the door and looking through the glass I saw Rex, our huge German Shepard eagerly wagging his tail in apprehension. The grizzled old cat cuddled as I cradled him in my arms. Immediately he began to purr. It was like a Model T with no muffler and missing on one cylinder. Rex lowered his head and retreated to the kitchen with a wimper of exasperation.

I stroked Silly Willy and nuzzled his cheek, he began to slobber, I didn't care, love overcomes a lot of gross stuff.

"Bubba's home! – Bubba's home - Poco's shriek came from the living room. This was my baby brother, James. The name Poco came from the Doctor that delivered him at The Lady of the Lake Hospital in Baton Rouge, June 1th, 1949. Our family was primarily blonde with fair complexion. James was a throw back to our Indian ancestry on my Momma's side. He had a mass of black hair, dark eyes and a complexion that was definitely not fair. The Doctor said if he had been a girl we could name him Pocahontas. The name Poco stuck with him, from then on.

Silly Willy made a move to leap from my arms as the shrieks startled him. I held on long enough to set him down. He dashed down the stars tumbling over a number of times and ran head first into my seabag, recovered and disappeared under the neighbor's house. He would be back when he got hungry.

Poco flew into my arms, "Bubba! – Bubba!" He hugged my neck and flew down the stairs calling. "Gray! – Gray! – Lynn's home -- Lynn's back from the Navy!" Both my brothers swapped calling me Lynn or Bubba, I never know why.

I think Gray, seven years younger, probably started it all and James Elvis [Poco] just used it from time to time. I could hear Poco as he traveled around the house calling Gray.

Daddy roused up from the sofa and stumbled from the living room. "Son!" He spied my bags, his brows knit, as he asked, "Is everything alright, your home so soon?"

I shook his hand and as we hugged, I began to tell him my plight. He listened politely then offered his advice. "I'll go get this straightened out for you first thing in the morning, Son!"

"No Daddy - like I said - I don't think it was a deliberate thing - I think it was just a paper work mistake!" Little did I realize how God works his plan.

"Well if you need me - just let me know!" He had already relaxed to his humped over stance. I thought how old he looked. At fifty-eight he was still hard as a rock and strong as a bull, but the weakened abdominal muscles from the massive hernia had permanently deformed his physique.

"Where's Momma?" I inquired.

"She went in early - Mrs. Wise is sick so your Momma's working both shifts." He replied.

"Daddy - that's sixteen hours." I said. "Momma's no spring chicken you know!"

Daddy rose to his full height, he always did that when he wanted to be profound. "Yeh! Mr. Wise -Twenty Year Old – she's a forty-eight year old woman!" He was being sarcastic. He relaxed with a little laugh, and said. "Besides they got a coffee pot!" My whole family was addicted to caffeine and I suppose the night nurses were as well.

"Say - Lynn, you want some chicken and dumplins - we gotta pot full from dinner?" Dad made the best chicken and dumplings I've ever had.

"Man that's great Daddy - I haven't eaten anything all day!" We made for the kitchen and Daddy pulled the trusty old pressure cooker from the fridge and placed it on the stove to heat. "How bout some collards and I'll put on corn bread?"

"Don't go to a lot of trouble, Daddy!" I pleaded.

He was quick to interrupt. "Don't sweat it, Son, I gotta eat and feed these boys too - so stir this." He passed me a bowl with corn meal in it, as I took the bowl, he reached for the flour, dipped about half a cup, dumped in the bowl. I began to mix the meal and flour.

I heard Gray and Poco running up the stairs. They were struggling to try and be the first to the top. Gray was thirteen, but Poco was sneaky and would grab Gray's foot, as he tripped, Gray would seize Poco by the belt and hold him back. Those were some pretty tough stairs, because this went on all the time. Daddy added the milk and a couple of eggs, poured the mix in a pan and placed it in the oven. I could smell the chicken and dumplings as they began to simmer.

Gray walked in and just looked at me for a moment. He spoke. "When we eat - I wanna show you what I built – Bubba - you can help me hold it down - cause it keeps blowing over before my experiment is finished and -------------!"

He began to ramble about a barrel and carbide gas and stuff that I really wasn't interested in, so I didn't pay a lot of attention to him. But it was good to be home.

As the evening wore on, I called and talked to Momma. She worked the third floor nurse's station at St Joseph's Hospital. She was busy and we planned to talk when she got home the next morning.

The "Ed Sullivan Show" had just ended, when the phone rang. Daddy answered as he probably thought it was Momma calling back. I could hear him talking to Uncle Gene. Uncle Gene was Momma's baby brother and had served in the big war as a radar man. He came home and had lived with us in Baton Rouge for a while, before getting a job at the Telephone Company. He now lived with my Mamaw and Papaw on 72nd Street in Cedar Grove, Louisiana. He was their primary care giver. I could tell from Dad's voice that something bad had happened.

I went to the bedroom door and Daddy held his hand up in a "don't disturb" fashion and I didn't. He hung up the phone and hung his head in a fashion I had never seen.

"What's wrong Daddy!" He sat silent, his head hung. I didn't press him any further.

After a few moments, he said. "Papaw has taken a turn for the worse; they are putting him in a home." I didn't have a clue as to what he meant.

"Daddy, what do you mean - a turn for the worse?" I inquired.

"Oh! – That's right - you've been gone - Lynn. - Papaw had a stroke and has had it pretty rough.- Gene just said Mamaw can't handle him anymore and since he has to work - an old folk's home is the only choice." Daddy's voice cracked a little.

My heart sank, Papaw had always been a towering figure in my childhood. He was close to ninety and had married my Mamaw late in life. He was part of that 1880 and 1890 Wild West we heard so much about.

When I would make my summer visits to Cedar Grove, he would set on the front porch and sharpen saws, knives and scissors. He must have been good because he worked at it all day long.

There was a box on the corner of the porch with dividers in it. Folks would just drop their tools off in the box and Papaw would sharpen them and put them in a different section of the box. If no one was around when they came for their tools, they simply left the money in a section of the box with a lid on it. The lid had no lock and Papaw said it was only to keep the money from blowing away.

Mamaw dipped, but Papaw chewed. His brand was Brown Mule and he got a kick out of offering me a chaw and watching my face as I reacted to the awful taste.

Papaw was from Texas and his mother was a Sniktaw Indian Princess. Momma tells the story like Sniktaw was a sub Choctaw tribe in East Texas and spelled the name backwards as Watkins to gain some notoriety. I don't know how much truth was in that, but Papaw's family name was Watkins.

There were some TV series in the fifties that glorified the gunfighter and I would ask Papaw how true they were. He would kick his rocker back against the wall, take a bead and spit a dap of tobacco juice on a little bull nettle bush by the porch. These cactus type plants would grow quite large, but this single plant stayed stunted by Papaw's continuous tobacco barrage.

He would look wistful and laugh. "Can't say much fer em – Lynn! - Fust off - they wears them scabbards -- only lawman and dudes wore scabbards. They got them fancy handguns too. Sho - they wuz hand guns around but most folk's just had rifles and as fer as a man telling someone he was awaiting fer him in the street! - Well that's jest plumb foolish! - The smart thing to do was shoot him from behind a bush - tell God he just up and died then go bout yo bidness!" He'd chuckle and softly say. "Yessuh! –That's a sho nuff fact!"

Papaw told me he had been a railroad lawman at one time, and I asked him if he ever had to face an outlaw. He mused for a moment, spat a load, and commenced this tail.

"Once I had the job o policin the trestles over the Sabine River and run up on ol Alligator Louis - or maybe it was Choctaw Charlie or - Shucks! -- It's was one of them varmints anyway! - I was a waterin my hoss on the Texas side an I looked up and he was a waterin his hoss on the Louisiana side! - I tipped my hat and said HOT DAY! - He tipped his hat back and said. " SHO NUFF!" - I asked him. "COMIN TO TEXAS?" - He answered. "NOT TODAY!" I said. "SEE YA!" - We mounted up and rode our separate ways!"

Daddy mentioned he thought it best not to tell Momma about her Daddy until she came home from work, so we turned in for the night. I slept on the sofa as Gray had moved into my bed and Poco was now in Gray's bed. Gray and Poco had always slept together before I left. I saw no reason to mess stuff up again. I went to sleep with Rex's head on my feet. It was good to be home.

Momma looked frail. Her hair had always been very light blonde, but was now evenly blended with not grey, but pure white. Her blue eyes were as bright as ever. I felt like I had been gone for years instead of not quite three months. She took the news of her Daddy with her typical fashion. She seldom showed emotion, except righteous indignation and that was always under control. I always thought of her as a hard woman and unfeeling at times, but I'm sure she only appeared that way to teach us kids to be strong.

At coffee on Monday morning, Momma suggested we give some serious thought to going back to Louisiana to see Papaw before he passed. She said. "God has sent you home just for this – Lynn - you watch - it'll work out."

I hoped she was right as I dressed to go to the reserve center. I drove my trusty Ford less than a mile to the Reserve Training center and checked in. As I started complaining to Willingham, the yeoman attached to the unit, he stopped me short and assured me there was no mistake, this was standard procedure.

I would be home for only two weeks and would be assigned a boat by the Naval Base in Charleston, S.C. He also confirmed how hard it was to get an assignment for only two years on a boat. Those guys want you for as long as they can have you. I was really beginning to think I may never make it to my boat.

Willingham did some paper work and went through some schedule listings, got everything together and as he laid my papers down he said. "You will report to the Charleston Naval Base by 0800 on July 16, of this year. - Your papers are FFA [For Further Assignment] which means they will assign your boat then. Here's your travel chit - it's by bus to Charleston - from there on it's up to them. Things will get tough from now on - so don't screw up – Wardlaw!"

"Willy! - You ever been to Sub school?" I didn't see any Dolphins on his tunic.

"Do I look like an idiot? I don't like any water over knee deep!" He kidded.

"Well don't tell me about tough - them three stripes on your arm don't mean diddley if you ain't done a hunderd foot free ascent!"

I felt like a mighty man, having said that, but it was just male libido talking and Willy knew it. Willy and I liked each other. He was good at what he did and he appreciated what Renny and I had done with the drill team.

He slapped me on the back and spoke low. "As far as the center here is concerned you ain't here! - Just report to Charleston by 0800 on the 16th of July and everything will be OK!"

I thanked him and drove to the Telephone Company Office. It too, was less than a mile away. There were no co- workers around, but some managers and the storeroom people were there. I spoke to Leonard Hadden, the company mechanic, Mr. Rushing the storeroom manager and saw Mr. Chester Harn. He joked at his surprise that I wasn't in the brig by now.

I drove back home and found Momma sleeping from her sixteen hour work day. I decided to wash my Ford and call Phyllis Michelis. Phyllis was a year younger than me, but was from an old elite Savannah family. Their home was a two story stately manor just off Forsyth Park in downtown Savannah.

Her Mom answered and told me that Phyllis had a new job; she was now the account manager at Mangers, an exclusive lady's shop on Broughton Street. I thought I would drive up that way later and surprise her. She was a good friend and we always enjoyed each other's company. She was never interested in heavy petting. I always tried, but to no avail, however, she never got angry and I don't think she ever turned me down for a date. She taught me how to drink what little I did drink. She was pure class and I suppose I was dating way above my head, socially.

As I was spraying my car to prepare it for washing, I felt a wave of concussion. I really don't think I heard anything, but I certainly felt a concussion. It was familiar. I had felt it many times when I would help my Daddy set up a house trailer near Fort Stewart and you could feel the blasts from the artillery range. As I proceeded to wash the car I began to hear the voices of my two brothers from the other side of the house.

They seemed to be in a dispute over something. I could hear Gray pleading with Poco.

Poco would say. "I don wanna! -- I don wanna do it -- Gray!"

I decided to investigate and lay down the hose. As I walked around the back corner of the house, I caught sight of Poco sitting on top of a rusty old 55 gallon oil drum. The sides of the drum were bulged out as if it had been subjected to a great internal pressure. There were some wires running from under the drum. Gray was nowhere in sight.

Poco caught sight of me, jumped from the drum and took no more than two steps before a blast sent the drum straight up and way above the roof of our two- story home. The force of the blast bowled Poco over and almost knocked me off my feet. My ears were ringing.

Poco jumped up and lit out down the other side of the house, screaming. "I tol you I din wanna do it! -- Gray! -- I tol you! -- din I tell you? -- Now I'm gonna tell Momma and she'll whip you for sure now -- and I don care – cause I tol you I din wanna do it!"

Well, Poco didn't have to tell Momma, that blast woke up half the neighborhood. She was at the upstairs window beckoning for Gray and James to report immediately.

Gray had built a log barrier to get behind as he would touch two wires to a battery and provide an arc in the drum that had a bucket of water in it. Gray had dumped a cup of carbide in the bucket, to form a gas. He had been experimenting with the blast and the drum would jump up a little and fall over. That was the small concussion I had felt earlier. But this time he had really loaded the carbide and it had set a little longer as he coaxed Poco into sitting on the barrel to keep it from falling over.

Needless to say, all the innocent intentions, pleading and explanations were to no avail. Momma wore Gray out. He had the" Heebee Jeebees" for at least a half hour. I caught the devil for not checking the first blast and stopping it from happening to begin with. She was a hard woman to reason with. This episode would become, like all the rest, a tale to delight and entertain our family and friends in the future. These kinds of happenings would make a book all by themselves.

Momma was too uptight to go back to sleep, so she asked me if I would care for some good ol Jambalaya for supper. That helped Gray get over his dilemma as we set out for Mr. Bryd's "Penn's Corner Grocery".

Momma had the shrimp, onions and spices, but we needed some pork and beef sausage and some bell peppers. We had learned to like jambalaya without crawfish, and used shrimp instead. It's not the same but still very good. Mrs. Denham back in Louisiana would say that the manna, God sent from heaven, was really jambalaya; they just didn't know how to spell it.

As we feasted that night we discussed plans to go back to Cedar Grove and see Papaw before he got worse. Mom asked Daddy if he thought their Ford would make it.

"Hey! - Mom! - Take my car - it's a '54 and yours is a '51! - I know mine will make it! - Haven't you been driving it to work?"

She agreed, that would make more sense, but thought their older Ford got better gas mileage. I argued that was because their car was an old flat head and mine had that new high powered T'Bird engine in it.

Dad told me of a new Ford at J.C. Lewis that was a good deal. He was a mechanic at the Ford place now.

Dad said that the dealership had received an order of police cars and there was one that didn't match the paint scheme as requested. I asked him how conspicuous would it be. He said I needed to see it.

Momma began to fuss at Daddy, telling him we could not afford a new car.

Daddy told her to be still and hear him out. He had a plan that he felt might work. He said for me to look at the car and then if I liked it, he would tell us the deal and talk to the Old Man. That was the affectionate term that separated the father and son at J.C. Lewis. Older men tend to want to deal with older men.

I wrote a letter to Yvonne and explained that it would be only two weeks before I got my assignment and maybe another week before I would be back in Groton. I hoped my optimism was evident in the letter.

I went by Phyllis's home around seven and she had just arrived home. She greeted me with a kiss and it was as if I had not been gone. We rode around that night and made the drive-in sweep, checking out old haunts. We stopped by to see some of her friends. I told her of my brief tenure at New London and dancing and skating and swimming, but never about Yvonne. I really didn't think I was stepping out on Yvonne, because Phyllis and I were more like romantic friends than romantic lovers, but I didn't want her to know of Yvonne. I suppose that was pretty low of me and really didn't speak highly of my honor. I guess all men are really just good for nothing bums to begin with and that didn't seem to bother me either. I had a lot to learn.

Tuesday morning I drove Daddy to work. The shop was behind J.C. Lewis on Oglethorpe Avenue. Daddy checked in and got his first assignment. He proceeded with his diagnosis and soon we went to the parts counter to get what he needed for the repair. Daddy asked Oliver, the parts attendant, to get his order up and he would be back in a little bit.

We walked up front to the show room and over in the corner sat a white over black two tone Custom 300 two door sedan. It seems as the police wanted Custom models, with four doors.

The Custom 300 had a gold inlay in the rear quarter chrome strip. The interior was a plain grey design with heater and no radio. It sported a big V8 but only a 2 barrel carburetor. The transmission was a standard three speed on the column. It was fairly plain but I did like the color scheme with the gold trim. The dual headlights were neat. I liked the car, and Daddy went to talk with the old man.

I waited around and soon I saw Daddy across the sales floor motioning me to meet him back at the parts counter. As I approached he put his finger to his lips in a signal not to ask about the deal. He picked up his parts and we walked out to the shop.

"The cars yours if you want it! - Go home and clean up your ' 54 and we'll talk to Momma tonight. - We need to make the best deal we can - either trade or outright sell your '54 or Momma's 51."

Dad's car was a '41 Ford with a 46 front end. He wasn't even thinking about parting with it. Momma's '51 was an old taxi that Daddy got a deal on and painted black. It was a good car but the rear end howled like crazy. Mommy said she didn't care because she would just turn up the radio.

I came and picked Daddy up at 6PM when the shop closed. Momma was up and had supper ready when we got home. We wrapped up the rest of that jambalaya. You may not believe me, but it was much better the second day. We often would make it a day ahead for special occasions just so the flavors would have overnight to marry. "AaaEeeeeee!- Believe me! -- It's some kinda good - now! – Don't you know!"

Momma was dead set against the debt of a new car, even if it was my debt, mainly because I think she knew what was coming.

Daddy outlined his plan. I would trade my '54 in on the "58 and the payments through Ford finance would be around forty bucks a month. While I was gone, they would make the payments and Momma would use the car. I would pay the insurance because the car was in my name. Daddy secretly told me he would cover the insurance while I was gone, just don't tell Momma. Momma saw that it was going to be a done deal so she hushed.

The talk then turned to the trip back to Louisiana. I had exactly two weeks before I had to report to Charleston. Mom hastily made vacation arrangements with St Joseph's Hospital and Daddy did the same with J.C. Lewis. We planned to leave Friday evening when Daddy finished his week. Night driving would be no problem with three adult drivers to share.

I went by the telephone company and arranged for the car to be financed by Telco Credit Union and really got a great deal. This would be a surprise for Daddy. I finally made it to the Ford place about 2PM. The new Ford was cleaned up and parked at the rear of the shop. I parked the "54 next to it and went in to sign some papers and turn in the keys. I would miss that '54, someone was going to get a good car.

As I was looking from the office window I saw one of the shop mechanics looking it over. I guess he liked it, because Daddy told me he bought it the next day. I told the sales manager that the check for the new car would not be there until Friday.

He said. "No problem! - the "Old Man" had set this deal up!" The manager said everyone thought a lot of "Pop", that's what they all called my Daddy. He alerted, Mrs. Marilyn Florie, the book-keeper to watch for the check. The sales manager told me Daddy had the keys and the car was ready.

I walked out to the shop and Daddy was all smiles. He pulled himself up from his slump and tossed me a set of keys. Take her home and put some of that new green turtle stuff on her, that'll really shine her up. I did just that, except I used Simonize, it was some hard stuff to wipe off, but it was worth it.

As I cranked up and started to back out, the radio blast almost knocked me out of my seat. I looked around in confusion, remembering that the car had no radio the day before.

I could hear my Daddy's distinctive laugh; when I looked up he was at the shop door grinning so big, that his uppers suddenly dropped down. He grabbed them before they came out, but it was too late, half the shop had seen what happened and was cracking up.

The sweet Old Man had thrown in a radio and Daddy had installed it that morning, it even had a rear speaker. Wow! Was I ever in high cotton? I spent the rest of the weekdays getting the families laundry ready and packing up my gear, so when we got back, I would be ready. We were going to be pressed for time.

My nights were spent with Phyllis and Thursday night we went to the beach. A new group was playing at the Brass Rail and we had heard how great they were. The word "great" did not do justice to this group. They were sensational and the guy on the lead guitar was out of this world. They had a simulated fight routine that they had perfected. An argument would begin and suddenly the whole group would erupt in a brawl. It looked pretty realistic and was over before anyone in the audience could react. As soon as the crowd began to respond to the fray, the lead guy would get up and get everyone's attention. He would explain how fast tempers can get out of hand and how quickly things happen, so sometimes it's hard to tell what really went on. As he is expounding on the incident the group is straightening themselves up and resuming their positions.

The leader now states how nice it would be if you could review what went on in slow motion. What follows was one of the cleverest routines I ever saw. It all starts when a guy leans over to pick up his trombone cup, now all this is in exaggerated slow motion. The bent over guy is accidently goosed by a fiddle player. Not knowing who goosed him, he takes his trombone and extends the slide and bops another guy, thinking he's guilty. This guy doesn't know who bopped him so he smacks the lead guy in the groin and the entire band is now in a grotesque display of dirty fighting complete with gross facial expressions. It was all in slow motion and hilarious. Phyllis was in tears.

Finally the house quieted and the lead guy, named Duane Eddy said they would like to play something they were working on. He told us it was a little different than most instrumentals and featured the sounds of a "Twangy Guitar and Horns" in what he called, a unique blend. He told us there was no need to call our DJ's and request it, as it is not even out there yet.

From the first two notes I knew it was going to be big. Duane Eddy treated us to a preview rendition of "REBEL ROUSER!" This was truly a fine show and this handsome young fellow was going places. Phyllis said, if he made it big, she hoped that he would get his teeth fixed. I hadn't noticed.

As we drove home slowly that night, I told Phyllis I was leaving the next day for our trip back to Louisiana. She slid over close to me.

"Well another six months of not hearing from you - so what else is new?" She laughed and we continued in silence. When I walked her to her door, she turned and gave me a short sweet kiss.

"Call me sometime - Goodnight!" She whispered and was gone.

We had packed light and the luggage fit nicely in the trunk. I drove the first shift with Momma in the front seat. Daddy could sleep on a gravel road and was proving it with the boys in the rear seat. Momma was very talkative and talked to me completely across Georgia. We had just crossed the river between Columbus, Georgia and Phenix City, Alabama when Momma offered to drive. I pulled into an all-night diner. Daddy roused up and suggested coffee and pie. The boys heard pie and nothing would do, but get pie. As long as I could remember, when we took road trips we always stopped for coffee and pie. Tonight was no different.

As we prepared to leave, an Alabama State Policeman pulled into the diner. He was driving a Studebaker Hawk. The engine was extremely noisy with a whistling sound. I asked him why it was so noisy. He laughed and said that he had the fastest police car around. It was a Studebaker prototype engine with a supercharger on it. The super charger accounted for the noise.

I said. "I bet you surprise a lot of those hot rod Chevys!"

Again he laughed and said. "Not really -- every time I chase some dude - the damn thing breaks down! -- It's embarrassing as hell!"

We all laughed as we loaded up and set out. Momma took over. She said, this was like her shift at work and she was ready.

Daddy climbed in the front seat and we three boys cozied up in the back. We were in Louisiana by dawn, and stopped for breakfast. Momma and I had egg sandwiches, Daddy and the boys had pie again.

Daddy took us on in. It had been Highway 80 all the way. When we hit Bossier City, we crossed the Red River into Shreveport, picked up Texas Avenue to Southern Avenue, took a left to Cedar Grove, took another left at 72nd Street and the second house on the right was it.

To our shock we found that Uncle Gene had bought the first house on the right and they had moved to it and rented out the old home. Well it didn't matter because Mamaw was on the porch waiting for us. I hadn't seen my Mamaw in seven years. She stood on the porch in her print dress with a half apron and drying her hands. She looked the same as always, with squinty little eyes and her dark hair in a bun. I had never seen Mamaw any other way. She was just plain ol, beautiful, sweet Mamaw. I cried.

We sat around the kitchen table that night after Uncle Gene got home from work. We must have talked till midnight. Uncle Gene's girlfriend came over and we met her. She was a single Mom with a sixteen year old daughter. She and Uncle Gene had been seeing each other for a couple of years. They didn't speak of any plans about their future and I don't think Momma or Daddy ever asked.

We went to see Papaw the next day and he was out of it most of the time. Momma would sit and rub his hand and talk of old times.

Papaw would lie very peaceful and then raise his head some and say something like. "Well - how are you" or "You don't have to go now - do you?" Momma would tear up, but she never broke down.

Momma spoke to Papaw. "Daddy -- L.Z. is here with Lynn and the Boys."

Papaw attempted to sit up and with clouded eyes he said. "L. Z. and Lynn!" Recognition clearly was on his face, but quickly faded and the haze came back.

He relaxed, once again, on his pillow with that empty look on his face. I cried again.

I wish I could say that it was good to see Papaw, but there was enough little boy in me to want to remember that tall old man as a gun totin railroad lawman that could shoot the eye out of the eagle on a silver dollar. I cried a lot on that trip.

We saw a lot of our old kinfolk that weekend and spent the early part of the week swinging through North Louisiana. We visited Daddy's sister, O.C. [Oceola] and her family, the Shaws, and the Stevens Family.

We then swung over to see another sister, Annie Glen.

I can't remember all the towns, but there was Many, Red oak, Leesville, Coushatta, Bunkie and Monroe.

On the way back we stopped at Uncle Wetma's in Monroe.

We visited the site where Bonnie and Clyde Barrow were ambushed and once again heard the story of how close Momma and Daddy came to being shot shortly before the actual ambush.

Daddy's family had a very large plantation in Bienville Parrish that burned down; I think some time in the twenties, as a result of a family feud with the Creasy family.

A lot of Daddy's kin, he was one of eleven children, were still in that neck of the woods. Daddy also held a special license, issued by J. Edgar Hoover, as a federal deputy, subject to be activated in a time of national crisis. He was also a friend of Bienville Parrish's Sheriff, Henderson Jordan.

Momma and Daddy had left Shreveport early on a Wednesday morning, May 22, 1934 to take care of some property issues in Arcadia, La. Daddy had broken his collar bone and Momma was driving. She was heading down Louisiana Hghway 154 outside of Gibsville when Daddy's friend, Sheriff Jordan stepped out of the woods and flagged them down.

Daddy's version goes like this; Sheriff Jordan shouted. "L.Z. – is that you?"

"Yeh- Henderson- you broke down- where's your car?" Daddy asked.

Sheriff Jordan replied. "Don't worry about that L.Z. - you and Irene must get that car off the road! - We're looking for that Bonnie and Clyde Barrow - they stole a Ford just like this except we think it's a four door! - If I hadn't recognized that big old push bar on the front of your car we might o blown ya'll to hell and back - now please get out'a here!"

Daddy told us, they shot Bonnie and Clyde the next morning at that very spot. I guess it pays to have friends in the right places.

We came home through Baton Rouge and saw some more relatives and friends, the Lees, Kilroys, Tessiers, Toyes and the Denhams.

Mr. Denham was suffering from a mild stroke and Mrs. Essie cried at how I had grown. She told me if I wanted to come back, they would give me the store. She said their two boys, Mac and Wesley didn't need it. She said I could run it and live in the brick house and take care of them. I cried.

Daddy's old shop was still there. It was open, and Wes, Daddy's old colored helper and friend still puttered around and had a fit when he saw Daddy. Wes was a thin wiry black man with skin that was shiny black. Daddy and Wes embraced and both cried alligator tears.

When we left Baton Rouge in 1951, Daddy had talked Mr. Denham into letting Wes keep the shop open. Mr. Denham was a man of his word and Wes had apparently managed to make it work. Wes's mechanical ability was limited but he was able to change belts, hoses and make minor adjustments.

When Daddy left, he had left a stock of belts, hoses, clamps and bulbs. Wes had kept track and went inside. He was back in a moment and proceeded to pay Daddy for the stock he used. My Daddy found it hard to speak thru the compassion that was welling up in him. It only amounted to a few dollars, but Daddy knew what pride was.

He thanked Wes, took the money and turned away to supposedly wipe his nose. He missed and wiped his eyes instead.

Suddenly Daddy spoke. "Son of a gun – Wes --Remember when I left in '51?" Wes nodded. "Well Bless Pat -- Wes – It was right before Christmas and I clean forgot your Christmas bonus – That has kept me awake many a night Wes -- So here is your bonus – six years late!"

He handed Wes a twenty dollar bill. Wes looked at it in disbelief then smiled and shook Daddy's hand.

Wes looked at me. "Young Mr. Lynn -- Yo sho has growd to a fine young buck -- you looks jist like yor Momma!"

I shook Wes's hand, it was like smooth leather. "I'll tell her - you said - she done good - Wes. You remember Miss Angela don't you?"

He nodded. "Momma is visiting her today. We are on a tight schedule. I must report back to the Navy this coming Tuesday in Charleston, S.C."

Wes frowned. I suppose that for a man that had never been over fifty miles from home, Charleston sounded far away.

We made our farewells and left in a deluge of tears. This part of the country and my life here will always be with me, in my heart and mind. But that's another book.

"Lynn - here's a package for you!" Momma was going through the mail as we were unloading the car. It's funny how you can be gone just a few days and it seems like everything looks strange when you get home. The Sharps had looked after the animals, but Rex was overjoyed. Silly Willy ran like crazy, he still wasn't used to the new car.

Momma handed me a box wrapped in brown paper. It was not big and as I opened it I could see it was a costume jewelry box. I opened it and was shocked to see my High School Ring. No note, just the ring.

"Momma' is there a letter for me?" I asked. Yvonne had returned my ring. I couldn't believe she wouldn't wait a few weeks.

The answer was no.

"Momma - I gotta run a quick errand - I'll take the stuff outa the car - get Gray and Poco to finish bringing it up! - please!"

She started asking all kinda questions, but I was in no mood to explain anything. Maybe I should have told her about Yvonne, because now I had to go find a pay phone and try to call her.

I backed out of the drive and as I drove away I could see Momma at the top of the stairs with her hands on her hips, calling me to come there, right that instance. I loved her but I was no kid anymore.

I went to the soda shop and thought I could get some coins from Jeanie. Jeanie was no longer there. The word was she was engaged to be married very soon. I still got five bucks worth of quarters, nickels and dimes. I found the pay phone at the corner of Penn's Corner and hastily got long distance to place a call to Yvonne's number in Jewett City.

It was Saturday afternoon. No answer. I waited around for maybe an hour, continuously trying, still, no answer. I kept the coins; there would be numerous attempts, still no answers.

CHAPTER V

CHARLESTON & NORFOLK

Charleston is a little over a hundred miles north of Savannah. There is no express bus, so the ride from Savannah took all Monday afternoon. The bus station was in downtown Charleston and as I walked out of the building I saw a city bus and the little marque read Naval Base. I whistled for the driver's attention and made my way over to the stop.

As I was crossing a small square I noticed a sign suggesting I try an old fashioned authentic Italian Pizza at this quaint little Italian Restaurant.

Arriving at the bus I asked the driver how often the buses ran to the base.

"Bout every hour or so." The driver answered.

"Thanks - I think I'm gonna get a pizza - before I report in!"

"OK with me –Buddy - see ya in about an hour!" He released the brake and that familiar air blast could be heard as the big diesel lurched off on its run to the base.

It was close to 1800 hours and I needed a good old fashioned Pizza after my disappointment in New York City. I walked back across the square and noticed how much old Charleston and downtown Savannah were alike. There were the same squares, massive oaks, stately manors and real Italian Restaurants.

I put my gear next to the front door and was shown to my seat by a young fellow with starched white frock and bow tie. "Wow" I thought, this place was really swank, and there was Italian music with Italian singers piped in the background.

Porzios was 1st and 2nd generation owned and managed in Savannah, but there was no authentic Italian atmosphere at all, except for Mrs. Porzio's accent. I felt as if I was in for a treat. After I saw the prices, I hoped the treat would be worth it.

The prices were so high that I ordered a small instead of a large pizza and still paid more for it than the large at Porzio's. I figured this was due to being in the tourist district as opposed to Porzio's being in a somewhat residential area.

My order came and the pizza could have been a picture on a menu or in a magazine. The crust was nice and thin with a texture that resembled Porzio's The crust roll was a nice dark brown on the high spots and faded to a light brown in the valleys. The sauce still bubbled under the smooth, oily, layer of mozzarella cheese that amply decked the top of the pie. The spices were liberally applied with the oregano quite evident. The ground beef was generous and well placed.

I broke two cardinal rules for eating pizza. First, I forgot to thank the Lord. Second, I forgot to check to see how hot it was. Either rule could be responsible for the damage that was inflicted with that first bite.

The pain was intense and the bite was immediately deposited on the plate, but way too late. The bite even passing the lips was way too late. My mouth was a mess. The pain with a mouth burn will subside fairly quickly, but the resulting damage will take weeks to repair itself and needs to be treated carefully.

I could already feel the blisters forming on the roof of my mouth. I was not a stranger to this injury, as it had happened before with not just pizza, but tomato soup, ravioli and hot oatmeal.

The incident had a direct effect on my enjoying what I think was a fairly good pizza. As I paid my tab and picked up my gear, I reflected on the agony of the coming days with my damaged mouth, particularly the damage to the roof.

The driver was right on time and asked how I enjoyed my pizza. I lied and told him it was as good as any I ever had. He informed me that I was lucky to have waited a bit on the bus, because the going home from work crowd was over and the trip to the base was less crowded. He explained that sailors were expected to give up their seats to civilians if it was crowded.

"I don't have a problem with that!" I offered, thinking of old folks and ladies.

"Oh! – Really!" The driver sneered. "What if it's a snotty nose teen ager with his collar turned up and chomping gum - Eh?"

"That's different!" I retorted.

"Thought so!" He looked at me in the mirror. "That's a base order – now - not a city order - ya understand?"

I nodded and reckoned it was the Base Commander's idea to try and improve or maintain a good relationship with the people of Charleston.

I left the bus and started walking to the base gate, when it suddenly struck me. I was within days of having my own boat. The thought of being on board of one of America's finest, having a place to lay my head, guys knowing my name and depending on me was comforting. I had been disappointed so much in the last few weeks, that I was beginning to feel a little sorry for myself.

It would be good to see Yvonne again and give her that ring back.

It's not good, if someone feels sorry for themselves. It diminishes their potential to be a benefit to anyone, but themselves. I put that thought out of my mind and relished the thought of my own boat. What would it be, a Tench class, Guppy 2A, or something even more exotic, like the new Albacore.

Reality snapped back as the guard barked; "Papers sailor! – Papers - where's yor head - Boy?"

I shoulda known it was a "Gung Ho" Marine. I have all the respect in the world for Marines and was only thinking this in response to his remark about my head. I also never understood why sometimes the gates were manned by Marines and sometimes by Sailors. I never pulled shore duty so I never found out.

I was directed to administration and checked in. I was assigned to Barracks A for further assignment. This was all very familiar as I made those last few steps to Barracks A.

I thought how ironic it would be to walk in and see Chief Hardy standing there. I'm sure he'd say. "Say! – Pirate! – How's it goin for ya?"

No such luck, it was a third class Yeoman with a pencil up his "Ya – Ya" and an attitude to match. I'm still a seaman so I guess we get all the gruff. The PO checked me in, assigned me a bunk on the first deck and told me I would be mess cooking [cleaning up] at 0500.

He smirked. "We ain't got no alarm clocks so I hope you're late - that way I'll have another ass hole to clean the shit house!"

I realized the "cuts above" I knew at Sub School were not around here. I thought I might put this guy on a little. Why not, I'm only here for a day or so, then it's off to my own boat.

"Hey Pen!" I quipped. "How about this head detail – shoot - anything's better than mess cooking!" His head snapped up at the mention of "Pen".

"You been busted or something?" I shook my head. He was referring to my use of "Pen", and I'm still a seaman, only old timers or guys that had been to sea a lot used that phrase for Yeoman. It carried a degree of respect with it and this PO recognized it. He softened.

"Naw! – You don't want that." He motioned toward the heads and lowered his voice. "It's after taps and is added to your workday, so don't volunteer. I nodded with understanding.

"Look - is there any other job – man? - I'm just waiting to be assigned a submarine and I'll only be here a coupla days!" I was playing on his mercy, if he had any.

"Ahh! - A pigboat sailor - how come I don't smell you?" He was back in his attitude mode and was referring to the diesel smell that permeates a submariners clothing. It will wash out but you can just walk through a sub and come out smelling like diesel fuel. I, personally, think there should be an after shave that smells that good.

He riled me a little, but I played my cards. "Look Pen - you're running low on ink here - I don't mind working - I just had rather not mess cook! - Help me out - Man!"

He heaved a sigh, and glanced at my barracks chit. "Wardlaw - my only options are mess cooking - the shit house and "Short Stay".

"Short Stay?" I asked with enthusiasm.

"Yeh - that's an island up on Lake Moultrie! - It's a fairly new dammed lake and the Navy is making some kinda resort up there.- We send a truck load up there every day to work on it-- all they take is their bathing suit and a towel - but I hardly ever assign anyone - mostly the names are sent to me from the FFA office so I can't help you there."

He heaved a sigh as if exhausted. "Mess cookin – 0500 - I hope your late!" He leaned over and directed my attention across a concrete assembly area that is affectionately called the "Grinder" and pointed out the chow hall. "Der tis - sailor boy - 0500!"

My Ruxton watch, the gift from Daddy, had no alarm feature so I slept fitfully that night. Luckily the other guys on mess cooking and scullery duty are not politely quiet people, so I woke up in time to get dressed. I noticed that some were in undress whites and some were in dungarees. A few questions and I found out if the PO said mess cooking, it was undress whites, if he said scullery, it meant dungarees. He didn't explain that to me so I dressed in dungarees, just to be abstinent. I was determined to not mess cook. I know that was not a good attitude but I couldn't, I mean wouldn't, help it!

It didn't go well with the dungaree outfit, so I volunteered to go change, however the guy in charge said I could clean tables, keep the deck clean or anything else that did not require me to touch food before it was served. He also informed me that I would be on scullery duty from then on. I really didn't care, work is work, but I wasn't getting my whites dirty.

As I was sweeping some imaginary trash near the side door of the mess hall, I heard the scullery boss call me. "Hey sailor - roll that boat [a rack with wheels] out to the truck in the front -- It's the truck for "Short Stay".

I push the stainless steel, buggy like, carrier out the side door and looked toward the front of the chow hall and there was a navy dually, complete with canvas cover and a group of sailors loaded in the back.

A cry went up as I approached with the buggy. It seems I had their lunches. There were about a half dozen guys in dungarees and had their bathing suits rolled up in towels.

I soon found out they spent the day digging small trenches to drain pools of water off this island into the lake. They spent the day working a little, then dashing off to cool in the lake then go back and drain some little pools, relax, eat lunch. I really think this was my kind of duty. I realized now why someone else assigned this work. It was a premium job and probably highly sought after.

I worked my first day and got a compliment from the scullery boss. He told me that was the first time he ever walked through the chow hall and didn't have to call attention to trash on the floor or on the tables.

No one instructed me on how to do the job, so I simply made it a policy to stand at parade rest at the head of a table. I supposed I was perceived as an observer. Most of the sailors that came through were recruits or apprentices that were waiting to be assigned. The rated guys knew who I was and didn't pay much attention. The younger fellows simply did a good job of cleaning up after themselves and I just watched and took care of business as soon as it happened.

When a meal session was finished, it was nearly two hours before the next session. There were a goodly number of tables and it took a little time to wipe them down. A quick swab of the deck and it was done. The job was really not bad, and I liked the down time between meals.

As I was finishing up the deck after lunch the boss sailor came by and asked where the other guys were. "Been by myself all day- Boss- sorry!"

"Sorry! -- Hell - it ain't your fault if the PO screwed up - why didn't you say something about some help?" He really seemed ticked off.

"Hey Boss – It's not so bad-I don't think we had a big crowd anyway." I didn't want any problems.

"It still gets me hot when the PO won't get up early enough to check the transfer list and have me a full crew! - This crap happens a lot! - If I had known this earlier - I coulda had you some help! - You done good sailor!"

I was confused; I felt he should have known the situation without anyone telling him. He had simply told me to do the job and didn't check to see if any other sailor showed up. I wondered if this went on a lot. Perhaps the fact that this section of the base was for further assignment meant that the personnel turnover was on a daily or even an hourly bases.

I had a lot of spare time between the meal sessions. It made sense to stay out of the way. I didn't get off until close to 1900 hours. I took a nice hot shower and was lounging in the social room when one of the guys from the "Short Stay "truck came in looking for a smoke.

Sailors in a FFA barracks seldom know each other and bumming a cigarette doesn't make you popular.

The guy was catching flack. "Screw you - mooch! -- Cost ya a dime, ya bum!"

He was actually reaching in his pocket for change when I motioned him over by waving my pack of Viceroys at him.

Say Man! –Thanks!" He quipped. "We got to hossin around at the lake today and my whole pack got dumped in a puddle! -They are totally ruined - Man! – I'm having a nicotine fit here!"

He plopped down beside me and lit up. He took a deep drag and said. "There ain't much to these things - Man!"

"What the Sam Hill you smoke – boy - Home Run?" I taunted.

"Hell no - but this crap ain't nothing compared to my Camels!" He retaliated.

"Lookin the gift horse in the mouth ain'tcha?" Again I taunted him.

He let out a little yelp and slowly spoke. "I'm - outa - here - first thing - in the - morning! My transfer is in, I'm going to Mayport and the Lake Champlain! Yoweee! Can you believe it! Florida and a carrier! Man I'm one lucky sailor!"

I was happy for him, I knew how good it felt to get what you wanted. We talked a little, I gave him a couple of my mild filter tips and as he left I noticed the name on the back of his chambray shirt, Mueller, yeh!   His name was Mueller.

I was up early the next morning and dug out my swim trunks, I didn't like the Navy issue so I brought my personal Janzen, it was reversible with black on one side and mild plaid on the other. It was suitable for any occasion. I wrapped it in my towel and stashed it inside the window ledge close to where the Short Stay truck was parked.

I went in and checked my section, everything was in order, and the chow hall would open in about ten minutes. I prayed my devious little plan would work.

The boss called out to me. "Wardlaw - you got two guys - show them the ropes and two young recruits walked my way.

"Hey Boss!" I shouted to the boss. "I'm going to Short Stay today!"

He looked my way and laughed. "Good luck with that one - Sailor!" He turned and walked away.

I showed the new guys where the rags, swabs, brooms and shit cans were. Sorry, but that's what the Navy calls them. I briefly outlined their duties.

The first wave of guys in the chow hall included the crew for "Short Stay." I was counting on the system to fail and not have a replacement for Mueller when the list was checked and I was going to be the guy out there with the lunches. If all went well, I would worm my way out of the scullery and into this ace of a job at Short Stay.

I saw the dolly being loaded with water and lunch cans. I kept my eye on it, to make sure that I would be the one to take it out to the truck. Soon I saw one of the mess guys push it into its position by the side door. I told the two new guys that I had to take the cart outside and if the boss came by, just tell him, I was working at Short Stay.

I pushed the cart outside and began to place the water and lunch cans in the rear of the truck. I stretched it out until some of the crew began to show. A couple of the sailors climbed up in the rear of the truck and lit their cigarettes; this was probably the best place to smoke. If you sat around outside, near the grinder, there was always some PO with his skivvies in a wad and would hassle you about something.

I retrieved my swim trunks and towel from their hiding place on the window ledge and tossed them to one of the guys in the back of the truck. He called. "What's this for?"

"It's my gear - Mueller transferred out and I'm taking his place!" I didn't offer any other information. I didn't lie either, I was fully intending to take his place. I was hoping my plan would work. It all hinged on the fact that transfer replacements were almost always delayed.

The crew began to show. I had counted the lunch cans, there were eight. I remembered that yesterday there were six sailors in the rear of the dually and two up front. I counted as they showed. The count was up to five in the rear and one guy in the passenger seat up front. There were two left.

I was beginning to get uneasy. If my idea didn't work then all I had to do was retrieve my suit and towel, push the buggy back inside and go back to work. The thought struck me that my name had to get on that list for Short Stay or I would be in trouble.

My anxiety rose as I saw two guys walking our way, one was the driver from yesterday and the other had a clip board in his hand. "Bummer!" These two made eight.

"Poop", my cleverly devised scheme was going to fail. I backed away so as to not be conspicuous.

The two stopped at the rear of the truck. The guy with the clip board called out. "All aboard!"

A couple of the sailors shouted. "Hold on! – We're one shy!"

One of the early arrivals spoke up. "That'll be Mueller, he transferred out -- That guy over there is taking his place - his gear in already on board - over there!"

He gestured toward my rolled up towel. I nonchalantly turned and started to push the cart toward the side chow hall door.

The clip board sailor called out. "Hey you - with the cart!" I turned and gave him the "Who me" thumb to the chest move. "Yeh you! – Come here!"

I held up the familiar "Hold on a second" finger and pushed the cart in the side chow hall door and then briskly walked back to him at the rear of the truck.

"Who assigned you to this detail?" he demanded.

I looked at him and played dumb. I shrugged my shoulders. "Hey! -- I don't know the guy's name – I'm just passing through – Maybe it was Admiral Halsey!"

He rolled his eye in complete exasperation, raised the clip board and proceeded to scratch through Mueller's name. He poised his pen to write. "What's your name, Sailor?"

The ride to Short Stay was close to an hour, but that was OK. The scenery was wonderful and it turned out that Short Stay was not an island but a little peninsular that jutted out into a new freshwater lake.

Lake Moultrie was one of two lakes that resulted when a new dam was constructed. The Santee and the Cooper rivers formed a complex that was very large and was being developed as a fishing and resort facility.

The day was just as described. A lot of hard work, a lot of dashes into the beautiful, clear sandy bottomed lake, a nice lunch, a short nap in the sun, more hard work and a leisurely ride back to the base. It was indeed a good day. I didn't even feel guilty about the underhanded method I used to get there. I couldn't wait for tomorrow. I was gonna work on a tan.

As I was preparing to go to chow, the barracks PO sought me out. "Hey! – Wardlaw! Man! – We thought you went AWOL. We liked to never found where you were yesterday. If your boss hadn't remembered you told him you were going to Short Stay and then found your name on the list – Hell - we woulda had a warrant out on you!"

My heart sank, I figured I had really screwed up this time. I played innocent. "Golly Gee - Man! - Am I in some kinda trouble?" I blinked my eyes in mock innocent shock.

"Naw – Man! - This kinda work assignment crap happens all the time - don't sweat it. - Look! – You've gott'a have your physical and dental stuff done so they can process you - report to the medical building at 0800 tomorrow and they'll get you started. - As soon as all that's done -- Man! – Your outt'a here!"

I could taste my boat. New London, here I come.

My one day at Short Stay was nice, but the pleasure was short lived. Friday at 0800 I began the medical stuff. I had no problems, I coughed, bent over and generally pleasured the doctors until one of the doctors said open and say "Ahhh"!

"Good God! - Boy! – What the hell have you got?" He gasped.

"What? – What? – What's wrong Doc?" I asked with alarm.

"You mouth – Sailor - surely you must know the shape your mouth is in?"

I had forgotten the pizza burn, there wasn't much pain, just aggravating shards of flesh dangling down and sensitive to heat. I explained, about the hot pizza, but he wasn't satisfied. He insisted I see the dentist right away. He arranged for me to go ahead of everyone else.

I expected the dentist to simply confirm that it was blisters and they would heal soon enough.

I thought the doctor was upset, man, you should have heard the dentist. Apparently he had never heard of a pizza burn, much less seen one. The "rigger marrow" that followed was one for the books. There was actually a suggestion made to bring charges against me for self-abuse.

I argued, it was simply an accident. I acknowledged it was careless, but purely accidental. I suggested they check my work record. I gathered my wits.

"You'll find I haven't missed a minute's work since I've been here and I don't care to remain here any longer than necessary - so gentlemen - please let me get outta here!" I spoke as calm but firm as I dared with two commissioned medical officers gazing doubtfully at me.

"The dentist checked my mouth again. "Umm! – Yeh! – They do look like the results of burns!"

"What did you do when it happened, boy?" Tthe Doctor questioned.

"I took a swallow of milk then finished my pizza - Doc! -- Ehh! -- After it cooled a little!" I added.

"Hell! - I would hope so!" Mused the dentist. He turned to the doctor. "I think he'll be alright. - Maybe we'll make a note on his MR about him being an idiot and let someone else worry about him!" They both laughed.

It was close to noon and I went to chow. I was very aware of my mouth condition now, funny how I had all but forgotten it till now.

When I went back to the barracks, the PO caught me and asked why I wasn't at work in the scullery. I played dumb and told him I thought I was finished with my jobs till I was transferred.

"No way – Jose!" Tell ya what - take off the rest of today - but 0500 tomorrow, it's the scullery and the scullery this entire weekend – now - shake your head and say, Si Senor!" He motioned for me to nod in the affirmative.

I really liked this PO, he was fair and really didn't BS much.

I feigned meekness and used my Spanish accent when I said "Si Senor e lo siento, jefe. I hoped I said. "Yes Sir and I'm sorry boss!"

It was Tuesday morning and I was trying to keep my cool. It is not a good thing to get in trouble with the U.S. Navy. The guys at Tripoli had tried it, the folks at Montezuma had tried it and the Navy had sent their little brothers to handle them. If I could get my hands on the SOB that cut these orders, he was gonna need some of those little brothers. I had my transfer; I was assigned to the USS Torsk, operating out of Norfolk Virginia. "What happened to my choice of duty?"

"How do I find the guy that cut this transfer?" I directed my question to the little wave at the counter that had Transfer Assignments wrote on it. I tried to look dignified. I had dressed in dungarees, contemplating an easy morning before I checked out.

The little wave looked flabbergasted. "Wha – What did you ask?"

"I - need - to - speak - to – whoever – cut – this – transfer!" I growled. She was completely at a loss. She was a third class yeoman, but clearly had never had any one give her any gruff.

I instantly felt sorry for her. "Yeh - I know and I'm the damn bully!" I thought.

She called a name and a first class stuck his head out of an office. "What's up sweety?" He almost hummed the words.

"This sailor's got a problem with his transfer - can you help him?" she hummed back.

"Poop - I'm done for!" I thought. This guy doesn't give a happy about anything but humming with this little wave.

I was cooling down rapidly. I was already resigning myself to whatever destiny, fate was dealing.

"Ma'am! - I'm sorry I lost my cool but my request was for New London Sub Base," I said in a somber tone.

The first class answered. "Sailor - you know you don't always get your first choice.

"Sure I know that - but I didn't choose Norfolk at all. I was promised my choice by the Commander of the Submarine Base at New London - in front of hundreds of witnesses!"

"Well now – That's different! - You must be one important --------- !" He glanced at my blank chambray sleeve as he opened my travel envelope and looked at my papers. He smiled and continued. "Oh! – He's a seaman!"

There was a mocking tone in his voice. I don't think the little wave cared for his demeaning approach to my problem.

He thumbed through more papers and made a mocking gasp. "My! – My! - He graduated Sub School with a 91 percent! - Yes! – Yes! - He's a smart seaman at that, but there is one little problem - smart seaman!" He paused to see what effect he was having on me. I tried not to give any indication that I was wavering, but I knew I was done.

He continued, " You see - you're a f--king reserve and f—king reserves don't get shit in the regular Navy – besides - no one here cut this transfer! - It came straight from Sublant Six - right out of Norfolk! - So if you want to talk to the SOB that cut your transfer - then go see him as soon as you get there!" He reassembled my package and slid them to me on the counter.

"Now I can offer you a transfer - one that I can assign! -- How about a transfer to the USS Brig - it's right here in Charleston?" There was a rush of cautious laughter.

How could I save face. I picked up my package and turned to leave. "I think they have a ship like that in Norfolk - I might take them up on it there!" There was another cautious round of laughter.

I thought of Yvonne, did she know something I didn't know?

As I walked back to the barracks, it struck me! I had my boat, the USS Torsk. Wow! What a name, Torsk, sounds vicious and intimidating. I didn't know it was Norwegian for Codfish. Torsk was a perfect name. It was Tuesday afternoon, July 22, 1957. I was going by train the next day to my boat. Things weren't so bad after all.

The guard at the gate of Norfolk Naval Base, looked at a clip board hanging on the wall.

"Sorry - sailor - The Torsk is at sea - she's due in Friday - You gonna hafta check in overnight -- Sit a spell -- We'll have a driver take ya over to the admin building shortly."

I sat on a long bench just inside the gate, but under an overhang. The light rain that was falling was a welcome respite from the grueling hot day. It was at least ten degrees hotter in Norfolk than in Charleston. Presently a jeep pulled up and the driver jumped out and made a dash for the guard post. The jeep had the canvas snap on sides that really didn't do a great job of keeping you dry if the rain got too heavy. The guard must have told the driver I was waiting. He came out of the post house and plopped down beside me.

"You in a hurry fella? - I'm bushed!" He feigned a pant and waved his hand in front of his face as if that would cool him off.

"Nah! – What's the diff?" I uttered. "I've waited three months for my boat - I get here and she's at sea - she won't be in till day after tomorrow.

"Which one you got - Man?" He asked.

"Torsk SS 423!" I replied.

"Well - you got a go getter - my boy - that's one diving bitch - that Torsk! - She's got the most dives of any sub in the world and her skipper ain't gonna lose that record! - He even takes her out when they are on 'non ops' and just "porpoises" up and down off of Virginia Beach.

The driver said he would like to let the rain play out a little before we left. The jeep didn't do a very good job of keeping us dry and the water splashed up on our whites when we dashed through it. The bottom of our trouser legs were already stained with dirty water. We sat and smoked. He enlightened me on the charms of Norfolk, Virginia.

"Shit City – that's what we call it. - Yep! - They really love us here! - Hell - they got signs that say -- KEEP OFF THE GRASS - THAT MEANS DOGS AND SAILORS! - The beer is even that 3.2 crap! - You gotta drink a case to get a buzz and it don't even make you fart! - If it wasn't for Ocean View and Virginia Beach - this town wouldn't have diddly!"

The rain slacked up presently and the driver dropped me off at the admin office.

The PO that checked me in seemed to be preoccupied with something. He mumbled at my questions and cut me short a few times. I can vividly remember this particular check in. Why I never said anything is beyond me, because this big "rigger marrow" is developing right in front of me. I saw it and never said a word. I suppose the last few weeks of disappointments and the fits of anger I had, were just wearing me out.

The check- in process was brief. The PO nonchalantly tells me I'm checking in on an overnight status and signs me into a log that plainly says, OVERNIGHT BARRACKS "A". I saw this typed on the top of the log page, I was the third name on the list. He then hands me my Barracks chit and I see in bold print, FFA BARRACKS "B", on the top of the chit. I saw it. It never registered that one of the biggest fiascos of my young life was about to begin. Stay with me, my friends and readers; because as true as every word of this story is, you ain't gonna believe it.

Another driver dropped me off at FFA [for further assignment] Barracks B. The PO checked me in. "Everyone up at 0500 - you're mess cooking!" He looked at the log. "Wardlaw!" He said, after noting my name.

This mess cooking was getting to be a pain. "Well - it's only one day – buddy - my boat gets in Friday!" I half laughed.

"Yeh! – Right! Everybody's ship comes in when they're here!" He laughed. "Pick a bunk-- 1st deck -- we'll get'cha up! -- Nighty – Night!" He laughed again.

I remembered that dungarees in the chow hall did scullery. I had rather work scullery than mess cooking and wearing whites. So I put on dungarees and followed the crowd. We went two buildings over to the chow hall.

I was the only sailor in dungarees. I screwed up again. My boss was a tall colored fellow, every one called him "Smoke". He didn't put up a fuss about the dungarees, but said tomorrow it would be whites with T shirt. No exceptions.

"Boss - there ain't but one tomorrow for me - my boat"s in tomorrow and I'm outa here!" It sounded good to say, my boat. I should have kept my mouth shut.

He put on the biggest grin I had ever seen and spoke with a pure ethnic accent. "Well! – I swan! – Boy -- If'n yo ain't here in de morning -- yo best be on dat boat -- cause if'n yo ain't -- I's gonna drag yo over here and stuff yo skinny white ass in dat dishwasher!" The crew that surrounded us roared with laughter.

I did work in scullery that day and Smoke did put me to work at the tray washer and the deep sink for cleaning the big cook pots. It was backbreaking work and constant all day. After the lunch meal was over, I let some sudsy water get away from me and wet part of the floor as it made its way to the floor drain.

Smoke came walking by and slipped in the suds, my heart stopped as he began a long legged flurry of slips and slides, with arms swinging wildly, it was a perfect comedy routine straight from Abbot and Costello when Lou Costello lost control on ice skates.

The kitchen crowd began to laugh and cheer, while Smoke held me in total terror. He would do leg splits, then leg crosses, then almost over backwards, all the while swinging his arms, and screaming. "Ohh! – Ahhh! – Ehhh! -- Owww! – Wooo!   Suddenly he stopped with legs wide apart and arms straight out, with no other movement except pure muscle strength, he pulled his legs together and lowered his arms to his side, tipped his hat and with a little bow, continued on his way.

The workers cheered and clapped. It was a magnificent performance. I grabbed a swab and went to work drying the deck, my heart pounding in my chest.

The day was finally over, it was close to 1900 hours. I was bushed and in need of a shower. I had thrown my gear in a locker near the bunk I had chosen. I opened my locker and immediately noticed my duffel bag was not as I left it. I had placed it on the top shelf with the zipper facing out. The bag was still there but the zipper was facing in. I knew something was not right before I ever touched the bag.

 I removed my duffel and saw it was unzipped about six inches. I had shaved that morning and simply stuck my new Remington down in the corner of my duffel and zipped it up. The razor was gone. My heart sank, that razor was a prized possession and I immediately felt the loss and a terrible feeling of helplessness.

I had been violated. I was among sailors, my friends, birds of a feather, fellow men at arms, bosom buddies. This had to be a thief that sneaked in from off base. It was a Communist plot. I felt almost sick.

I went to the PO Office to report the theft. The PO was sympathetic and told me I bore some blame for not having a lock on my bag. I was becoming angry and with a conviction of integrity I said. "A sailor in the US Navy should never have to lock anything up!"

He stopped writing, and looked up at me. "Sailor - you are absolutely right - but sadly that's not the case and you have just learned a valuable lesson - now give me a description of your razor."

Being the naive soul I was, it never occurred to me to write down the serial number of my razor, but I did give a thorough description, including a small crack in the case from when I first dropped it at Sub School.

My shower was not enjoyable. I even thought I would check the other heads and possibly find the thief using my razor. I figured a thief would not be that stupid. As I was drying off I saw this guy shaving with a safety razor.

"Hey Buddy -- Uh! – I know this is asking a lot -- but somebody stole my electric razor today and I was wondering if I might use your safety razor -- you know -- just to get by for tomorrow?"

He looked at me, as if he couldn't believe his ears, he just stood there with lather on his face, a clean swipe on his cheek and the razor poised in his hand.

"Look! – I know it's a personal thing an---------!" He broke in.

"No – Man! - It's not that! -- You see -- I can't believe this -- Some guy up on the second deck tried to sell me an electric razor a couple of hours ago! -- He said it was a gift and he needed some money -- He only wanted ten bucks for it -- What kinda razor was yours?"

"It was a Remington Rolectric –It has two curved steel heads on it and it's grey --I answered.

"Man! – That's what I saw -- He's probably sold it by now -- Lemme get dressed and I'll go show you the guy!"

I really thought we would have no success. I described the razor to my new friend, even the crack. My new friend was going to introduce me as a potential buyer.

As we reached the second floor, my friend led the way. He pointed to a tall kid with a pocked marked face sitting on a lower bunk. He was talking to a couple of fellows standing nearby.

My friend approached and ever so casually told the kid he found a guy who needed a razor and this sounded like a good deal. He pointed to me, I smiled.

"I hear you got an electric razor to sell!" I said cheerfully.

"Shit! - I reckon!" He responded with no hesitation. "Got it as a gift but it hurts my face - Hell! – I'll take ten bucks for it! – It probably cost forty brand new!"

I could tell from this guy's language he was nothing but scuzz. He reached in to his locker and pulled out the grey case that was so familiar. He pulled the top off the case and there sat my razor with the cord neatly folded beside it.

I took the case from him and held it up for admiration. My friend and the other two guys stepped closer to have a look. "May I take it out and check it?" I asked.

"F--king A! -- My man! – Shit! -- Plug er in over there and try er out!" He was eager to make the sale.

I removed the razor and opened the shaving head and there was the identifying crack. I turned the razor head to my friend and casually pointed to the crack.

"Damn - it's your razor!" He muttered. "Son of a bitch – Son of a bitch!" He turned to the pocked faced sailor. "You're a thief! -- You're a G-d damn thief!"

The observers stepped back and their body English immediately said. "We don't know this guy!"

The accused began to stammer. "Uh! – I uh! --- It really wasn't a gift -- Uh! -- You see. Uh -- I found it in the head this morning and figured the guy that left it was transferred. Uh! – I was gonna pick up a few bucks! - Uh! -- I didn't know it was yours!" He directed his lies at my friend.

I was still holding the razor as I spoke. " Well - You see Mr. Thief -- It ain't his razor -- It's mine and I just showed him the mark that proves it's mine and you lied about the head -- Cause I didn't even take it to the head this morning -- I plugged it in and shaved right in front of my locker! - You-- Mr. Thief -- opened my locker -- stole my razor -- this very razor – right out of my bag this morning!"

The thief eyes grew wide and I could tell he was thinking of his next move. I guess he realized if he gave in now it would be an admission of guilt. He set his course.

"Gimme my damn razor!"   His hand darted out to grasp the razor, I attempted to jerk it away, it hit the floor, the top spun off and another piece of plastic broke. The fury began to whelm within me. I could feel my ears getting warm. My body was instinctively getting tense, my muscles were becoming taut.

I kept my cool and bent over to pick up my poor wretched razor and the pieces.

The thief shouted. "You son-of-a-bitch! -- You broke it!" He grabbed my head with both hands and gave me a violent push backwards. "I'm gonna whup yo G—d damn ass now!"

I don't remember the guy even making a fist or raising his hand. I don't know if he was bluffing or if he didn't have the time, because I never attempted to use my left jab.

My tense body had kept his push from moving me back very much and as I rose it was just natural for my right cross to lead the barrage that I unleashed on this poor, wretched, pock marked , low down, sneaky, snake in the grass, thief!

The frustration of the last few months, the suffering I had felt was unjust, the disappointment at my present assignment and situation, all came to focus on this low life as my right cross caught him squarely on the side of his head. I don't remember how many blows I landed on him before my friend and some more guys nearby, grabbed me and kept me from punishing him more.

He lay back on his overturned bunk and began to moan. He was still doing a slow squirm, mixed with garbled mumbles when the PO arrived. He was in no condition to run away or offer any kind of resistance. I felt a tremendous sense of relief. I looked around the room and saw the faces of the men that were watching. I saw justification in their faces.

I attempted to explain, but the PO cut me off. "Save it for the SPs and Duty Officer!" He said. "Let's go to the office - you'll wait there!".

He turned to the observers. "You guys don't go anywhere -- the SP's are gonna talk to all of you! -- Now listen! -- They'll talk to you guys individually! -- So get you story straight before they get here! -- I've been through this before -- There are two people involved here -- Your account as to what happened here will decide what happens to each one of them -- So get it straight and all tell the same story! -- GOT IT!" He left, escorting the two of us to the PO office.

The wait seemed forever and the thief, once he regained his senses, began to try and worm his way out and began to accuse me of assault. The PO cut him off and finally told him simply to shut up.

The SPs finally arrived. I immediately knew they were full time Provost Marshall Staff. They were professionals all the way. It took the better part of an hour for them to do the preliminaries.

When they left, the thief was taken away in handcuffs and I was placed under the watchful eye of the PO. That wasn't bad. I was supposed to go to my boat tomorrow afternoon. I had no idea how late I would be.

I was loading the tray washer the next morning when the runner [PO's messenger] came to the scullery and said to hurry.

Hurray! My boat was in. "Not!" I was being summoned for Captain's Mast at 1000 hours. My heart stopped, next to court martial, Captain's Mast was a serious thing. I guess it was for fighting in the barracks.

Luckily, my white trousers were not too dirty, so I pulled on my white jumper, slipped on my tie, I needed a shave, but there was no way. My razor was taken as evidence against the thief. I had no idea when, if ever, I'd get it back.

I was escorted by a SP from the PO office to the Admin building, second deck to the Conference room of the Base Commander. Yep! The carpet was green.

A PO came into the room. "All rise!" He gave the Commanders name, rank and position, then stated the charges against me. I was correct. The charges were sorta fancy, instead of reading I was charged with fighting, it read, I was charged with assault on a fellow serviceman within the confines of a Navy sanctuary and etc. I knew I was a done duck.

This was Thursday, July 25, 1957 and my boat was due in that afternoon. I was sure I wasn't going to meet her. My heart was breaking. Now I'm twenty years old. At age twelve I was shot by a moonshiner, I didn't cry. At age thirteen, I fell on my hunting knife, I didn't cry. I had been whipped by my Momma a hundred times or more, I didn't cry. I could feel the tears welling in my eyes. I prayed and set my jaw in a supreme effort to keep them back.

"What is your plea, sailor? - pay attention!" The sharp tone of the Commanders voice jolted me back to reality. He repeated. "I said -- You've heard the charges against you - what is your plea?"

"Yes sir! - I did it! - I hit him!" I stated, in a matter of fact manner.

"Look Son - I know you hit him - but why did you hit him?" The Commander looked at me with raised eyebrow. I guess I am dense. I always thought I knew the score, but I didn't know what he wanted me to say. I knew, he knew the whole story and I wasn't going to lie.

"Sir - he stole my razor an--------- !"

The Commander raised his hand. "Hold on - sailor! - I know the whole story - but there is something I need to hear from you! – Now - tell me - why did you beat the crap out of that boy?"

"Well Sir - I was angry an---------!"

The Commanders hand went up again. "Son - I've got five depositions here from eye witnesses that said this little prick hit you first! - What say you to that?"

"No Sir - he never got the chance - you see I ----------!"

Again, the Commander's hand cut me off. "Sheesh! – Boy! - Will you ever get it right?" He shook his head in exasperation. "Listen to me! - Did this thief put his hands on you?"

I thought for a second, suddenly I knew what he wanted, I still didn't want to lie to him, but how could I dispute five eye witnesses.

Yes Sir! - He grabbed my head and pushed-----------!

"CLOSE ENOUGH!" Cried the Commander. This Mast dismisses the assault charges against the accused on the grounds he acted in self-defense! - He is hereby remanded to the custody of the Provost Marshall! - All leave - transfers or re-assignments are here-by put on hold - pending the court martial of P.D. Delcort - for which L.Z. Wardlaw is the prosecuting witness!"

It is possible to be relieved and disappointed at the same time. I was no longer in trouble, but would I ever get to my Torsk?

I was getting used to the scullery. The scullery was the name given to the cleanup area of the galley. The galley is where the food is prepared. The chow hall is where they eat it. The duties of keeping tables clean fall under the scullery gang.

A few days later I was cleaning tables, it was really the best duty in the whole deal. I talked Smoke into giving me the job in case I got called away.

As I looked up, I caught sight of a line of prisoners coming in for lunch. They had on dungarees with "stockade" written across the front and back. Third in line was Delcort. He caught sight of me. His reaction was dumbfounding. He began to wave and called my name as if we were old, long, lost friends. I couldn't believe the way he carried on. I tried to ignore him.

There were about ten prisoners, connected together by a line attached to a webbed belt that each wore. I saw Delcort talking to one of the guards.

The prisoners made their way through the chow line and sat in a special, cordoned off section of the chow hall. Presently the guard called me over and told me that Delcort really needed to talk to me.

"You don't hafta talk to the dick head unless you want too and I hafta be present! - You hafta remain across the table from him and keep your hands at your sides at all times!"

I was curious as to what the little ass hole could possibly want to talk about. I walked to the table closely escorted by the guard. I stopped across from Delcort.

"Hey! – Man! – Look at these!" He pulled the sleeves up on his chambray shirt to expose a mass of vulgarity in brown tattoos. I was shocked at the array of crudely drawn naked women and filthy words that literally covered his arms.

I turned to the guard with a questioning look. "Don't look at me - Man!" He pleaded. "The little bastard's crazy - he stole some laundry ink and with a straight pen did that to himself in only two nights!"

Delcort blurted out. "Man -- You gotta help me! – Man! – I'm broke –Man! - I need some money! -- Please! -- Help me out!"

I turned to the guard. "Can you believe this? - I'm the guy he stole from and he wants money from me!"

Delcort blurted out! "Yeh! – You're right -- It's your fault I'm in here! -- Man! -- You owe me!" I looked at the guard in disbelief.

The guard said. "Alright - That's enough - Talk times over!" He turned to me. "You gonna give him some money or what?"

I couldn't believe my ears. A quick glance told me that all within ear shot was waiting for my answer. I reached into my pocket and pulled out the contents, my Ronson lighter my lock key and seventy-two cents.

I handed the change to the guard and growled. "When ya'll get back to the brig - help him stick this up his ass and you'll both have a good time!" I walked away. I didn't hear any laughter.

I was relaxing in the lounge after my shower. I had salvaged a broken injector razor from the trash and managed to shave with it. The handle was broken in half but the blade still had a good edge on it. I was getting low on money. Payday was in two days. I could make it. I had a half pack of Viceroys left. I felt sure I could make it till payday.

The PO runner came in and began to tell folks goodbye. It seems his request for sea duty had come through. He was on the way to the West Coast. He had his car and was given five days travel time. He was pulling out that night. Driving from Norfolk to San Diego in five days was not impossible but, he would be exhausted when he got there.

As I sat there I began to think of his job as runner. It was a pie job. You never got dirty, did a little work, like straighten the desk, keep pencils sharp, run messages and errands and get the mail. I rose from my lounge and made my way to the PO's office. He was nowhere around. I surveyed the office closely. I had been in it many times but never checked it out as a possible work place.

I made my mind up to try the "worm game" one more time. I went to bed and set my head clock for very early.

I didn't sleep soundly and was up at 0415 hours. I dressed in clean white trousers, my new Stedman tee shirt; I liked the tight fit around my neck. I gave my shoes a quick shine and pulled a clean jumper over my head. I shaved and dashed on the old spice. I was getting low but still had a full bottle of Aqua Velva. I made it to the office at 0440 hours. The floor watch was asleep on the bench by the door. I scared the poop out of him. He would have been in big trouble if the PO had caught him. I pull the coffee pot out and handed it to the watch.

"Fill her up - I'll cover for you!" I said. He looked at a loss for words.

"I can't leave my post!" He retorted somewhat sheepishly.

"Don't you do a walk through when you get everyone up?"   He nodded. "Same difference and I'll give you a cup - when it's ready." I announced.

I noticed he was a seaman apprentice and probably not as gullible as a recruit would be, but he headed for the head just the same. He was not gone long; I suppose he didn't want to be gone when the PO arrived.

"Who are you? – Uh! – I mean what 's your job here?"   He asked cautiously.

"Oh! – I'm sorry -- I'm the new runner! -- The other guy has transferred and I'm the new man -- The PO should arrive any minute!"   It was about a minute or so till 0500. I took the trash can and removed all the trash and stuffed it in a brown paper bag that was conveniently in the trash also. I walked into the dorm and placed it in a big can for the cleanup crew to dump. As I walked back into the PO office I saw him coming up the walk.

I waited until his hand was on the door handle and called to the watch. "0500 Man! – get em up!

The PO walked in the door just in time to hear my call. The apprentice hadn't moved, the PO looked at me, then turned to the watch. "Well - get em up!"

"Morning boss - coffee will be ready in a minute! -- Hope you like it!"   I acted as if I had everything under control.

"Alright - boy what's up - you in trouble again! He quipped.

"No! – Boss - you see - your runner got his orders and I'm taking his place." I didn't lie, but it was still a fabrication.

"Fine!—Fine! – Now tell me where this decision came from!" He asked.

I had been this route before, a little lying may be in order here, I thought. "UH! – I don't know where it came from—Boss -- I just follow the orders!"   I lied a little.

"What's your name again?" I told him. "Yeh! – Wardlaw! – Now - listen Wardlaw -- Don't try to bullshit a bullshitter -- You see - I make the decisions as to who the runners are around here and who stands watch and who works where -- So you're just trying to get a cushy job ain'tcha?"

I lowered my head, I was not ashamed of what I did. I was ashamed because I got caught.

"Look! – Boss! - I should'a been on my boat last Friday and here I am doing scullery and waiting as a witness in a court- marshal that I have no control over and I figured this was a good place to be in case I was needed or something!" I suppose I was close to pleading.

He looked intently at me. "That's really not a bad idea! - Lemme check out this coffee and think about it? -- OK?"

I nodded in agreement, then offered this. "I don't mean to rush you – Boss – But - I need to either go to the scullery or let Smoke know something -- He told me if I screwed up he would stick me in the tray washer!"

He cracked up at this. "Alright! – Alright! – I'll give you a try -- Your first job is to go tell Smoke you got a new job -- After that - run by the mail room - pick up the mail and get me a paper and if this coffee ain't any good! -- I'll fire you when you get back!"

The coffee was good and I had a new job.

The line stretched half way around the Admin Building. Pay day was a big event for a sailor. We were paid in cash. Only rarely were we paid by check. I patiently waited my turn and finally reached the pay table. On nice days they set up a series of tables out in front of the Admin Building.

"Nothing here for you - Wardlaw!" The PO stated as his finger went down the "W" list.

"What ! – Check again - Please! – Man - I'm about broke!" I pleaded.

"Sorry - kid! -- There ain't even a Wardlaw on the list!" He replied.

I moved away, dejected and confused. I walked back to the barracks, trying to figure why my name was not even on the list. A sailor gets paid twice a month, on the 1st and the 15th. If either of those dates falls on a weekend, then they are paid on the Friday before. This was Thursday the 1st of August, my first day on active duty was the 16th of July, so I was a day shy of two full weeks. I reasoned that was why I didn't get paid. I considered wiring home for some money, but the only real reason was for cigarettes, so I put it out of my mind.

The PO kept a basket under the counter for lost or left behind items. There was an assortment of keys and strange coins the cleanup crew found and placed in the basket. Once in a great while we would get a request to take a set of keys to the Admin Office to be forwarded to the owner. The PO had just such a request when I arrived back at the office.

"Wardlaw! – Look in the basket for a set of GM keys with a blue Navy fob on it."

I pulled the basket out and there was a red and white box of Marlboro Cigarettes right on top. I set them to the side, and sorted through the mass of keys. Sure enough there was a set that matched the description. "I think we got em - Boss!"

"Check good -- We don't wanna send the wrong set!" The PO was very particular about his job and his work ethics as well. Further investigation left no doubt; this was the only keys that matched the description. The PO placed them in a small manila envelope along with the request and his initials. "Take em to Admin and make a mail run - Got it?"

"Sure thing - Boss! – Uh – About these cigarettes -- They're gonna get stale just sitting here." I spoke casually, I really didn't want him to know how badly I wanted them. The PO was a non-smoker. A non-smoker can't understand the drive that nicotine can place on a smoker. All smoking sailors can control their desire to smoke and sometimes go a day or more without smoking as part of their dedication to duty. But the desire is intense all the same. The PO looked up and said. "Go ahead -- Take em if you want – But - if someone comes looking for em -- I'm sending em to you! – Got that?"

"Got'cha Boss!" I shouted as I darted out the door, envelope and cigarettes in hand. The cigarettes were in one of those new flip top boxes and were a little longer than most brands. Marlboro had been a girly cigarette when I was a kid. I could remember how the young society girls would smoke them in the lounge at Momma's riding academy, years before. Now they were being touted as a man's brand with the big signs featuring different men in adventurous occupations. I think there was even a sailor on one.

I delivered the envelope to Admin and as I was leaving a young Lieutenant stopped me. "Sailor! – No Smoking allowed in here!"

I wasn't smoking, but suddenly realized I still had the cigarette box in my hand. "Sorry sir - I wasn't thinking!"

"Well – Sailor – Stow em! – Stow em - now!" He barked.

"Yes Sir - right now!' I attempted to put them in my jumper pocket; the size of the box caused my pocket to protrude and really was unsightly. He shook his head in disgust and walked away. I beat it out of there in a flash.

As I proceeded to the post office, I realized why most sailors smoked Camels, Phillip Morris, Lucky Strike, Chesterfield or Kools. These were all short cigarettes and in a soft pack. You could place them in your jumper pocket with no problem. I moved the box to my sock and the feel of the hard box was very noticeable. I vowed then and there not to buy cigarettes in a box.

The next couple of weeks went by fairly uneventful. I picked up a few bucks playing checkers in the lounge. We would play and the winner got a dime for every man he had left on the board and a quarter for every king. I would have to wait sometimes two or three days between playing, to allow my opponents to transfer away so the new guys wouldn't avoid me. It kept me from being completely broke.

One afternoon, this guy came looking for me. "Hey you! – You the hot shot checker ace - I been hearing about?"

I stood. "Well I play - if that's what you mean?"

"Yeh! – That's what I mean - I hear you play for money - that right?" He seemed cocky."

"Sure - if you don't put too big a price on the men." I answered.

"I don't understand - don't you just bet on the game." He asked.

I was beginning to think he just thought he was a checker player. "Let me explain - you see - when the game is over - the loser pays the winner the agreed amount for each of the winner's players left on the board."

He knit his brow. "'That's stupid - why not just bet on the game and the winner gets the money?"

"Oh! - No!" I lowered my voice as if confiding in him. "That's gambling – man - We'ed get thrown in the brig for that! -- This way the winner has earned the money by keeping as many men as possible on the board - the loser pays the winner for each man left - it's like professional checkers - you get paid for your skill and that's not illegal." It was pure hogwash, but I thought it sounded pretty good.

"Oh! - Yeh! – I see now!" My challenger announced. "Let's go get it on!"

A crowd was gathering as we set up the board.

"I want red!" My opponent stated.

"Fine with me!' I had never found any advantage in moving first or second. I also didn't have any certain strategy. I just played and enjoyed it and mostly won.

I had an Uncle, Dennis LeBorde, who was married to my Aunt Versie. I spent the summer of 1949, with them in Compton, California. We played every night. I never beat him. I played every day at work with Mrs. Essie Denham in Hope Villa, Louisiana. I could win against her, but not every time.

I explained the value of each man and the kings. The challenger laughed at the small change idea, and suggested a dollar for each man and five dollars for each king.

I suddenly realized this guy was either a pro or a complete idiot. I only had a little over two dollars.

A fairly large group had gathered and I was beginning to feel uneasy. This guy was a loud mouth and I could sense, he was a bully. I wanted out of this deal, but how. I didn't want to tell everyone I was broke. I certainly didn't want to back off as if I were afraid to play him.

I decided to be as honest and humble as I could be. "Look – Let's do this -- Let's play for a buck a man and two bucks for a king - how's that sound?" I figured I was good enough to keep him down to a final king.

"OK – But I don't like pussy bettin and that's what this is!" He spat the words out.

"Easy now - remember we ain't betting -- We're paying the winner according to his skill." I warned.

"Yeh! – Whatever! – My move!" He made his first move. The game was on. I couldn't believe a man could run his mouth the way this man did and not play better checkers. I had two kings and three men left on the board, two of my men never left my home row.

Boy was he pissed. I fully expected him to demand another match. He stood and unloaded a barrage of profanity. He had made no move to pay up.   I grew tense.

One of the other guys came over to him and pulled him to the side and spoke too low for anyone else to hear. The crowd was all murmuring about the match and I realized that this may become a fiasco.

The conversation ended and the guy seemed a little less hostile. "You're a damn ringer - that's what you are - a damn ringer - but I asked for it -- I looked you up -- I asked you to play – But - I think you still suckered me!" He threw seven crumpled dollars on the board and walked out.

I picked up my money and walked over to the guy that spoke with my opponent. "I appreciate whatever you did - my friend - I thought I was in trouble for a minute - thanks!"

"No problem - I just told him - I heard you whipped a guy's ass over a razor - so what did he reckon you'd do over seven dollars!" We both laughed. I bought the guy a coke. To be honest, I didn't feel right about the money, but I kept it.

"All Rise!" The Military Courtroom was not crowded and I recognized a few faces as being present the evening that I encountered the thief. The court was introduced, but I saw no jury.

The charges were read against Delcort, as he sat in a chair up front, in full view and looked as complacent as one waiting for a bus. His eyes scanned the room and when he saw me, he half grinned, and raised his handcuffed hands in a slight wave. This was one weird guy, I thought.

I couldn't believe the list of charges, in addition to stealing and defacing himself, with the laundry ink tattoos. He had collected some uniforms from the laundry and stuffed them into a makeshift dummy. He broke a glass window in his cell, on the third floor and pushed the dummy between the bars, then called a guard, claiming someone had jumped to their death.

The guards removed him from his cell and took him to the duty officer. The duty officer had been cleaning his 45 pistol and had placed it in his desk drawer, unloaded with the clip removed.

Delcort was standing beside the officer with hands cuffed in front of him. The duty officer was seated at his desk. The duty officer opened the desk drawer to remove a pad to make notes on, when Delcort saw the pistol, he grabbed it, cocked the pistol, placed it against the duty officers head and pulled the trigger.

I was dumbfounded at the charges. This was one crazy, mixed up young man. He had pleaded guilty to all charges. The defense wanted to plead temporary insanity. The court presented test results that pronounced him sane enough to know right from wrong.

The only reason that I, and other witnesses were in court was to identify the accused. Each of us stood and pointed out Delcort when the instance of our encounter was read. I looked at the Duty Officer when he stood and wondered if he had thanked God for that pistol being unloaded.

The verdict was six months hard labor and a bad conduct discharge. I thought that was lenient. Apparently the charges for the pistol deal were not as serious as one would think. Delcort had testified that he knew the gun was unloaded and was just joking.

The court martial was adjoined and I was released. I could now proceed with all pending transfers, assignments and leaves. The court clerk removed the Exibit #1 tag from my razor and handed it to me.

"USS Torsk! - Here I come!" Well, at least that's what I thought. I told you, you wouldn't believe it.

I fully expected the Navy to proceed with the precision that our history has shown it to have. I mean, I expected a jeep to show up and take me to my boat. I asked my PO. "What's next Boss?"

"Just hang around until you get reassigned." He answered.

"I shouldn't need to be reassigned – Man! - Just get me a jeep and take me to my boat!"

"Listen – Wardlaw - this is the FFA Barracks [for further assignment] - if you are already assigned then you shouldn't be here - but you were sent here - therefore you are mine until I receive orders that say otherwise!"

I felt relieved that all the legal stuff was over and I had received no notice of my assignment being canceled. The Officer in court that morning had said I was released to proceed with my assignment. I stressed this to the PO.

"Wardlaw – look! - This is outa my hands -- I tell you what -- tomorrow is payday – you can have the morning off! -- Be first in the pay line then go to Admin and see what they can do for you -- If you'r not back by 1300 hours - I'll have the SPs on your tail -- Savvy!"

"Aye! – Aye! -- Sir!   I did a comic salute and proceeded to dump the waste basket. I really concentrated on my work for the rest of the day. It went fast; I caught up on my laundry that afternoon. It was easy with every one off at work.

"Sailor -- I'm sorry but you are not on this pay sheet. Again I complained, the Marine guard took my arm and escorted me from the line. "If you ain't on the list-, you ain't gonna get paid! - Sailor!"

I jerked away from him and stepped back to the pay clerk, we were again outside the Admin Building. I could tell the guard was angry.

I quickly asked the clerk. "What can I do to get paid? - Please tell me!"

He held his hand up to stop the guard as he was about to grab me. "OK – Second floor of Admin is the paymaster - get them to pull your pay records and authorized me to pay you and I will! -- That's what it'll take!"

The Marine forcefully pulled me away and uttered. "Don't try that again!"

I was angry. I looked down at his hand on my arm and slowly raised my eyes to meet his.

I spoke softly, slowly, but firmly, no one else could hear, but him.   "My Friend! -- Don't put your hands on me again!"

He dropped his hand in shock.   I immediately walked away without looking back.

No one at the Pay Masters counter could find any information on me. It was as if I didn't exist. No one really seemed to take an interest. Everyone had jobs to do and the clerk that handled the miscellaneous stuff was at a total loss. I could tell I was causing quite a stir, but at this point, I simply didn't care. I started thinking that causing a stir was the only way I would get any results. It was evident that everyone just wanted me to go away.

A cute little second class wave stuck her head out of an office and called me over. "You're causing quite a disturbance – Sailor! - Are you sure you're on the right base?"

She was a doll, with dark red hair, creamy white skin and not a sign of a freckle. Her green eyes seemed intelligent. Her question was definitely not intelligent.

"Am I on the right base? Dag Gum girl - do you think I just went "poof" and was here?" I quickly ran through the scenario that transpired since I arrived.

She listened intently, then asked me to sit tight a minute and left the room. In a moment she returned. She had a different look on her face. I thought maybe she had verified my story and felt sorry for me. I sure felt sorry for me.

"Wardlaw - your records are at the Provost Marshall's office -- If you go get them and bring them back to me and I will straighten everything out." She gave a pensive smile.

The Provost Marshall's office was across a grassy area in front of the Admin building and just a brief walk away. I walked into the building and noted the two armed Marine Guards at the door. The traditional long counter was there for the purpose of conducting business.

I addressed the PO that stood to assist me. "I came to pick up my records - if you don't mind." I made up my mind on the way over that I was gonna be a nice polite, sailor boy!

"What reason would we have your records for - Sailor?" The question surprised me. How did I know for what reason, I didn't know! I kept my cool and continued to be polite.

"Eh! – I'm not sure   - maybe it's cause I was prosecuting witness in a court marshal and ya'll are holding em so's I wont get transferred accidently!" I thought that sounded pretty good and it seemed to make sense.

"What's the name - Sailor?" He thumbed through a rolodex file as I gave the information. He stopped thumbing and pulled up a card. He glanced quickly at me and asked. "Serial number?"

I answered, "457-94-66!"

He removed the card, slammed the lid on the Rolodex, and called loudly. "Guards arrest this man!" I thought he was making a joke.

The guards weren't in on it, if he was. They moved with swiftness and precision that only dedicated training will provide.

"What's the joke - Man?" I cried.

"Being AWOL is no joke in this man's Navy -- Sailor -- You been AWOL for nearly three weeks now and you ask -- WHAT'S THE JOKE?"

My legs went weak. "What next?" I thought, as the marines strong armed me to the Duty Officer's office and sat me in a chair next to his desk. I was in a stupor and I thought. "Is this where Delcort stood when he pulled the pistol on that Officer!" In a few moments the duty officer walked in and without looking at me, threw my records on his desk.

"Decided to turn yourself in – Eh – Sailor! – I hope for your sake it was worth it - cause you in a pile of crap now!" Contempt was in his voice.

I couldn't believe my ears, here I was, sitting here, being treated as a criminal and I had done nothing but want to serve my country on a submarine.

"Sir - I have not set foot off this base since I got here, weeks ago! -- I've worked every day in the scullery till I got the runner job at Barracks B -- You can check with those POs - they will verify that I was working!"

The Duty Officer looked me full in the face for the first time and I instantly recognized him as the officer in court that testified against Delcort. "Damn! – Boy! - I know for a fact you were in Court yesterday!" There was a long pause and neither of us spoke.

He turned and picked up the phone. The series of calls that followed pieced together the story of a snafu that is one for the books, or at least this book.

When I arrived at Norfolk that first night, the PO was somehow distracted and assigned me correctly on his log. He logged me in to Barracks A, which is for overnight stay.

The chit he gave me was for Barracks B which in FFA [for further assignment].

The only record the Navy had was Barracks A and I wasn't there. So when the Base came to take me to my boat on that Friday afternoon, I was reported AWOL and my records were turned over to the Provost Marshall, therefore I didn't get paid.

All the while I'm slaving away in the scullery, tracking down a thief, standing for a Captain's Mast, running errands for my PO and not getting paid.

The very guy that is arresting me is the same guy I had sat by in court, only yesterday. I told you it was unbelievable, but now it is a matter on record.

The Duty Officer looked at me. "Young fellow - you have really had a raw deal! - you just relax now!"

The guards had gone and he turned once again to the phone, and placed a call to transportation. He introduced himself and stated he wanted transportation and a porter, apparently he was asked for the purpose of the request. He looked at me and smiled. "Let's say it's for VIP transportation and baggage assistance. Have them report to the front door of the Provost Office!"

"Get me the berthing on the Torsk at the DE Piers!" He called from his office to the PO at the counter. "And pack up the folder on Wardlaw!"

He turned his attention to me. "I'm going to give you a paper!" He began to type. "You keep this with you -- should any problems arise - simply give them this paper."

He smiled and said. "We'll send a message to your reserve unit and have them clear up any problems with your family." I reacted to this. He was expecting it.

"Hold on now -- We sent a message day before yesterday -- It's standard procedure for them to contact your parents - in case you go home -- they were to encourage you to turn yourself in - at your reserve unit -- chances are - they haven't contacted your parents yet - so either way you are covered."

Sir! – You don't know my Momma - she'd drive all the way up here just to give me a whipping if I did go AWOL!" Everybody cracked up.

The driver showed up in a 56 Chevy four door with a sailor to act as a porter, both were in dress whites. The Duty Officer took him and the other sailor into the office and spoke to them privately. I waited on the bench by the door.

"Let's go Sailor!" The porter said as he came out of the office, the driver lingered behind, but caught up with us as we reached the car.

The porter opened the back door and with a slight bow swept his hand in a motion for me to enter. I did so, and he got into the passenger seat.

As the driver pulled away, he turned and said, "Paymasters office first -- Am I right?"

"I really should tell my PO why I'm late – Guys - he said he would report me AWOL if I weren't back by 1300 hours."

At this the two sailors howled with laughter. The driver said through his laughter. "I don't think the Base Commander would give you any shit right now!"

The porter looked at me and said. "Man! -- We gotta hear this whole story - the Provost Marshall said to take care of you as if you were the Admiral's son! - He said you were the victim of an awful mistake and to see to it that you got paid -- Got your gear and to escort you with greatest care and courtesy to the gang plank of the USS Orion -- Pier 22 at the DE piers! He said your sub was tied up on her outboard side!"

The driver was a third class boson [boatswain] mate and the porter was a seaman, they listened intently as I unraveled the story that had brought us together. I was nowhere near finished when we reached the Admin Building. The driver parked right in front, in a restricted zone.

The porter reached into the glove box and handed him a stack of cards.

The driver shuffled through them and pulled out a card that had two navy anchors on each side of large blue letters that read VIP. He placed it on the dash. They then each placed a band around their right arm that read, ESCORT.

"Let's go – Mr. VIP!" They were going to enjoy this. The porter took my folder and placed it under his arm. The two men stepped to each side of me and we stepped off as if on parade. They truly did escort me into the building and right up to the Paymaster's Counter. Everyone looked up and the expression on their faces ranged from awe to confusion. The little red head noticed the change in the room's atmosphere and stepped from her office.

"Well! – Look whose back!" She glanced at the escorts and raised her eyebrows, she was impressed. "Looks like somebody's gonna get paid!" She extended her hand and took my folder from the porter.

The driver and porter stepped back and assumed parade rest, one on each side of the door. It was so quiet that you could hear the wristwatches ticking. I don't reckon anyone here had ever seen a VIP before.

The little red head read the cover sheet and sought out the Pay Master's Duty Officer. We could hear her on the phone tell him. "I know Sir – But I don't think this can wait!" There was a pause. "Yes Sir – I understand Sir - but Sir - I don't think this SHOULD Wait! -- AYE – Aye –Sir!"

She hung up the phone. "The Duty Officer is on the way!" She exclaimed.

We could hear him clumbering up the stairs. He was one of the Navy's "not too fine a specimen". He was overweight , red faced and very unhappy at being taken away from whatever he was doing .

"This better be damned important - young lady!" He addressed the little red head. She simply gestured toward me as she handed him my folder.

He looked at me and for the first time saw the escorts. "Who the hell is this - the Duke of Assbury?" He grimaced as he read the cover letter, he glanced up at me a few times and then shifted through a few pages of my records, reached in his pocket for his pen and said. "Damn!"

He placed his initials on something and snapped the folder shut. "Pay the son - of--------- eh! – Sailor! As he exited the door, I heard him say again. "Damn!"

My pay up to date was a hundred and five dollars. I really felt better and continued my story as my escorts delivered me back to Barracks B. As I walked in the PO started.

"Wardlaw - you heard me say 1300 -- Here you are over an hour late an ----!" He caught site of the escorts. "Oh! -- Shit! - Wardlaw - what've you done now?"

The driver broke in. "Hey Wardlaw - you want his job - you can have it if you want it - you know?"

I laughed and briefly explained what had transpired. He stood transfixed as I explained.

"Know what – Wardlaw -- I'm gonna follow through on every new guy that comes through here from now on -- If I had verified that boat assignment you said you had - then none of this would have happened." I think he was truly sorry.

I loaded up my gear and the porter would not let me carry a thing. The guy said this was what he was paid for and he was having a blast.

On the way out, I shook hands with the PO and reminded him to get a new runner before morning or he would have to make his own coffee.

We stopped by the chow hall and got everyone's attention with the escorts marching at my side.

I told Smoke goodbye and he wanted to know who I was. "I'm Wardlaw – Smoke - you know me! I worked in here for you!"

He went into his "Step and Fetch it" routine.

He kinda humped over and began to rub his hands in anxiety and his eyes grew exceptionally wide as he said with quivering voice. "Nawsuh! – I doesn't knos you -- Nawsuh! – I thots I knos you! – But - I don't knos you! -- You ain't dat nice lil white boy dat lik'ta bus my ass wit dem suds! -- Nawsuh you ain't dat boy!"

The escorts looked bewildered and I had to laugh. Smoke straightened up and embraced me. Suddenly he jumped back and put both hands over his butt and ran off in a high step gangling run, shouting.   "Don't torpedo me - please don't torpedo me - Mr. Submarine!"

 We were still laughing as we reached the car and pulled away. I was on my way to my Torsk.

CHAPTER VI

MY TORSK AND NATO

The escorts were really enjoying this outing. I had finished my story and they both agreed, I should write a book about it. They made a big deal out of the screw-ups, but somehow I didn't agree. I still thought the Navy was a very good, proficient and vital part of our nation's defense. I could understand how mistakes can be made, with the amount of work that most navy personnel have

to do. It's easy to overlook an obscure mistake. I also felt it was partially my fault.

I distinctly remember noting the different barracks numbers when I checked in. I just did not do anything about it. I made a mental note to myself, never let a question, or doubt pass until it is clarified. I figured it may someday save a life.

The driver drove the Chevy right on the pier, this was a "NO NO" for normal vehicles, but my escorts were playing it to the hilt. The driver stopped at the brow of the Orion, and the porter jumped out and opened the door for me to exit.

As I stepped out, the driver came around and said. "Man! – It's been great -- We wish you lotsa luck!" The porter reached in for my seabag and duffel. He hoisted my bag on his shoulder and picked up my duffel. The driver led the way and the porter followed as we walked up the brow.

The USS Orion was the Submarine Tender for Subron 6. The Orion's boat deck was quite high so the brow had a mid-platform and the brow finished its accent in the opposite direction.

We had drawn some onlookers by driving on the pier; there was now quite a few sailors watching as well as some officers from the bridge.

They saw an unusual sight, a car doing the taboo of driving on the pier, then the Blue Navy VIP sign in the window of the car, and two official escorts providing VIP treatment to an ordinary seaman.

The topside watch stood there in amazement with his jaw agape.

The driver whispered to me. "Don't step on deck yet." I paused on the top step of the brow. The two escorts stepped on deck; the porter sat my gear down and stepped to the side of the driver.

The driver addressed the topside watch. "This special detail has delivered their assigned charge to the USS Orion as ordered! – Do you accept the charge?"

The dumbfounded watch muttered. "Aye – Aye --- EH! – I – We – accept the charge." The driver and porter faced left and as they passed me they stopped, came to attention and gave me a fine hand salute. I returned the salute, and restrained a tear.

They never looked back as they left.

I turned toward the stern of the Orion and gave another salute and then faced the topside watch. "Request permission to pass across to the USS Torsk?" I stated.

"Are you a new crewmember?" He asked cautiously.

"That's correct." I replied.

"Well - you must check in with the squadron first. - Name?" He pulled a clip board from inside the watch podium.

I gave him my name and his finger began to move down a list. His eyes grew wide, he looked at me. "Spell it -- P-Please?" I did. His trouser's leg began to shake.

"OH! – NO! – Please God! -- Not again! -- I prayed!" YEP – AGAIN!

The watch grabbed the PA mike and called for a guard and the Duty Officer to report to the quarterdeck on the double. I thought he was going to pull his 45, but he didn't, he just raised a finger and waved it in a "Don't move fashion." I didn't, but reached in my pocket and took out the letter the Provost Officer gave me.

Two sailors came in a rush asking. "What's up?" The watch told them to just watch me, I had been AWOL. They positioned themselves on both sides, and eyeing me with caution.

The onlookers were really getting a show. I suppose it was confusing. They had witnessed the arrival fanfare and now the same guy is being placed in custody.

"Yeh! – It is one for the books!" I thought.

The duty officer showed and the watch pointed me out and showed him the AWOL notice on the list.

"Been on vacation – Huh - Sailor?" He quipped.

"No Sir - nothing like that at all!" I handed him the letter.

He read it and in a moment, addressed the guards. "As you were -- Men! -- You may return to your duties!" He ordered me to follow him to the ward room.

He motioned me to take a seat and left the room, soon to return with a number of other officers. None of them addressed me at all. They simply read the letter and made subdued comments, frequently looking my way. I saw no nods of approval or sympathy, just murmurs, like, "Sheesh! – Damn! – No Way! –"I'm not believing this!"

They then decided to call the Provost Marshall and confirm the letter. He regretted the call. The Provost Marshall was apparently very upset, thinking the letter was more than sufficient and apparently told him so. I was immediately ushered out and released to continue across to my boat.

I'll never forget that first view of my Torsk. I stepped on the top step of the brow on the outboard side of the Orion. It too was a split gangway that led down to the deck of the USS Sailfish. There were five boats tied up, out board of the Orion. The Sailfish, the Argonaut, the Torsk, the Runner and the Sea Lion.

The Torsk was the third boat out from the Orion and seemed to be in a class all by herself. To me she looked longer, cleaner, leaner and meaner than any of the rest. The flag at the stern seemed to wave more than the others. She was a beaut!

I kept the letter from the Provost Officer out as I crossed the boats to my Torsk. I knew full well that I'd need it again.

The topside watch was a slender guy, named Gangloff, he appeared about a year or so older than me.

I had my bag on my left shoulder. I sat my duffel down on the deck of my Torsk, but before stepping onboard, I paused and turned toward her colors as they flapped in the summer breeze on this late afternoon of August 15, 1957. I could feel the tears welling in my eyes, I didn't care. The weeks of frustrations, disappointments, trials and trouble were swept away by the presence of my most treasured destination, The USS Torsk - SS423.

"Request permission to come aboard?" I choked back the tears.

"Permission granted!" Came the welcome reply as the watch stepped forward. I stepped on my Torsk for the first time. The feeling that overwhelmed me was beyond this written word. "All was well with my world!"

"The name's Wardlaw - I should have been here a month ago - but I was delayed - I had to send a man to prison."

Gangloff looked at me and glanced at his clipboard. "You may wind up there yourself - if you can't get out of this warrant here!"

"Yeh! – I've been through this all day - call your duty officer and I'll show him this letter - it'll straighten everything out."

The watch picked up a hand mic and keyed it to call below deck. He called for the duty officer, gave a brief explanation and hung up the mic.

In a moment a huge colored guy came up through the forward torpedo room hatch and motioned me to follow him, as I reached for my gear, he growled. "Leave it - you ain't staying – playboy! - just bring your papers!"

Well, I just thought all was well with my world. I didn't even think of smart mouthing this colored sailor. He was a hunk, not just big, but defined. He was perfectly proportioned with rolling muscles that stretched his tee shirt and outlined his pecs and abs. He was a classic example of a heavy weight boxer.

I followed him meekly to the ward room of my Torsk. The smell of diesel was extreme to a new comer but welcome to one who had already learned to love it. The steady drone of the pulse of the sub was comforting, I needed comforting.

The colored sailor motioned to the door of the ward room. "Sit – wait - don't touch or say nothing till Mr. Burkart gets here - got that - playboy?"

I nodded; he was definitely brow beating me. I was in no position to do or say anything about it. I wondered if this nightmare would ever end. I sat and savored the few earlier moments when I first arrived, somehow I felt it was going to be alright. I looked around and realized how small and tight everything is on a submarine. I didn't care, it was my boat.

The curtain parted on the other end of the ward room, and a Lieutenant entered and sat down. He looked at me sternly and leaned forward, he fairly hissed his words. "We don't want men like you, on this submarine!"

The words cut me to the quick, the tears once again welled in my eyes, but my sudden fury kept them at bay. I was as angry as I had ever been in my life. I wasn't angry at Mr. Burkart, or the Navy, or the colored guy.

I guess I was just angry that nothing ever seemed to go away. I was sick and tired of it all, I wanted to start submarining. I wanted to work, sit around and shoot the bull, go to sea, live a sailor's life.

My brain screamed. "WHEN WILL IT END?"

I slowly rose from my seat, pushed my envelope toward Mr. Burkart, handed him my letter and leaning over the table spoke low but with deliberation.

"Sir! –Mr. Burkart -- I'm not gonna try to explain all this to you - but what you just said is the most unfair thing I've ever heard an officer in the U.S. Navy say!"

He looked stunned. "Sir! – I'm not trying to be disrespectful - but after you read this letter and you still feel the same way - then you can do whatever you feel is right!"

I sat down. I could tell he was on the verge of getting angry himself, but he controlled himself and opened the letter.

He read for a moment, then looked up at me. He seemed amused. "Son - you scared the hell out'a some folks, - you know that?"

"No Sir! – I sure didn't want to do that! - What are you talking about - Sir? - You see – Sir - none of this was my fault and----------!" He cut me short.

"Wardlaw - did you read this letter?" He was examining the envelope the letter was in, as he spoke.

"No Sir! – Was I supposed to? - The Provost Marshall Officer simply told me to show it to anyone that needed to see it?"

"Well – Son --To tell you the truth - this letter does not explain any details concerning your AWOL period - just that you were a victim of circumstances -- but it definitely - tells me if I give you a hard time - it will have a serious effect on my career!" He stood and extended his hand. "Welcome aboard - Sailor!"

As he walked me back topside, he called. "Brown - come help Wardlaw with his bags."

It turns out, Brown was a steward, for the wardroom and was a heavy weight boxing champ in the Navy. Brown didn't like the idea of helping me.

"Mr. Burkart - I thought we was gonna keel hawl this little prick?" He muttered.

"Come on now – Brown - it was all a mistake - he's alright!"

As soon as Mr. Burkart was out of sight, Brown dropped my duffel bag and hissed. "Carry it yoself, playboy!" I picked the duffel up and made my way to the chow hall.

The cook was "Catfish" Woodson, a slender colored fellow that had a personality that could charm a great white shark. He was finishing up preparation of the evening meal.

Catfish greeted me with a smile and shouted. "Halleluyah! -- Got me another mess cook! -- Whoah! -- Stow that gear and rattle them pots and pans - - Boy!"

I asked, "Where do I bunk – Man - I just got off da bus?"

"You ain't seen the Chief yet - Boy?" He quizzed.

"Boy! – Boy! – How many boys you know - just been AWOL three weeks and got away with it!" I shouted in a whimsical way.

"Whoah! - You dat boy?" He looked at me in amazement. "Sit down dere an I'll get da Chief -- He gotta talk to you anyhow!" I pushed my gear between the tables and sat down.

As he ducked to go through the forward hatch, toward the control room he called back. "Put up dem plates and stuff by the sink -- so they be outta de way when we eats.

I shouted back. "Yassuh boss - rat now - boss!"

I heard him as he trailed off. "Haa! – Haa! – Haa! – You'll do - Boy -- Yassuh! -- You'll do!"

He returned presently with the Chief. He introduced himself as Hal Wright, Chief of the Boat. "Everybody calls me PAPPY and that's fine - cept you hafta know when to use it and when not to -- OK?" I nodded, even though, I wasn't sure what he meant.

"You may hafta swap bunks – Son - less'n you want the waterfall -- It's always vacant – Cause no one can handle it!"

"Waterfall?" I inquired. All through sub school and even on my cruise I had not heard of the water fall.

"Yep! – Come on – I'll show you -- who knows - you may be the first!" We squeezed our way through the crossway to the double row of bunks on the port side, just aft of the chow hall bulkhead. He pointed to a vacant bunk on the very top, inboard row. At the bulkhead end was a metal tray hanging from four little flexible chains.

"Know what that is - Sailor?" He asked.

"Yes sir -- That's an AC driver [a type of air conditioner compressor] - I'm pretty sure." I answered.

"Pretty close -- You know it sweats a lot and that tray always has water in it -- if you bump it! -- It'll wet you and its ice water! -- So no one wants this bunk!" He told me.

"I'll take it! -- I'll take it! – Chief!" I stated. " I'll make it work - now about this mess cooking!"

"Oh! – You volunteering to mess cook?" He exclaimed hopefully.

"No! – No!" I exclaimed. "You see Catfish said -------!'

"Aw! -- Don't fret Catfish -- He's always funning with the guys! -- Now if you want mess cooking -- that's fine -- but I'd rather have you in my deck crew -- especially if you can paint. -- I need a painter – bad!"

"Paint? – Chief I was born with a paint brush in my hand!" I boasted.

He laughed. "That's not exactly what I had in mind - but you'll see bright and early tomorrow -- my boy-- yes indeed - you'll see!" He turned and walked away.

I checked the tray above my bunk and found it to be about a 16 X 16 inch pan, hung by four very flexible chains at each corner. The object was for the condensation from the air conditioning compressor to drip in the pan. This was not the evaporator coil, so the condensation was only the moisture collected on the casing of the apparatus. The pan did not have a drain. The liquid that collected in it was exposed to the atmosphere and therefore would evaporate long before it ran over. It did, however, always have liquid in it and the chains allowed it to remain level as the boat rolled when at sea, if it was bumped or moved, it would dump the ice cold water on whoever was asleep in the bunk. The pan was not much more than a foot above the bunk, so it required some expertise in getting in or out of bed and even some caution in turning over. I was always aware of it and had no problem.

I stowed my clothing under my mattress, that's where the locker actually was, the mattress is lying on a stainless steel frame that has about a four inch depth to it. The lid is the base for your four inch mattress. It is very space saving and quite ample for most of a sailor's gear. There were also some small lockers to hold taller objects, like boondocks [work boots], and tall objects. I looked around the quarters that was officially called the after battery compartment. It housed the chow hall or galley, the crew's quarters and head, on the upper level. On the lower level was the freezer, cooler, dry storage and about one hundred twenty or so one cell batteries, each cell was an entity of its own and was replaceable. Each cell produced one volt, but believe me, that was a huge volt, which means it created massive amps.

I changed to dungarees and turned my whites inside out. I neatly lay them out under my bunk. They would be perfectly pressed for the next dress occasion.

The chow hall was packed as I walked in to see twenty-four of my companions for the next two years.

"Hey -- new meat! -- I'm first-- com'er honey!" Called a grizzled engine man sitting on the back row.

"'Dog-gone Collins - there ain't no room now!" – Exclaimed a radio man sitting next to him.

"Hey! -- That's fine - cause the little darlin's gonna sit on my lap - aint'cha honey?" I instinctively knew this was all jive and decided to play along.

I threw up my arms and rushed between the tables and leaned over the radioman and began showering the ugliest engineman I had ever seen with exaggerated caresses and kisses all over his head.

The crew went wild as the astonished man cried out. "What de hell you doing Boy!—Damn! -- Stop dat -- shit - Man! - Stop it!"

The crew began urging me on. "You asked for it Collins! – Hey! -- Man! – You called him over! – You can dish it out - but you can't take it - can you – Collins?"

I stopped and looked at him and he sheepishly said. "Get the hell away from me - Boy!"

I feigned being crushed. I stepped back and made a pouty face. "Aw! -- Now you've hurt my feelings - I thought you was gonna love me and you really wanted to fight! - OK! – Do we fight in here or go out on the pier?"

It grew quiet, I figured I just overstepped my boundaries.

I stuck out my hand. "My name's Wardlaw - and you don't know how glad I am to meet you – Collins -- and all you guys!" I addressed everyone but needed to mend my bold action with him. I gave him my biggest childish grin.

He wiped his hand on his pants leg and took mine in that giant paw. He didn't smile, but looked at me and asked. "You ain't really, you know, funny are you?"

I leaned a little closer, but spoke loud enough for all to hear. "Naw - are you?"

Once again the chow hall erupted in chaotic laughter. It was quite a first crew encounter.

I was asked about the AWOL thing and began the first of many recitations about my ordeal. It always led to one of those "can you top this sessions," where someone would tell of their "snafu experience."

The next morning we were up at 0600 hours. The morning cook was Hersey, he had the blackest, curliest hair I ever saw on a man. He was a great cook. As I sat down, he pointed his spatula at me. "How many and how you want em?"

"Two - with yellow runny and the white done." I answered. He flipped his spatula with a skillful flick of his wrist, caught it without even looking and proceeded to prepare my eggs.

"Toast or cornbread?" He called. I chose cornbread. He served me hash brown potatoes with two perfectly cooked eggs and a huge spoon of thick baked beans and crisp bacon, with a slab of cornbread on top.   It was on a seafoam green glass plate. I was impressed.

"Just say - over medium from now on and that's what you'll get!" He smiled and pointed to the sink area with his spatula. "Cups and silverware are there -- you gotta handle them yourself."

I knew from my brief time in the Navy that grits were not on the menu. I asked. "Do you ever serve grits?"

Hersey looked and answered. "Well I can cook em - but I don't know how many sailors would eat em! – Gee - most of these guys never even heard of em!"

A burly second class fire technician that sat across from me, spoke up. "I'll eat em -- any time you fix em -- Curly!" He looked at me. "Where you from - Sailor?"

"Savannah, Georgia for now - but my old home was in Louisiana -- I'm Lynn Wardlaw. - How bout you?"

"I'll be! – Bud! – I'm from Clyo – that's just up the river from Savannah. - I'm William Jones - everybody calls me Jonesy. -   Good to have you aboard - how long you been in?"

"Two or three month - counting sub school. I've got three years of reserve though!" I reported. I could tell from his reaction that being a reserve for three years did not impress him.

"Well - if I decide to go home for a weekend or something -- maybe you'll want to ride down and share gasoline -- you can have someone meet you near home." It was a nice offer. I never took him up on it though.

I was summoned to the ward room as soon as breakfast was over. There were four officers finishing their coffee and Pappy was there.

The chief, Pappy Wright, introduced me to: Mr. Sheehan – LtJG, Mr. Bibby – Lt, and Mr. Mobley – LtJG, I had already met the XO – Mr. Burkart.

"Have a seat Wardlaw." He indicated a chair at the foot of the table. The ward room is also where the officers take their meals, hold meetings, lounge around and hold captains mast. I was not comfortable.

Mr. Bibby noticed. "Young fellow - we have all read the letter you brought with you and understand you have not read it. - Is that correct?"

"Yessir - that's right - was I supposed to read it -- cause the Provost Officer never said to read it?" I was thinking I was in trouble again, maybe there was something in the letter I should have done.

Mr. Burkart spoke. "No - you see sailor - the letter was never sealed -- It was given to you in case you needed it and you used it -- looks like -- three times and never once read it -- Is that right?"

I nodded and answered "Yessir."

Mr. Bibby again spoke. "Why didn't you read it - Sailor?"

I was slowly getting angry again. If I had done something wrong, "Dag Gummit," just tell me and let's get it over! Maybe it would be best to simply answer the question.

"Sir -- the officer handed me the letter and told me to show it to anyone I had a problem with -- that's what I did. -- It never crossed my mind to read it."

"Alright – now – Sailor - let's hear your story from the beginning. -- This letter has every ones attention -- but no details -- except you have been wronged."

I retold the entire story, minus Yvonne, but including the choice of duty promise. I only told of the snafus. They listened in mute attention, I didn't tell em about my emotions either. When I finished, I asked Mr. Burkart if I should read the letter.

They all laughed, and Mr. Burkart said it was astounding that I had not read it and they were now convinced that I had, indeed, not read it.

"Alright, Wardlaw - here's the deal." Mr. Burkart leaned back in his chair at the head of the table. "If you want to transfer to New London -- we'll send you back to the base here in Norfolk and they will transfer you to a boat in New London. You'll be in New London in less than a week - how's that sound?"

I was flabbergasted, it was what I had wanted. All the trouble, anguish and disappointment was gone.

I thought of Yvonne, suddenly the shock hit me. She had sent my ring back. No letter no message, just the ring. There was a force at work here, something out of my control. No matter what I had done, no matter how hard I had tried, no matter what I had planned, that force had me sitting here, in the ward room of the USS Torsk.

I yielded completely. God's plan was at work.

I could feel the tears once again. I blinked them back and stood with a new resolve. "Mr. Burkart – Gentlemen – Chief -- If ya'll will have me -- I'd like to stay on the Torsk."

"Atta boy!" said Mr. Bibby. The officers all stood and Mr. Burkart began to tear the letter up in pieces, not regular pieces, but little bitty pieces.

"Welcome aboard sailor!" We all shook hands. I genuinely felt they were pleased to have me.

Pappy called. "Come on – Sailor -- you got some painting to do. -- We gotta show Europe how pretty we are!"

We stepped into the corridor and the Chief stopped and looked me up and down. "I think we got a painters suit in just your size!"

The boat had just been repainted from bow to stern with that familiar grey paint. The task at hand now was to shade the flat black paint on all surfaces that can be seen from above. As I looked at the other four boats in our nest I could see how the scheme prevailed. The general look was the same on all the boats, but you could tell that the same hand had not done them all.

Each boat had its own crew and each painted their own boat. It appeared as if I was the chosen one to blend in the black. I thought maybe this was a grunt job that fell to the newest and most unqualified man, but something told me that the resulting appearance of the boat depended a great deal on the way this black was shaded

As I was being instructed on the use of the power sprayer I reflected on the way the school stressed the importance of camouflage on a submarine. The grey paint was on the surfaces that were visible from the sea surface and the black was on the surfaces visible from above.

The areas where the two paints met had to be blended, or faded, so that a distinct line would not attract the eye. When at sea, a long straight line of contrasting colors, would immediately, catch the eye. I donned my paper suit, complete with paper shower cap, shoe covers and mask. I began to spray very carefully on the forward deck areas that were wide and would not overspray the grey.

The paint was thicker than most spray paints, but the pressure was higher also. The paint gun could be adjusted for width and amount of paint. It took some practice, but soon I was feeling confident with my work. At the end of the work day, which was 1400 hours on Friday, while in port, I had the deck done, and had shaded the sail. I knew the area where the deck rolled over to the sides of the superstructure would be much harder and probably a back breaking job. That however, was a weekend away. I was going on liberty as a full-fledged sailor for the first time. " Yoweeeee! – Norfolk here I come!"

Bummer! Norfolk was just as described. I really don't know what I expected. I went downtown and found a side street that sported an arcade, a few doors down was a burlesque house that was featuring some renowned stripper.

I put some coins in a movie machine and turned the crank, the girls would do a little jerky dance and just when they were about to take off some revealing clothing, the machine would stop for more coins. The next show was a different girl and she too, would want more coins to continue and so on. I thought how stupid I was, to keep feeding coins in these things and looking over my shoulder to make sure no one from my boat saw me watching girly shows.

I moved uptown and went to a movie. Glen Ford played a guy that had to get an outlaw on a train by 3:10 to Yuma. I stopped at a drugstore and picked up some electric pre-shave lotion to make my whiskers stand up for my Rolectric. It's alright to laugh if you want to.

I caught the bus to head back to the DE piers. The city bus stopped at a point a little distance from the base. A base bus would then come by and pick up the sailors and take them on a special route that was within the base and at the piers.

I got off the city bus and walked into a little grill where most of the sailors would get a burger or coffee, while waiting for the Greyline [Navy grey bus]. The shore patrol would make frequent stops and check the waiting sailors, if you were out of line in the least, you were in trouble. There was no love between Norfolk and the Navy.

I ordered a coke and as I sat there a sailor tried to open the door. He was so plastered he couldn't figure how to open it. It was standard glass door, framed with metal, a bar across the middle and a handle on one side. You just pulled the handle and it opened, but not for this guy. His white hat was askew, his neckerchief was cocked, his tee shirt was out under his dirty jumper, his laces were untied and he was a total mess and couldn't talk.

All he did was mumble under his breath. He tried to grab the door handle numerous times. He could see the handle and as he wobbled back and forth he would aim his hand at the handle and make a swipe to pull it open, miss the handle and his motion would cause him to stumble backwards almost into the street.

I couldn't help but laugh, and at the same time felt ashamed for a fellow sailor being this drunk.

I rose to help him with the door.

The young lady behind the counter stopped me. "Hey! – Hey! – Fella! – I don't want that drunk in here. - If you let him in -- I'll call the Shore Patrol and they'll take you too!"

"But Ma'am - he's gonna fall out there in the street and maybe get run over!" I exclaimed.

"Tough shit - Sailor -- at least he ain't in here -- if you wanna help him that's fine -- but do it outside and not in front of my place -- got that?"

I did. I went outside and pulled the guy over to the bench by the bus stop. He immediately wanted to lie down. Someone had left a tray of french-fries, loaded with catsup on the bench and he proceeded to lay right in them.

I began to talk to the drunk, hoping to bring him to some sort of sensible condition. I got some napkins and proceeded to wipe as much catsup from his shoulder as possible.

He went fast to sleep, luckily we were the only two there, so the lack of seating was not a problem. It was close to 2000 hours, so it was really early for a Saturday night. I wondered how a guy could get this bombed this early. He must have been at it all day. I pondered, why me?

Why was I so bored that I was returning early and run into this guy. I had to stop pondering because the bus showed up.

I managed with great difficulty to get the guy up and called to the driver. "How bout a hand here – Buddy - we need a little help?"

The driver called back. "Screw you and your buddy - I'll drive ya - but damned if I'll carry ya!"

"Hey that's great - maybe it'll be you someday!" I shouted back.

"If it is - just leave my ass - cause that's what I'd do to you!" He cursed.

I managed to get the drunk to the door, but it was like he was filled with jello. There was no help and every bone in his body was like rubber. I was literally stuffing him on the bus.

The driver finally got up to help drag the poor guy on. He cussed the whole time and said he wasn't gonna help me get him off. I didn't tell him I wasn't going to be on the bus, to get him off.

We waited about fifteen minutes and three more sailors showed up. As the bus pulled away, the lights from the diner caught the sleeves on one of the sailor's arm, it read USS Runner. I knew the bus would now stop at the DE piers. The Runner was sister to my Torsk and tied up alongside her.

Boy, was the driver mad when I got off with the other sailors. He called me names I can't spell and as he pulled away, I shouted. "Just ride him till he wakes up!"

As we walked along the sailor from the Runner asked me which boat I was on.

"I'm a new guy on the Torsk." I replied.

Ahh! – You're the AWOL guy? He quizzed.

I had to laugh. "Man! – The scuttlebutt sure gets around - don't it?"

The guy asked. "Heard you whipped six guys and dragged em to the brig and locked em up yourself! -- That so?"

I stopped, we were in front of the telephone center and I wanted to call home. I looked at the guy. "That's ridiculess – Man! - It was only three guys and the marines locked em up!" I turned and walked into the phone center.

Dad answered and was really glad to hear from me. I did not mention the AWOL issue, hoping that he would, if they had received any word. I could tell that all was well, they had no clue and I left it that way. I wired fifty bucks home and watched a movie topside with about thirty of the crew, my new family. There wasn't a bad egg in the bunch.

We had a brunch on Sunday, a young seaman named Ferrand held a Bible study in the forward torpedo room. I didn't go. I slept in, if you can call it that. At night it seemed that everyone took care not to slam the chow hall door. It is attached to the bulkhead at the head of my bunk. During the day it is slammed repeatedly without regard to anyone sleeping. I would learn about selective sleeping in the weeks to come, but that luxury was not mine yet.

I fell in love with Sundays on the Torsk that first weekend. The brunch was special, a wide variety of breakfast fare as well as lite lunch venue. It was from 1000 to1400 hours. No big meal at night, just sandwich stuff and whatever we had left over from brunch. We always had an early movie and then a night flic. It was indeed a relaxing time and prepared a guy for a strenuous Monday. I spent a lot of the day roaming the boat and getting used to the layout.

The Torsk was about 312 feet long. That's exterior length, now take away the forward and after trim tanks and super structure and that left around 230 feet of interior space. The widest beam was less than 30 feet, including saddle tanks. The interior width was around 15 feet, when you add piping, cabinets, lockers and equipment, that leaves squirm room only.

Except for forward and after torpedo rooms, there are two decks. The upper deck was for operation and crew. A crewman could stand erect in most all areas we had to operate in. The lower deck was for batteries and storage and the bottom of the engines and electric motors were located there. The headroom on the lower deck was restricted in many cases.

No amount of training can prepare a man for the change in his life style, like living on a submarine. The training we went through was designed to weed out the men that had super egos, identify men with inflated images of self-importance, and reduce the chances of personality conflicts. The training is usually very accurate, however, should a man suffering from a case of meitis [me, I, syndrome] slip by; he will soon be discovered and if he can't make the adjustment, he will be removed from the submarine program.

Its little things, like trying to sleep late on a Saturday or Sunday. At night the door from the chow hall to the sleeping quarters is opened and closed with care to allow men to sleep in peace. The same care is given to this door when at sea, because when underway the operation of the boat is the same day or night. There is always someone who needs sleep. When in port, however it's different during the day. The stainless steel door is mounted on a stainless steel bulkhead and is spring loaded to shut, it's quite loud. A sailor is sleeping in and the door slams next to his head. I know of that which I speak. The average person would think that the door slam is inconsiderate, however a submariner's thinking is, why should that bother me and soon it doesn't bother him anymore.

Submarine sailors learn little things to do that make life easier. Normally there is never a time to lounge around when at sea. A submariner sailor seldom gets a long sleep and soon learns to put his head down and go straight to sleep and wake instantly, ready to perform whatever duty he is called on for. We normally sleep fully clothed when operating. One of the little things, I spoke of, is noticing everything going on around you.

A sailor may not know who stands every watch nor has every duty assignment, but a little observation will tell you the whole story. A glance at a duty station will identify who the man is and what he's doing. A quick look at the clock will tell you how much longer he will be there. If you happen to be in the sleeping compartment at the change of a watch, don't get involved in a task that will interfere with the watch change.

Here is an example how important it is to learn the little unwritten details that make life easier on the Torsk. I was much rested that first Monday and was up maybe ten minutes before reveille. Both toilets were occupied when I went to the head, so I proceeded to shave and brush my teeth. The stall door opened on the aft john, and a machinist mate named Brinkley stepped out, he was still tucking in. He could tell I was about to enter the john.

"Hold on!" He glanced at my name on my chambray. "Wardy - you better wait a bit!" He glanced at his watch.

I laughed. "Is it that bad?" I was thinking of the smell.

He grinned and at the same time the PA called "Reveille! – Reveille! – All hands up and turn too with the daily routine! – Reveille! – Reveille!" He looked at me and pointed up the corridor toward the control room.

The guy sitting on the first throne spoke up. "You shouda let him learn the hard way - Brinkley!"

"Naw! – Some one warned me - so I'm passing it on!" He pulled my shirt sleeve and directed my attention once again up the corridor.

I could not hear what was happening, but I could see crewmen moving out of the corridor and then the chow hall door opened. I could see that a man in a bunk had reached out and was holding the door open and through the control room hatch came Pappy Wright. He was moving at a brisk pace and was barefoot, in his tee shirt and skivvies. His left hand was over his fly and his right hand was stretch out in front of him. Brinkley was holding the hall door to the head open.

Pappy dashed by me, reached for the stall handle, pulled the door open and out came his hose, his aim was remarkable, the pressure was considerable and he heaved a sigh of relief as the stream began to ring against the stainless steel bowl.

I looked at Brinkley, unable to comprehend what I had just seen. "Say thank you - Brinkley! – I just kept you from getting "pissed off" -- Wardy!" Everyone laughed, including Pappy.

That happened every time Pappy slept over four hours. Someone would pass the word. "Pappy's sleeping in!" We would be prepared. I might mention, "Yes some sailors did get pissed off!"

I quickly caught on to the rhythm of the paint gun. The paint pot was an aluminum pot that held close to five gallons of paint. The pressure hose put pressure in the pot and pushed the regulated amount of paint to the gun. The gun then sprayed the desire pressure and syphoned the paint into the mist. The whole thing was adjustable and had very little over spray. I finished the entire topside about 1400 hours on Tuesday.

Pappy was pleased and it felt good to stand on the main road and look at the Torsk from a distance. She was indeed a lean, clean, mean machine and I loved her. She sat pretty high in the water as she was tied up next to her sister boats. We had raised her to expose more tank top area; we then put a list on her to paint one tank top and then the other. We cycled the vents later in the day and lowered her after the paint had dried.

In the process of painting the Torsk, I asked when we were going to sea. To my amazement I was informed we were out-fitting the Torsk to be a part of a NATO Operation and a visit to Leharve, France and Portland, England. We were scheduled to depart 0800 August, 31 1957. The balance of the week was spent on spit and polish. The Chief sent Jim Givens, Dave Cummings and me to the conning tower for a special assignment. "Report to Lessor, he'll clue you in."

Lessor was a second class quarter master and a war veteran. He was ex-frogman, and had been caught in an underwater blast. The entire back of his body, neck, back, legs and arms were damaged by the concussion. Every pore that was exposed was imploded and remained that way. He was a hero in my book. The man was one of my mentors.

"Alright you guys – we're going north in Artic waters and then on to the British Isles and Northern France." Lessor showed us a stack of pages and some clippings. He also brought out some books. "These books have all the navigation information that is referred to on our charts -- these pages are updates and these clippings are corrections and changes. -- You guys got the rest of the week to get em right.-- The pages are a direct replacement -- the clippings will be glued over the original line printed in the book."

He pointed out some bottles of glue with the little rubber nipple that you just spread the glue on with. "You guys work up your own system -- but all three of you must be aware of every action and result. -- That will reduce the chance of error -- cause an error can kill us all. -- Got that!" He barked. We all nodded.

We worked out a system and soon realized that a page may be replaced more than once, so we went through all the pages and clippings to identify duplicates and picked the most recent. There was no need to replace a page and in ten minutes replace the same page again with a more recent update. Same went for clippings. We probably cut our work in half by doing this. The pages went fast. We even found new pages that required a clipping to correct a line or paragraph. The navigation books had such information as to the description of lighthouses, the height above sea levelandshorelinedescription.

Our navigation charts contain important information, but if more written information is required and there is no room on the chart, then you refer to the navigation books. A good navigator will study a location intensively if he must operate in it, especially if you are submerged.

We finished early Thursday afternoon. Lessor was pleased and called Jack Britton, the first class QM. Britton informed us that Mr. Bibby wasn't going to believe we had finished so soon and was sure to check everything out. We said we better double check, he agreed. We had kept the removed pages. So we divided them into the three books we worked with. Picked out the most recent of each page and clipping. We placed the removed material in order and started through each book. We checked each new page or clipping and found each one to be the most recent.

It took less than two hours. We found no mistakes. We were still a day ahead. We didn't say anything to Lessor until the next morning, and he put us to work polishing up the bright work in the conning tower. I liked it up there. Little did I know, it would soon be my second home.

Pappy asked me if I had any art experience. I thought and told him I took an art course in school and painted a picture of my horse, Champion, with the help of my Uncle in Compton, California. Uncle Dennis was an artist for North American Aircraft and had painted the pictures of the F80 Shooting Star, for Lockheed and the F86 Sabre Jet for North American. The paintings were done before the aircraft ever flew, but were done in such detail that you would think they were photographs. He gave me a copy of each and I proudly displayed them on my wall at home.

Pappy said that would do and gave me the job of painting a new brow canvas to display when we got to France. I worked on it, in what little spare time I had. It was a picture of a Fighting Torsk [Codfish] with a cocked white hat, boxing gloves, and a grimace on its face. The fish was at a slight down angle across a 3' by 10' canvass that was laced across the metal brow that connected the boat to the pier when we were in port. The fish was in the foreground of an orange circle with a green border and had a periscope protruding from its back. The boats name was boldly blazoned across the bottom of the canvas. The small drawing, I was to paint from, had the name on a small banner at the bottom. In reality the name was much too small to identify the boat at a distance so the Navy had suggested the bold name at the bottom for the brow painting only. I really felt privileged to have this assignment. It was a daunting task.

I had duty Sunday, but Givens, Cummings, Johnny North and I decided to go to Ocean View on Saturday. It turned out to be an unusually cool and damp night. We played every boardwalk game and all but had the place to ourselves. There was simply no crowd and still fewer girls.

We drank a lot of beer and even though I don't like it, I was buzzing a little. I suppose we were all flying low as we discovered the roller coaster. There was no one on it and the operator was kicked back in his chair under a giant umbrella, chewing on a cigar. It was a quarter a ride, I treated, and handed the guy a dollar and away we went. I don't know if this was the greatest roller coaster in the world or if the 3.2 beer was telling me it was, but we hollered and yelled and genuinely enjoyed it. The ride stopped and we all jumped out and like a bunch of school boys, ran down the exit ramp and right back up the entrance. Givens handed the operator another dollar and away we went again. It was a blast.

As we slowed at the end of the ride, Cummings was holding up a five dollar bill, in anticipation of another round and change. The operator snatched the bill from Cumming's fingers and away we went again. I think he put it in high gear, because in short order we were not yelling and hollowing nearly as loud. At the end of that breathtaking first drop there was a hard left turn. The motion of the car would throw you against the right side of the car. My side was beginning to hurt, so I leaned far to my left and placed both hands on the left side of the car and placed my head down on my extended arms, my left ear was on my Ruxton wristwatch. I did this to keep from crashing into my right side again. We whipped around that first corner and I felt a shock on my left arm and heard my beautiful, self-winding, Ruxton wristwatch make a loud "SPWOONG" sound. It was done for. I suppose the constant movement of that roller coaster wound it so tight that every spring in it broke. I was heartbroken. I didn't feel so good either.

When we finally slowed, the operator looked at us as we approached and held up a finger in a "One More Time" request. Eight hands began to wave NO! – NO! – NO! He grinned and we stopped. We were coasted out and I was heartsick over my watch. We went back to our Torsk. I placed my watch in my locker with all intent to have it repaired and hit the sack.

Tuesday we got underway early and headed across the bay to load a fresh supply of torpedoes and take on munitions.

I went on the helm as a trainee under the tutorage of Catfish Woodson, the cook. Yeh! He was the cook, but he was the deck officer's first choice for that special detail called "Maneuvering Watch." I was at the wheel for the second time in my life, it felt natural. Catfish let me do it all, offering suggestions and speaking in clear distinct tones, gone was his "Yassuh -- Boy" stuff. The man was a first class submariner sailor. I couldn't have asked for a better tutor. Leaving the berth was a simple operation, but getting into our position to load torpedoes at the munitions pier was a different matter. It is impossible to write a description of the regimentation that occurs to berth a submarine.

The helmsman cannot see and relies solely on voice command from the deck officer. The deck officer wants the submarine to move in a manner that puts it alongside a pier in a specific spot. He has voice control, only, he calls his commands down the upper conning tower hatch to me, the helmsman. I do whatever he orders. The helmsman takes no orders from anyone else unless the deck officer releases his command.

Our Captain was E.P.K. King, a graduate of Annapolis and the son of the Ex-Governor of Hawaii. He loved the Torsk as much as I did. It may have been his first command. On occasions the Captain would asked the deck officer. "Do you mind if I park her?" I would hear the information command. "The Captain has the bridge!"

I would generally acknowledge by saying, "Aye – Aye – Sir!" then turn and call down the lower hatch to the control room. "The Captain has the bridge!"

If we were submerged the term would be, "The Captain has the con!" because, obviously, he wouldn't be on the bridge.

I must have done alright because I heard every "Very well" response.

I heard Mr. Wiseman shout to the deck crew that manned the bow and stern lines. "Cinch em up good boys - we gotta lotta fireworks to load!"

He called down the hatch. "Good job Wardlaw - tell Catfish to go burn some biscuits - we got a new maneuvering watch helmsman!" I turned, Catfish was already gone.

It felt strange, when the engines shut down. The comforting vibrations of those massive Fairbanks Morse diesels were gone and the boat almost seemed to be resting. It was very quiet in comparison to being underway.

We rigged our boom, that was kept stored under our deck superstructure, and a couple of guys began some maintenance on it by chippling or sanding rust and corrosion. The loading crew pulled four fish [torpedos] from our forward torpedo room and moved two of them aft and loaded them into our after torpedo room. The other two were sent to the ammunition storage. We then took on six new fish to max out our capacity. Some of the fish were older models that we were going to fire and just let them sink and some were practice shots that we would retrieve after firing. We also had some hot ones too.

We left with a full complement of armament. Seldom did a U.S. Submarine go to sea without a quota of hot torpedoes. We were in the midst of the late fifties cold war and our guard was always up. Someone had to stand up to those Russkies!

It was well after 2100 when we made it back to Norfolk, we tied up along-side pier 23. I was alone at the wheel on the return trip. Mr Bibby had the bridge and it went smooth as silk. When we tied up and everything was secured, I requested permission to come up on the bridge.

Mr. Bibby replied. "Come on up - Wardlaw."

I looked around and saw the Orion, our tender, off to port, she was all alone at pier 22. The other subs were spread around the piers.

I looked out over the bay and saw the running lights of the Runner as she was approaching. She intended to tie up along our port side. Our deck crew was waiting to take her lines. It was a thrill to see the sailors on the Runner, throw their hand lines to our deck crew. Our crew would then pull the hand lines in with the heavy mooring lines attached and make them fast on our cleats.

Mr. Bibby turned to me and placed his hands on each of my shoulders and squared me up in front of him. I felt like a little kid. "Wardlaw - you had quite a ride to get here - you know that?"

I nodded. "I think you are supposed to be here, sailor!" I thanked him and started to go below.

"By –the - way!" He added. "'This is your boat - when not underway -- you don't need to request permission to go anywhere on your boat." I thanked him again. He was a good officer.

We spent all day Wednesday carrying stores from the Orion to our boat. It was backbreaking labor. We probably had fifty of our crew lined up down the corridor of the sleeping quarters on the Orion as we waited our turn to load a case of lettuce, or some other vegetable on our shoulder. Some of the guys carried the forty pound sacks of flour to a huge roller cart. It was neatly stacked and a half dozen of the crew would start pushing the cart from pier 22 to pier 23, where the Torsk was tied up. We were only a portion of what was happening. All the boats had the same operation going on. The piers were crowded with carts being pushed, trucks of supplies being unloaded and sailors carrying supplies on their shoulders. It was a massive display of preparation.

When we reached our boat, all the supplies had to be passed by hand from man to man and down hatches and stored away in a proper place. The officers worked right alongside the enlisted men.

Catfish was preparing the evening meal, and would not let anyone store anything in his dry storage room. He made us set it on the deck and between his peeling, stirring and putting stuff in the oven; he would dash down the ladder and store the supplies himself. Pappy told him he was going to work himself to death.

He told the Chief. "Pappy - if you wants to eat it -- I gotta cook it -- to cook it -- I gotta find it and I'll never finds it with dem melon heads storing it -- so leaves me be!"

Pappy retorted. "Yassuh! – Mr. Catfish! – Yassuh!" The respect between the two men was evident.

From the Orion to where we were moored was well over a quarter of a mile, if walking. The Orion now had to replenish in order to be prepared for her next supplying venture. It was a classic example of how a plan can work when you work the plan. I felt honored to be part of it.

It was Friday August 30, 1957 and payday. As we were lined up for our money, some of the first guys in line ahead of us were beating it out to the Western Union Office. Our curiosity got the best of us and we found out we were getting four paydays in one, and a lot of the sailors were wiring money home. I got paid a little over two hundred fifty bucks. I wired a hundred home to Daddy. Man I felt rich. We were not scheduled to return from the NATO operation until the 23 of October, so that was four paydays, three in advance. I suppose that's the only way it would work and it suited us just fine.

We backed out of pier 23 at 2300 hours on August 31, 1957. We were in route to be an integral part of the NATO Exercise of 1957. I was at my wheel.

"Port back one third!" Came the order. I answered.

"Very well! - Left full rudder!" I answered. "The ships whistle sounded one long blast. That's ship talk saying we were underway.

"Rudder amidship!" Came the order. I answered.

"Starboard back one third!" Another order. I answered.

I called out. "Rudder is amidship! – Answered starboard back one third!"

Mr. Wiseman replied. "Very Well! – All stop!"

My reply. "Answered all stop!"

Mr. Wiseman. "Very well! – Left full rudder – Starboard ahead one third!"

My answer. "Left full rudder – Starboard ahead one third! I had already spun the wheel to port and gave some information. " Rudder is approaching left full, Sir!"

"Very well! - Starboard stop! – Rudder amidship!"

Sometimes a new order will come before a confirmation can be given for the last order, when that happens you act on the new order and forget the old because it makes no sense to confirm an order that no longer exists. Here's an example. Mr. Wiseman just ordered; "Starboard stop! – Rudder amidship! -- before I can confirm, he orders. "All ahead two thirds!"

I answer, "All ahead two thirds," and don't mention starboard stop because it now must go to two thirds ahead, but I must acknowledge, "Rudder amidship! – Answered all ahead two thirds!" I must inform him when the rudder approaches the amidship position. We are now in the bay and heading for the channel. Seldom do we steer a course in a channel. The deck officer will visibly sight markers or buoys and give orders like. "Come left ten degrees!"

I answer and check the present heading only to know when the ten degrees is reached. I will answer when the new course is reached.

The deck officer will respond. "Very well!"

Now I haven't mentioned the enunciators. These devices have a knob in the center and two dials that indicates the speed and direction of the propellers. There is an enunciator for port and starboard props. They are officially called engine order enunciators, but really don't change anything on the engines.

The engines turn generators that power electric motors that turn the props. When I received a speed request, I turn the dial in the center of the enunciator and the needle goes to the requested speed. The sailor manning the electric controls, in the maneuvering room, reads a dial that duplicates my request and he instantly pulls handles, turns knobs, flips switches and makes the electric motors turn the props as requested. He immediately turns his dial to agree with the request and when I see his agreement, I report to the deck officer with the familiar, "Answered" response. This seldom takes over a few seconds. It is truly a remarkable scenario. The working bond between a deck officer and the helmsman is necessary for a submarine to maneuver effectively.

On my cruises as a reserve, we never went far out to sea. Believe me, the sea is different when you get to really deep water. We continued to dive and operate with the Barbero and Runner. We would be the target for a run and then swap around and perform S1R's on the other boats.

I would race to the after torpedo room and unroll the new brow piece and paint a little every time I had a few moments. I was beginning to think, maybe, I wouldn't have time to finish it. Then again, France was nearly a month away, maybe, I was worrying needlessly.

The next night, September 2, at around 0230, I returned to the bridge after my break. I brought coffee for Mr. Mobley and Tighe. As I called up the hatch for Mr. Mobley to take the coffee, he said softly. "Hurry –Wardlaw - the lights are on - you don't want to miss em!" I had heard of the Aurora Borealis, but had never seen them. Mr. Mobley told us that this display was not nearly as spectacular as some he had seen. We swapped the watch around quickly and called some more of the crew to see the display.

A lot of the old timers weren't interested, but I was fortunate to watch a good half hour of the "Northern Lights." There would be a flash and ripples of white light with an edge of maybe blue or purple light, occasionally the lights would perform like a curtain and undulate. It was strange because I noticed no reflection of the lights on the water and even though they were very noticeable, they really had no great brilliance. They faded off to our east and were gone by 0300.

The sea had become a huge plane of gentle swells; it was by no means smooth, but seemed to swell in gentle upheavals that spanned hundreds of yards. The swells were so far apart and gentle that there were no white caps. As the boat cut through the dark water at close to 13 knots, the bow would rise gently and then softly descend downward in time with the swells. As the bow would gently submerged and disturb the fluorescents that lived in the water, they would react and cast a quick flash of light under our bow. It was as if someone under our boat took a flash bulb picture of us as we went over them. The fluorescents were visible when the ripples left the sides of the boat as she swept through the sea. Sometimes we would see a great flash of light deep under water and realize we had startled a great school of fish and their sudden flight disturbed the fluorescents.

I went off watch at 0400 and hit the sack immediately. I slept like a log, but was up at 0700. I shaved, brushed my teeth and bathed with my wash cloth; it took, maybe a half cup of water. We dove as I was finishing my eggs and hash browns. We immediately went to battle stations. I sopped my toast on the plate to get the balance of that delicious mixture and one handed it into a pocket book sandwich, with the other hand I placed my plate and silverware in the sink and lit out for the wheel.

I took my position at the helm and already the Skipper was at the battle scope picking up the range on the Barbero. We made another S1T run on her and then surfaced. This operation took less than ten minutes. I went below and began to clean the after battery deck in the sleeping quarters. I was tempted to slip in my bunk and go back to sleep. I probably could have done that and gotten a little more rest. My conscience kept me on my knees. I had finished the little nook where I slept and was scrubbing the deck in the rear section of my bunk row, when I felt the boat begin to veer to port, in a moment we veered to starboard, and picked up speed. I could feel the increased vibrations of the screws. Something was up.

An electrician named Dilks was coming through the corridor. "Dilks! What's going on?" I asked.

We're target for the Runner." He replied.

"Ok - but why the zig-zag and speed change - we usually just stay straight." I remarked.

"Well that's when we play like a dummy - this time we're playing smart and we know they are there and are being evasive -- it gives them good practice."

I thanked Dilks for the heads up, and went back to work.

I was hoping to get the entire deck in the crew's quarters done before lunch. I went back on watch at 1200. It would be nice to get off watch and not have the rest of the job to finish. Our deck cleaning method was simple. We take a pan of clear water, a steel wool pad and a clean white rag. Dip the steel wool in the water and scrub a section of the tile. Wipe it with the rag and check to see how much dirt came up. The condition of the rag tells you if the tile is clean. No soap is used ever on the deck. We never put anything slippery on the deck. Too much slippery stuff gets on it by accident. Slips or stumbles when an emergency occurs could be disastrous.

"AHUUUGAH! – AHUUUGAH! – Dive! – Dive!" Forget cleaning the deck, I thought. I knew battle stations were soon to follow. Yep! The time I felt the boat level off, I knew we were at periscope depth. The boat's PA cried "Battle Stations Torpedo!" I stashed my bowl and pad in the port drain run and headed for the conning tower.

"Angle on the bow - mark!" Exclaimed the Skipper. "Range to target - mark!" Mr. Bibby would record the angle and distance and another man would enter the info in the TDC [torpedo data computer]. This electronic computer cut the computation time for the firing resolution to a minimum. Back during WWII, it would take some few minutes to reach a firing resolution. With the TDC it took seconds and the info was electronically sent to the torpedo. The S1T this time was a real torpedo. We had loaded two older fish that were no longer in our current arsenal as mainline weapons and fired the first at the Barbero. It was an old Mark 23 Model O expendable.

The torpedo we fired at the Barbero had no warhead. The data fed to the TDC was altered and was designed to miss the target by a certain distance. All of this information is recorded, every angle, degree, course, speed, depth and time.

The time is recorded to the split second. The target also records the information of their statistics and will report the sighting on the fish as it makes its run. When an operation is completed, all this information is compiled and sent to the Naval Department and the results are compared and each boat in given a grade.

The Naval operation review team actually takes an overlay of the operation area and puts tiny mock boats on the overlay. They then retrace the data supplied to them from the various participants and can judge the effectiveness of the boat's operation. It's that simple.

The Torsk is on the board at the location, speed, course, depth and time reported. The Barbero is placed in its reported scenario. Draw a line for the course the torpedo takes from the Torsk and if that line intersects the Barbero. "Pow!" The Torsk gets credit for a kill. It works and is very accurate. The information reported by the boats in also very accurate. It is very obvious; if the information is flawed a shadow of doubt is cast on the boats credibility. It is a matter of honor and credibility to be accurate.

We had dived at 1044, ran the S1T and surfaced at 1123. I hadn't gone far, because I heard Captain King tell Mr. Bibby that it felt so good firing that real fish that he wanted to send one to Bill Crowder on the Runner. We weren't surfaced much more than five minutes before we plunged again and went after the Runner.

The clang of the battle station alarm sounded as we reached periscope depth. I knew it was coming and had stayed in the control room to be close. I climbed back up the ladder and took the wheel, from Clyde Derricot. He told me the course and plummeted down the ladder to take his post in the forward torpedo room.

The Captain turned his hat around, yes, just like in the movies, and placed his eye to the scope and began calling the conditions of the target. Angle on the bow, range, speed, Mr. Bade the exec repeated and recorded the info and the computer operator in-put the data. In a few seconds we had our firing resolution and the Skipper ordered, "Fire two!" I could imagine a tremble as the air blasted the Mark 23, Model O expendable fish from its tube and on the way to the Runner. I wondered how it felt to be theoretically doomed. I was soon to find out.

We secured battle stations at 1152. Our noon meal was ready and we were still down as I ate early and went to take my watch at the stern planes. We were at 100 feet and making three knots. The order came to surface. "Five degree up bubble!" Came the order. "Blow main ballast!"

The Chief of the boat repeated the command as he worked the valves and levers to force the high pressure air into the ballast tanks. We broke the surface in a few moments and the order came. "Secure the high pressure! - Turn on the low pressure blowers!" The Chief answered and performed with rapid precision as the deck officer headed up the ladder. We stowed the planes and followed him to the bridge to take our lookout post.

As I ducked under the faring and came up in my lookout port, I saw the Runner off our starboard after beam at about 1000 yards and she's was going down. The bow plummeted under the waves as giant spurts of water was blasted up from under her deck by the air gushing from the open valves that allow the sea water to fill her ballast tanks. She glided smoothly under the sea and I could see the bubbles from the air still escaping from the hidden crevices in her superstructure. She left a trail for a short distance and was gone. It was a sobering site.

Mr. Mobley, the deck officer told us that we were the enemy now. We were playing the part of an enemy ship that was stationary in the water and the Runner was going to have to dodge imaginary mines and line us up for a shot.

"Keep a sharp look out for the torpedo now – Boys! – It's a real fish just like we shot! - It's a dummy but if their aim is off - we may get hit. - We don't want a big dent in our hull – now - do we?"

"All stop!" Called Mr. Mobley.

"All stop!" Came the answer from the helmsman below. "Answered all stop!"

"Very well!" Mr. Mobley brought his glasses up and began to scan from the bow to the starboard quarter. I scanned from the beam aft, then back to the bow. I found that it was best to scan with the bare eye, and then use the binoculars if you spot something. Time dragged slowly by.

The time came to rotate our watch. Mr. Mobley told us to forget it. "Stay were you are and don't break your concentration on spotting that torpedo!" Time continued to drag. The sea was relatively calm with a few white caps, spread out maybe twenty to thirty yards apart. Mr. Mobley and I saw it at the same time. I picked up a splash that caught my eye; it was out of sync with the white caps. I put my glasses on the splash and there she came, just like in the movies. Twenty feet of speeding torpedo just under the surface and leaving a bubbly trail.

"Torpedo off the starboard quarter - Sir!" I called.

"Got it - Wardlaw! - Forty degrees off the bow!" He dropped his glasses, leaned forward and squinted his eyes, he leaned a little more.

Suddenly he cried "All back full!"

The helmsman answered and I could hear the "ding ding" of the enunciators as they sent their message. I heard the "ding ding' as the maneuvering room answered and immediately the boat shook with the torque of the huge twin props as they dug into the water and began to pull close to 1600 tons backwards. We backed maybe twenty seconds.

"All stop!" called Mr. Mobley.

The Helmsman answered, the shuddering ceased and the boat continued to back a little then sat still. We watch in awe as the missile passed closed to 25 yards across our bow. Mr. Mobley's keen eye had seen a perfect shot and had he not backed us down, that missile would have struck us amidship at over 35 knots. That would have put quite a dent in our starboard ballast tank. It was a hopeless feeling, seeing that potentially deadly dart coming at us. Had the fish been two feet deeper in the water, we may not have seen it in time to steer clear.

We could hear the UQC [under water telephone] squawking our call name "Luna Light – Lunar Light" as Captain Crowder from the Runner was calling to boast of his nice shot, to Captain King.

He said "Evan, we heard you backing down so I know you saw the fish -- we set it for a surface run to make sure you saw it. -- We killed you – Buddy -- You know that don't you!"

"We'll wait to see what the NRT [Naval Review Team] says!" replied our Captain. "Say - Crowder – What error did you put on paper?"

"Thirty yards off the bow - Buddy – See ya next exercise!" The UQC went quiet. The captain moved our recorded position to the spot we were in, after backing down. He was a true gentleman, and wasn't going to cause the Runner a problem with a right on shot. He wasn't going to deny the Runner a kill either.

We were somewhere off the coast of New Foundland Island. The water depth was around 700 feet, and the water temperature was getting colder.

Our daily operations were constant cleanups, man overboard drills, battle stations, sonar drills. We moved away from New Foundland, the water depth went to over 3000 feet. I worked on the brow painting in the few spare minutes I could find.

We continued to sail northeast and by Saturday, September 7, we broke out the special cold weather gear for topside watch. The water temperature was now in the frigid zone and the sea was giant swells that rose to fifteen or more feet.

The gear was a suit that zipped up the front with a sealed zipper, a hood that had a rubber pressed fit seal around the neck, gloves and boots that sealed to the suit. The suit was a rubber impregnated light weight fabric that once the wearer was sealed inside did a most magnificent job of keeping the wearer dry and relatively warm.

This was my first encounter with heavy water. Heavy water is when you are completely engulfed in water. The sea can come at you in many different ways. The sea can have large waves that are close together and the waves will actually pass over you. This is not so bad, you are under the water for only a second or two and you can steel your body against the force of the water. But it can get mean. The sea can have waves that reach twenty to thirty feet high and be far apart. The boat is only 312 feet long and if the waves are two hundred feet apart it can be perilous. The submarine will ride up the crest on a twenty feet wave, as the boat slices through the wave the center of the boat reaches the apex of the wave. The entire front half of the craft is now twenty or more feet in the air. As the wave moves aft the forward weight of the boat takes control and the sub plummets into the trough between the waves. The propellers will be completely out of the sea and the boat will vibrate violently as the screws spin in the air. The subs 1600 tons will crash down the back slope of the swell and the boat dives under the next wave. The wall of water will hit you at your speed plus the speed of the sea. The lookouts and the OD [officer of the deck] are submerged sometimes twenty or more feet under water. You must hold your breath and be ready to flip your glasses of water, wipe your eyes and take a quick scan as you crest the next wave. The sea can be so ferocious that the look outs must be strapped in to prevent being washed away.

This type of sea is especially dangerous. There is the constant impact of water, and also the limited visibility. Other ships nearby can be completely out of view if you are down between swells and they are also.

We spent long hours submerged now as we were engaged in an exercise called "Fish Play II." We had set our clocks ahead one hour a few days earlier, to coincide with the current time zone.

We went to silent running as we stealthily stalked the Runner and Barbero. They too were running silent and stalking us as well. The propellers on a submerged boat are much quieter than when on the surface. They don't cavitate [pick up air] and the engines don't run. We actually listen to the sounds that are generated underwater. It is not a quiet world. Schools of fish make sounds as they flash by. It takes a good sonar man to pick up on these sounds. A skilled man may be able to tell the difference between the size of the schools and the size of the fish as well. Shrimp will drive you crazy. If a school is any size at all, the thunderous clicking sounds will make your listening devices useless.

Whales have a soulful moaning sound and they are varied, I suppose with their mood and anxieties. The presents of a submarine doesn't seem to concern a whale a great deal.

Porpoises or Dolphins, now, that's another animal altogether, they are curious and playful. We could imagine what they were saying as we could hear them all around us. Some of the guys would listen to a Dolphin call and make a comical interpretation.

A dolphin found one of our hydrophones, it is a waterproof microphone that protrudes from the boat about five inches and has a metal frame to protect it. I suppose that we were the only thing solid for hundreds of miles and this giant mammal needed a back scratch. SCRONNNCH ---- SCRUNNNCH – SCRIMP-SCRIMP-SCRIMP – Weeeeeeee! – Whoooooo! – Wahhhhhhh! We prayed he would leave us and go scratch himself on the Barbero or Runner. The operation was useless for us. Budda Phillips interpreted the whistles. "Ahhhh! – That's it! – right there! – Ahhhh! No! – Don't stop! – Up a little! - Yeah! – Right there! – Uhhh! – OHHH! - I wish I had a cigarette!" That blew the run silent mode; the crew erupted in uncontrolled laughter.

Suddenly, every one grew quiet and found something to do, as the Chief stuck his head in the forward torpedo room hatch. He whispered loudly. "What de hell's goin on in here, boys?"

Budda replied. "Danged if we know Chief. That blamed porpoise is making so much noise we can't hear anything!"

Bromley crossed his eyes and almost burst out laughing. Welsh goosed him and he buried his face in his pillow to control himself.

The Torsk had been to sea for sixteen days now. The only operation we had not done, was guide a missile and that was our primary job. Our part in the NATO operation was to act as the enemy and stop a combined surface fleet of Canadian, Norwegian, British and American ships. We were in route to the North Sea. The North Sea was to be our patrol area.

We were on the surface running dark and listening for radar. We were doing about six knots when the Captain decided to dive. We went to 90 feet and were at close to five knots for a short time. We heard a "Bravo Call" on the UQC. It was the USS Grouper SSK 214, one of our allies in the operation. The Skippers wanted to swap movies. That was swell, we had seen ours at least three times each, since we left Norfolk.

I was not on watch and asked Mr. Bibby if I could throw a hand line to the Grouper. Mr. Bibby told me OK, but a lot of folks were watching and if I screwed it up, I better be prepared for the ridicule. I wished I hadn't asked.

I picked up a hand line and Collins had one also. He looked at me and said. "You got one shot, boy, and that's it! We want dem movies!"

The coiled hand line was one hundred feet of 3/8 nylon rope, it was soft and supple from frequent use. The monkey's fist was tight and dandled with anticipation. I held the line in my right hand with my index finger between the coil and the line going into the monkey's fist. The tight little fist added just enough weight to the end of the line to act as a missile.

The sea was calm and the water had a thick look to it. The sky was overcast but visibility was good and the two boats were only about 60 feet apart. I stood on deck with Collins as my backup. With a side arm swing, I unleashed my hand line with all my strength. My eagerness to succeed and inexperience caused me to put way too much power in my swing. I immediately felt that familiar sickening pain that is a result of hyperextension. My aim was perfect though. The line sailed straight in front of the sail on the Grouper and went taught as I held my end.

Collins whistled and softly said. "Somebody's been practicing!" I hadn't practiced enough to know when to pull up and stop that hyperextension, though.

The high line transfer went well, and we swapped four movies. It was always an adventure to swap movies at sea. The boats never discussed the names of the movies, we just swapped movie for movie, so it was always a gamble to see what gems we would come up with. Two of these, were jewels, "Elephant Walk" and "Johnny Concho." The other two were movies we had already seen. So we knew we would see a lot of elephants and a lot of Frank Sinatra.

The high line transfer took place shortly after 0600 and it was fully day this far north. The transfer took about fifteen minutes and we were clear and going our separate ways. We had been operating independently for a few days now and were looking for land.

The southern coast of Iceland came into view at 0637 on the morning of September 15, 1957. We changed course and headed south. We were now going to play our part in "Operation Strike back."

The entire time we were operating with the Runner and Barbero and even the encounter with the Grouper, we had to keep hidden. The Navy monitored all reports of contacts and the evaluating teams would grade us on how well we stayed out of sight.

In addition to our drills and practicing torpedo shots at each other we had to dodge commercial ships and aircraft as well. We spent our nights on the surface, running dark. If we saw lights of a ship, we listened for radar, if radar was not heard we would silently slip by and the unsuspecting souls would never know that a deadly predator was just off their beam. I would train my binoculars on a merchant sailor leaning against the side rail of his freighter; he would light a cigarette and draw a drag in complete security, never suspecting that death was looking straight at him.

The water was still frigid as we caught sight of Halten Light on the Norwegian Coast. Activity really picked up now as we entered the North Sea, we dove repeatedly to dodge aircraft and merchant ships. We were constantly getting radar hits when on the surface. We were nearing the operating area for "Strikeback." Our job had changed, we were now going to patrol an area and wreak havoc on the enemy fleet.

Our operating area was in the middle of the North Sea. The Torsk was doing what she does best, running silent at 300 feet. We were pros at this now. If an alarm was set we passed the word by whispers and hand signs. Every man working in a compartment was constantly bending over and glancing through the hatch at the men in the next compartment, watching for hand signs. If battle stations were set, a sailor would pass the word by taking a fighter's stance and throwing a few punches, and the men seeing this would pass it on. Some of the guys would simulate firing a 50 caliber machine gun by putting his fist together and vibrating them in mock recoil.

We had been "on go" for "Strikeback" for over ten hours. That's a long time to run silent. It means the heat in the boat builds, because of no air conditioning. The air handlers are run at a very low speed for silence and less vibrations. The cooks don't stir anything. Talking is at a minimum and in whispers. The boat is trimmed to as near neutral buoyancy as possible so we can use the low speed to change depths without having to increase power. We definitely don't want to pump any air. It is very peaceful, and can lull you into a false sense of wellbeing.

The sonar room reported that there was a lot of noise on the surface, but could not identify anything. This was strictly from listening only; we dared not use our pinging sonar. Sonar would be a dead give way to our presence. The Captain went to the sonar room, located at the entrance to the forward torpedo room. He returned and discussed what he heard with Mr. Burkart and Mr. Bibby. He said it sounded like the entire surface fleet but it was like listening through a wall. The sounds were everywhere, fast screws [props], slow screws, little screws and big screws. The sounds were weak, but he couldn't put his finger on it.

"I don't think they are far away. It's like our volume is on low." Mr. Bibby suggested the amplifier may be malfunctioning.

Captain King said, "Sonar checked it and it was the same on the back up amplifier." We went to battle stations; I was already on watch at the wheel, so I didn't have to move.

"Bring her up to 200 feet easy, Control!" The Skipper whispered.

The word was passed by sound powered phone to control. The planesmen slowly put a little up angle on the bow and stern planes. The hydraulic pumps worked at a slow pace and hopefully would not be heard over all the other noise that was in the water. The Captain turned on the UQC [under water telephone]. The noise was there and indeed sounded low. It didn't sound far off; it was very distinct, just low. Captain King twisted the volume knob wide open and the hollow sound of space gave evidence that this amplifier was working, but the surface noise didn't get that much louder. We could definitely hear props turning. Many props.

"Ease to 100 feet, Control!" The Captain commanded softly. The Torsk's planes responded sweetly, but we didn't rise as smartly as before.

Captain King could be a bit impatient at times and was watching the depth gauge in the conning tower. He darted to the lower hatch, crouched and hissed down to Mr. Sheehan. "How about that depth change -- Mr. Sheehan?" His voice had a note of sarcasm.

"She slow coming up Captain! -- I think we are under a thermal layer." The Captain went back with his ear in front of the UQC. The depth gauge finally reached 100 feet.

The sounds were much more distinct now but still did not seem to be any louder.

We had been making slow turns, just enough speed for our planes to be effective.

The phoneman informed the Captain that Mr. Sheehan reported a thermal layer of almost 15 degrees. That is extreme and the difference in water density is keeping the submarine from rising as quickly as desired.

"Hell, we can't tell what's going on down here and the fleet may just sail away. We'll miss them if we don't do something. We may have missed them already!"

There was no doubt; the Skipper had made up his mind. "Bring her up to periscope depth -- smartly now! -- Mr. Sheehan!"

I could barely hear Mr. Sheehan's command. "Full rise on the planes boys! Level at 55 feet. An agonizing moment passed. "We're not rising Captain!" Mr. Sheehan's voice was tense. "This layer's got us!"

Here is some more of the physics that play such an important part in the operation of a submarine. A thermal is when a layer of water of varying depths will have a significant difference in temperature. The density of water will change with temperature. The submarine has been trimmed to match the density of the water you are in, so if you encounter a thermal layer where the water is suddenly warmer, then the submarine has negative buoyancy compared to the present water. Our slow speed couldn't penetrate the layer. There was no time to go through a lengthy process of re-trimming the boat, the simplest solution was speed.

"Make turns for 6 knots - Maneuvering!" The phone man re-layed the command. The boat responded and rose rapidly, I could hear Mr. Sheehan order the planesmen to compensate so we wouldn't broach the surface.

"WHOOMP – WHOOMP – WHOOMP!" The surface sounds were deafening. Whatever was subduing the sound was gone. I reached for the UQC knob and turned it down without being ordered. It was a natural response on my part and it was an arm reach away. Mr. Bibby gave an approving nod. I felt relieved. The Captain didn't even look as he was already crouched to meet the battle scope as it came up from its recess in the deck.

Captain King swung his hat around and placed his eye to the scope as it emerged from the deck hole. He raised his hand in a hold fashion and Mr. Bibby stopped the scope ascent.   The Captain's fingers began the "ease her up" motions, and then his fist closed in that "hold it" mode.

"WooWee! – Lowe – We're in the middle of the fleet.   There's the Champlain! – Angle on th---------------!"   The noise on the UQC once again was annoyingly loud. The Captain swung the scope around to our stern.

"SOUND COLLISION! – SOUND COLLISION!" His command was urgent. I reached for the alarm handle and as I pulled it down the boat suddenly rolled violently to starboard. The alarm sounded and the lower hatch shut with a bang. The roll pulled me away from the alarm so it did not sound long, but our training paid off.   There was no impact of any kind, just a pronounced roll to starboard.

Captain King was still at the scope and began to pull at his right earlobe. He swung the scope as he watched the destroyer that nearly rammed us speed by at over 30 knots. Captain King said it was so close that he couldn't see any grey as the white of the ships numbers passed by the scope. He said he was sure he saw their Captain sitting on the john as a port hole passed us by.

It was a close call. We were at periscope depth, which placed the top of our sail faring close to ten feet below the surface. A destroyer draws nearly seventeen feet of draft. The water being push by the speeding brow of the ship actually pushed our boat out of the way and we escaped a collision by only a few inches.

The destroyer never knew we were there. She was probably chasing our ghost image on sonar. The thermal layer will actually deflect a sonar signal and make the target seem some distance from its actual location.

We all quickly recovered from our near miss and the officers were back at the mock war.

"Left ten degrees rudder!" Came the order.

I answered in a subdued tone. The Captain was back on the scope giving data on the USS Lake Champlain CV39. She was one of our finest carriers of the Essex class. We fired three fish at her. The fish, of course, were hypothetical, but for realism the torpedo tubes were loaded with air and we fired three green flares to meet Navy regulations.

The resulting scenario was to duplicate real life conditions. The sound of the giant air burst was to simulate the torpedoes as they left the tubes. The flares were fired to coordinate with the hypothetical blast as the torpedoes hit their targets.

"Right full rudder! – All ahead full! – Take her to 70 feet!" The Captain knew we couldn't stay there.

The resulting action from the surface fleet was instantaneous and expected. The UQC noise became, once again, almost deafening as the destroyer escorts and destroyers reacted and began to swarm at where we had been.

"Rudder amidship! – Make turns for 4 knots! – Come to periscope depth!" Ordered the Captain. He met the scope as it was on the way up and quickly scanned.

"It's the Essex, men!" I could tell by his body English, he was excited. Can you believe we're lining up the Essex. The USS Essex CV9 was one of our most revered carriers and we were going to sink her. The data flowed with that usual precision and we unloaded three more torpedoes from our deadly make believe arsenal along with three green flares.

"That's two for the books - fellows! – Now we gotta hide! – Pray that thermal is still there! – Fire three false targets and take her down to 300 feet Mr.

Sheehan!" The Captain straightened his hat and gave one of his few smiles, cocked his head and gave a tongue "Clich!"

The Captain was a happy man. "Now - just don't get us sunk - Boss!" I thought.

We reached our depth and the Captain gave orders for all stop. Luckily the thermal layer was still at around 100 feet. We could clearly hear the flurry of action on the surface and the UQC began to squawk of "Ringers". Ringers are weak depth charges that are loaded with yellow phosphorescent paint. The charges are dropped and when they detonate the paint will stick to the target if they are close enough to cause any damage.

We could hear the sonar pings as they wildly sprayed the depths with their penetrating rays. The thermal layer was very effective as we only felt a few explosions anywhere near us. The paint is designed to stick for some time and a review team would later look us over for telltale signs and assess our damage.

Our area was in the North Sea between Scotland and the huge inlet that separated Norway from Denmark. The Inlet led to the Baltic Sea and Russia, via the Gulf of Finland. The land masses were only about three hundred miles apart. The water was around six to seven hundred feet deep. Our test depth was 412 feet and we seldom went deeper than 350 feet. Our mission was an apparent success. If all went well and the Navy's review team agreed, we may very well have saved the country from an imaginary invasion, by theoretically sinking or disabling two major air craft carriers.

The intensity on the surface did not decrease. The Captain went to his room to rest and gave the con to Mr. Donahue, a Lieutenant Junior Grade, with instruction for the boat to go to sleep and hover at 300 feet with a minimum of power and noise.

I was relieved at the wheel and went to my bunk with a "pocket book" baloney sandwich. I was exhausted. I would take a bite of the sandwich, doze off and wake up some time later and continue to chew it. Six hours later I awoke and as I walked into the crews mess I took the last bite of my sandwich. The movie "Elephant Walk" was just starting. The surface fleet had moved on and the war was in someone else's yard now.

The movie was enjoyable and we were to see it many times before the final ten days of our sea duty would end in Le Harve, France. The fleet operation part of "Operation Strikeback" ended and we were back to operating with the

Runner and Barbero. We had moved north again to reach waters that were not in the main shipping lanes. We were targets for our sister boats and we theoretically sank them so many times it was simply routine. We also drilled intensively on man overboard, chlorine gas, collision, flooding and repel boarders. We all felt like the repeated drills were superfluous and the emphases placed on reaction speed and accuracy was uncalled for. Little did we know that these drills were going to save our lives, in the very near future.

I found some more time to work on the brow painting, it was coming out beautifully. I began to work on the giant name across the canvas. Sleep was calling.

"Johnny Concho" was on his knees in the street as his tormentors mocked him. I bent over the water fountain for a drink, before my nap. We had seen this movie enough by now that the crew would say the lines along with the actors. Budda Phillips would ad lib words for the side winder rattlesnake at the beginning and kept the crew in stitches.

I was starboard lookout at 0200 that morning. The Torsk was running dark. Our instructions were to keep close watch for ships. We were at the extreme top of the North Sea and were operating at the southern tip on the Norwegian Basin. The Soviets used this stretch of water as a short cut to the mid and lower Atlantic. We were well aware of their presence as they observed our "Operation Strikeback." We probably planned it in this location to show off for them. The cold war was in full force in 1957. We pictured the Russians as being buffoons and primitive submariners, compared to us. I'm sure this was unfair, but I suppose it is a natural thing to think less of your opponents in any untried contest.

It was a nice night with a mild sea of light chops around two feet. The weather had warmed up nicely since our northern passage to get here. Tighe and I were playing Irish tunes on our harmonicas. Mr. Craig had given us permission to smoke, but he told us to keep the cigarette under the faring so the glow would not be seen from the sea.

Mr. Craig asked us if we could play "Danny Boy." As I looked at him a dim flash caught my eye over his shoulder.

"Tighe! – What's that in the water off the port quarter?" I called.

Mr. Craig spun around and asked. "Range Wardlaw?"

Before I could speak, Tighe cried. "Torpedo wakes! – Sir - two of em - twenty yards apart! - Closing fast!"

It was dark, but the luminous wakes of the two torpedoes were a dead giveaway.

My body actually went numb with shock and I had a buzz all over. Our trained minds instantly calculated that no effort we could make would save us from this impending doom. I thought how it would feel to die, would I feel the blast, would I feel any pain. Perhaps if I jumped from my lookout port I could clear the side and miss the blast, but what chance would I have adrift in the North Sea in frigid water and no life jacket.

Mr. Craig's training caused him to instinctively sound the collision alarm and the upper hatch closed immediately, sealing us outside to die in the sea as the rest of the crew would perish from the blast or a slow death on the ocean floor.

I cast a last glance at the missiles as their trajectory indicated impact on our port beam, forward of the conning tower. I turned my back and steeled myself for the inevitable. All sound and movement ceased, it was as if time itself stood still. "Lord – Please accept my spirit!"

Nothing happened. I turned to look at Mr. Craig. His face was blank. Suddenly from beneath the Torsk, on the starboard side, right beside the sail, the water churned with luminous light and two giant harbor porpoises came straight up from the sea in a brilliant splash, as if to say. "Ta Da! - Here we are!"

My body went limp, I think I heard Tighe's sob of relief. I said a quick prayer of thanks. These beautiful creatures had seen us from afar and were unaware of what they appeared to be as they sped toward us at 30 knots, just under the surface.

I felt sorry for Mr. Craig as he had to explain the unscheduled collision drill. I don't think anyone could fathom the emotions we went through unless they had experienced this precise encounter.

The porpoises stayed with us for the rest of my watch. Darting and jumping in a game of chase and "let's scare the big fish!" You could watch every move they made as they swept through the luminescents of the water. Their giant leaps would make luminous splashes that were breathtaking. I had to have some sleep.

We spent the day on the surface, we were released from our independent operations and were heading south through the North Sea. I was pretty rested by this time and had seen "Elephant Walk" and "Johnny Concho" at least three times each in the last ten days.

I went back to my brow painting. I unrolled it on the deck of the after torpedo room to review my handiwork. I went numb all over. I could feel my body buzz in disbelief in what I saw. I had painted "U.S.S. TR", when I last worked on the piece. I couldn't believe that I had painted an "R" instead of an "O". I suppose it was from fatigue. The paint was dry. I wanted to cry. All the trust put in me by the crew and now my work of art had a giant fiasco right in the middle of the name. I sank to the floor in desperation.

I thought of a cartoon I read as a child. Sheriff Phillip Flynn would seek refuge in his bed whenever something went wrong. My bed called to me. We were only a few days from France. I dressed the "R" as best I could with white paint to block out the lines that didn't match an 'O'. It was evident that I couldn't repaint the correct "O" until the paint dried. I gingerly put the painting away. I never mentioned my blooper to a soul. I prayed for God to give me some help. I suppose I expected a miracle. I didn't sleep well.

My watch was 2400 to 0400. I was starboard lookout when we caught site of the lighthouse at North Foreland, County Kent, England, at around 0230. We were entering the English Channel. I felt we were on hallowed waters. Remembering my history, I thought of Dunkirk and the heroic actions of the Brits in that evacuation. I looked off the port side and imagined the flickering of artillery that would have lite up the sky on that northern French shore in 1940.

Mr. Donohue was first to sight the South Foreland Light, it was about four miles north of Dover. It was strange to see the glow of Dover in the distance. How romantic it was to see the glow but never behold these places we had only heard of. I wondered if anyone in Dover knew that an American was only about fifteen miles away, thinking of them.

My watch was up at 0400 and as I approached the narrow passage by the radio room. I saw Carlton, a third class radioman working inside the radio cabinet. I started to say "coming by" so he could squeeze in to allow me passage. I never got the chance.

Carlton's body went rigid. He gave an involuntary "'Unnhh!" and began to collapse. John Christ stepped from the radio room. Christ and I caught Carlton. He was still conscious but disorientated. We helped him to the mess hall and got "Doc" Johanson to threat a bad burn on his left arm. He was lucky, that radio voltage can really be dangerous. I hit the sack.

It seemed I had just put my head down when I woke to hear Doc telling someone to take it easy. "Sure it burns - but we caught it in time! -- Just hold still! -- It'll quit burning in a minute!"

I swung from my top bunk, careful to avoid the water fall, to check on who was burned now. As I opened the door, to the mess hall, I saw Zwick, a third class electrician, with his head tilted back and trusty old Doc washing his left eye out with water. He had splashed battery acid in his eye while working in the forward battery storage area. This was a night for injuries. Doc looked haggard. I know he was tired, but Doc never complained. He had a tough job.

I sought my painting, the gusto was gone. My idea of a masterpiece was tarnished as I proceeded to finish the lettering. It actually didn't look too bad, from a few feet you would not notice the white paint on white canvass where I had covered the excessive "R" lines.

Suddenly a thought occurred to me. I began to outline all the letters with a white outline. I thanked God for the thought. The brow piece really looked good, but anything God does will look good, so it's no brag. By the time we made port in LeHarve, the brow canvass would be dry. "Hallelujah!"

Ahhhh! Man, those Navy breakfasts were something. I sopped the remainder of my baked beans and egg yokes with a half piece of toast. I deposited my plate in the sink and drew a second cup of coffee. I carried my coffee with me and headed for the head. I planned to clean all the stainless bulkheads in the after battery head before we made port In LeHarve. I filled my pan half full of water, got two clean clothes and a dab of detergent. This detergent was not for the deck. It was a dab. That means one of the rags had a finger pushed into it and dabbed in the detergent. That was all it was. This cloth was now the cleaning cloth and the only reason for any detergent was to cut the body oils that hands would put on the stainless panels with normal use. I washed and wiped dry the entire head area, including shower stalls and johns by 1130 hours.

Word was passed that the maneuvering watch would be set soon. Everyone knew I would be at the helm so when I entered the crews mess, room was made available for me to eat early.

Catfish was cooking and grinned at me. "Better you din me -- on dat wheel -- boy -- I was sho tired o dat thing! -- Georgia boy-- I's gonna bake you a pecan pie one day."

That set everybody off. "I'll buy you a watermelon—Catfish -- if you'll bake me a pie!"

Another shouted. "Catfish -- I'll take yo sister to da ball -- if you'll bake me a pie -- Wooo! --Dat's one ugly gal!"

Catfish slammed his big spoon down to get everyones attention, then slowly made a bugger picking motion with his finger.

"NO! – CATFISH! – NO! -- We didn't mean it! - We love you Catfish!" Everyone clamored for forgiveness. Laughter prevailed and Catfish laughed the loudest. I loved these guys. I was only half through when the maneuvering watch was set. I rolled a pocket book sandwich with whatever was on my plate and headed for the wheel.

As I ducked through the hatch to leave the chow hall, I stopped and called back. "Valet parking for LeHarve, France - coming up!" You could have heard the cheers in Paris.

I took the wheel from Francis, a seaman that was onboard when I joined the crew. He was always a bit sarcastic, but was a good worker and a good sailor. I think he may have resented me because I had more time in grade. He was still hopping bunks. Apparently he didn't like the water fall bunk and I think he may have resented me taking it. Mr. Wiseman still had the deck when I went on the wheel, but was relieved by Mr. Sheehan at 1200 hours.

"All stop!" Came the command from Mr. Sheehan.

"All stop!" I replied. "Answered all stop!"

"Very well!" acknowledged Mr. Sheehan. I could hear small craft activity along the port side and presently I head the distinctive French accent of our pilot. He was the honorable, Capitaine Duvanel.

Captain King came to the bridge and assumed the con. "All ahead two thirds – come left to new course 090 degrees. Captain King was calling the shots.

I answered. "All ahead two thirds! – Come left to new course 090 degrees!"

The enunciators answered. "Answered all ahead two thirds! At new course 090 degrees!" I only had to move two degrees. Captain King did not acknowledge. I knew he heard me. Why did he do this to me?

I repeated loudly. "ANSWERED ALL ------!" He cut me off.

"VERY WELL!" He was heated.

I made up my mind to do that every time he ignored my response. He may have just been testing me, I don't know.

We started steering by left and right degrees. I knew we were lining up for something. The helmsman never gets to see where he is going, he simply follows orders.

From my brief experience I didn't feel like we were tying up this soon. I was right, from the bridge discussion I found we were going into a lock. The purpose of a lock is to equalize the difference in water levels. Most of LeHarve's harbor is subject to tide changes, but it is shallow. The lock we were entering was to some deep water berthing that was part of a series of deep canals that ran parallel to the Seine River.

It was nice, not to have to station a line watch, to constantly adjust mooring lines to keep with the tides. It took no more than five minutes in the lock before we were out the other side and proceeded to tie up in Bassin Bellot, South Quay next to the USS Pompon - SSR267.

CHAPTER VII

FRANCE AND ENGLAND

There were five American ships in LeHarve. The USS Tringa, ASR16 was a submarine rescue ship, we bought them a lot of beers. We were there along with the Runner and the Grouper. The Barbero was not with us. I suppose she chose a different liberty port. The Pompon carried the Squadron Flag.

The new brow canvas was laced onto the brow and I was told "Well done Wardlaw!" Little did they know how despondent I had been, only a day ago. I did notice when the early morning sun shone through the canvass, the darker black of the "R" error was noticeable through the white paint. No one ever mentioned it. I loved these guys.

Red Donaldson and William Jones were selected for shore patrol the first night in LeHarve. An agreement must be reached between the local law enforcement and the U.S. Navy for the shore patrol to have jurisdiction in a foreign port. The shore patrol is only armed with a "billy stick" and some training is required on its use. It is a very effective weapon and its intent is for defense and to disable without doing internal damage.

I went on liberty with four other guys from various boats. We shared a taxi into downtown LeHarve. We had been told that LeHarve had received extensive damage from air raids during WWII, but the recovery was magnificent. It had only been a little over ten years since the war and I saw no visible damage. The buildings were only three or maybe four stories high and it all looked old Europe to me. There were numerous trees and long narrow boulevards with walk ways.

The shops were small and neat. Tables lined the sidewalks in front of restaurants and coffee shops. It was a scene that Gene Kelly could have danced through without any Hollywood help. The taxi driver took us to an office of some kind to exchange our U.S. money for French money. I got twenty bucks worth of francs. I thought I was rich. I had twenty-five 200 franc notes and ten 500 franc notes. We separated after our money deal, and I proceeded on my own.

I found a small camera shop and bought a nice little camera. The man was very helpful, but spoke very little English. He did tell me the camera would use standard 120 American film. I paid him what seemed an enormous sum of money, but it amounted to less than ten of our dollars. The camera did nothing special, it simply took pictures, the focus was automatic and it had no flash, but I was happy. It was the new style that had a thumb knob on top to advance pictures and you held it up to your eye to sight the shot. It came with a black case and strap to hang around your neck. I thought I was in high cotton.

As evening wore on, I had walked around much of LeHarve's old section of town and came upon a club that was quite crowded with our sailors. There were at least a half dozen from the Torsk and maybe twenty more from other boats. Some of the guys were already on the down side of a binge that should have ended an hour ago.

"Hey! – Wardy!" Came the slurred words of one of our torpedomen. "Come on over here and meet this purdy lil thing on my lap, she thinks you're ze cutez zing!"

I held my hand up in the "No Way!" sign and proceed to a table with two guys from the Tringa. They made room for me and I offered to buy them a drink.

"Thanks, Man, but we haven't paid for anything all night. That big guy over there is handling everything." He pointed out a first class quartermaster from the Runner at the bar.

I caught his eye and he motioned me over. I asked my table pals to hold my seat and made my way to the bar. The place was quite crowded. "What's up, boss?" I quizzed.

Don't spend your money on any Tringa man in here tonight, France is footing their bill!"

"What the Sam Hill you talking about, Man?" I asked with disbelief.

"We're buying their drinks with black market francs, so just pay for your stuff and don't worry about it, OK?" I had no clue what he meant, but it was much too noisy and the men were way too drunk to discuss anything, so I returned to my chair, ordered a beer and looked the place over.

The girl brought my beer and took three hundred francs, that's almost a buck and a half in American money. I didn't argue with her, but I nursed that beer for almost an hour. French beer is no better than American beer, but what could I do? The place was in turmoil with half-drunk sailors and locals that were trying to carry on conservations in broken English.

There were a lot of women fraternizing with the guys and every once in a while a couple would leave, hand in hand and I knew a deal had been reached. The girls definitely weren't dates and hadn't arrived with the guys. We had only been In LeHarve for around five hours.

I saw a fellow crewman leave with a good looking blonde and figured she was his high school sweetheart that had flown to France to meet him. I chuckled under my breath at my humor.

I talked a bit with the men from the Tringa and found that the main reason our NATO operation was held in the North Sea was for depth concerns . The North Sea is large enough for a big operation but is from 500 to 700 feet deep. In case of a submarine accident, any depth over that would be way too deep for a rescue operation.

I told them about our near miss from the destroyer and they agreed it was a close call. They got a big laugh when I told them of the Porpoise attack. They wanted to know if we messed our pants. I told them there wasn't time to even think of that. We all had a good laugh.

I had noticed, the public toilet facilities in LeHarve were very different from the states. In America, we have a great deal of privacy in our restrooms. Generally the toilets have partitions between them and doors that close. The urinals are mounted on a wall with a little partition between them and there are seperate rooms for men and women. Not In LeHarve. The street toilets for the public had partitions and doors, but were open at the bottom and your head was above the partitions. I had avoided using them for that very reason.

I could ignore the call no longer. I had to go. As I worked through the crowd I passed the bar and noticed a good looking brunette sitting alone near the restroom door. She half turned and smiled at me when I passed, but did not attempt to speak. I felt sure she was with someone and they had just stepped away.

I entered the small room, there was a sink then a stall with a half door. Luckily, the room was empty; I entered the stall and proceeded to take care of my pressing problem. My back was to the door. I heard the door open as I began my delivery. Out of politeness I did not turn around, feeling sure the next patron would patiently wait.

A woman's voice in perfect English said. "It's hard to get used to men and women using the same bathroom at the same time - isn't it?"

I had heard it was hard to stop your stream once you had started peeing. Don't believe it. If you are peeing and a woman surprises you with a question, the stream stops all by itself! I could feel my ears getting hot with embarrassment. A man tends to be always aware of himself in the presence of a good looking women. He will posture himself to show his best side and try to look masculine and strike poses that make him look appealing. Standing in a stall, in total shock with your pecker in your hand is not one of those poses.

I half turned and saw a pretty blond, dressed in a tweed wool suit accompanied by a man of slight build. She was probably in her early thirties. I couldn't tell about the guy.

She continued to talk of the European openness about sex and I finally had to let it go. It sounded as if I had turned on a high pressure hose. I tried to move the stream to the side of the bowl to soften the sound, but I don't think it helped.

The man spoke up. He had, I think, a German accent. He asked my boat's name, and went right into the possibility of smuggling his wife on board to get her back to the states. She would insert little bits of correcting information about losing her passport and getting into some trouble by accident and she just had to get home to Cincinnati. He would follow later when his passport was ready.

I told them to find some sailors with the Tringa name on their shoulders. That ship was much larger and had more room to hide someone than a submarine. I've never been to Cincinnati, so I don't know if she made it or not. I beat it out of there.

I was heading back to my table when the brunette stepped from the bar and blocked my path. In hesitant English, she spoke. "Zailor Boi – You are no like zee ozer zailor boiz here! -- You pleeze come wiz me for tonight!" She gently took my hand and headed for the door.

I heard a voice call out. "Uh Oh! – another cherry bites the dust!"

The club door shut off the sounds of the rowdy crowd. The brunette looked to be in her early thirties. Her hair was glistening black and cropped straight across the front. Her earrings dangled and sparkled in the light of the street lamps. She was shaped well and endowed with all the physical charms a woman needed. Her lips were just pouty enough to be interesting and the makeup was perfectly applied. I wondered if she was all real. I felt, somehow, I was going to find out, for sure.

I floundered for words. I had never made a deal with a hooker. As a matter of confession, it was only my second intimate relationship. The first was set up for me at a telephone school in Albany, Georgia and paid for by a bunch of guys that knew I was innocent. I think they were in the closet, watching.

She held my hand as we walked down the street and talked as if we were on a date. I tried to tell her I didn't have a lot of money. She obviously was a high class hooker. I had noticed she sat at the bar and looked around, never once did she join in the flirtations that dominated the club.

"Zailor Boi -- do not speek of zee monee – pleeze! -- A lady doz not speek of zee monee."

We walked quit a few blocks and entered a section of town that had some very nice homes. Presently she stopped at the steps of a brick three story home; it was not very wide and had no front yard.

She whispered. "Pleeze -- not to make zee noiz - my Zailor Boi! -- Zee naborz are ze soft sleepeirs- no!"

I placed my fingers to my lips in a mock "Shhhh!"

I learned more about a woman that night than all the other nights of my love life. It would not be fair to place this woman in the category of a common hooker. She never did place a money figure on our liaison and she simply lay there as I dressed to leave. I left a ten dollar bill on her chest of drawers.

As she walked me to the door, she made me promise to be quiet and not to come back again. I asked her why she would not come back to the club with me.

She replied. "When zee peepol zee us come in - zey weel know what we do - - wee? -- Zat iz alright for zee manz -- but not so alright for zee ladez -- no!" I liked this lady!

I didn't realize how far we had walked and I felt sure the lady had taken me to her home. She definitely was not an all-night worker and I hoped changing the ten spot into French money would be no problem for her.

I found the club; it was well after midnight as I walked in. The atmosphere was chaotic. The guys had been at sea for a month and were dry. Not anymore. Some were already stupefied and many others were on their way. I had to take a leak again. I scanned the club for the blonde and her guy. I looked at my old table and my Tringa buddies were gone. Maybe they struck a deal. I made my way to the head

I pushed the door and someone was a little close inside. A voice called. "We in here! - Man!" I could see the stall was empty, but someone was at the sink. I didn't want to be rude so I looked around the door. There was a sailor leaning over the sink and a very tall colored sailor standing next to him helping to hold him up. I started to squeeze by when the colored guy spoke again. "Hey! – F— ker! – I said we's in here!"

I suddenly felt empowered and was ready to give him my best shot if he played his card.

I came in and boldly replied. "I see you - but you ain't in the pisser and that's where I'm going!" I proceeded to take my leak, keeping the colored guy in my peripheral. As I zipped up, I turned around thinking the guy at the sink was sick. I was shocked to see blood was spattered all over the sink and was dripping from multiple places on his tunic. "This man has been stabbed!" I exclaimed.

"Look F—ker! – I told you not to come in here! – I'm helping him out!" I could tell the colored sailor had been drinking. Suddenly I recognized the sailor at the sink. It was Watkins, a third class torpedoman from the Torsk.

"This man's from my boat! - He needs help!" I told the tall guy.

"You better not get this man in no trouble - white boy! – You hear me?" He shouted as I darted from the room. There was no time to hassle with a drunk trying to be a big shot.

As I dashed for the front door of the club I shouted to a group of sailors from the Torsk. "Watkins is hurt -- he's in the john -- help him till I get someone!" My intent was to find the police or the shore patrol.

The Lord in his infinite wisdom saw fit to place Jonesy and his shore patrol mate exactly at the front of that club as I dashed out. Jones was the second class electrician, from Georgia. I met him when I first came on board my Torsk.

"Jonesy! -- It's Watkins -- he's in the head in the club -- he's hurt bad – Jonesy -- we gotta help him!"

Jones was off like a shot. He pulled his way through the crowd and with the help of his SP partner, helped Watkins out to the street and laid him down. They did some first aid and arranged for transportation for Watkins.

All the while, the tall colored sailor kept throwing insults at me for getting Watkins in trouble. There was a tremendous amount of racial overtone, but I was concerned about my shipmate and really did not pay a lot of attention to him. Finally a couple of sailors from the Tringa quieted him down and got him to leave.

The next day I found out that Watkins was coming down a flight of stairs at a nearby hotel where he had been, when an Algerian lifted his wallet. Watkins felt the theft and accosted the guy. He was stabbed numerous times in his arm, neck and face. He recovered, thankfully. Jonesy was unusually cool toward me after that. It was a long time before we ever talked about the incident.

We met a young French boy that hung around the boat at lot. He was about seventeen and spoke a little English. He never knew his Dad, but said he was an American sailor. His Mother told him he was the most wonderful man in the world but had to go back home. I suppose the boy hung around American ships thinking his Dad would return one day. He was a good kid and told us of the important places to visit and what to watch out for. We called him John.

I asked about the black market francs I had heard of in the club the first night in LeHarve. Here's how it works. An American sells his clean American cash on the black market and can get as much as twice the going rate in exchange for French francs. He then takes the francs to England and exchanges it for British money. When he gets back to the States he then exchanges the British money back to U.S. currency and can wind up doubling his money. I'm glad I didn't get involved in it. I think it would trouble me thinking I may have helped some Russian spy in Washington get clean U.S. money.

I pulled duty the second day in LeHarve and that's when I met John. He wanted to swap two for one French cigarettes for American. I gave him a pack of Viceroy. I wound up giving him about eight packs when we left as I had gone back to Pall Mall for that full tobacco taste. John told us about a grand restaurant in LeHarve that served a full seven course meal and was very elegant. We decided to give it a try the next night.

That night we watched "Elephant Walk" for the umpteenth time. It was close to 2300 hours when the elephants made their stampede through the sprawling African ranch.

The continuous calls of the wild beast were deafening. "Eeyaaaagh! – Eeyaaaagh!" Push a wall down! "Eeyaaaagh! – Eeyaaaagh!" Run through a straw house! "Eeyaaaagh! – Eeyaaaagh!" Crush a slow native.

The chief of the boat stuck his head through the hatch and cried. "The Captain says to turn that damn thing down!" Tolley, reached and turned the sound down.

The elephants continued their rampage in full volume. "Eeyaaaagh! – Eeyaaaagh!

Suddenly the Captains head appeared in the hatch. "Turn that damn thing off!" Came his stern command.

Tolley clicked the off switch on the projector. The room went dark.

The elephants screamed on. "Eeyaaaagh! – Eeyaaaagh!" Everyone looked bewildered.

The lights flashed on and so did the elephants. "Eeyaaaagh! – Eeyaaaagh!"

All heads turned to the source of the deafening elephant crescendo. Two drunks were curled up in the corner under the after battery hatch and were harmonizing with the elephants. "Eeyaaaagh! – Eeyaaaagh!" We had to pour water on them to stop the elephants trumpeting. That's the only time I ever saw our Captain really laugh. He turned and sat in the hatch, buried his head in his hands and laughed heartily. He then stood and made his way back forward to the officer's quarters, slowly shaking his head, from side to side, in disbelief.

John North, Jim Given, Dave Cummings and I caught a taxi to the Grande Resturaunte and treated ourselves to a full seven course French meal. The restaurant had the customary Maitre d'. The waiters were in tails. It truly was grand. They would not let us in the main dining area; we were seated in the bar in a fine booth against the wall. Opposite our booth was the bar that ran the full depth of the building. The entire bar was wood paneling. Behind the bar and also running the depth of the room were three rows of wine bottles. There were hundreds of wines on display.

A full formal meal takes some time to consume and we enjoyed each course. I ordered escargot and immediately regretted it as the other guys began grossing me out. However it was quite enjoyable. I've never had it since, but at the time it was quite nice.

As the meal progressed we became curious of why so many bottles of wine. Our waiter could speak no English but he was fluent in Spanish and I spoke a little Spanish. I'm sure it was a funny sight as the formal dressed local society began to come in, to see a group of American sailors speaking Spanish to a French waiter.

The waiter informed us that this classy restaurant was famous for serving every brand of wine that was a product of France. He stood in profound sincerity as he made his statement.

Each one of us raised our eyes in equal profound exuberance as we all came to the same thought. How wonderful it would be, to truth-fully state, we had tasted every wine that France had to offer. We made our proposition to the waiter. He thought for a moment and excused himself to go speak to the bartender. We could hear their discussion, as fruitless as it was.

The bartender, I don't think believed we wanted to try each bottle. It seemed that you were offered a free sample to make a selection before buying a bottle. But we wanted a taste of each.

We finally reached an agreement. We chipped in and raised 5,000 francs. I'm sure the waiter and bartender would split the money.

We told the waiter to start on the bottom left and proceed to the end, and then do the same on the next row up, and so on. The wine goblets were very small, just big enough for a little sip that you rolled around on your tongue and then you would take the rest in a single swallow. "

"Ahhhhh! We were zee mastair connoisseurs – Monsieur - S'il vous plait!"

Every wine had a different taste, I'm sure a true wine drinker could tell each history, but for us, it was peach, grape maybe strawberry or whatever. Some were good, some were awful. A couple actually burned my lips.

The bartender cleared our first set of glasses. There were sixty in all, and I was fancying myself a drinker. I had just downed fifteen swigs of fifteen different French wines and I felt fine. I mentioned that perhaps this wine was watered down and was not the real stuff. Some of the guys, who had more drinking experience, assured me, it was the real stuff.

Man! I really had to take a leak. I stood and called the waiter to ask direction to the restroom and it took some hand signs for him to get the message. As I turned to follow his directions, I noticed a table in the high class section had been observing me. The ladies seemed quite amused at my hand language, describing my urge, and I'm sure my red face amused them even more.

"Oh well!" – I thought. "They don't know my Momma so it doesn't matter."

I followed the directions down the regal hall to the first door on the left; it had a symbol of a top hat on it. This must be the right place. I opened the ornate opaque glass and brass door to a huge room, it was tiled, floor to ceiling. A huge crystal chandelier hung from the center ceiling. Directly beneath the dangling masse of sparkling crystal was a magnificent fountain. The water spewed gently from the top and poured down in little rivulets from layer to layer into a giant circular basin at floor level.

On the far wall was a series of porcelain toilets with those familiar short partitions separating them. The places smelled of lilac.

I approached the fountain to better appreciate its beauty when I was appalled at the cigarette butts that danced in the basin. How could anyone deface a beautiful masterpiece this way? The lights went out. I seemed to be falling.

Darkness, I vaguely remember my nostrils burning, like when you get water up your nose while swimming. Darkness again.

I was in the rear seat of a vehicle and I was sick, very sick. I told whoever was driving I was sick. The driver spoke Greek or something and kept telling me he was "ne parlying angels!" I finally made the vomiting sound and he stopped. I really messed up someone's sidewalk flower box. Darkness again.

I woke up in a bunk that was not mine and buck naked. Man, I was thirsty. I stumbled a few steps to the chow hall and poured a cup of water.

"Georgia Boy! – Easy on dat water!" - It was Catfish. "Yu gotta load o wine in yu - ifin yu drinks too mucha dat water, yu gonna be drunk all over again! -- Boy! - Yu wuz a stinking mess when yu came in last night - Yu wuz lucky I was baking -- or yu'd lost yo dress blues - Dey's drying in the forward engine room - Pour yu some coffee and go light on de sugar - Dat sugar'l push dat wine right back in yo head an yu'll be back in La – La - Land!"

I don't care for unsweetened coffee, but I took Catfish's advice and drank a cup. It did clear my head some.

"What time is it, Catfish?" I asked.

"Yu blind, Boy – Yu ain't got no watch? - Can't you see me wit da flour on my hands- You know we bakes at night and I'm late now! -- I'm late cause I washed dat pee and tobacco outa yo blues and hung em in da engine room! -- Yu needs to shower whilst we still on France's water and clean up dat bunk we stuffed yu in last night -- cause at 0800 we gonna rise an shine and make plans to leave dis place and go see da Queen!"

I rose to take my thick head to the shower, and mumbled a thank you to Catfish.

"Hey! – Georgia Boy! – Pappy's gonna talk to yu first thing now!'

"Why" I answered.

"Man, Yo sho was drunk las night - It woulda been funny ifin yu didn't stink so bad! -- WHUEEE! – Yassuh - yu wuz sho a little stinker - Done fell in a pisser - Man! --How yu gets so drunk yu falls in a pisser!"

He was still mumbling about how a white boy could be so dumb as to fall in a pisser, a French pisser at that. "Hell! – He coulda stuck his head in our john, it least it woulda been American piss!"

I was tired of hearing it and took a shower. I felt somewhat better and cleaned up the mess on the bunk, where I slept it off. I checked my blues. They were none the worst and I really began to appreciate what Catfish had done for me.

Our blues are a wool blend, Catfish had thoroughly washed all the urinal mess out and rinsed with cold fresh water. He then squeezed the water out and blocked the wool to dry in the controlled heat of the engine room. Blocking the wool and drying slowly will allow it to keep its shape and not shrink. I owed him a deep debt. I didn't realize how much of an influence this man would have on my life.

I dressed in dungarees and went topside to get some air. I'm sure I was still buzzing a little as I rested against the sonar doom, forward of the sail. We had liberty 'till 0800 and I figured all the guys were back on board. I wanted to check on Watkins.

I heard a taxi stop at the head of the pier. It was comical to see Tolley, a second class engineman, unfold from the back seat of that small French taxi. He fumbled through his tunic pocket and just gave whatever he had to the driver. It must have been adequate. The driver pulled away, as Tolley swayed and took those little half steps that drunks take.

The topside watch was Burt Pierce, a first class electrician. I had dropped back into a daze as my head was still thick from last night's wine. I realized I was not a drinker.

Pierce's voice brought me back to reality. "Wardy! – What de hell's Tolley doin?"

I looked up to see the 6'4" Tennessee mountaineer, gracefully unfolding his arms in a ballerina fashion. He would hunch one shoulder forward and undulate his arm. He then turned his head the other way and repeated the process with the other arm. His arms slowly rose to a lofty height and he rose on his toes. He arched his face skyward and proceeded to mock a graceful bird in flight. Gone was the drunken stagger.

Tolley could have been a nightingale. As he flew in lofty circles with a flurry of his wings he whistled beautiful bird sounds. He whistled chirps, lilting lines, and the haunting strains of the whippoorwill. He was truly a master at this bird whistling. He put on a dazzling display of a magnificent song bird returning to his nest.

He did two circular paces at the brow and finished with a wide swing to line up with the narrow walkway that spanned from the pier to the deck of the Pompon. He flew straight across the Pompon brow, to the delight of the watch and a couple of observers, who were cheering him on. He made a short loop on the Pompon and flew across the Torsk's brow. He extended his wings in a glide pattern and flew straight off the port side of the Torsk into the bay.

We all stood in mute shock as he surfaced and wildly splashed the water and continued to try and whistle. I gathered my senses and grabbed the life ring. A gentle toss that was actually more of a drop, placed the ring, right in front of Tolley.

By this time, Pierce had set the man overboard alarm and a number of sailors came topside, as well as quite a few from the Pompon. Sailors from the nearby boats were gathering on their decks to observe. Tolley did not appear to be in any distress, but made no effort to grab the life ring. He continued to thrash the water as if he were a bird and still was blowing, as if to whistle. Finally a couple of guys stripped down and jumped in to assist Tolley to the side near the tank tops. We threw them some ropes and they secured him in a lift harness in order to pull him aboard.

Once onboard, Tolley stood erect and slowly looked himself up and down. He was being flooded with questions. He did not reply. The remarks about his performance had drawn no response as well. Suddenly he began to softly cry, not sobs or wails, just soft little crying sounds.

The crowd began to plead with Tolley. "What's wrong, Man! – Tolley, are you hurt? – It's alright, Tolley! – Can we help? – What is it, Man?" Tolly cried on.

Suddenly he stopped and slowly pulled himself erect and with quivering lips, loudly proclaimed. "A BIRD CAN'T FLY WHEN ITS FEATHERS ARE WET!"

Silence. But only long enough for what Tolley had said to sink in. The laughter resounded all over the bay. We were treated to a classic example of a man getting caught up in his own performance and bringing it to a stupendous climax.

We put Tolley to bed and covered for him till well after noon. I rinsed his blues and blocked them alongside mine in the engine room. It was my pleasure, and my head was clear.

Pappy caught me as I was finishing breakfast. He told me I had disturbed the Captain last night and that was a No! No! Mr. Bibby wants a word with you right after Quarters. "Yes Sir!" I answered.

"Save them Sirs for the brass, boy, you gonna need em!"

"You don't have much experience drinking -- do you -- Wardlaw?" Mr. Bibby's voice did not carry any tone of reprimand, but was to the point. Mr. Bade, the exec, sat in silence at the head of the ward room table.

"A beer and a Tom Collins, once in a while, Sir! - Am I in big trouble, Sir? – I didn't know I was drunk, Sir, honest!" I began to tell the story exactly as I remembered it. I could tell they fought to keep from laughing at my fall into the urinal. They were convinced I simply thought it was a splendid fountain. They also made some comments about how a sailor, could possibly think they could drink that much wine.

Mr. Bibby told me I made so much noise in the corridor of the officer's quarters that the Captain had to rebuke me. "It didn't help the situation any, when you told him." Skipper, you're a swell guy, no matter what everyone else says!"

I could feel the color leave my face. Mr. Bibby assured me that I had not committed an unpardonable sin. They viewed it as poor judgment due to inadequate alcohol experience.

Mr. Bibby became very official as he stated. "Ward law - it is the decision of this hearing that your actions were not out of willful disdain for your country - your ship or your commanding officer - Therefore this punitive action will not be recorded in your records - You are hereby restricted to the confines of this vessel until 1600 hours on the 5th day of October, 1957!"

I replied. "But, Sir, We'll be at sea that whole time!"

Mr. Bibby dropped his jaw in mock surprise. "Son of a gun – Oh well! – Nothing can be done about it now! – Suck it up, sailor!" I really like these guys.

We departed LeHarve at 1835 , October 4, 1957. We cleared the lock and in short order the French pilot left us by small boat and we were in the English Channel, headed for Portland, England. We finished dinner and the crew set up for a showing of Johnny Concho and Elephant Walk. I headed for the sack. It was one of those unusual times when my watch fell on our departure from Leharve, therefore at 2000 hours I was off. I felt pretty sure that we would pull no drills, since we were scheduled to tie up in Portland early the next morning.

I passed through the chow hall on the way to my bunk. I saw Jonesy sitting in the back corner with his head in his hands. Tolley and Red Donaldson were sitting soberly at the tables. "Somebody die?" I asked jokingly. I immediately regretted that question, what if someone close to one of these guys really had died.

Lambert was rolling out dough for his night baking. "Didn't you hear - Wardy?" He looked gloomy.

I shook my head in a negative manner. "Them damn Russians have put a space ship up in space to spy on us!" My legs went numb as Red rose and left the chow hall. There were tears in his eyes.

We had all thought of Russians as a bunch of boot kicking, vodka drinking buffoons. They bore the brunt of many a crude American joke.

We began to gather more accurate details as other shipmates came through with updated information. It seems that it was a satellite called "Sputnik" and was transmitting signals back on conditions in space. The "Sputnik" was orbiting the earth about fifteen times a day. We couldn't believe a bunch of throwbacks to the last century could have pulled off such a feat. From then on, every blip or beep that we heard had a new meaning. What else did these Cossacks have that we weren't aware of? We now had an adversary that was worthy of our caution. It affected our entire outlook on the cold war.

I had showered that morning, before we left France. I slept between my sheets in my skivvies. It was a rare treat, but I slept soundly. I had the strangest dream. I seldom ever dreamed of women. This night was different. A faceless lady visited me and consoled me in a warm embrace that was gentle and sweet. There was no intimacy, just soothing comfort and security. I awoke refreshed, but still worried about the Russians and starving to death.

We were running low on stores, having been to sea over a month and took no supplies while in France. Our breakfast was powdered eggs and potatoes with, as always, that fresh bread that Catfish and Lambert did so well. Our cooks could even make the powdered stuff quite tasty.

Catfish claimed that Lambert, the senior cook, was better at the baking than he was. These guys were the basis of the moral on the Torsk. Cooks did not stand any watches. They were scheduled to cook meals and bake at night. They did their own thing. No one ever complained. Cooks did pull special duty on drills, battle stations and maneuvering watch, but their regular workday was strictly cooking. Hersey was the quiet one in the bunch and generally handled the big dinner operations. His specialty was, roast, pork loins and other major meat dishes. These guys worked long hours and hard, but also got to sleep long hours as well. We were careful during the day not to disturb the cook as he slept. We allowed them to bunk in dark, quiet corners and always looked out for their attitudes. We knew the terrible things an angry cook could do to the food and we would never be the wiser.

Our cooks prepared the same food for the officers that we ate. The stewards would come and pick up the officer's food and make the final preparation and presentation. The officers ate in the ward room.

At 0800 on the morning of October 5th, 1957, the maneuvering watch was set and we entered the Portland harbor. At 1000 we secured the watch and were tied up on the starboard side of the USS Piper SS409. We were moored at "Q" pier, Darby Yard, Portland, England.

Liberty went down at 1600 hours. My restriction was up at that same time. I went ashore with Francis, Givens and Richard Moore. We had dinner at a nice restaurant in Weymouth. I ordered liver and onions. There was a sign on a board next to the entrance that told of a dance in honor of the visiting Navies at the Queens Ballroom. It did not seem to interest the other guys but I made up my mind to go. I wanted to dance with some of the Queen's hand maidens.

We had caught a taxi into Weymouth because we were told that's where the action was. The action in England is not the same action as in France. The British are most proper indeed. It was nice to be able to speak to folks and understand them, well, almost understand them. It was strange to hear two distinct dialects spoken by two people from the same town.

The proper Brits spoke a rolling very precise English. The ordinary folk spoke a curt, cocky type of English. I found that the term "Bloody" is used in the same context that we Americans use "Damn". "Ars" is the same as "Ass" – "Ducky" is "Honey"or"Sweety". The British are great for giving things nicknames. Incidently, we were drinking with some British sailors and found they use an "F" word much more than we do. Their version of the word is "Friggin". We made up a song about no friggin in the riggin and the pub owners asked us to leave.

I was embarrassed and left immediately. Jonesy from the Torsk called me "Chickenshit" as I exited. It didn't matter, the beer was not cold and was black and was even worse than American beer. I don't know why I drank it. I found a pharmacy and bought an English version of Sen Sen. I didn't want to take my beer breath to the Queen's Ballroom.

The Ballroom was only a few blocks from the downtown district of Weymouth and was an impressive building. I entered the regal doorway and was impressed with a highly polish hardwood dance floor. The walls were hung with gorgeous draperies. Between the draperies were paintings of Britain's greatest heroes. Statues and suits of armor were placed in mock, but imposing guard positions. It truly was a piece of old England. I felt honored to have been invited, even if it was from a sign in a restaurant.

I couldn't believe my eyes. The light was not bright but the chandeliers gave more than enough light for me to see.

There stood one of Savannah's debutant beauties that graduated a year before me in high school. My mind made some quick calculations. I had been out of school three years. She had been out for four years. She would be in her last year of college if she had come to England for her education. Debutants frequently take their education abroad. We would be about the same age as I was a year older than most of my class.

We simply knew each other in school. She was way out of my class I thought, but here she was. My mind told me. "She's here - this dance is in our honor – therefore - she has - more or less - told me - she's is in my class!" I searched my mind for her name.

Oh! Well! Here goes.

I walked over and decided to simply stand by her side and see how long it took for her to recognize me. She was talking to some friends and I remarked how well she had mastered that most proper British delivery.

I thought how she was much prettier than I remembered. She glanced at me and politely moved to the side thinking I wanted to pass. I saw no recognition in her eyes at all. "Oh Well! – It's been four years!"

I stood as if I were intent on her conversation. She glanced again and I gave her my warmest smile and let my eyes play along her lovely face. I looked out of sincerity, but I don't think she understood. The look got her attention.

"May I help you?" She asked with a concerned furrow of her brow.

My ploy was a failure. I lost all my coyness. Her distinct proper English accent, told me, she was not the girl I knew.

I made up a name. "Mary -- I'm Lynn from Savannah!" I still half way expected her to react with astonishment and remembrance.

She stood silent and then politely extended her hand. "Lynn -- I'm so very sorry! - I'm not your Mary -- but I am Leslie -- from Weymouth! -- Will I do for the present?"

Man! – So much for being cool. I must have stammered a bit as I shook her hand. I proceeded to explain how much she looked like Mary and she listened politely.

The dance was a regal affair. The orchestra that played would have done well in any American dance hall. I didn't bother dancing with any other girl, but Leslie. She danced well and was particularly pleased with our fast dancing. The shag was known in England, but had not caught on like back home.

I remembered the rhetoric that Martha Coatsworth would chant to me as I was learning. "Step -- Touch – One – Two -Three – One - Two! Step – Touch – One –Two -Three – One – Two!" I softly chanted them to Leslie as we danced to "Glow Worm," and soon there was no need to chant anymore.

As we walked from the dance floor she hugged my arm close to her breast and whispered. "Lynny - I've been to quit a few of these dances - but never have I had such fun!"

I told her that I was sure the Queen was much too busy to come tonight, but was there a possibility that Princess Margaret would drop by. She thought that was hilarious and rushed off to tell her friends. I could hear the peals of laughter around the room as she made her rounds to tell everyone of the sailor that wanted a dance with the Princess. I was quite popular.

All good things must come to an end and the band played "God save the Queen" and then "The Star Spangled Banner." It was quite stirring. Leslie had other things to do and I looked her up to say goodnight and thanks for a great time.

"Must you leave straight away? – Lynny -- I would so much like to talk a bit more!" She asked softly.

"Eh! – Sure! – I don't have to report back until dawn!" I replied. I didn't mean it to sound like a pass.

She laughed. "I don't mean to talk all night - you silly goose -- but!" She paused as if to measure what she was about to say. "Perhaps you would consider seeing me home?"

"Wow!" I could not have planned it any better.

I waited for her to meet with some of the officials that set up the dance. She emerged from a room off to the side of the dance floor presently and we walked out to the side walk. I made sure to walk on the street side, remembering my Momma said that's where a gentleman should position himself. It was a little past 2300 hours and I offered to call a taxi.

Leslie protested with a pouty face and taking my arm, she spoke in that so proper English. "Oh! – Lynny – I would so much rather walk - it will allow us to talk and become much better acquainted." That made me happy.

As we walked, she told me of the surrounding buildings and their wartime history. Weymouth was a short distance across a little bay from Portland. Portland was a major target of the Nazis in WWII, because of its shipyard and port. She could remember the whistles of the bombs as they fell and the screams of the dive bombers. She said it seemed as if it would never stop. On occasions, German planes would dive and shoot a stream of bullets through the roofs of homes in Weymouth. It would cause water leaks when it rained and was a general nuisance.

I took her hand as we crossed a street. I did it as a courtesy gesture, but she held on and we walked hand in hand until we reached her home. Leslie's Dad was captured by the Germans in 1939. He was a railroad man, and was imprisoned for the war. He lost a leg in the camp, but after the war he acclimated to the leg loss and was once again employed by the rail system in England. Her Mom was a homemaker.

We walked up the few steps to her home, which was one of the three story units in a long building. No way to the rear of the homes unless you went around the entire block. We stopped at the door.

Leslie turned to me, and took my other hand in hers. "I would so much like for my parents to meet you – Lynny -- but it's quite late and they are surely asleep by now."

I told her it was OK, perhaps another time.

"Oh! – How delightful!" She almost squealed. "Can you make it tomorrow about two in the afternoon?" -- My father will be home by then and I would so like for him to meet you!"

I was a little stunned by how quick this all was moving, not that I minded, you understand. I had the 0800 to 1200 watch on that Sunday morning and would have no problem getting a standby for the rest of the day. It was Sunday and no work was scheduled, so a standby was an easy "I.O.U." I agreed and she gave a happy little jump, pulled my hands to her breast and gave me a quick sweet kiss, turned and entered her home.

Luckily I remembered we only made two turns from the Queen's Ballroom to Leslie's home, so retracing my steps was not a problem; however I didn't realize how far we had walked. I was getting concerned that I had gone wrong somewhere, when I looked to the right at St. Thomas Street and saw the little bridge that led to Portland, I knew where I was. I soon met up with a couple of other sailors and we shared a taxi to our boats.

Sunday dawned cool and foggy, I mean really foggy. The air was filled with a thick white blanket of mist that gave birth to a hundred fog horns of different pitches. It was almost comical to hear the differences in their tones. Some were deep and resonant, others, almost like the little squeeze bulb horns on a child's tricycle. Fog tends to dampen all sounds except that which is on the water.

As I stood my topside watch, quite often, I would hear the sounds of a boat as it pushed its way through the water. The sounds would be alarming as I would strain my eyes in anticipation of seeing a ship suddenly crash into our side.

The fog contained constant tinkling of bells and the predictable blast of the marker buoys. I'm sure the local boaters and fisherman were used to this fog, but I wasn't. It was the most trying four hours of top side watch I ever endured.

Fortunately we were moored alongside the Piper and didn't have to adjust our mooring lines. The Piper however was subject to Portland's huge tidal difference and maintained constant line adjustment.

The fog was so thick, the topside watch on the Piper could not see the lines from the watch post and had to constantly walk and test the tautness of the mooring lines with his feet. I would cover his post as he inspected. We shared the mooring line crew with the Piper and kept them busy. If you miss the time to adjust your mooring lines by just a few minutes, you are in big trouble. The mooring lines are not little ropes. They are very substantial and as the tremendous weight of the boat is stressed on these lines, they will draw so tight that you are unable to loosen them. It is very important to keep a close watch on your mooring lines.

I was beginning to worry about my 1400 hour date at Leslie's home. The fog lifted somewhat as the morning wore on and by noon the taxis were running. Ferrand, the Preacher's son stood by for me, but I had to agree to take his 0400 to 0800 watch on Monday morning. .

There were three of us in the taxi as we crossed the bridge into Weymouth. I had explained to the guys about Leslie and they couldn't believe that I had hooked up the first night and was going to a girl's home to meet her parents on the second day in port. We only went a few more blocks, to drop off the sailors in the center of town and the driver turned back to carry me to Leslie's. I knew what street to take from St. Thomas Street but failed to make note of Leslie's street.

The driver was a nice chap and asked questions about the houses and surroundings. I remembered the homes were brick, and not painted. There were no lanes between the houses and when I told him there were only three or four steps up to the door, he stated. "We're on - mate!" and drove me to the center of the block where Leslie lived. He knew his town.

The fog had lifted and I could see the corner where I turned to go downtown. I was making a mental measurement as to which door was Leslie's, when a door opened and Leslie softly called, "It's the one with the lion's head knocker - Lynny!"

I hoped my brisk walk was not a giveaway as I hurried to her door. It would be nice to have a little of that British aloofness.

Leslie gave me a sweet but brief kiss at the door and whispered. "They are waiting - don't expect any gushing – Lynny - they are quite reserved."

Her Dad was standing on his one leg and had his hand on the wall rail for support. Her Mom was dressed in a proper blue flower print dress that accentuated her blue eyes. I extended my hand to Mr. Saunders as I acknowledged Mrs. Saunders.

I immediately turned my focus back to Mr. Saunders and he removed his right hand from the rail and placed his left hand on the back of a huge easy chair in front of a blazing coal fire. His grip was manly and his hands calloused. I was very familiar with hands like these. My Daddy, Uncle Bud, Uncle Gene. Every telephone man and helmsman on submarines has these same hands.

Mr. Saunders noticed. "Not a stranger to working with your hands - are ya - lad?"

"No Sir!" I replied. "Climbing poles and steering submarines are kinda rough on them."

"Rough on stockings too - I fear!" I didn't catch his meaning right off, but when Mrs. Saunders gave him a pinch and a look, I caught it.

We talked briefly and Mrs. Saunders told me she was pleased to meet the first sailor that her daughter had every brought home to meet them. I noticed that our blue eyes were much alike and I was curious if she may be of old Scottish blood. I never asked.

We had a pleasant visit before Leslie suggested we go walk about town. The fog had lifted, but she told me it would be back, so I needed to be back on the Torsk before 2200 hours or the taxis would stop running.

Somehow the walks with Leslie were not nearly as long as when I'm alone. We walked to the center of town and she was giving me the grand tour. We held hands and it was as if we had known each other for years. The buildings were very close, I'm sure it had something to do with the narrow streets. This town was built long before automobiles and the streets, though now paved, required great attention if you were to drive. Some of the streets went to the very edge of the buildings, others had sidewalks, but they didn't have the extreme edges that we have in the states. It was common to see a car drive on the sidewalk as they navigated around town. I realized why the English had such small cars. There wasn't room for anything any larger.

I told Leslie, I knew why the British drive on the wrong side of the road. I had to clarify this concept, as she had no idea that we thought they drove on the wrong side. I dropped the idea of my little joke because I thought she would not understand it.

In a moment she questioned me as to why I thought they drove on the wrong side of the road.

I thought. "Well here goes! – You see – Leslie - these streets are so narrow and the drivers spend so much time on the wrong side -they just decided to stay there!"

She looked at me with a complete blank face. I figured, I had really screwed up.

As I looked into that beautiful angelic face, I thought how much she looked like the girl back home and I was with her.

Suddenly a flash of understanding sparkled in her eyes and she began to laugh in pure delight, she had caught on. She grabbed my arm and hugged it to her breast, a felt a brief nostalgic flash. I remembered France.

"Lynny?" Leslie's voice brought me back. "I know a lovely pub that serves a fine roast beef if you would like to join me?" I was caught by surprise. Did she mean that she was planning to have dinner without me or was she offering to pay?

I needed to clarify this situation. I looked at my watch, it was 1730 hours. The time had flown by and she probably felt I was thoughtless. "Leslie – Please forgive me - I was lost in your charms and forgot the time. Please! -- Have dinner with me at your lovely pub?"

"Well - since you put it that way. What's a lady to say?" She took my arm and we walked to a nice little pub near St. Thomas and Bond Streets.

The meal was very good, the beef was tender and succulent and the cabbage was cooked just like home. The potatoes were new to me. They were cut and boiled with peeling on and covered in a buttery clear sauce heavy with spices. They were excellent. I tried an English beer again. I told Leslie how I felt about beer and it was embarrassing to be out with a group of sailors and not drink a beer. Leslie said she thought I would enjoy a Shandy and she ordered one to go with my meal. It was by far a better drink than other beers. It had that familiar beer taste but was almost lemony. It went pretty well with the meal.

I tried my hand at darts and the local gentry had great sport at my expense. They shouted. "We hope ya ain't the bloke what aims them torpedoes, mate!" The Brits laughed heartily at this well put joke.

There were a couple of British sailors in the pub as well. I felt a bit uneasy at first, but they fell into an atmosphere of gaiety and I soon relaxed.

It was getting late and when Leslie and I stood to leave, the locals all raised their glasses in a salute to the bloke that couldn't hit a dart board with a torpedo. I really enjoyed this night.

Leslie and I hadn't walked half a block when a sickening thud came to our ears. A young man on a scooter had pulled out of St Thomas in front of a bus on Bond Street. The man was lying on the ground in front of the bus and not moving at all. I could see the thick red pool of blood beginning to form as his dark locks were matted to the pavement. The bus was not going very fast, and had fully stopped with no brake squeal. The scooter was on its side only a few feet from the impact. The victim had struck the back of his head on the pavement.

I ran to his side, knowing not to move him. Moving him could cause further damage if there were any broken bones. The bleeding had to be stopped. I jerked my neckerchief from my neck and quickly folded it into a hand sized pad. I gently placed the neckerchief under the back of his head and applied direct pressure on the massive split in his skull. I noticed, from the peculiar twist in his left arm, that it may possibly be broken.

"Has anyone called an ambulance?" I cried. A fairly large crowd had gathered.

"Indeed! – Indeed! -- The lolly will be along presently!" -- Carry on -- young man -- carry on!" A stuffy and very proper male voice called out.

I hadn't forgotten Leslie, but the man needed some help. The crowd was quiet and very reserved. No one else came to help and I began to feel conspicuous. I called. "Is there a doctor here?"

There was no answer but I heard a lady's voice say she had heard that in a movie once and immediately a group began a discussion on what movie it was and who said it. It went from Cary Grant to Van Johnson or Alex Guinness and so on.

Finally I heard the ambulance as it jingled its way through the narrow lanes. It pulled behind the bus and as an attendant rushed up, he called out. "Dicky - we'll need the gurney!"

An answer echoed back. "Righto Chief!"

I told him of the head wound and my suspicion of a broken arm.

"Ye done good! – Mate! -- We'll take 'er from 'ere -- thank ye ever so!" He placed a large gauze pad over the head wound as I removed my neckerchief.

I stood and felt I had done all I could do. I walked back to where Leslie waited. She took my arm and hugged it close to her breast. That must be a European thing with women and it made me warm all over.

"Careful Leslie - There is a lot of blood!" I warned.

"Never you mind - you kind - kind man - let's go straight home and we'll clean you up! - I think the fog will hold for a bit."

We went briskly by a different route, but it made sense, the town was laid out in crisscross streets and we simply approached her home from the opposite direction. I admired the ability this lady had in walking, I think she walked everywhere.

Her Mom and Dad left us in the living room and retired early. I said early, it was already 2100 hours and the fog was heading in. Leslie washed the blood from my neckerchief and proceeded to iron it dry. The iron was an old cast iron relic that she placed on the gas stove to get hot. They had no refrigerator. I asked about food storage. She said they stored very little. They went to the market almost daily and picked up what they needed for their meals. Fish and chips were a major meal fare in England.

I had hoped to get a little closer to Leslie that night, but I could see it was not going to happen. I needed to catch a taxi very soon. The neckerchief was a little damp as I rolled it and tied it around my neck, but was going to be fine.

I pulled Leslie to me and she stopped just short of my lips and whispered softly. "That was a wonderful thing you did for a perfect stranger tonight. I was very proud of you!"

The kiss was fabulous. I had to have more, but my reserve told me. "Not tonight!"

"Leslie - I will be here only until Thursday – please -- we must spend some more time together." I pleaded.

"Lynny -- I must work! -- I'll try for holiday Tuesday -- if you can arrange it -- we'll take a train to Dorchester and I'll show you to my co-workers at the County Hall."

I agreed, "But Leslie what about tomorrow?" I asked.

She smiled, "You know where I live and I'm home by five."

Another kiss, this time it had a different meaning and my reserve was going fast

"Don't push your luck!" A little voice spoke to my conscience. "Good night Leslie!" I was out the door.

I started for St. Thomas Street. Luckily I saw a taxi approaching as I reached the corner. I had a taxi all to myself back to the Torsk. I didn't like footing the whole bill, but it was much too far to consider walking from Weymouth to Portland and the fog was coming fast.

I slept hard for the four hours before I took Ferrand's watch at 0400 Monday morning.

As I relieved David Paine topside, I could hear a heated commotion at the stern of the Piper. They had missed their timing on the stern lines and the weight of the boat had pulled the line so tight that it had to be cut. They were in the process of attaching the new line. It really is not a loss because the old line will be spliced into another old line and reused at some other mooring job elsewhere. Mooring lines have a great deal of stretch ability and last an amazingly long time. We sailors also know how to make splices that are actually stronger than an un-spliced section of line. The line may break at the splice, but not in the splice.

The fog was even thicker this night than before. We had to feel our way everywhere we went. Luckily none of our sailors had stayed out late, but it wasn't a dull watch. Normally the topside watches would converse in the wee hours of a lonely morning, but not tonight. I suppose we were afraid of who was listening.

Man, we couldn't see much further than we could step, so we stepped with caution. It's a strange feeling to walk your deck that is very familiar, and find it to be much further than you remembered. You also hear strange sounds. The foghorns and whistles are bad enough, but when you hear a splashing in the water that your imagination tells you is a person swimming, you get the willies. I heard someone swim all over that bay, and suggested a roll call from all the boats.

It was amazing to hear a guy call his name and boat. You know he is 500 yards away, but he sounds like he's right alongside. Every boat answered and we continued to hear our swimmer. We never did find the source of the splashes. Perhaps it was just fish jumping, we'll never know.

Breakfast was lean and Hersey told everyone that we had stores on the way. The word was passed that there would be no early liberty until we had unloaded and stored the supplies.

It was strange to see so many vegetables. We had lettuce and cabbage up the "yagh yagh", there was a ton of meats. We were going to give lamb a try. It was obvious we had bought English stores. Lambert and Hersey had gone with Mr. Dowe, the supply officer and had purchased stores at an English wholesale distributor. We were very low on dishwashing powder so Lambert picked up a jug of liquid that was concentrated. The potatoes were a smaller variety than our Idaho spuds, but I told the guys if our cooks could get that recipe from the pub, where Leslie and I had dinner, Sunday night, we would send a ship to England just for potatoes.

Francis made a crack about how I was in love with Leslie, he did it in a taunting way. He twisted her name to sound like Lesbian. It really fried me. No one was looking and I grabbed a handful of his shirt and put him against the bulkhead.

I got very close to his face and slowly growled. "One more time and I'll break your face!" I released my grip and immediately went back to work. I never heard another word from him.

We had the stores tucked away by 1300. Catfish held lunch for us so the trucks could clear the pier. We had soup, which was very good, we knew it was a hodge-podge of everything we had left over, from the last week.

I found the Chief and asked permission for a day of leave to go to Dorchester the next day. Pappy said he would ask Mr. Burkart if I could do that. I knew that liberty was available after 0800 in the mornings while in a visiting port. There were exceptions like this morning when everyone was needed to get the stores onboard. But I was leaving the locale and needed proper papers to do so.

Mr. Burkart found that Dorchester was less than fifty miles from Weymouth and told me I would not need any special papers and that leave papers were not necessary. I asked permission to leave prior to 0800 to catch an early train with Leslie.

Mr. Burkart looked at me intently. I knew something was bugging him. "Mr. Burkart – Look! I'm just going to meet some folks with a girl I met in Weymouth. She works for Dorset County in Dorchester and wants me to meet her friends - that's all. I'll be back tomorrow afternoon. We're having dinner at a pub in Weymouth.

Mr. Burkart relaxed and said he thought I was going up there to meet her parents.

I told him, that I met them the second day we were here.

"Wardlaw! You're not planning to go off and marry this girl are you?" The question stunned me. I just looked at him.

"Look if this is serious - When we get back to the states – I'll help you with the legal work -- but I won't have you running off and marrying some girl in a strange country -- after less than a week -- Hell! – Boy! - You have no idea what kinda crap that will stir up!"

"Mr. Burkart -- I swanee promise that won't happen -- I'd have to talk to my Momma and Daddy before I did anything like that!" I think he got a little tickled when I said that, but I would never consider such a thing without my parent's knowledge.

He told me I could leave whenever I saw fit.

I met the train when it came in from Dorchester that afternoon. A lot of people from Weymouth and Portland worked in Dorchester and I thought I had made a mistake thinking I could find Leslie in that crowd. I needn't worry, I heard her call to me long before I would have seen her. She was all smiles as she ran to meet me; she threw her arms around my neck and rose on one tiptoe with the other foot raised behind her. She showered me with superfluous kisses and started giggling.

She whispered in my ear. "I've seen this scene in so many old war movies - I simply dared not miss the opportunity to act it out! – How did I do?"

I pushed her away and said. "Terrible - we must do a retake! – stay right there!" I rushed off to the gate she came through -- I turned and called. "Leslie - Darling - I'm back and ran to her waiting arms. As I embraced her she placed her hands on my chest and cried -- "Stop! --------My name is Mary!" The crowd that had stopped to witness this little charade laughed and some even applauded. I think I heard a lady say she had seen that in a movie. I was really beginning to care deeply for this girl.

It was a hearty walk from the train station to Leslie's home. I asked if there was any information on the young man that was injured the night before. Leslie stated that the newspaper said he would recover after a lengthy stay in the hospital.

We stopped at a market on the corner a few blocks from her home and I bought the Saunders dinner for that Monday night. It was my first encounter with fish and chips. I was amazed to find it was nothing more than fish filets and French fries; they were wrapped in wax paper and newspaper. I'll admit the fries were much crunchier than our fries at home. The British use more salt and vinegar. I missed catsup on my fries.

Leslie and I walked downtown and spent hours sitting in an open room on a pavilion that jutted out into the bay at Weymouth. There were no lights and except for an occasional sailor looking for a place to rid himself of his excess beer, we were alone in utter darkness.

There was no reserve in our relationship now. We were totally engrossed in each other, but we dared not enter that blessed state of ultimate intimacy, it is reserved for another place and time. I felt the first pangs of love; it physically hurt and was frightening.

I didn't want to leave Leslie that night, but it was necessary. We couldn't stay in the cabana all night and she had a reputation, as well as her parents to be concerned with. We slowly walked to her home and we lingered at her steps until a neighbor came out, for whatever reason, and piddled around in a planter at the footsteps. I kissed her one more time and started for my Torsk. That faceless lady came again that night as I slept. She held me close and comforted me.

I thought I was going to have to walk the entire way to Weymouth that Tuesday morning. I was off the boat at 0530 and there were no taxis anywhere in sight. I knew there were people in Portland that were heading for Weymouth, but I guess none came by the piers. As soon as I reached the main road to Weymouth a motorist stopped and offered me a ride.

He introduced himself as a Mr. Peters. He was a barrister and remarked that he knew a Wardlaw from Edinburgh, Scotland, also a barrister. They had collaborated on some legal work on properties on the northern shore of the Forth River in County Wardlaw, Scotland. I told him that we were probably of the same blood line, as my ancestors had come from Scotland to America in 1720. He was a friendly man and drove me straight to the train station.

As I sat and waited for Leslie, I wished I had asked him to drop me off at her home and we could have walked together. I thought that may not have been a good idea. I could have missed Leslie and not knowing the route she took, could have fouled everything up. She had suggested I meet her at the station by 7:00AM and that was best. I was very early, not even 0630 hours. I sat at the first bench inside the gate, so I could see her as soon as she arrived. The crowds began to arrive and soon a car pulled up and three girls and a guy got out, Leslie was the last out and saw me as soon as I stood. I guess it was their equivalent of a car pool.

"Lynny, I would like you to meet my friends!" She said as she graciously introduced me to her companions. They all worked at the County Hall. "We must hurry along now - or we will be split!" I think she meant that the compartment would be crowded and we could not all sit together. I really didn't care as long as I sat by her.

She was dressed in a neat light brown tweed skirt with matching jacket. She wore a gold silk blouse. Her shoes were brown to match the outfit, but not as stylish as the outfit. They were a simple design with maybe a one inch heel. Her hair was naturally curled and a little less than shoulder length, just right to kiss the back of the neck without having to brush the hair aside. Her makeup was there, but not noticeable. This was the first time we had been in a group where she knew everyone and the conversation was not all directed at me. She held my hand and as she talked to the others she would always look them in the eye, but her hand language told me that I had her attention. It was nice to hold hands with her.

We sat in a compartment that seated eight comfortably. The people, in the group I was traveling with, were all well-educated and spoke very proper English. I was very self-conscious of my southern drawl, and tried to speak as proper as I knew how, but the ya'lls and any word with an "o" would slip out as "aw" every once in a while. Leslie never said anything, but the guy in the group would slip a bit of cockny in his conversation to mock me. Every time he would insert a bit of British profanity in his speech, he would put this pious look on his face.

I was getting tired of it and after a bit of vulgarity, I faked a little laugh and leaned across the aisle and whispered in his ear. "I hope you don't talk a lot in your job - it will be difficult for you to speak with no teeth and swollen lips!" My eyes were stern and my gaze piercing as I gave another laugh and sat back in my seat.

The color left his cheeks and his gaze immediately went out the window to the hazy countryside. He never uttered another word and was first out of the car when the train stopped. I didn't even feel sorry for him. Leslie sensed something was wrong but never spoke of it.

The ride was less than an hour and Dorchester was a beautiful town. It was a lot like Weymouth and Portland. There was no big city atmosphere or big city buildings anywhere to be seen. In front of the County Hall was a square where I sat and waited for Leslie to go inside to make arrangements for me to come in.

She introduced me around to people she worked near and then asked me if I would be terribly disappointed if she were unavailable until noon. I think she may have had trouble getting off work to spend time with me. I didn't mind and told her I would walk around and see some sights. She apologized and told me that Dorchester did not have much to offer. I assured her it was alright.

I walked through Dorchester and admired its beauty. There was a military base there that had an extensive history. The Brits have had some rough times through the years. The British people have endured countless invasions and are much the same as Americans.   America is a mixture of different ethnic backgrounds, due to people coming of their free will. England has been invaded by different European people and just absorbed them.

I met Leslie at noon and we had lunch at a nearby pub. The rest of the day went fast and we took an early train home. The girl was fast becoming a fixation with me. I knew I was leaving in two days and should just back off. I began to think of what Mr. Burkart had said about helping me with marriage plans. I didn't realize I was projecting that impression, and had not thought about it, until now. It was not a bad thought, but I kept it to myself. I remembered Yvonne and realized that the U.S. Navy was very demanding and I didn't want to hurt anyone else, so I never addressed anything of a marriage nature to Leslie.

We had the living room to ourselves as her folks retired early. We both fit into her dad's easy chair and nestled in each other's arms. I told her of my young life in Louisiana and Savannah. She told me she never knew anyone, that had that much adventure. She examined the scar on my wrist from a hunting knife accident and then turned her attention to the scar on my forehead from a 22 rifle shot. I never mentioned to her that her Dad had seen much worse than anything I had been through. Apparently her Dad had never mentioned any details of his wartime capture and imprisonment. I felt he was a true hero.

I had dinner Wednesday night with Leslie's parents in the small kitchen on the second floor of their modest home.   Her Mom fixed corned beef and cabbage. I had never had corned beef before and fell in love with it. It has been a favorite ever since.

We almost spent the night in that big chair and those pangs were in my chest again as I kissed her for the last time that night. It was the wee hours of the morning as I walked away from that trim figured beauty that had stolen my heart. I remembered her sweet angelic face, as she stared after me in the dim light of the street lamps. There were no tears in her eyes but that wistful look of lost love was there. I cried enough for the both of us. The pain in my chest was real.

I deliberately walked all the way to St. Thomas Street and across the bridge and would probably have walked all the way to Portland, had a taxi not stopped. The taxi already had a fare, Jerry Shallock, an electrican mate from the Torsk. He offered to share the Taxi and I accepted. The tears had dried by this time. Neither Jerry nor I shared the reasons for our late return that night. I really hoped he was not hurting like me.

The faceless lady almost tucked me in that night. I don't remember even climbing up in my bunk, but she was there and comforted me until reveille.

The heart ache was excruciating as the ships whistle sounded at 1600 hours. The whistle meant we were clear of the pier and under way.   I had spent the day topside. I would fabricate some deck choir to do so I could keep my eyes on the pier. I fully expected Leslie to come running down the pier with tears in her eyes calling my name. That's what Hollywood would do if they were directing this heartbreaking scenario. She never came and as the commands began to come to maneuver the boat I imagined in my mind the route we took to leave port.

I called up to Tighe on starboard lookout. I knew that there would be a long jettie that extended from the mainland. "Anyone on the jettie, Tighe?   He answered negative. I fantasized that Leslie was running down the jetties calling my name, hoping to catch a last glimpse of her love.

Mr. Sheehan voice brought me back to reality. "Mind your helm - Wardlaw!" There was nothing wrong with my steering, but Mr. Sheehan, in his wisdom, knew I had to refocus on my job. He was right and it was the only time in my entire career that I ever had to be told to "Mind my Helm!" It didn't help the chest pain though. It was real and it hurt terribly. Something deep inside told me it was pyscological, so I blinked back the tears and tried to put my broken heart to rest. I didn't want my Torsk to know that I cared for anyone else.

We stayed on the surface all night until 0947 on Friday, October 11, 1957. We dove the boat on what came near to being the last dive of the U.S.S. Torsk SSG423.

The Captain was on the bridge as I finished my watch and was relieved. I heard him tell Mr. Dowe to pull the plug in a little bit. He also mentioned that sonar needed a new mentality when listening for the Russians. He was going to his quarters. I went to my bunk to stow my cap before turning to, on ships work.

"AHUUUGAH! – AHUUUGAH! - DIVE! – DIVE!" Came that exhilarating claxon and voice command. I could feel the boat as she seemed to take a deep breath like a swimmer would, before a plunge into icy water.

Something was wrong. We had dived many times and always there is an attitude that prevails in making a dive. The boat always noses down, sometimes just a little and sometimes a very pronounced down angle. The boat was diving stern first. We are not designed to dive stern first. The angle was not just a slight down bubble as we call it, but was fast approaching twenty degrees.

The crew was frantically grabbing something to hold on to, there was no panic, and the officers were giving commands to correct the situation. The commands were not helping much and I could hear men calling out their thoughts as to the problems. I held on to my bunk and placed my feet against the locker that was at the end of the crossway to our row of bunks.

I could hear the thuds of bodies as crewmen lost their grip and fell the length of the corridor to crash against the door to the head. I heard no cries of pain or terror. I knew the fate of our boat was in the hands of the men in the control room. I could hear voices suggesting the after torpedo room was flooded. I felt the boat begin to shudder violently and knew we were all ahead full. The maneuvering room was OK. That's where the propellers are controlled from.

Suddenly there was a great swooshing sound as the high pressure air was released to blow the water from our safety tank. This tank in always full of water and is designed to compensate for a flooded conning tower. My ears began to feel pressure, I knew we were in trouble. We had been to 350 feet before and we never felt ear pressure, but it was there now. I wished I could do something, but I was completely helpless. It was all I could do to simply hold on and not plummet to the after wall of the crews sleeping quarters.

My Torsk began to complain. Her groans of pain were a result of compressed metal that was straining to hold pressure she was not designed for. We were well past our designed test depth of 412 feet. We had always heard that the Navy's published test depth was only half of the actual depth that a sub could handle. I had never seen that in writing and I was certain that we were about to find out.

Remember, I wrote about the physics of how a submarine depends on the proper trim and buoyancy to operate efficiently under water. When that buoyancy gets too far past the neutral state, you sink and you sink fast. We were no longer diving, we were sinking. I remembered the feeling I had when we saw the torpedo wakes coming at us, in the North Sea. To us, they were real and we were helpless. Death, again, was imminent. I was going to die; I expected the hull to split and the cold water of the North Atlantic to sweep me away.

The creaks and moans were more pronounced now. Blowing our main ballast tanks would prove fatal. They are not designed to withstand any pressure at all. If we had enough pressure to blow that much water out then the external pressure would simply crush the tanks and our doom would be sealed. The only way out was by power, pure power, and the batteries were being called to do their best.

My eyes began to burn as the batteries began to heat. They were called on to provide full power and not just push us through the water in a state of neutral buoyancy, but overcome whatever was making us sink, stern first.

I prayed; "Lord! - Please accept my spirit!" I tensed my body and once again thought. "I am going to feel what it is like to die!" The lights flickered out, and the emergency red lights took over. I shut my eyes and could feel my Torsk shudder in her throes of agony. She was trying. I could hear distant voices. "Depth's holding! – Sir! – Flooding in the after room! - Sir! Down bubble decreasing! – Sir!" Somehow the Captain had made it to the control room.

I heard Mr. Bibby's voice call. "Captain – should we seal off the after room?"

"Negative – I think we're holding tight! – But we got fitting leaks everywhere!" The Captain's voice was cool and steady.

That's when I noticed a red mist in front of the red emergency light. The water was coming through a pin hole at a fitting through the hull and as it sprayed it dissipated in a red mist, reflected by the emergency lighting.

The deck was quite wet. "We're coming up!" a loud voice cried. The cheers were even louder.

I noticed the down angle was disappearing and my Torsk had ceased to groan. The shuddering continued and the caustic sulfuric fumes were beginning to burn my nose. I heard the air exchange system shut down. Someone was wise enough to know not to spread the deadly fumes through the whole boat. I noticed the red mist had disappeared.

It seemed an eternity in red silence. Suddenly I was startled back to reality.

"AHUUUGAH! – AHUUUGAH! – AHUUUGAH! – SURFACE! – SURFACE! – SURFACE!" It was Mr. Dowe's voice on the speaker. Another eternity passed, then the rush of compressed air as we blew our main ballast tanks. My legs went limp as I felt that familiar roll that told us we were no longer submerged. "Set damage control!" Came the call. I struck out for the tower.

As I passed through the control room on the way to the helm, I reported the water leak in the crews after battery sleeping quarters. As it turned out we had over twenty such leaks reported and even some minor injuries as a result of pinhole water leaks. Some of the crew had somehow passed under some of these leaks and the water pressure had actually bruised the skin.

I never felt it at the time, but across my left shoulder was a ten inch mark as if I had been lashed with a wire. We collected our thought and wits and began the process of analyzing what went wrong. The Runner and Cavalla came to our aid and were standing off the starboard and port beam as we wallowed in the North Atlantic.

My vantage point at the wheel put me at the center of all the data that flowed to be analyzed. I will try to explain in terms I hope will be understood. The mistake made, that brought about this near disastrous dive, was a result of a modern invention and a lack of concentration on a most important detail.

We had just received a new invention that was designed to cut paper work to a minimum. It was called a Xerox machine. The yeoman had made some new copies of the "Rig for dive" check sheets. This is all well and good except for one little thing about these copies. The paper was like a thin photo paper and would store static electricity and stick together. It was not a matter of rubbing the papers between your fingers to separate them because they would cling to each other. The duty officer that rigged the boat for dive had missed a crucial page.

A submarine depends on a number of precise conditions to operate efficiently while submerged. It must achieve neutral buoyancy in order not to require excessive power to push through the water. If you have positive buoyancy the boat wants to broach or skim the surface and you must use more power in order for the bow and stern planes to force the boat deeper. If your buoyancy is negative then the same thing applies to keep from sinking too deep.

Now we must make sure the boat is trim, that is to be level forward and aft , and starboard and port. The sideways trim is not a problem as the ballast tanks flood evenly. The "Christmas Tree" is a panel of red and green lights that reflect the condition of the tank valves. The Chief of the boat and the con officer are waiting for the light confirmation on the panel. "Green- board! – Sir!" is the signal that confirms that all is normal for a dive. That was the case in our catastrophe. The board was green because the problem did not occur with the tanks that control the dive.

The problem was with the forward and after trim tanks. These tanks are designed to balance the only load on a submarine that constantly changes. Clean fuel constantly changes as it is used by the engines. The fuel oil in the saddle fuel tanks is subjected to sea pressure and as it is used, the sea water takes its place and there is no weight problem. The fuel goes through a fuel oil purifier that separates any water intrusion and debris from the fuel. The clean fuel is then stored in two huge tanks inside the submarine, one forward and the other aft. The forward clean fuel oil tank is compensated for by adding or removing water from the forward trim tank. The same operation controls the weight aft.

The page that the duty officer missed was to trim the boat for the condition the inboard clean fuel oil tanks were in at the time of the dive.

We were running on the after clean fuel tank when we entered Portland Harbor. It was nearly empty, but was of no concern; we had ample fuel to moor the boat. The forward clean fuel tank was full. During the week in Portland, the fuel was transferred from the forward clean fuel tank to the after clean fuel tank. No water was added to the forward trim tank to compensate for the 16000 pounds of fuel that was no longer in the forward fuel tank. That fuel is now in the after tank and no water is removed from the after trim tank to offset the 16000 pounds added to the rear of the boat, that's what the missed sheet was to take care of. Mathematically it meant the Torsk dove with the stern 32000 pounds heavier than a normal trim.

Now, the submarine has for all practical purposes no buoyancy of its own, because we have deliberately set about to make her efficient by achieving neutral buoyancy. Long story short, the Torsk diving condition was like having eight hundred concrete blocks tied to her stern.

Our problems were just beginning. We finally pulled ourselves together and made a list of the reported leaks, but decided that a dive was necessary to see if any leaks would require any immediate attention. A special damage control team made a trip through the boat and checked everything we could think of that excessive pressure could have damaged. The Captain gave the command to the bridge to make six knots and we would trim the boat making sure that the missing page was double checked.

The maneuvering room reported the motors were laboring and the temperature alarms were sounding. We came to all stop. The Captain and the engineering officer went to the maneuvering room to investigate the problem. The propellers are at the end of two long steel shafts that go through the lower part of the boats stern. They connect the propellers to the electric motors. The housingss for the shafts are called the stern tubes. Obviously there can be no bearings for the shafts to turn in because the spans for bearings would allow water to flood in the boat. The stern tubes have a teak wood bushing on the inside and outside of the stern tubes with rags dipped in thick water proof grease stuffed into the housing for lubrication and water seal. The extreme pressure of the depth, we went to, was sufficient to force the outer seal and grease coated rags into a confined space that was actually binding the propeller shafts. The stern of our Torsk had reached over nine hundred feet. God was watching out for us.

The captain ordered all engines to run and began to cycle the motors on and off. Gradually the shafts began to loosen to the point we could make turns without over heating the motors. The stern tubes had always leaked, as is common on all ships that have propeller shafts that protrude under water. Our shafts had quit leaking due to the new pressure that nature had put on the packing.

The Captain gave the command to make six knots. All went well, we breathed a sigh of relief. The Captain had considered pulling us out of our return home operation due to the mishap. The decision was made to continue and we made a test dive to ascertain any leak damage and its severity. We were amazed to find absolutely no leaks at all. We had numerous personnel in every compartment and even in the channels that led to each bilge. We found no leaks above normal even at 400 feet. We were all relieved at our good fortune. The leaks that had manifested themselves were all due to excessive water pressure and would require X-ray to locate.

We surfaced and took our station 1000 yard to port of the Runner, we could see the Cavalla about a half mile beyond the Runner. We made speed of twelve knots, but not for long. The water began to get a little rough and our propellers began to vibrate terribly. The lack of support on the shafts due to the rear teakwood bushing being compressed was causing the shafts to vibrate badly. We could make some speed and everything would be smooth until a wave with a sufficient valley in it would allow a prop to get a gulp of air and the cavitation would set in. The only way to stop it was slow down and gradually pick up speed, only to have it happen again shortly. The Commander of the Sixth Naval submarine was on board the Runner. Captain King and Mr. Burkart had a UQC conversation with the commander and agreed to continue with the programmed operations.

We performed very well when submerged and spent a lot of time snorkeling in choppy seas. We completed all of our assigned operations. The only difficulty was getting to our next station for operation in time. We never missed our queues but we had little rest and the strain was telling on everyone.

We spent all day at battle stations on October 13. We would fire a MK 14 exercise shot, locate the fish, breakout the boom and retrieve the fish, stow the boom. Dive the boat, go to battle stations and repeat the operation again.

I went 37 hours without sleep. Mr. Bibby talked Mr. Burkart into putting Catfish back on the wheel for some "Refreshing of his skill." I slept for a heavenly six hours. Catfish said the pecan pie was cancelled. I didn't care. The faceless lady fed me pecan pie the whole time I slept.

We were getting closer to home now and I could see the change in the water. It was still deep water but the sea ran much closer together now than in the North Atlantic. The waves were close together and still any speed over about 9 knots would start that awful vibration. We began some sonar drills. Actually the drills were simply listening exercises.

We were snorkeling and listening late on the afternoon of October 14, when we caught site of a destroyer about 8000 yards away. We secured from snorkeling and began tracking her by sound.

The Navy knows what they are doing. We are on station, which means we are where the Navy told us to be at a precise time. We are doing what the Navy told us to do. We are patrolling a certain area.

The Navy has also told a number of other ships to do certain things like; transgress this area and seek out the potential enemy. We all keep detailed records. All of these operations are scrutinized by a review team and every ship is rated on their results. It is not good, to not measure up, and quite often an up and coming young officer will have the results of these operations decide his Navy future.

We spent the afternoon and well into the night tracking not only this destroyer but a number of other Navy vessels as well. We made simulated runs on a number of ships including a cruiser. We also did our best to hide and escape from repeated depth charge runs on us. We searched in vain for a layer to hide under, but their sonar was locked in on us. I could hear the pinging on the hull. We had to resort to firing false targets that had some good results. We would fire a target and immediately the pinging would subside. The Navy would evaluate our efforts. The destroyers broke off the attack and we were left to hover in that quiet comfortable bliss of silence.

We surfaced and began charging our engines. The fall chill was in the air. I knew that cold weather was on the way. I mentioned this to Mr. Wiseman. He laughed and asked. "Wardlaw – How would you like a vacation in a tropical paradise for a few weeks?"

"Missuh Wiseman! – now don'tcha know you ought'n fun a po ol county boy bout sumpin like dat!" I threw him some cracker lingo.

"Well! – po ol country boy -- when we get patched up from our war wounds and get through with our Philly yard trip -- I'm gonna take yo country ass to the Caribbean and show you some Puerto Rican coota! -- How about dat, Zack?" I guess he read my records and found my middle name, or maybe it just rhymed so he used it. He never called me Zack again, so I guess it simply rhymed.

I got off watch at 0400 and the chow hall, was empty. I wrote Leslie a letter and told her, as best I could, about our near disaster. I had difficulty putting my emotion into words without sounding wimpy, so I tore the letter up and just wrote we had a near miss.

My stomach began to feel funny and in a few moments I was lickity- split to the head. Man, I almost didn't make it. It was not a normal movement. It was loose and didn't want to stop.

I was not seated more than a minute before I heard. "Damn! I shit my drawers -- Damn! – I ain't done that since I was a baby!" The head door opened and Benbow came in and took the other stall. He continued to voice his disbelief in messing his skivvies.

Suddenly the door opened and Jack Bonner cried. "Someone out! – Now! - or I'll shit the deck!"

I grabbed my pants and pulled them up enough to clear my feet and stepped out the door.

Bonner already had his skivvies off and they were on the floor next to Benbow's. They were soiled also. It was a perfect opportunity to make fun of two guys messin in their skivvies, but something told me not to do it, after all, I had just made it myself.

As the early morning progressed it was evident that something was going around. No one seemed to have any nausea, but the majority of the crew had the runs. It seemed to let up about mid-morning, but mid-afternoon was wild.

I didn't have any more problems after my first bout but some of the guys were really suffering. We were fortunate that our exercises were over and the Torsk and Runner were operating independently. That meant we made up our own games. By the second day of the outbreak we had to surface and allow the crew to come topside to take care of their toiletries. The smell in our Torsk was overpowering.

This is not a pretty picture, but I will tell you as it happened. The Torsk slowed to maybe three knots. The crew came topside by way of the after battery hatch and through the conning tower. No shoes, socks, or pants, skivvies were optional. All were directed to go aft of the conning tower. Some brought their clothing with them. They didn't intend to dress, but to wash the crap from their soiled clothing. A salt water hose was in use to wash the excrement from legs, feet and soiled clothing. When a man squatted, the other men, behind him, gave him at least six feet clearance, for obvious reasons.

Some of the crew had no symptoms at all. The officers and Chiefs were not affected. I was no longer having a problem. Those of us that were apparently OK, were doing just what we trained for, someone else's job. The cooks were not affected.

I can't bring myself to ask you to picture this, but there were forty-seven men, squatting on the after-deck of a submarine and squirting anything that was within six feet of their asses. Leave it to a sailor though. The jokes and one liners started.

"Hey! – Jonesy, I thought you didn't give a shit!"

"Hey! – Mac! - You wouldn't shit me, now, would you?"

"Oh Well! – I've always enjoyed a good shit - but this is ridiculouse!"

"What do you get if you shit in one hand and wish in the other?"

We would then dive the boat and allow the sea to clean everything up only to surface again for the same ritual. Captain King said that would be a perfect way to win a war. Give the enemy the running shits. A man can't fight with pants around his ankles and won't fight naked. The dilemma was growing and something had to be done.

On Thursday the 17th of October, a helicopter arrived with a three man medical team. They boarded by lift line and looked like foreboding figures from outer space in their white overalls and breathing masks.

They went straight to work. One of the team began to do water samples; another began to examine some of the crew that had the worst symptoms.

They came to the chow hall and determined there was nothing airborne, so they removed their masks. They sat at the table nearest the wall and were reviewing their findings. One of the team had taken some samples of the excrement and had determined the cause to be laxative induced and voiced some suspicions of sabotage.

One of the team members walked over to where the mess cook was washing dishes. He picked up a freshly rinsed plate and rubbed it between his fingers.

"Hey! Guys! We may have something here!" He walked over with the plate and handed it to the two and said. "Rub it between your fingers".

They did so and immediately requested to see the detergent the mess cook was using.

The approved method of washing dishes on a submarine is to draw a sink full of hot water with the detergent in it and next to it is a sink full of hot rinse water. Every sailor knows to sop his plate with a piece of bread or wipe it out in the trash container. The plates are never loaded with food debris. The mess cook then washes the china or silver with a rag and dips it in the rinse water. It is then set in a tray to drain and dry. Between meals the dishes and cups are placed in racks hanging on the bulkhead above the drain tray.

The medical team determined the English detergent; Lambert had purchased, to be extremely concentrated. In America, concentrated means just a little stronger, in England it means just what it says. Our one dip in the rinse water did not get all the detergent off the plates, cups and silverware.

The Officers and Chiefs had their china and silverware washed with American detergent. Some of the crew not affected simply got plates from the wall rack that had been washed with our previous detergent.

The team said the detergent was safe to use, but limited the amount in the wash water to a tablespoon only. They also said to change the rinse water twice as often as previous.

The team departed in less than four hours after their arrival.

By morning we were back to normal. I was enjoying a healthy helping of bakes beans, hash brown, fried eggs, corn bread and bacon when Carl Bryan walked into the crews mess. He had it particularly rough with the runs.

Catfish called out. "Say – Bryan! I heard you had de running shits. - Is it so?"

Bryan soberly replied. "Is it so? – Catfish! - It's so so - I can't touch it with a powder puff!"

The crews mess erupted in laughter, so loud, that it brought the Chief to see what was up. It was good to have things back to normal.

We continued to operate with the Runner and the Piper. We sank them at least a dozen times and they sank us an equal amount. We were still plagued with the vibrations if we tried to make too much speed. The Captain had given the maneuvering room the prerogative to adjust turns as they saw fit to maintain a desired speed. The crew in maneuvering could sense the vibration well before it started shaking violently and could back off and usually stop it before anyone could tell. The Captain had also lowered our profile in the water and lowered our stern by over filling the after trim tank. We could generally make 9 knots for a considerably long run without the vibration becoming a problem.

CHAPTER VIII

NORFOLK AND PHILLY '57

We moored in Norfolk, Virginia alongside the USS Grampus SS 523 at 1635 hours on October 23, 1957. We were gone from our home port eight days shy of two months. We had been at sea and operating for all but ten days of that time. I had two encounters with death, one imaginary and one real. It made a difference in how I breathed every breath, took every step and thought every thought from then on. The next moment may be my last and there is absolutely nothing I can do about it. I realized how fleeting life is and can end in an instant. It was sobering.

A lot of the guys made arrangements to take a week of leave starting the next day, Thursday. We got loads of mail that morning and my letter to Leslie went off in our outgoing bag. I had two letters from her. One postmarked the day after we left port, October 12, the second was postmarked Monday, the 14th of October.

I waited until 1600 hours, when we quit our topside work, to open Leslie's first letter. I retreated to my secret cave deep in the sail, to a little platform just in front of the main induction valve. I had found this reclusive spot while checking for rust on a routine inspection. It was secluded and no one else cared to go there. I opened Leslie's first letter.

Her handwriting was magnificent. She told me how she felt as she imagined me sailing from Portland Harbor. She was on the train coming home from Dorchester and began to think of me as I steered the boat through the offset jetties and out to sea. She mentioned some of the private moments we had spent together and how she cherished them. I think she really missed me. She told me she planned to go to the Fair that weekend and would tell me about it in her next letter. I decided to get cleaned up a little and go to chow, before treating myself to her second letter. It was a wise choice as I was soon to find out.

We were pigging out on the balance of the English meats we had loaded up on in England. Hersey had made a stew from beef, lamb and pork. He had used the balance of the small potatoes and some canned carrots. It was thick and savory, laced with large chunks of onions. We had a choice of eating it from a bowl, or over rice. I chose rice. It was a double platter. Hersey was a master at meat preparation.

I had a nice shower and put on clean dungarees, before my meal. It was a nice evening until I made my second twenty foot crawl to that secret spot.

I opened Leslie's second letter. She began it, "Dear Lynny, I missed you so much these past few days." She then told me how things didn't seem to have the same impact as they used to have, and she thought she just had a case of the blues. It was only her second letter, but altogether different than her first.

Leslie then wrote of her most unusual experience. She was at the Fair with some of her friends from the County Hall. She wrote that she was stunned to see me standing at a booth with some other fellows. I was in civilian clothes. She left her friends and ran to me. To her embarrassment, of course, it was not me, but an American exchange student going to medical school in England. She said his resemblance to me was uncanny.

I often wondered if this guy simply slid right into the slot I left. I thought of the irony that she met him the same way I met her. I wrote another letter to Leslie but avoided getting too pushy. The weeks went by and I realized I had heard my last from Leslie. The faceless lady visited again. Her company was welcomed, even if only in a dream.

We spent a couple of days in the shipyard at Portsmouth to have new packing placed in our stern tubes. The yardbirds did not even attempt to remove the original packing. They simply filled the void with new greased rags and placed a new teakwood bushing on the outside of each tube. . We had the only stern tubes in the US Navy that had no leaks. On our return across Chesapeake Bay we let her rip. Twenty plus knots and smooth as silk. Captain King was all smiles, one of his greatest pleasures was outrunning the Runner. We were sister boats and often we would stretch it out. Captain King was an ace at trimming the boat for surface speed. I won't tell you how fast I've seen her go, at least not right now.

We spent the better part of the next month operating in Area 19 Alpha, off of Kitty Hawk N.C. It was our state side operating area. We added a new training note to my routine. Ever since I had been on board and studying the boat's operating system I had seen our boat's designation as USS Torsk SSG 423. The SS stands for submersible ship and the G stands for guidance. Our primary job was to guide a Regulis missile when it was launched from the after deck of the Barbero or Growler. We had yet to drill in this area. We set the missile guidance detail a number of times during this month of exercises. My duty station was, as usual, the helm. We had a missile guidance room below the control room that was off limits to all but the missile guidance team. We called it "Combat." It was full of science fiction type screens and scopes that I knew nothing of and was not part of our qualifying curricular. A sailor had to be cleared for "Top secret" to go in the Combat center. I was only cleared for "Secret."

Subron Six had two missile launching submarines. The Barbero and the Growler. We had operated in the North Atlantic with both, on our NATO operation. These submarines carried the Regulus missile. The Regulus I and Regulus II were the American updated versions of the German V1 rocket. The launching submarine would fire the missile and the Torsk or another guidance boat would position themselves to guide the missile to the target. The launching boat had the easy job. They would surface, position themselves and pull the trigger. As soon as the missile left the deck, they could dive and vamoose. The guidance boat, on the other hand, had to remain on the surface and track the missile to confirm its trajectory and send correcting data to the missile.

The success of the launch depended on the accuracy of the guidance boat. I had not been on board for any launches, but we received word that after our yard period in Philly was finished we would get plenty of action.

We moored in Norfolk one crisp Thursday afternoon. We had been in Op Area 19A for four days. A message was waiting for me from the Red Cross. My Papaw had died. I was devastated and very angry that the Navy hadn't notified me more timely.

Mr. Burkart explained that our weekly exercises put us in an area that was critical to our nation's defense. He explained that my parents were notified that my return home would be delayed and had decided not to wait for me.

I spent a sad night with the faceless lady comforting me. I was glad I had the chance to see my Papaw last June. I flattered myself thinking I was the only one he recognized. My memory went back over the visits when I sat at his side, listened to his yarns and watched him spit tobacco juice on that stunted bull nettle cactus. I cried.

On Saturday afternoon, I found my way to an Army – Navy store near the base. They were advertising a sale on custom Navy Blues. I bought a set of thirteen button original bell bottomed blues. The jumper had some nice oriental stitching on the inside of the cuff. I don't know what the original price was, but the twenty-seven dollars I paid, took a healthy cut out of my liberty money. They threw in a child's set of Navy Blues. The set was just the right size for Poco.

Thirteen buttons was the name of the old style trousers the Navy issued at one time. After WW II the zipper became fashionable and my issued uniforms all had zippers. I liked the classic fit and flare of the old style blue so I splurged and bought a set. I never regretted it.

We had spent the week operating with the Barbero. We had simulated numerous missile launches. On Friday, November 15th we highlined Commander C.W. Styer from the Barbero and spent the day drilling, then made our way to Norfolk. The Barbero and the Growler were the two missile boats on the east coast and one was always deployed for our nation's defense. We were going to port, so the Squadron Commander rode home with us.

I decided to spend the weekend on board my Torsk. It was comforting to lounge around the familiar old girl and take time to study her construction and systems. I had been on board a little less than three months and had already completed my qualifying exam. We had six months to qualify, but most sailors completed their qualification in around four months. There were three of us in the same group, Jim Givens, Dave Cummings and myself.

The chief of the boat had assigned us a final project. We had to draw a plan that would allow us to blow the crews sanitary tank [poop tank] through the ships whistle. The concept was intriguing and we had plowed through the plans of the Torsk in a vain effort to find a link that would allow this theory to materialize.

It was Sunday afternoon, November 17, 1957 around 1500 hours. Cummings and I had the boat's air systems plans spread out on a table in the chow hall. We had just finished a late brunch and had some sandwich stuff lying around on the table along with strawberry cool-aid. We were engrossed in our assignment when I heard someone ask what the date was. There were probably a half dozen guys in the vicinity and no one knew. A quick trip was made to the control room and a look in the open log book showed us the correct date.

It suddenly struck me. I was twenty-one today. I made the announcement and all turmoil broke loose as everyone ganged up on me and I got a red belly, along with hair burns and towel pops. It was not really painful, but you must give your buddies their satisfaction or they just get meaner. I was lying on the deck on my side and of course my field of vision was at an angle. Suddenly it hit me.

"Dave – I've got it!" I jumped to my feet and straightened the crumpled plans on the table. "Look! – It's the angle - Man! – We've been trying to hook up the lines and that won't work - but look - let's say the poop tank is full!" I made a slight line at the top of the tank that held the crap and stuff. The line was just a little lower than the opening of the low pressure line that supplied the air to blow the crap out of the tank. Dave Cummings was getting the idea.

"Let's pressurize the tank - just like we were going to blow it - but don't open the dump valve. - It's got pressure in the tank! Right?" Dave nodded. "Now - we shut off the air to the piping system and vent the pressure out of the pipes!"

"Let me finish!" cried Dave excitedly. "We then put a list on the boat and the liquid in the sanitary tank will cover the opening where the air-line comes in. When you open the air valve the pressure in the tank will force the crap into the air line and when we take the diaphragm out of the ship's whistle the shit will hit the fan!"

WOWEEE! – We did it Wardy! – We did it! We gonna qualify in three months! Wait 'til Givens hears this -- He's gonna shit!" We all cracked up.

We made imaginary plans as to how we would request permission to place a ten degree port list on the boat under the pretense of cleaning tank tops. We would then remove the diaphragm from the ships whistle and request a whistle test when the crew was at quarters, in the morning.

We all drew a mental picture of sixty men lined up neatly on the foredeck for quarters with the officers all neatly squared away facing them when the ships whistle blew and covered them with crap from the knees down. I'm sure they'll put that in a movie one day.

Jim Givens came back from his leave late that night and we shared our dream with him. He was all for it. The plans, of course, did not work out. We made our request for the list on the boat and of course the Chief denied it.

"We'll be in Philly for over a month and get the tanks blasted. - So why clean them now - that's dumb!" Pappy growled, then raised his eyebrows and asked. "Any other strange request you boys may want to make?"

"Yeh! - Chief – Would you please stand in front of the ship's whistle for us?" Givens requested.

"Oh! – I see- you guys think you have it figured out don'tcha? Well let's hear your plan!" The Chief was definitely pleased.

We gave him the theory and he complimented us on our thoroughness. "Most guys forget about the whistle's diaphragm -- you fellows did good -- this could be a record!" The chief was definitely pleased.

We operated for two days with the Commander of the Sixth Submarine Division on board and went through some intensive missile guidance drills. It was a grueling two days. We moored back in Norfolk on Wednesday, November 20 and spent the balance of the week pigging out on our stores and getting rid of munitions and anything that would not be necessary during our yard period in Philadelphia, Pennsylvania.

Sunday morning, November 24, 1957, the Captain presented, Jim Givens, Dave Cummings and me with our coveted silver pins. We had our "Dolphins."

Words cannot bear witness to the emotions I felt as that pin was placed above my left pocket. I was now a full fledged, bona fldu, dyed in the wool submariner.

We cleared the dock at 1254 hours for Philly. I had a maneuvering watch of about an hour and a half to clear the Chesapeake Bay. Pappy told me to hit the sack. I had a rather long, "deal at the wheel", coming up, as we navigated the Delaware River to Philly. I slept nearly eight hours.

I took the wheel at 2335 hours, that's twenty-five minutes 'till midnight on November 24, 1957. Our pilot was C.K. Shell, as we entered the Delaware River, at 2341 hours. It was an intense six and one half hours at the helm, with no break. Coffee was brought to me and a cheese sandwich on hot fresh baked bread, compliments of my buddy, Catfish. Man! That was a fine sandwich. Two slices of still oven warm bread with a light coat of mayo and a nice slab of mild cheddar that is soft from the bread heat. When you take a bite you have to raise the sandwich and lower the stringing cheese into your mouth. I would take a bite and everyone in the conning tower would watch to see if I could catch all the cheese. I was a pro at this and would even exaggerate the cheese strings to make it exciting.

We docked at the Philadelphia Naval Yard at 0549 on the morning of November 25, 1957. A new adventure awaited me.

The crew moved from the Torsk and took up residency in a fine set of barracks. We were on the second deck and the chow hall was on the first deck. The chow hall boss was a Chief Commissaryman with considerable service. All of the cooks reported to him and it worked out fine. The cooks, that weren't cooking, were free to keep an eye on the civilian yard birds that were doing contract work on their boats. These yard birds were civil service employees with close ties to the US Navy. They are well trained and dedicated to their jobs and took a great deal of pride it their workmanship.

We were allowed to wear civilian clothes while in Philly. Civvies didn't hold a great deal of appeal to me, but it had its merits in a big city. It immediately removed a sailor as a threat to the local gentry. The shoes however were always a dead giveaway. I bought a pair of penny loafers at a shop on Market Street just off of city hall. I was astounded to see a pair of Savannah Oxfords on display at a price considerably higher than we paid at home. Alan Barry's was an exclusive men's clothing store on Broughton Street in Savannah. Mr. Barry had designed a shoe a few years ago that apparently had swept the country. The oxfords had a crepe sole close to a half inch thick. The toe and heel of the shoe was pebbly, reddish brown grain leather and the saddle was dark, smooth, brown leather. Every boy in high school had a pair, or wanted a pair. I bought a loafer with a leather sole, specifically for the dancing advantage.

The weather had started to turn cold. A couple of guys and I buddied up with Johnny North and took his 56 Chevy to a discount clothing warehouse. We outfitted ourselves with a pretty good selection of civvies. I was the only guy in the group to buy new shoes. I was a little flat until payday, but that was OK, I just wanted to dance.

I did not go ashore anymore that week until Saturday. We had a payphone on our barracks floor and the number was published in the phone book. It was listed as "transit personnel" assigned to the Naval Yard. It rang constantly, mostly curious women looking for a sucker. But that's how the men got their personal calls. It didn't take long to learn to identify the hucksters. Sometimes it was fun to talk trash, and sometimes it got us in trouble.

We made a date to attend a party on Friday night. Four of us piled in Johnny North's Chevy and drove to a bad section of town. We decided to turn around and get out of there when a group of teens blocked the exit on the street. Johnny floored the Chevy and the gang stepped back preparing to hit the car with boards and chains as we went by. Johnny handed Jim Givens a cast iron replica of a German Luger. "Hang out the window and aim it at anyone that looks like they want to hit my car!" Johnny cried. It worked like a charm, as Givens brandished the Luger, the gang split and were gone in an instant, leaving little dust devils in their wake.   We made plans to learn the bad sections of town so this would not happen again.

We heard of a dance at the YWCA in downtown Philly that Saturday night and decided to give it a try. The dances at the "Y's" were always chaperoned and drinking was not allowed. That didn't bother me, but the other guys wanted a little wilder atmosphere for their liberty nights.   Johnny North would probably have stayed with me, but Jim and Dave said they heard of a club in Jersey that had half price drinks for service men.   They dropped me off at the "Y" and struck out for Jersey.

We had worn uniforms that night because the party was supposed to be for servicemen. The "Y" was packed. There were a set of stone steps that led to the massive oak double doors and the ballroom was to the right of a majestic foyer. The fine wooden floors looked as if they were perfect for the jitterbug. I stood in the doorway to the ballroom, fully conscious that my silhouette was accented by the bright lights of the foyer. It was the first time I had worn my new dress blues. My eyes slowly became accustomed to the subdued light in the ballroom as I stepped in and surveyed the room. I was looking for someone that was looking at me. Believe me, it saves a lot of time if your potential victim ---Eh! – I mean potential date is already interested.

"Bingo – Wow – Whatta beauty!" She was clearly not a teeny bopper. She was dressed in a green party dress and well put together. Her hair was cut in a close crop and her bangs swirled to the left. She had a full head of hair but it was short. The sides swirled in a gentle sweep behind hers ears and came to a point under her emerald earrings. The back of her hair tuned under in a gentle roll that glistened under the ballroom lights. Generally a dish water blonde has difficulty with a catchy hairdo, but this lady had it mastered.

I took my time to make sure that she was indeed watching me. She turned to a younger lady by her side and whispered to her and made a motion my way. The women couldn't tell that I was aware of their actions, the foyer lights kept anyone inside from seeing any details of those coming in. I made my way to their side of the dance floor as the band started playing "Harbor Lights." I walked directly to the attractive lady and without a word extended my hand to request this dance. She accepted.

There is something about music and dancing that bridges a vast expanse of time. The lady was an exceptional dancer, by that I mean she instinctively knew how to follow. I think she was impressed.

"Do you bop?" She softly asked as the music died away.

"Well! – Yeh!" I answered. "I'm Lynn Wardlaw - from Savannah, Georgia. We're up here in the Naval Yard getting some work done." I noticed she was not as old as I first thought. I think her party dress is what threw me off.

Most times the girls at a "Y" dance are generally high school age. This "Y" was different. There were plenty of women well passed their thirties and all were fairly good looking.

My partner and I danced quite a few times before I offered her a coke and we found a table where we could talk a bit. Her name was Deloris, the younger girl was her sister Nan. They came to all the "Y" dances, simply because they liked to dance.

We talked a great deal and found it very relaxing to chat. I made it a point not to monopolize the conversation and every time a good song was played I would ask her to dance again. We were having a fine time.

Deloris had a good job. It seems she was an accomplished speed reader and had a job, proofreading books before they went to press. She was twenty-two, a year older than me, but I wasn't going to let that bother me.

Her sister, Nan, was a totally different type of woman. She was a flirt and kept at me with sly remarks and innuendos. I thought how disrespectful this was to her sister, but then, Deloris and I had no commitments to each other, so I suppose I was fair game. I didn't like this role reversal; I wasn't used to it and really didn't know how to react to a lot of her advances. I was glad when a Marine asked her to dance. She spent the rest of the evening wooing him and that was fine with me. I really liked this Deloris. She suggested I call her Del. That's what her friends all call her, so it was Del from then on.

She was very nicely built. She was not the "Gaa! Gaa!" looker, but was all there in the right places. She was quite striking in that green dress that flared to just above the knees. The legs were shapely with cute dimpled knees and nice slim ankles. She was quite pleasing to behold. It was a nice night and my ride home on the subway passed pleasantly as I went over the night in my mind. I did not offer to see her home. I was not going to press my luck. I reasoned that we would be in the yard until late January, 1958, so there would be plenty of time.

I remembered how I had messed up in the past by moving too quickly. I didn't want that to happen again. The faceless lady kept me company till dawn.

The Torsk's primary function was to guide missiles. Plans were underway to construct the first of a series of submarines that would have the capacity of launching dozens of intercontinental ballistic missiles. The first on the construction table was the "George Washington". This meant that our missile guiding capabilities would not be needed much longer.

The Department of the Navy decided we would be converted to a sound boat. Our job would be to listen to our potential enemies and track them. We were having some sophisticated sound gear installed on the bottom of our bow. There would be one hundred and ten sensitive hydrophones installed in a semi-circle under the very front of our boat. It was covered with a fiberglass dome that resembled a huge wart on the chin of my Torsk. I thought how this was going to affect our speed when we wanted to stretch out and race the Runner. Oh! Well! Progress must be made.

I dressed in civvies that Saturday night and didn't even ask what Johnny North and the guys were up to. I caught the subway straight to the City Hall stop and walked the few blocks to the "Y". As I walked in the front door, I saw Deloris standing by the door to the ballroom. She waved, smiled and motioned me to come on in. She led the way to a table were Nan, her sister, was sitting with the Marine from last week. There was another couple there as well.

I felt honored, this was a preset gathering and I was obviously included. "Hey! – Del!" – I asked. "Does this mean I'm your date for the night?"

"If that's the way you want it - Sailor Boy!" She responded with a coy look.

"Suits me fine!" I exclaimed. "I walked into this place and get picked up by the best looking gal in the house! -- it don't get any better than that!" She smiled.

It was a great dance. The group that played was younger than the week before and played a lot of "Rock and Roll" stuff. I was pretty tired at 11:00 PM when it was over.

I asked if I could see Del home that night and she agreed. She wanted to walk. I wondered if she had been to Europe. We walked to the Town Hall, then headed west on Market to South 21st Street. We went one block south to Ludlow Street. On the corner was a little bar that I would spend quite some time in the future.

Deloris lived with her parents, two sisters and a brother in the two story brick building that was an extension of the bar. Deloris had an older brother in North Philly who had a nice home. I would spend some nice weekends there as well.

We stood in the hall as we made our good nights. I kissed her and she responded. I felt good about our relationship. I definitely didn't want to get into another heart wrenching affair like Yvonne and Leslie.

I was holding Deloris in my arms when a car drove up outside. There was a brief delay; I suppose long enough for a goodnight kiss before her older sister came into the house.

Del introduced me. The older sister was in the university and was taking fencing lessons. She had her foil in a cloth case with the handle exposed. She was a larger woman than Deloris, but had that chiseled Norwegian beauty in her face.

I had hardly kissed Deloris again when I heard the youthful, vibrant footsteps of someone running. The footsteps left the pavement and cleared the three small steps that led up to the door and her younger brother flung the door open. His mouth fell open as he saw his sister in the arms of a total stranger. I had to admire the spunk of the sixteen or so year old boy as he stammered, "Everything OK here?"

Del spoke. "Its fine Alfred - this is my friend – Lynn - we've been to the "Y" dance."

"Swell! – Good to meet'cha - see ya later!" He disappeared into the house.

Del invited me in to sit and talk, but I passed it up. I asked her if she would like to catch a movie the next day, Sunday. She agreed and I asked her to pick one out. I told her I would be by to get her around 2:00PM.

I felt pretty good about the night, and was relieved that she was going to a movie with me. I was getting used to walking. It was a straight shot from the corner a block away to Market Street, turn right and you could see the great spire of the Town Hall. The subway terminals were in the basement of the Hall. It was then a straight shot south, under Pennsylvania Avenue, on the subway to the Naval Yard.

I was back in the barracks by 0200 hours. I slept great, but was beginning to get dry skin from the steam heat in the barracks. I never realized how steam heat would dehydrate a person. I was told just to drink more water.

I kept company only with Deloris while in Philly. I never cared for bar hopping, the girls you met there were not the same cut as the girls you meet at social dances, church and other functions.

Christmas passed and Del and I exchanged small gifts. Her sister was getting involved with the Marine and I don't think Del cared for the relationship. She never talked about it but she shied away from any double dating. We were always alone on our dates. She seemed perfectly happy with the way things were going.

I asked Del about the New Year's Day Mummer's Parade. She said that every year, she and some friends went to the Catskills for a skiing trip. That left me with no agenda for New Year's Day.

Some of the guys thought it would be nice if we all went in our uniforms and spent the day in town. We actually had a sizable group of sailors as we found a spot to watch a magnificent display of pageantry. There were dozens of banjo bands, mostly sponsored by fire stations from around Philly.

The Mummers were a special group that wore fancy costumes and gigantic feathered headdresses that rose high in the air. The Mummers held lines tied to the ends of the headdresses to keep them straight. They would do a kind of smooth high stepping strut that kept time with the nearest band that played. They would dip and bow, then move back with high steps and make a slow strutting turn. Some would do their own dance, and some would have a routine that a dozen or so performed together. The routines were spellbinding.

We were having a few beers and a lot of the guys would mimic the Mummers and do a little strutting dance. We enjoyed it, but the locals didn't applaud our efforts.

A sailor from another ship in the Naval Yard joined our group and told us of a club, not far away that he heard was loaded with broads. I didn't relish the idea, but my buddies were all for the broads. Have you ever heard that if something sounds too good to be true, it's probably not true. Well! We were about to see living proof of that fact.

We found the fabled "Club 13" a few blocks away. It was a two story brick building with no other building attached to it. The Club sat on a corner and had a parking area around the two sides away from the street. We approached from the side street and found the back door open.

As we walked in, there was a stair case leading to the second floor. We noticed about six or eight cars in the lot, but there was only one guy at the bar. We each ordered a draft beer and sat at some booths to enjoy our cold brews.

We joked a little about how the place was supposed to be loaded with broads but they probably ran off when they saw the Navy approaching. Girls are afraid of the big guns the Navy carries around, joked one fellow. Another quirped something about how women can't handle the rapid fire of a sailor. It was all ego talk. The bar keep didn't seem to mind, as we were the guys paying, at the present.

One of the guys had to take a leak and found his way upstairs to the head. In a moment we heard him stumbling down the stairs. He rushed to our booths and in a hushed but excited voice said. "Fellows -- there's another bar upstairs -- just like this one and that's where the women are -- guys!" He stopped to take a breath. "There's at least a dozen! -- Man! – We're in the wrong bar!"

In a flash the eight or ten of us in the group headed for the stairs. I was not that enthused and brought up the rear. I heard the bartender laugh as we thundered up to the second floor. The biggest difference between the two bars was the lighting, this bar was very dim, but indeed, there were women. It seemed as if they were all overdressed. Some had on sequined dresses and the woman at the end of the bar had on one of those long feathery things around her neck.

The women immediately turned their attention to us as we crashed in. It was not like we made a dignified entrance by any means. We took seats at some booths and a couple of guys went to the bar and sat by some ladies. The guy that alerted us to the Club 13, made his way to the woman with the feathers. She appeared glad to see him as her arm went around his neck and she began to nibble on his ear. He looked back at us with a grin as if to ask. "Am I doing alright?"

A few of the guys began to talk with some women as our vision began to adjust to the dark. A woman asked me if I would care to buy her a drink and join her in a booth. I declined. She then said she would buy me a drink if I would join her in a booth. I told her I was nursing a rash and would not be good company. She gave it up and promptly returned to the bar.

Well, to set the record straight, here is when and how it happened. It was Wednesday, January 1st, 1958, around 3:00 PM, on the second floor of the Club 13 in Philadelphia, Pennsylvania.

The sailor that sat by the feathered lady suddenly pushed away from their embrace. He began to wipe his mouth and started mumbling. He appeared to be terribly confused.

One of the guys at my table called to him. "Hey sailor -- that tonsil tickling too much for you?"

He staggered to the booth and stammered. "She's gotta dick - Man! – The broad's gotta dick!"

The confused statement was loud enough for those nearby to hear and the women broke out in a raucous laughter. It wasn't a woman's dainty laughter, but the deep laugh of men. It suddenly struck us, these were not women, but men dressed as women.

We made a mad dash for the stairs. If you hear stories of how the sailors cleaned house in this affair, don't believe them. All we wanted was to get out of there.

Once on the street we gathered together and, of course, the "'woulda– shoulda– coulda!" statements started flowing. We suddenly realized that two of our group was not with us. We looked back toward the club expecting to see them emerge, but they must have decided they liked the company. We didn't check on them either. So much for "No man left behind!"

We worked hard on our Torsk, some of the jobs we did ourselves. We buffed the bubble that was on the bridge. The bubble is a plexiglas quarter dome that protects the Officer of the Deck from waves and wind while at sea. Over the span of a year it would get dull and the use of a buffer and pumice would bring it back to its original clear condition. We also laid new deck tile throughout the boat. Lessor taught me how to lace the wheel and I really enjoyed that project. After the lacing and dead end designs were finished, I painted the wheel with green shellac. It was truly a beauty and I felt a rush of satisfaction every time I placed my hands on her from then on.

I was careful not to get too involved with Del while in Philly, but it's hard not to have feelings for someone as sweet and pretty as this lady was.

It was not as hard leaving Philly as it was Weymouth or Jewett City, but, I still wished I didn't have to go.

I remembered Del crying as I kissed her that last night; she told me she loved me. I told her that was not my intention. I didn't want her to fall in love with me.

She asked me. "What am I supposed to do? - You fill my every moment - if I'm not with you --I'm thinking of you - I can't help it!"

I told her, I didn't know if I would ever be back and I was sorry, I didn't want to hurt her. It didn't help matters any, she was still crying as I left.

We left the Naval Yard the Middle of January, 1958 and went straight to Norfolk to reload munitions and supplies. We lost our Executive officer, Mr. Burkart, and picked up a new one, named Mr. R.B. Bade. I think, maybe, he was an interim.

Caribbean, here we come. It was the topic of every conversation. Some of the guys had been there before and painted a picture of a tropical paradise that was every sailors dream. They had a little chant they did. "Five and two! – I love you! – Ten and four! -- I love you more!" I would find out how true this saying was. The faceless lady went to San Juan with me.

CHAPTER IX

THE CARIBBEAN

We left Norfolk at 0812, Monday, February 3rd, 1958. The ship's whistle sounded just as a commotion began in the control room. The Executive Officer, Mr. Burkart, called the bridge and ordered us to tie up a brow line for a transfer. It seems as Lambert, our boss cook, was having an appendicitis attack. The transfer was made and we continued to back out into Chesapeake Bay. Little did I know how this occurrence would affect my next few months on the Torsk.

When the maneuvering watch was secured I struck for the kitchen. I knew they were now short one cook and thought how I could help Catfish. He was a good man and I really owed him.

A new sailor was sitting at the rear table of the chow hall. He was a seaman with dark hair and steely eyes. His nose had a pronounced crook in it to the left.

I spoke. "Wardlaw – from Savannah, Georgia." He looked up and tilted his head back in acknowledgment. He gave a sorta nasal snicker. I sat across from him and extended my hand.

He answered. "John F. McGovern - from Syracuse, New York." His hand shake told me he was, indeed, a man. He looked to be my age and was wiry. He definitely had a nose problem. I suppose he was about my height, but I probably outweighed him at least twenty pounds.

The chief of the boat came in and gave "Mac" the welcome aboard talk. Mac had just made it that morning. If he had missed us, he would have stayed in Norfolk at the base until we returned and missed our trip to paradise.

Mac had finished sub school and took some leave back to Syracuse and just did get back in time to catch us. I didn't get any details but he was very melancholy about his girl back home. I suppose she told him she wasn't waiting. I knew what that felt like.

Catfish began to work on me about cooking while Lambert was recuperating. I really thought he was joking. He pointed out all the perks, like no other duty except maneuvering watch, battle stations, man overboard party, and missile guidance party. The menus were all preplanned and it was a simple matter of knowing how much to cook, how long to cook it, how much seasoning to put in it and when to start its preparation.

As an example of how caring Submariners are for each other, we always sat a plate aside for Jim Takas that contained no salt and nothing that came out as roughage. Jim had a severe hemorrhoid problem and didn't want to miss this San Juan Tour.

The Chief of the boat, Pappy Wright, came in and set down beside me. Catfish was not putting me on. The boat was actually asking me to fill in as cook, on this cruise.

I told him I had cooked eggs and grits, fixed cereal, fried bacon made cornbread and tea.

Pappy asked me if I ever fixed peanut butter and jelly sandwiches. "Yeh! – for my two younger brothers."

"You got the job! –Wait till Mr. Bibby hears you volunteered to help us out. He thinks you are the best thing that happened to this boat in a long time!" I was glad that no one else was in the chow hall but Catfish, Mac, the Chief and me. Man, I would never live down being an officer's pet. I still felt honored.

In the next few days I got to know Mac better. He had been a golden gloves boxer since he was fourteen, and the nose was a result of some fights that proved to him that he wasn't as tough as he thought. His speech was always a bit nasal as a result of the nose damage. He joined the Navy to get away from Syracuse. I never found out why. He simply said, if he was going to be a sailor he was going to be the best and that was on a submarine. He joined our little group of Jim Givens, Dave Cummings, Johnny North and me. We were the fabulous five.

My cooking experience was not a great success. If it had not been for Catfish, and Hersey, the Torsk would probably have mutinied. I think I was chosen because I could tolerate abuse without losing my cool. I was insulted continuously and called all kinds of names. They never played any tricks on me, but when I resorted to the bugga flicking motion one day, I thought the whole crews was gonna whip my ass. Catfish said they were just having fun.

The crew did help a lot. If we needed potatoes peeled, we simply washed them and put them on the chow hall table. The mess cook would peel a few, and then set about other duties and as men would have a few minutes they would stop and peel some potatoes. We never had a problem with getting a meal ready.

Catfish and Hersey would check everything I did and the meals all turned out good. I sent some roasted pork loin to the ward room for Officers Mess and Brown came back, fuming about it being too rare. He ranted and raved and made a case out of it in front of everyone. I finally told him that I would be glad to take his place as Commissary Man to the Officers and he could cook the pork loins any way he liked. That really pissed him off and he told me how lucky I was that he was a professional boxer and if he hit me it was like using a lethal weapon. I told him I was glad too.

Hersey was the meat specialist and said Brown really did me a favor, if the officers had seen the meat it could have been serious. I always let Hersey check my pork after that.

I found the time to apologize to Brown also. Brown and I would talk from time to time. He had spent some time in Savannah and knew the layout of the town. He liked to brag about the telephone girls that he had dated and always wanted to brag about his conquest. I felt it was all put on and didn't let it bother me, I never heard a name I recognized anyway. Brown told me of a Navy boxer, from Savannah, named Spellman. He knew him from his early days in Navy boxing. I often wondered if it was Coach Spellman of Commercial High School in Savannah.

The next five days were a quandary for me. Between cooking and the drills, I was in a daze most of the time. We set missile guidance party so many times it was now a natural thing. We sank the Runner, the Barbero and a couple of new comers to our operating group, the Argonaut SS475 and the Medregal SS480. These subs also made their practice passes on us as well.

We finally got a moment to catch our breath and I heard the Captain laugh as he sounded the "Man overboard Alarm." Yep! - He had a well-trained crew; he knew it and was going to keep it that way.

We moored in San Juan, Puerto Rico on February 8th at 0735 on a Saturday morning. It was indeed a paradise. I went topside before I took the wheel on the maneuvering watch and saw the island in the distance. It was mountainous on the eastern side and as green as anything I had ever seen.

When we moored, I went top side again to observe, up close, this tropical paradise. It left me speechless. We had moored at the famous Banana Piers in San Juan. We tied up next to the Argonaut at pier 12. There were four other boats in port and a fast attack class transport, the USS Monrovia APA 31. The Caribbean was safe for the present.

We received news that the Sputnik satellite the Russians had placed in orbit had crashed to earth. There was little elation at the news. The Russkies had still beaten us at this space thing, and we worried at what they may have that we didn't know about. It was a cloud that stayed over us on every operation.

San Juan was as predicted. Yes, there were swaying palms and people walking around in pants cut off at the knee and sandals, with straw hats and flowered shirts. The breeze blew constantly and the clouds were little puffs of white in a blue expanse that was breathtaking. Off in the east you could see the mountains rise in a profusion of green.

Cries could be heard from the workers nearby. "Mira! – Mira! – Que pasa! – Amigo! – Viene aqui - por favor!" We were sealed off from the general public but were close enough to hear the heartbeat of San Juan, Puerto Rico.

"Arriba! – Arriba!" Liberty call went down at 1600 hours. The sailors flooded from the ships. Some sailors ran as if they were afraid it would all be gone before they got there. The fabulous five kept their cool. We didn't want them to know we wanted it that bad. We must maintain some dignity.

Every automobile in San Juan is a taxi. It was fifty cents wherever you wanted to go, within reason. We all piled into a taxi and went to downtown Old San Juan. Immediately we found the car with the loudest horn and the driver with the longest arm always had the right-of-way.

Everything was within walking distance of the huge shady square in the center of the old section of town. There were TV sets on high stands and people were watching from benches set up in front of them. There were various mariachi bands playing and island dancing was everywhere.

I had never seen so many hookers in my life. You could immediately tell a hooker from a girl that was just downtown shopping. The innocent girl didn't see you; she simply went about her business and paid a sailor no attention. It was as if you weren't there. If a sailor attempted to force a girl into a conversation and she was reluctant, the local gentry would step up in numbers and the sailor would get the message in a hurry. There is always that one stupid sailor that won't observe the rules or doesn't care, that gives the Navy a bad name. San Juan liked the U.S. Navy.

The fab five made their way to a club on the last street before the green roof district. That was a section of town like the bowery in New York and was officially off limits to sailors. This last street was tempting. I don't know why anyone would want to go any further, Man, whatever you wanted was right in front of you.

There she was, dainty and young, she called herself Nelwaya. She said she was diez y siete, seventeen, but I didn't believe her. She aggravated the pure life out of me. I think the girls working a club must have a secret code they use and actually pick out the men they want. It was nearly 2300 hours before my new friend, Ron Rico, he lived in a bottle, talked me into following Nelly to her place of enjoyment. It was five and two. Five for the girl and two for the room. She was playful and put a lot of antics into our liaison. It was enjoyable and I learned some more about women.

As we walked back to the club I asked her if she wanted to go to a movie tomorrow. She told me she didn't work on Sundays. I said "No! - No amor - just a movie. "

She stopped dead in her tracks. The look of disbelief on her face was shocking. I thought maybe I had committed some unpardonable sin, as if I had not done just that.

"Yu no want puta - jus take me to cine?" I nodded. She paused and with an air of mistrust, asked. "Por Que?"

"Este cine es Elvis Presley y me gusto! – Su es Nelly y me gusto!" She understood my broken Spanish. She couldn't believe I asked her on a date. I couldn't either and don't know why I did it.

"Muy bien!- Me muchacho!" she beamed and told me to meet her in the park downtown at 2:00 PM. I didn't go back to the club. I didn't care to see her make another date. I didn't care for the girl emotionally, but I think, I had to do it differently. I guess I felt any relationship, worth having, should have some effort in it.

She didn't look like the same girl. Nelly's hair was pulled back and her make-up was conservative. She had a simple print sundress on that was white at the bottom and blue and orange flowery brocade at the top. She wore white pumps and carried a small fold over white purse. She didn't look seventeen. She took my hand and for a moment I thought she was going to skip. She told me it was her first real date, just like in America.

Don't go to an American movie in a land where English is not the primary language. "Jail House Rock" was widely acclaimed, but I had to wait for us to get it on board the boat to really enjoy it. The movie was in English, so it had Spanish subtitles under the picture. The subtitles covered much of the picture at times and the youthful audience read every word out loud, so hearing what the actors said was useless. The audience was quiet for the songs, but they danced in the aisles when Elvis performed. No more movies for me in a San Juan Theater.

When the movie was over, Nelly and I, went to a little ice cream parlor near the square. The guy behind the counter didn't want Nelly in the place, I could tell, perhaps he knew her and didn't want the reputation of his store tarnished. When he brought the ice cream over he pointed at Nelly and hissed, "Puta!"

I was ready and pointed back at him and hissed. "Cabeza mierda!" That's close enough to "shit head" that he got the point.

Luckily the sundaes came in paper cups, so we exited to finish our treats in the square. He watched in mute astonishment, as we left. I was enjoying treating this little girl like she was somebody. She was feeling pretty good about herself too.

Nelly let me take her home that night and I met her parents and family. I was terribly confused at this situation. The home was large and stately, not in the best condition, but well kept. Her father was still dressed in Sunday church clothes and her mother was a typical, doting Latino Mom. The family was large with numerous active kids and some teens that appeared around Nelly's age. I was not neglected; however, no one attempted to engage me in much conversation. Nelly was an integral part of the family and shared in managing the kids.

I don't think they knew what she did. I saw numerous pictures of family members in social activities and even saw Nelly at her confirmation. The family was staunch Roman Catholic. I didn't stay long, but was invited back for Sunday dinner one day. We didn't make any definite plans on the dinner, so I wasn't that enthused. I mean – Stop and think! – You get invited to Sunday dinner at the home of your hooker. I went back to my Torsk.

I was recounting my day with Nelly to my buddies, Mac and John North, when Mac made his little nasal snicker and took my face in his hands. He gently moved my face around as he examined it.

"Damned if he don't look normal, but he's got to be crazy as hell to romance a hooker!"

John put his hand under his chin and gave that Italian devil sign, where you wave your fingers. These guys weren't the kind to blab all over the boat. It was good to have buddies you could depend on.

Many times, when in port, we would tie up alongside our tender, the U.S.S. Orion. The Orion had a ships store and I had been looking at some very nice wristwatches. I really liked a gold "Citation," I think by Bulova. I simply couldn't get far enough ahead with money to afford it. I bought, instead, an Aquacade by "I don't have a clue!" It was supposed to be tested waterproof. It had a new type stretch metal band that wouldn't pull your arm hair. It was very nice but also very loose. I hadn't figured how to tighten the band yet.

Monday morning we went back to war. The crack of dawn saw us drawing a bead on the USS Wood DDR715. We just practiced an attack. It was a weird feeling to track a ship and they don't know you are there. Captain King was at the battle scope and observed the ship as they looked for us. He remarked as how there were at least a dozen sets of nocs [binoculars] searching and he knew none of them saw us. We surfaced just off their port beam and they were astonished at our close presence.

We received three observers from the Wood to accompany us on our simulated attack. They kept quiet as the Captain and Officers did their jobs with that usual precision. We made an S1T [Simulated-One-Torpedo] attack on the Wood. From my vantage point at the helm position, I could observe the faces of our guest. It was obvious that knowing your ship's going down has a psychological effect on you. We surfaced and transferred the observers back to the Wood.

We dove again, to make another S1T attack on the Wood. This time the observers were there to tell them how we operated. Captain King knew this, and figured that the first step in defense is to put distance between you and your enemy. We dove and immediately went full speed under the Wood in a straight line opposite of where we dove. We had off loaded the observers to a small boat that had to get back to the Wood and then be winched aboard, before they were ready to get underway.

The Captain was right on. We were well ahead of the Wood as she turned and began to put that distance they thought was so important between us. I was amazed at Captain King's reasoning; the Wood was heading straight for a text book shot at her starboard beam.

We drilled and re-drilled. The Captain covered every possible scenario that could cause us a problem. Our reactions were second nature to us now. I would spend time thinking of dire possibilities that could present themselves, and what my actions would be if they should happen. It became very evident that you must be aware of all that is transpiring around you at all times. It could save your life. Everyone makes mistakes and the more people aware of your actions is like insurance that you get it right.

We rendezvoused with the USS Kittywake ASR15 and began a search and rescue exercise. We sailed away to an out of sight distance and then without any electronic sensoring, we dove the boat and gently lay her on the sandy bottom. We were at 150 feet. We were simulating a sunken submarine that needed help.

The Kittywake had to find us and launch her rescue mission. We released our forward escape buoy. The signal didn't sound right. The sonar man determined that the buoy did not make it to the surface. That would reduce the effectiveness of the radio beacon immensely. We simply sat and waited.

The Kittywake did their job. We lounged on the bottom for about four hours when we received the signal from the Kittywake that the rescue pod was ready. We only simulated the rescue. We had tracked the sonar blips from the Kittywake as she realized that there was no escape buoy to locate us by. She had commenced listening with her UQC and heard the signal underwater. She then used her pinging sonar to pin point us. We had no buoy on the surface, so the Kittywake lowered a grapple and snared our buoy. We now had line contact to guide the escape pod. Mission accomplished. It was found that the line on our escape buoy fouled and the buoy was only about fifteen feet above our deck. You can believe that line was checked closely on every deck inspection from then on.

We surfaced and received the ORI [Operation Readiness Inspection] Team from the Kittywake to transport them to St Thomas in the Virgin Islands. We tied up opposite the Orion, our tender, at 1830 Hours. Liberty was not authorized. I went to sleep.

I was roused up at midnight. By this time, the watchman knew everyone's special method of being awakened. All he had to do, for me, was lean around the corner and shine the light in my face. I instantly woke up. Oh! By the way! I was no longer in the water fall bunk. When I started cooking, somehow, I graduated to the next bunk down and stayed there for my entire tour.

We left St Thomas a little after midnight. It was only a twenty minute maneuvering watch and I figured I would get a little more sleep before I had to start breakfast. I didn't make it to the head before the Captain called a fire drill. I knew what I wanted to burn, his rack. I immediately regretted the thought. He was a good Captain and I respected him.

Later that day we were snorkeling around the island of St Croix, taking pictures of her shoreline. I was helping Hersey with dinner when James, the mess cook, cried out in pain. He was forcing a plastic net trash bag into the garbage tube when a can top sliced his wrist. I found out why people slice their wrist when attempting suicide. The blood was profuse and was everywhere in short order.

Doc Johanson took care of James' wrist and I finished his mess cook duties. A lot of other guys helped also, no one wants to eat in a blood spattered mess hall.

We continued to operate for the balance of the week. I realized that an American Naval vessel never just cruises around with nothing to do. Every minute is planned. Even the unplanned time is scheduled and the Captain will find one of his pet projects to pursue. Captain King loved to sneak up on the Runner. And then challenge her to a race. Generally this was when our operations were over and we were headed for a weekend port call.

We operated with the USS Vesole DD878 and acted as her target. She never located us and then our turn came. We surfaced and exposed ourselves. This was to start the exercise. We dived and immediately the Captain turned and went full speed away from the Vesole. His theory was, the skipper of the Vesole had communicated with the skipper of the Wood and had been informed of our tactics. A sub needs enough time to get information to feed the DTC in order to get a firing solution and then enough time to make the shot.

Our Captain was uncanny; the Vesole was steaming straight across our bow. Their skipper had decided to charge straight at us with the assumption we were going under him to wait. He thought he was distancing himself, but was lining himself up for a perfect shot. Ever since we aced the NATO operation, Captain King's reputation had become legendary. It was a feather in your cap to sink us and an accolade to escape an operation without a green flare.

In the NATO operation we used all electronic gear as if we were in actual combat, but in these operations it was restricted. We operated without pinging radar. It was up to the ships involved to be honest, especially when you can hear the pinging with your ears as the electronic pings bounce off you hull.

We had our firing resolution and gave the Vesole three shots of air and then that dreaded green flare. We surfaced and exposed ourselves.

We dived again, the Captain stood at the scope in deep thought. "Do the same thing! - Right full rudder! - All ahead full! - Make depth 60 feet, Mr. Wiseman!"

I did my thing and answered. Mr. Wiseman answered. The Captain did not acknowledge, I turned to answer again and the Captain abruptly turned his head and gave a quick nod that he heard me. I understood, but it always bugged me when he wouldn't acknowledge. No other officer on board did that. This little quirk in Captain King would rear up and bite him in the ass in the near future.

Once again the Vesole lined up for a perfect shot. Captain King had figured the Vesole's skipper would never expect us to use the same method twice. Three more air blast and another green flare, proved, we had their number.

We exposed ourselves and the Captain said. "One more time boys! – Damn - I'm almost tempted to give em one! -- No I'm not! – Dive the boat - Mr. Wiseman!"

The usual precision chaos occurred as the lookouts cleared the bridge and slid, clanging down two ladder flights, the air rushed from the top of ballast tank valves as thousands of gallons of seawater rushed in. The OD [Officer of the Deck] pulled the upper hatch shut and the helmsman [me], stepped up to turn the dogging wheel to draw it tight to its seal. The sound of the dive claxon has hardly faded before we are in fighting form.

The Captain called for a water depth reading, he didn't consider the fathometer as a fighting tool. "A short ping only!" He ordered.

The answer came back "600 feet - Sir"

He answered. "Very well!" Maybe it was just me he didn't want to talk too. He paused for a second.

He had a plan. "All stop! – pump us to 300 feet - Mr. Wiseman! – Go to ultra-quiet! Tell sonar to listen carefully and keep me informed!" We were using listening devices only.

This meant we were going to slowly sink right where we dove and hopefully disappear from any surveillance from the Vesole.

Here's the picture, this operation had started with the Vesole hunting for us. She had no success at all. We had evaded all of her approaches. We now have two kills on her and the success of a third is very remote. We were about to find out just how shrewd our skipper was.

Sonar reported the Vesole was high speed in the opposite direction figuring we had not done the same thing as the first two times. The Vesole steamed away and we thought that two out of three wasn't bad. Captain King didn't lose faith though. He ordered sonar to listen for any change in sound from the Vesole. He kept glancing at his watch.

Each exercise has a certain amount of time involved in it. If a submarine has not achieved its kill in the required time, it is useless to continue. A surface destroyer has a speed over 35 knots. Our submarines under extreme speed could not get more than maybe 11 knots while submerged. If the distance is too great the sub cannot possibly catch its prey, so we must wait.

We are in the exact spot as when we made our last shots and the Vesole is speeding away. Captain King glanced at his watch and asked Mr. Bade what's the exact time we dove. He continued to glance at his watch.

The Captain was almost talking to himself as he stood pensively. "Now! – Vesole! – Now! - If you got any sense at all - turn now," he softly muttered.

Sonar reported the Vesole was reversing course and was now at full speed back across our path.

"Got'cha big boy!" - Periscope depth Mr. Wiseman!" The Captain was at his best. Three more air blast and another green flare. The Captain's reputation skyrocketed.

The UQC blasted a congratulation that compared him to the "Red Baron." I thought it strange, because no one liked the "Red Baron".

The Vesole's Captain had chosen what he thought was the only way to prevent a third kill. It didn't matter which way you went, just watch the time. At the time when you calculate your enemy is just beginning his track on you, reverse course and go to full speed, you pull away from his effective range. You can now reduce speed and as long as you are faster than your enemy, you are safe. In case the enemy had gone the other way and is waiting, it is no use, because the distance between you will take too much time and the exercise will terminate before the sub can get a shot. Captain King had seen to it we hadn't moved. We were half as close as the Vesole thought. "KABOOM!"

We dropped anchor and took three guys on our after deck from a helicopter. It was around noon. We were in a cluster of islands on the north eastern shore of Pueto Rico. We could see Puerta Del Soldado, Isla Culebrita and Puerta Este. The water was beautiful. We could see 60 to 70 feet to the bottom, no great detail but you could see it.

We received an officer and two enlisted men by helicopter at 1400 hours. They were LTJG Hussey and two first class enlisted men, Simpson and Gaskin. They departed at 1510. This was always a mystery to the crew. We never found out why these men spent a little over an hour on board our boat.

Another mystery, we lifted anchor and it was not there. The water was only around 75 feet at the deepest but the anchor was simply gone. Generally if the anchor is snagged, the strain on the chain will tell the tale. It was as if the anchor was just disconnected. We left a marker and the marker line was too short, as we were preparing to get underway when a lookout noticed it drifting away. We had to run the marker down and add line to keep it in place. We knew we weren't dead on the anchor location, but hopefully close enough for a salvage crew to find it. They would look; an anchor is not a throw away item.

We moored in St Thomas at 1752 hours and liberty went down immediately. I went to town and found it very pleasant. There was a much larger African population in St Thomas than in San Juan. San Juan was old world type styling, but St Thomas was old world all over. I found the people very friendly; however, I spent very little time in town. I can tell you nothing about the night life or the women. I spent most of my time in the little bay where we moored, or at the UDT [Under Water Demolition] complex that was at the head of our pier.

These UDT guys were the epitome of naval excellence, lean, mean and dedicated. They were respectful of submariners, but had little tolerance for other service personnel. They showed movies at night on a big screen in a patio between their barracks. We were welcome to watch, but kept a sharp eye out in case we were in a frogman's favorite spot.

These guys had a daily routine that would kill a normal man. They were up at 0400 hours, and a quick jog to small boats that took them out to sea. I heard two miles, five miles, don't matter to me, it was a long way. They hit the water with only their suits, a knife, mask and flippers. Now the hard part, they must swim the distance to the beach, not just any beach, a special beach that had a pole with brass rings on it. This pole is 5 miles from the chow hall, if you want breakfast, you must have a brass ring. It doesn't stop there, if you don't check in at breakfast, you don't get lunch, the same for dinner. Man! - That's brutal.

On the seaward side of our pier was a mountain ridge that spanned from the sea around to town. Across the ridge was the airport. The ridge next to the sea had a population of ponies. I don't think they were Shetlands because a Shetland generally has a large head. From across the bay they just looked like little horses. James Brown would fish from the stern of our Torsk as we watched the little horses graze and frolic on the ridge.

One day we noticed a disturbance on the ridge and saw a sailor in dungarees astride one of the horses. The animal was not broken, we could tell that, but the animal's size kept him from just bucking the stupid sailor off. There was quite a ruckus going on when the animal suddenly bolted and ran right off the cliff. We saw the animal with rider fall about twenty feet before they disappeared behind some jutting rocks. We heard the "Yee Haaas!" of the sailor, but his call was now a long scream.

We ran to report the tragedy. It was not long before the Coast guard boats swarmed around the point and personnel could be seen on the ridge. Later that day, each of us was called to the ward room to give our statements as to what we had seen. The Coast guard and search personnel had found nothing. The owner of the horses found none missing and the Navy, including the UDT unit had no one missing. We knew what we saw, I think!

Back to combat on February 24th. We sank the Argonaut with a massive S6T and ran target for her. She had a good crew and was a sister ship of the Torsk. She made a S2T run on us.

We worried about the next operation. Operation Springboard required us to be target for the USS Wood and the USS Vesole. We had an area to hide in and the two destroyers could use all tools at their disposal to find us. The Torsk had aced both of them pretty good recently.

The mission was launched at 1234 hours and the Wood and Vesole, being miles apart, were told the general area where we were. They steamed at full speed to rendezvous and plan their strategy. We were on station at 1644 when the Wood and Vesole were given our location that would allow them to find us within a two hour search period.

I can't believe how shrewd our Captain was. We immediately went at them full speed on the surface until we heard the first echoes of their surface radar. Captain King dived the boat and made full submerged speed until we were just inside our restricted area. The water was too deep for bottoming but we went to three hundred feet and hovered.

We went to ultra- quiet. We cut the air blowers. There was no ventilation. Nothing was running except Budda Philip's mouth. He whispered "Please - nobody fart!" Nobody has every mastered a whispered laugh. We thought we were lost.

The Wood and Vesole zipped past us in a straight pattern with their sonars on full sweep, but they didn't see us. How they missed us we'll never know. We could hear the ships tearing up the operation area, but we were apparently just out of range. We stayed at our hover for an hour and a half.

"Crank em up - Mr. Bibby - let's make em mad!" smirked Captain King. "All ahead two thirds! – Make your depth 100 feet! - Come to course 326 degrees!"
The affirmative answers were all "Very well," except for mine. I knew he heard me, so I didn't press it.

We headed straight for the center of where the search sounds were coming from and made no effort to be quiet about it. We could hear the sonar pings all around us. Suddenly the pings changed tone a little, or so it seemed. "They got us - Con!" came the word from sonar.

"Periscope depth - Mr. Bibby!" The Captain was in Hollywood again. Around went his hat as he stooped to meet the battle scope and eased it up by hand signals. "Woo! Wee! - Here they come - boys – ready two green flares!"

Mr. Bibby exclaimed. "Captain we're out of order if we attack them!"

"I'm not gonna attack em - Lowe! – I'm just gonna rub their noses in it - check the time!"

"Son of a Gun-----------! – The op is over in two minutes!" breathed Mr. Bibby.

The Captain smiled and said. "Yep! – It'll take em over three minutes to get here and they are almost within our range now. Ready the flares!"

Captain King looked at his watch, held up his hand with five fingers showing and counted. "Five – Four – Three - Two - Flares away! " He looked at Mr. Bade and winked. "How long before the flares break water - Mr. Bade?"

Mr. Bade answered. "Not over five or six seconds - Captain!"

"Good - we have about ten seconds left in the operation."   He made his way to the UQC and boldly announced. "Great game gentlemen - drinks are at the Club 21 in San Tuce - I'm treating!"   There was no answer, just the sound of propellers growing faint in the distance.

We surfaced to see the two destroyers steaming away. The Captain knew the destroyers were not going back to San Juan, and neither were we, not right then anyway.   He turned the bridge over to Mr. Donahue and left the stage.

The lights went out and the collision alarm sounded, reporting fire in the maneuvering room. I wished it was the Captain's bunk again. The Torsk gave a hard thump and immediately began to slow. This was not a drill. We had a problem.

The port motor began to arc when placed in circuit with the generators. There is no way to disconnect the propeller shafts from the motors. To work on the port motor, we had to lock the port shaft. That literally meant that a device was tightened down on the shaft to prevent movement. The repairs to the motor winding were completed in less than an hour. We watched a movie and made a night with no drills, alarms or mishaps.

It didn't help me much, I had to cook. By this time I could handle a meal pretty much on my own, but still the jokes persisted.

A sailor would announce! "Chow Down!"

Someone would ask "Who's cooking?" then the answer.

"Wardy!" Another would groan. "OH! Shit!"

If Jonsey was around he would say "Chickenshit!" I wondered what was eating on him. I would find out in a few months.

I was still the helmsman on all special details, but now as a cook, I found, I had less spare time than before. I will never understand why we drilled as much as we did. If you picture your Navy as just sailing around, free as a breeze, carefree and at ease, well, forget it. It ain't so, Joe!

We made our first trip to St Croix and anchored next to the Runner around midnight. I went to sleep and was up in less than an hour to take us back to sea. Thankfully the maneuvering watch is only 15 minutes. I went back to the sack only to be up again at 0400 to prepare our breakfast. Breakfast done and I was off for six hours before dinner. Hersey would get everything started and I would pick it up at 1600 hours and finish up.

I was telling my troubles to the faceless lady when I felt the Torsk grow limp. I was instantly awake. It was 1330 hours. I knew from experience now, within a few minutes we would be relaxing on a swim call or going to war. Why did I even consider a swim call.

"AHUUUGAH! – AHUUUGAH! – DIVE! – DIVE!" Down we went with no headway. We were going to attack somebody. I suddenly knew why we tied up next to the Runner for about an hour last night. The two best friend skippers were planning the rest of the week's operation.

I roused myself, cleaned up a bit and made my way into the galley. There were a few scraps left from lunch, so I slapped a pocketbook together and drew a cup of milk. I looked at Catfish. "I'll bet we go at the Runner in less than an hour, Catfish!"

"Yu bin reading the Capn's mail - Georgia Boy?" He quizzed. The "Battle Station Call" came. I winked at Catfish as I ducked through the hatch.

It was 1326. I didn't expect the attack this soon. I took the wheel from North. The Captain was already at the scope drawing a bead on the Runner. We made a S4T pass and surfaced. It wasn't long before we were at it again, this time the Captain, fired an expendable MK16 Mod 7. He ran it at a depth of 40 feet. It cleared the bottom of the Runner by a little over 10 feet. He told his

Runner Buddy to "Sit on it!" on the UQC. We surfaced and secured battle stations. I dashed to the galley to help Hersey get the meat going.

"The Captain's gonna be a sad guy soon as his buddy transfers - Wardy." Hersey said, as he was preparing some beef loins for me to slice steaks. I pulled off my chambray and donned my apron. I gave my hands a quick wash and turned the loin platters to begin slicing the steaks.

"Careful of the carving knife – Wardy- I worked on it last night."

He did a magnificent job, the damn knife was so sharp, it went through the loin and to the bone on my left "bird" finger. There was no pain, but I felt the knife rub along the bone. I jerked my hand up to look at the finger and the gap was from the first knuckle from the nail to well past the second knuckle. It was on the inside of the finger and the finger was so surprised that it hadn't felt the pain or even started bleeding yet. I knew my eyes would tell my finger what had happened, so I grabbed a cloth and put pressure on the gaping wound before the bloody torrent began.

I got Hersey's attention with the cloth wrapped on my hand. "What! – No! – Wardy! – You shitin me - Right?" I nodded negative. "Damn! - Boy! – I told you that knife was sharp!"

I felt sorry for Hersey and softly said as the pain set in. "Yeh! – Thanks! – If you hadn't told me – I would have cut my stupid hand off!" I could tell the cloth was not going to hold much longer. I looked up and saw Mac enter the chow hall, he noticed the cloth and the red beginning to show.

I mouthed a request for Doc and Mac vanished back down the corridor. In a moment the Doc arrived and began the slow process of stopping the bleeding in order to start the stitches.

Hersey was supposed to be off now and I was supposed to continue to prepare the meal. The man continued his work as if it was perfectly normal. I had to admire that.

The Doc put nine stitches in the finger and wrapped it lightly. He didn't offer any pain killer and I didn't ask. The men watching would try to erk me out with, "Euuw! – Oooh! – Ouch that hurts!" The skin would stretch when the needle tried to penetrate.

Doc was an extremely wiry man, I had not noticed that he was in his skivvies and shirtless. He was not gaunt but there was not one once of excess meat anywhere on the man. The little bone protrusions on the top of a man's shoulder that is a small round lump on most men were like little horn nobs on Doc. His humor was very dry. He handed me two small rubbers that you roll over a bandaged finger to keep it dry. "Don't put em on your pecker by mistake – now - Wardy!" He smiled.

I finished my dinner preparation that night, but I think every man on board did some little something to help. A brief investigation was held to answer Navy protocol.

Anytime a sailor is injured by his own hand or action, it must be determined if it was done on purpose or accidental. The Navy uses the term "Not due to his own misconduct" to excuse the sailor. It was hard to lift anything heavy and every time I would think my finger was getting better, the rubber would start filling with blood again. Catfish and Hersey agreed for me to cook breakfast every day. The baking at night took the biggest hit. We really missed Lambert, he was a baking artist. But no one complained.

We spent most of our time the rest of the week at missile guidance stations. There is little maneuvering in missile guidance so I got relieved of wheel duty, for a while, anyway.

We moored in St Thomas that weekend. I got some much needed rest. I found that if I slept on my right side with my left hand hung over the bunk bag of the water fall bed above me, the finger would not throb. If I tried to sleep with the hand any lower, the throbbing kept everyone on the boat awake. The healing was on the way.

Monday, March 10th, 1958. The war waged on. As the dawn came we were diving and looking for the Runner. It was drills all day long. When a drill would end we immediately went back to our regular routine then drop it all to drill again. We were like a pro boxer. As we steamed alone, we never just went "ho hum." We shadow boxed by doing simulated attacks. There was no target, but shame on his ass if there was.

We picked up a new playmate as the day grew. The USS Correy DDR 817 was at our mercy. We fired an expendable MK 14 Mod 3A and then fired another fish exactly like it. We secured the exercise and retrieved our second shot.

Down we went again and this time we were target for the Correy. It was a hard day.

We managed an undisturbed breakfast, but then it started with missile guidance. Thank goodness we were not going to attack anyone. I stayed in the galley. The finger was doing much better. The guidance party was secured and I knew immediately we were bound for something special. I could feel the boat go into that maxed out stretch that our Captain knew so well

Our boat was a Tench class submarine that was designed to make 20 to 21 knots at flank speed on the surface. I am often called a liar, but there are many of us that have been on the bridge when the Torsk and the Runner would stretch it out and make 26 to 27 knots. The Torsk could gradually pull away from the Runner and that would tickle our Skipper. He never showed that speed to any other boat, I know of.

We slowed and the word came that brass was on the way. The commander of Sub Div 63 transferred from the Argonaut to the Torsk. We made for St Thomas and moored at 1441 Hours. The piers were full of Navy ships.

I thought how crowded that little place was going to be with that many sailors on liberty at the same time. Our tender, the Orion, was there, along with the USS Angler SSK 240, the USS Hardhead SS 365, the USS Becuna SS 319, and the USS Croaker SS 246.

Not to worry, Our Captain doesn't like crowds. The brass disembarked and at 1910 hours we blew our ships whistle and were off again.

"Budda" Phillips joked about making one of our whistle stops.

Lessor quirped. "We just dropped in for dinner in St Thomas."

I might mention here, that Lessor's wife was a very famous fashion model out of New York. They were very lenient with each other's life style. She knew Lessor was a lifer and he knew she was a world renowned model. We saw her once when she flew in to St. Thomas to spend the week end. She was drop dead gorgeous and truly seemed to be in love with Lessor. She had flown to France and Lessor had met her in Paris, when we were there just last September. Remember I told you of Lessor's UDT accident. Apparently he was her hero as well.

We spent the next couple of days operating with the Barbero. We all knew that something was up because we did a lot of one on one drills with the Barbero. Her main job was to launch missiles. Our main purpose was to guide them to the target. We broke off our drills with the Barbero and she steamed away.

We made a dash for home and moored in Norfolk on Sunday morning at 0700 hours, March 16, 1958.

CHAPTER X

NORFOLK AND THE STORM

Monday at 0500 hours I was up and ready to start breakfast, when Pappy dashed through the chow hall on the way to his morning hosing. I called a warning, "PAPPY'S COMING THROUGH!" In a few minutes he returned and asked me how I liked cooking. I told him it was OK, but I had thought I would not have to do so much outside work.

"My question to you, son, is this, do you want to be a cook right on? I was looking over your record and you're well past rating time. Don't you want to specialize in something?"

"Sure Chief -- but I don't want to be a cook always!" I answered.

"Good - cause we don't want you to cook always!" I wondered how he meant that. "As soon as you finish breakfast - report to me – topside –we've got some painting to do!"

"Your joking – right -- Chief?" I couldn't believe what he just said.

"No joke – sailor -- by the time you get through with breakfast, we'll have the focsle ready to spray – besides -- Lambert's back and we got a new cook coming in a month.

My cooking days were over. "Hallelujah!" – I guess!

The top side painting went well, we only had some touch up to do on the spots where we cleaned rust and corrosion. It is amazing how quickly salt water will eat at metal.

That night Lambert baked some of the best little fruit tarts I ever ate. They were a favorite of our Captain.

I'd like to draw a picture of my relationship with Captain King. I respected the man immensely, but had never been around people who were naturally aloof. Captain King came from a long line of Hawaiian aristocracy; his father was only a few terms out of the governorship.

I was an enlisted man and only a seaman at that. I had no idea that Navy protocol often embraced a vocal barrier between the commanding officer and the enlisted personal.

It was Ok to say, "Good Morning Captain." Don't expect an answer and don't go further by asking, "Did you sleep well?"

I grew up with Submarine and Navy movies. In the movies, the crew always calls their Captain, "Skipper." That's the term that is used to display the love and respect of the crew. That's in Hollywood. In the real world, on the USS Torsk, you don't greet your Captain with "Morning Skipper, how's it goin?" I really had to concentrate to break the "Skipper" challenge.

There is shipboard protocol that is absolutely necessary. Announcing your presence, when entering certain areas that are hazardous or have a lot of activity is necessary to prevent accidents and injury. The Captain sometimes neglected to do this. I suppose he had a lot on his mind, but still it can cause a problem.

When anyone is working in the conning tower, and must move across the ladder leading down to the control room, there is a procedure that one must follow. You place both hands on the rails that are waist high on each side of the ladder hole and simply swing your feet across the ladder opening to the other side. The protocol here is any time someone goes up or down a ladder, he must announce his intention. "Up ladder!" – Down ladder!" This was normal protocol and all personnel did it. Well, almost all.

I don't think I was any different from any other sailor on the Torsk. I was constantly aware of what was going on around me. As the scene changes, I made mental notes, because our lives depended on this. We start depending on all things to transpire as they should. If an alarm is sounded, it was natural for some protocol to be dropped. "Up ladder! – Down ladder! – Coming through!" is not necessary because we are expecting this, as a result of the alarm, but on the average work day or when simply moving around the boat, it is necessary to observe this protocol.

I was absorbed in my work in the conning tower. I had to move across the ladder opening from the control room and as I swung my feet across, I kicked the Captain square in the back of his head as he silently came up the ladder. He cut the bridge of his nose on the top step of the ladder. He was visibly shaken and, of course, the personnel in the control room came to his immediate aid. The wound was not serious, but I was limp with fear and exasperation.

All I could think was, "Why me?" I was just working and minding my own business, but I still felt guilty and was worried about the Captain. I wondered what was going to happen to me.

I had already been cautioned by the Chief of the boat to not converse directly with the Captain and was reluctant to say more than, "Sorry – Captain - I didn't hear you!"

I never heard a word of official reprimand or disapproval about the mishap. The story went that the Exec and Mr. Sheehan both were witnesses and told the Captain he did not announce himself. I suppose, his constant lack of acknowledging my command responses, finally caught up with him.

I was on the last stages of my painting the topside of my Torsk. I carefully roped off the sidewalks on both sides of the sail and placed a warning sign. I had finished the grey touch-up and was shading the black shadow on the port side. The sail tapers down in the aft section and requires a broad black swath that must blend into the starboard side. I had already completed the starboard side. As I swung the paint gun in a downward motion to catch the trailing edge of the sail I heard the Captain utter a very profane word.

I lifted my finger from the paint gun trigger and looked around the back of the sail. Captain King stood there in his fine dress tans with the upper right of his jacket, half of his face, and hat, perfectly matching the black paint on our Torsk.

"Captain – Sir - I'm Sorry - I didn't know you were there!" He never said a word, he simply turned and stepped back over the ropes that blocked the sidewalk and disappeared below deck. I never heard a word of reprimand or caution. He was, indeed, an honorable man.

I enjoyed my time cooking for the Torsk, but my first love was in the conning tower. I was in the center of the action, what did not transpire in the conning tower was in the control room, right below and the open hatch kept me up to snuff on all that was going on.

Mr. Bibby was a mentor to me. He taught me to read charts, operate and read the DRT [dead reckoning tracer]. This device traces your path on a piece of paper while submerged and was dead accurate. It had inputs that read speed, course, depth and angles. It is difficult to pin point an exact location while submerged. You must come to periscope depth and get a star shot or a Loran reading, this can be dangerous, but the DRT will allow a submarine to retrace its path or reach a new destination without revealing its location. The DRT will not compensate for underwater currents, so the instinct of the officers is of key importance.

The Loran is a device that picks up signals broadcasted to give you a location. You must use formulas on the Loran signals to further adjust your location to be exact. It's very complicated. Mr. Bibby took a lot of time to explain the complexity of navigation. I took a great deal of pride in the conning tower and spent a lot of my spare time up there alone.

I was posting new updates in our navigation books when I saw a light flash in the control room. It had been very quiet and I was absorbed it my pasting of navigation up-dates. The flash was followed by a din of noisy activity. I moved to the ladder and called "down ladder" before zipping down to the control room.

I looked down the corridor and saw two guys carrying Crist to the chow hall. I dashed to help and Doc was already giving Crist mouth to mouth. That hi-voltage radio electricity had zapped another one. Crist mumbled something to Doc about no "frenchin" and we knew he was back with us. His forearm had a pretty bad burn but he would be OK.

The upper conning tower hatch was a different animal. Perhaps it was because it got such abuse. Every man that went up or down that hatch put his hand on it somewhere, he would grab the dog wheel, one of the dog legs, the upper edge of the hatch or some part to pull himself up or lower himself down. Every time the boat dived, it was slammed shut with all the power and weight the Deck Officer could put on it. The dog wheel was turned fast as a man could turn it and the dogs were latched down with all the force the helmsman could muster. When it opened, it was spring loaded to raise and slam itself into a locking lever that held it in place until the next dive. It led an abused life, and I suppose it sought revenge from time to time. It was not choosy as to its victims either.

We watched a lot of TV during the three weeks we spent in Norfolk. The press made a big hoopla about Elvis Presley joining the Army. A fellow named Krushchev became the honcho of Russia. We received word that our Navy did not have any more battleships in service. We had decommissioned the USS Wisconsin.

We began to hear about a guy named Castro starting a rebellion in Cuba. We were told we probably would not get involved, because Batista, the present leader, had aligned himself with the syndicates in the U.S. and Europe. The governments of these countries had problems catching criminals, because they would simply fly to Cuba and were safe. I suppose these countries felt that Castro would not shelter the criminals. It appeared we would let Cuba handle the rebellion without any intervention from the U.S.

We hit the high sea again on April 7, 1958 at 0800 hours. The upper conning tower hatch claimed a victim at the first dive. James Hicks, a third class torpedo man hit his head on the hatch as he cleared the bridge. He received quite a blow and fell into my arms as I held the wheel. He was totally unconscious, you can always tell, it's like there are no bones in the body. It is difficult to hold a man up, pick him up and even carry him. The fourth man on watch immediately took Hick's place and he was carried off to a table in the chow hall. I heard a little later, he came to, only to pass out again. He must have had a very bad concussion.

We had a normal week at sea in our operating area. We most always operated in area 19A or 19E. Now, remember, when I say a normal week, it means drills and more drills, exercise, dive, surface, snorkel, fire fish, retrieve fish, rescue man overboard, repel boarders, put out fires, stop flooding, collision drills, battle stations, lose hydraulics and steer manually, eat in a rush, catch maybe two hours sleep and go to war again. The Torsk held the world's record on dives by a submarine. We were not going to lose that title while under Captain King's watch.

A very rare situation developed on our last day of this week of operation. Our OP area was out to sea from Hatteras, North Carolina. This area seldom has a really smooth sea. We were making a smooth 20 knots in a perfect state "O" sea. A "O" [Zero] sea means that it is perfectly flat. The sea was like a glass pane as far as the eye could see. The only ripples were from our sleek bow cleaving through the glassy sea.

The flying fish were out in force. Flying fish really cannot fly and must have a semi-vertical plane of water to exit. They get a fast swimming start and exit the front side of a wave and glide on their large gossamer fins. The only wave for miles was from our bow and the flying fish made the most of it.

The starboard lookout reported an object in the water. It was a practice torpedo and was not an expendable. Apparently one of our sister submarines had fired the fish in a rough sea and was unable to find the torpedo for recovery.

As we got closer we saw why. When a practice torpedo is fired and is to be recovered it will inflate with a charge of air that floats the fish with the front end out of the sea about six feet. Somehow the fish was floating, but flat in the water. The boat simply could not locate the expensive missile.

We cruised next to the torpedo and came to all stop. The Captain called for the torpedo recovery team and that put me on the wheel. The recovery team began to break out the torpedo boom when the Captain had an idea. He asked Pappy Wright how long would the boom operation take. He didn't like Pappy's time estimate and ordered the boom secured. The Captain decided that since the sea was so smooth we would simply flood down and float the fish on deck and lash her down and take her in for the 500 dollar reward for her return. That money would throw a nice ship's party. Captain King sent Pappy to the control room to man the air manifold.

We had a least 40 men topside and the plan was carefully explained to all. We put four swimmers in the water with life jackets to maneuver the torpedo. The men removed their shoes and socks and carefully placed them on the bridge. Some of the guys had flared dungarees and simply pulled the legs up and did a sailor tuck. The Captain and the rest of the crew just pulled their trousers off and put them on the bridge with the shoes. The Captain and the men were on the deck and the Officer of the Deck was on the bridge. Pappy Wright was on the manifold, in the control room, that controlled the valves to the ballast tanks.

The plan called for Pappy to open the ballast tanks valves in increments that would allow the boat to gradually sink just under the sea surface and the swimmers would simply push the fish on deck and we would blow up under the torpedo and tie her down. "Piece o cake!"

All was set. All hatches were secured except for the upper conning tower hatch. The shoes, socks and trousers were all high and dry on the bridge. The sea was so smooth that it was almost uncanny.

I heard the Captain call. "Cycle the vents!"

Mr. Mobley was the OD and repeated the order. "Cycle the vents!"

I relayed the call. "Cycle the vents!"

Chief Wright answered the order and I heard the thunderous rush of air as the vents opened and shut. Silence followed. Apparently we had not moved.

"Cycle the vents again!" Came the Captain's call.

All the voice relays were made and once again I heard the vents cycle. Silence again. I heard someone say. "Shit! - We aint sunk an inch- If I hadn't heard the vents -- I'd swear they ain't working!"

Two more cycles followed, still no change. The Captain patience was wearing thin.

"Tell the Chief to open the vents – I'll tell him when to shut em!" The Captain was in command and we relayed the order. As the swoosh of air followed, it suddenly changed. I knew that change. I had heard it a hundred times, it was water, the tanks were full and we were going down.

I had no more than five seconds. I turned to my right and reached for the upper hatch lanyard. I pulled the hatch shut and dogged her down, as I released the handle it immediately started to rotate open.   Mr. Mobley was trying to get below. I knew that wouldn't work. I grabbed the locking wheel and held it. I heard the rush of water as it swept Mr. Mobley away. I reached and sounded the collision alarm.

I called down the lower hatch. "Chief we're diving!   Everybody's floating. Blow something - Man! - Blow something now!"

The depth gauge read 65 feet when the chief hit the air to the ballast tanks. We were on the way back up, but it was not a rapid thing. Our sinking momentum had to be stopped before our surfacing momentum could take over and that put us below 60 feet, before we started back up.

The Chief was on top of it now and had some sailors collect life jackets. The jackets were being stacked at the base of the upper conning tower hatch. I felt the familiar sound change when the conning tower cleared the sea. I called to the chief that we were up and he ordered the upper hatch open and two men to get the life jackets topside ASAP.

Mr. Bade the new exec was the first officer up to the bridge. "Where are they?" I heard him call.

One of the sailors   handling the life jackets cried. "There! – There! – Off the starboard quarter, Sir!"

"That's over a thousand feet, how did they get that far away? – Right full rudder – all ahead two thirds!" came Mr. Bade's command. I answered and swung the enunciators to relay the command. It seemed like forever before they answered.

Mr. Bade took us back to the floating crew. I could hear the cries of glee from the crew as we eased up and they began to climb up the side of the boat.

Someone cried out. "They're sinking – shithead - the sons o bitches are sinking! – Pull the damn strings - Dumb ass – Pull the CO2 cords!"

The sailors topside in their eagerness to get the life preservers to the floating crewman, were tossing the jackets over the side and they were sinking as soon as they hit the water. The jackets are flat and you place your head through a loop at the top and fasten it around your waist. There is a CO2 cartridge on the each side of the front of the vest that inflates the vest. The vests were sinking because they were not inflated. This flat vest was used on submarines to save space.

"Hey Cap'n! – Looka me!" I recognized "Budda" Phillips voice as he called. "I'm a whale – Cap'n! – Look I'm a Whale!" I could hear him blow water and the laughter was a relief.

The Captain told him to shut up. He did.

I suppose that the emotion that went through these men was extreme as they suddenly saw their boat slip from under them and was silently gone. They had no way of knowing that the upper hatch was shut and not a drop of water got in the boat. They probably thought we were lost and they would be floating for days unless some ship came by. As soon as they saw us surface and start toward them, the feeling of relief blew into an air of exuberance.

Mr. Mobley almost drowned. He saw the hatch shut and thought he had time to open it and get below before the boat went down. He later told me, I did the right thing in sealing him out. He said, the water rushing up through the decking drove him into the overhead of the bridge and almost knocked him out. He admitted that if he had opened that hatch, the boat would have been lost. I think all the shoes were lost, and at least a half dozen life jackets.

We rigged the boom and retrieved the torpedo the correct way; however, we did lash it to the deck.

It seems that our plan was feasible and would probably have worked. It had been done before, many times in stealthy approaches and rescue operations, during wartime. We failed to take two things into consideration. The first thing was headway. We had no headway to break the surface tension of the ultra-calm water. In school we would sometimes do an experiment with a needle floating in a cup of water. The water has a physical property that makes it stick to an object. It's called surface tension. The sea had our boat in a grasp of surface tension and we kept letting in more water, until our negative buoyancy was so great the surface tension broke and we sank like a rock. We were in the Gulf Stream and the current at 60 feet took us over a thousand feet to the north.

We sailed back to Norfolk for the weekend and collected our bounty on the torpedo. Mr. Bade, our executive officer for the last 5 months left us and Mr. C.W. Brink, an ensign joined our family. We also welcomed Mr. K.R. McCally, a young Lt. I was elated when Mr. Bibby got promoted to Lieutenant and was appointed as our new Executive Officer.

We were back at sea that Monday with the Commander of Comsubdiv 63 on board. This time we dived the boat as soon as we hit international waters and set a much deeper southern course than before. It seemed we were hugging the coast. I heard the term "Operation Springboard" and knew it was going to be a missile mission. The Barbero was off in the distance and was going further out to sea. We stayed submerged and snorkeled our way down the eastern seaboard.

Normally we sailors simply carry out orders and don't ask questions, so seldom does the average sailor know the whole operation. I was on the wheel and heard mention of the LV 109 Lightship. I knew the LV 109 Lightship was at Savannah. It was about 10 or so miles out from the entrance to the Savannah River at Tybee Island Ga. That's my neck of the woods. The chills went over me as I thought of attacking my own home. It was a game, I knew that, but the feeling was weird, never the less.

It seems our mission was to surface and be in position and guide the missile fired by the Barbero to the target. The target for our launch was the Savannah River Site, just south of Augusta, Georgia, a complex for the manufacture of nuclear weapon components was being constructed at the site.

This operation was the same as all naval operations involving multiple forces. All the various entities are given locations, times and operations to perform. Obviously we couldn't fire the real missiles at the target, but use the information given by a carefully laid out plan. The missiles are fired by simulation. The information is transmitted to us with a built in error. We receive the info just as if it were coming from an inbound missile. The Torsk crew then does its comparison and finds the error and transmits the signals to correct the missile's trajectory. The powers that be, may accept the signal, or send more signals that tell us we over corrected or possibly a crosswind had shifted the missile's course and we had to correct again. Our job was to stay with the mission until impact.

We had surfaced at dawn's early light and I could hear the tension as the lookouts and OD kept a keen lookout for air craft. We not only had naval aircraft to watch for, but Hunter Air Force base was located in Savannah. The base was a part of the Strategic Air Command and even though most of Hunter's air activity was cargo, they had a coastal patrol as well.

We had all our hardware at its extreme height, missile tracking gear and radar receivers. The exercise was developing well. The data we received was putting the missile right on course. Then a slight deviation to the north forced us to correct the course, naturally the guys monitoring said we went too far and sent a new error that pushed the missile too far south.

The Captain laughed, he had anticipated as much and had the solution ready. The new results held and the time ticked nervously by.

Mr. Bibby looked at his watch and did some quick calculations. "About five minutes away and good bye A Bomb Plant" he said nonchalantly. I wondered if Momma, Daddy and the boys would survive the fallout. I shuddered at the thought, if we could do it, why couldn't the Russians do it. I felt a little sick.

"Ten – nine – eight –!" Mr. Bibby began the countdown. I counted in my head as we sat dead in the water. "Three – two – one – KABOOM!" He grinned and called the Captain in Combat. "I show it's a done deal – Captain – congratulations - shall we dive and slip away?"

The Captain did nothing the simple way. "No Mr. Bibby! Let's stay right here and see what comes around!"

In the real world, this would be like shaking the hornet's nest. The enemy hears about the destruction of their prime location and seeks revenge. The Torsk likes a good fight.

Mr. Bibby shrugged his shoulders and passed the word top side that our mission was a success, but watch out, the hornets were on the way.

All elevated gear was lowered except the radar receiver. We could have a swim call, it was so quiet. We would occasionally get a radar flash, but no repeats and no locks. We had been up for over fifteen minutes past our objective, but were still about six hours until "Operation Springboard" was over. It would have been so simple to submerge and stroll out of there, but that would have been way too easy.

"Radar watching us Captain!" Came the info from radar.

"Where from and how far?" Called the Captain.

Radar informed us. "South and from a surface craft - they haven't locked on us yet - we figure they are over 35 miles away - Sir. If we dive now they will probably think we were only a wave top!"

"OK – Mr. Bibby - take her down and let's set on the bottom and see what happens!" The Captain was still itching for a fight.

I don't know exactly how far from the mainland we were but the continental shelf was very nearby. It's called the "Hundred Fathom Curve" in this part of the ocean. The water drops from around 250 feet to 600 feet very quickly. We sat down on a sandy smooth bottom and took a slight port list to rest and see what happens.

What transpires will always be a mystery to me, but I really think the Grand Master of all plans, the one who is in ultimate control, was bound to teach us a lesson in humility.

We sat on the bottom and went ultra-quiet; missile guidance was not an intensive exercise that required all departments to be poised, ready but not poised. Everyone was relaxed and the Captain put the UQC on broadcast, so all could hear. Everyone on board was listening to the shrimp and an occasional dolphin. We could hear currents as they would push a slug of freshly loosened sand against a hydrophone. The Captain gave permission to completely stow the radar mast as we had it still aloft as we dove. It was uncanny to hear the hydraulics as they lowered the shaft and sat it in its cavity. It made a clanking squeak. "We need to fix that" Budda commented. So much for all quiet.

It was not a trying time. We all felt invincible. We could hear the faint pings on sonar, a lot of pings. The sounds were coming through the UQC and weren't aimed at us. Still, what we heard sounded like the entire US Naval fleet was out there looking. We had only dived as a result of one little radar sweep that was never locked. The sonar sounds drew closer. There were, indeed, a lot of them.

Sonar reported that the pings were not a searching ping but from a fathometer, a continuously running fathometer. The approaching vessel was sounding the bottom. A fathometer is sonar but simply shoots down or at a programed angle and its purpose is to identify depth and type of bottom surface. We relaxed. The ship wasn't looking for us. We turned on our sophisticated sound gear that was installed in Philly and soon found the vessel to be going from left to right and apparently looking for the hundred fathom curve. The vessel was over 15 miles away.

I was sitting at the foot of the hatch from the bridge, relaxing when I began to hear the screw beats of the approaching vessel. The whole crew was keenly aware that this vessel was going to pass very near to us. The whole time we tracked this approaching ship we had never considered it a threat at all. Now it was coming straight at us.

We could hear the screws and the fathometer pings. "THRUMP - SHUSH! – PING-RNG-PING-RNG--THRUMP-SHUSH!—PING-RNG-PING-RNG - THRUMP-SHUSH! They were bearing down on us. We were now concerned but not alarmed. One foot to the side, or no one looking at the fathometer screen and we were missed. There were any number of reasons to pass overhead and never know we were there.

The mystery ship passed directly over us from forward to aft. It traversed our 312 feet length every inch. We held our breath. The screw beats and pings were deafening. We didn't need the UQC to hear them. We were about to relax as the ship cleared our stern and began to move away.

The Master Planner thought otherwise.

"THRUMPA – THRUMP - THRUMP – THRUMPA – THRUMP - THRUMP!' The ship was backing down. We heard her turn and began another pass, this time we heard her searching sonar. She knew we were there. We expected our skipper to spring to action, pull us off the bottom and launch a S2T attack.

Captain King passed the word. "All Quiet - Boys! – Maybe they'll go away!"

The surface craft cruised back and forth over us, undoubtedly tracing our outline on a scale map.

The UQC was delivering every noise of the search to us. The clang of the ships battle station bell rang clear to our ears. We heard the clang and scrapping of the depth charge racks as they readied the depth charges. Our Captain stood by the UQC with mike in hand. Every time someone would comment or attempt to ask a question he would use his "finger to lips" sign of silence.

The UQC now had a voice as the Captain of the ship, over us, sent this message. "Unidentified submarine! – Identify yourself! – We repeat! - Identify yourself"

Yep, they knew we were there. Captain King placed his finger to his lips again.

The UQC continued. "This is American warship! – USS Robinson DD562! – demanding immediate identification!" The Captain's head nodded negative.

The voice on the UQC informed us we had ten seconds before "Ringer One" would be fired.

The Captain stood firm. "Mark – ringer one! – PATOOM! ----- SPLASH! ------- Silence ----- Ka-plink! – WHOOOM!" We felt the concussion, our Torsk shivered, she was not used to this abuse. Hollywood would have us blast off the bottom, outrun a destroyer that could run circles around us, torpedo her and sail away into the sunset. In the real world we simply played possum.

"Mark ringer two! – PATOOM! ----- SPLASH -----Silence -----Ka-plink – WHOOOM!" Once again our magnificent Torsk shuddered in disbelief. The phosphorescent paint depth charges were dead on. As the barrage continued we actually heard a couple hit our deck before the "Ka-plink" of the firing pin.

The UQC spoke again "UNIDENTIFIED SUBMARINe! – Mark RED! - I repeat! - Mark RED ringer one in ten seconds! – Nine! – Eight! ----------------- This was the real McCoy!

The Captain instantly brought the UQC Mike to his lips and announced. "USS Robinson – This is Lunar Light! - I repeat! - Lunar Light!

He changed his voice and displayed one of his rare, humorous interludes. In a rough European accent he stated. "We ak de Russon Submarine - Son of de Bolshebitch- and vish de asylum of your budeful Charleston Harbor – Dah!"

It seems our conqueror was a Navy Destroyer from Norfolk that was destined to become a reserve training ship assigned to Charleston and was conducting a fathometer training class for reservist. The USS Robinson DD562 was not a participant in our "Springboard Operation,"

The Captains agreed on our surrender terms and the Robinson backed off 300 yards and we blew to the surface.

I was on the wheel and did not see the topside scene. But Johnny North and Dave Cummings told me about it.

The Robinson was on our starboard side and the entire crew and reserve classes were topside when we surfaced. Johnny said the ship actually had a port list due to the mass of sailors along the rail. Dave said their jaws were hanging open so wide they were scooping sea water.

We were covered with yellow phosphorescent paint. No doubt about it, we were dead and at the hands of a reserve training ship, not even in the operation. We knew what humble pie tasted like.

We tucked our tail and slowly sailed to Norfolk. I was glad I wasn't topside when we tied up. We moored at 1814 hours on April 10th, 1958. That was a Thursday afternoon and a lot of sailors saw us, think how embarrassing it was for the fabled killer elite ,the USS Torsk, to slip in port covered with that telltale yellow "I got killed" paint all over her. "Man!" I had just painted her a couple of weeks ago.

The new cook was waiting for us when we docked. He had been on the pier since early that morning. He was not a huge fellow, in fact he looked like a sixteen year old kid. He was only a seaman apprentice. This was his first boat and his first cooking job. He actually wanted to be a cook, and felt a U.S. Navy Submarine was better than any cooking school he could go to and he even got paid for it. His name was Karl Kettlehut and he was good from the first day on.

Water pressure is a magnificent cleaner. We worked for two days to water blast the yellow paint off and touch up our beautiful Torsk. We took great pride in our girl's appearance. We could pick her out of a nest of boats without ever looking at her number. She was, leaner, cleaner and meaner than any of the rest. We loved her and we were going to show her off. We were going to

Baltimore, Maryland for the weekend. It would be my first time to host visitors on board my Torsk.

The maneuvering watch was 13 hours as we navigated up the Chesapeake Bay to Baltimore. The trip was a real lark because we had 23 boy scouts on board for the journey. The boys were intently curious and asked all kinds of questions. I allowed each one to take a turn at the wheel, but I had to keep a keen eye on some of them. They would turn the wheel just to see the effect it would have on the boat and us. I took a couple of head breaks, but ate my favorite cheese sandwiches at the wheel. I thought I would be exhausted but I hit the beach within a half hour of liberty call.

Baltimore is a great Liberty town. I spent Friday night singing in a country and western bar about two blocks from where we were moored in the "Inner Harbor." I knew a lot of Hank Williams songs and performed "Love Sick Blues". You don't have to be a good singer to please a whisky soaked crowd of red necks.

There was not a bad bone in the crowd and everyone seemed to like me. I didn't pay for any drinks.

As the night wore on I was feeling pretty good and decided to do "You are my Sunshine" by Jimmy Davis. I gave a brief story about him riding me on his horse when I was four.   He boarded his horse at Broadmoor Riding Academy in Shreveport, where my Momma was manager.

A lady at the bar began to make moves on me. The old saying about "women looking better at closing time" did no apply to this woman. A week of closing times would not have helped her. I silently slipped out and went back to my Torsk. The faceless lady kept me company the rest of the night.

We spent the Saturday showing visitors through our boat. It was a new experience for us. There was no set program as to who worked where. We just moved around and each took a turn at answering questions and providing information. There was always a crowd at the after torpedo room ladder and the forward torpedo room ladder. Ladies didn't realize that it was best to wear slacks if you are visiting a submarine, but the sailors didn't mind helping them up and down the ladders, no, they didn't mind a bit.

Monday morning saw us bidding farewell to Baltimore. Hick's head was healed enough that he got in some trouble in Baltimore and the Captain saw fit to restrict him for two weeks. We steered down the Chesapeake Bay and out to sea to perform a series of drills that put the edge back on our response time. Captain King was a believer in repetition. He felt that instantaneous response was a most valuable part of the success of any operation. We owe our lives to his conviction.

We performed a heavy line transfer with the USS Argonaut SS 475. At the completion of the exercise we dropped anchor in Chesapeake Bay and simply rested for the night. We moored in Norfolk alongside the Cubera SS 347 shortly after noon on Thursday, May 22, 1958. The USS Sailfish joined us at 1930 hours. We rested for the weekend.

The weather was getting worse by the hour. A subtropical depression had formed in the Gulf and had moved across Florida over the weekend. The winds were not that high but it was following the Gulf Stream up the coast and the water was getting very rough.

We received a report that it was going to hit the northern coast of North Carolina. That meant Norfolk and Chesapeake Bay would be directly in its path.

The U.S. Navy gives a Captain the prerogative of riding a storm at anchor in a bay or going to sea to ride the storm. A ship cannot safely be moored alongside a pier when the water gets too rough.

Captain King made the decision to go to sea and try to get outside the storm area. It was a toss-up as to which decision was best. If it is a high wind, full force hurricane, it would probably be wise to ride it out at anchor on the leeward side of a landmass. However this was a low wind depression that had a lot of rain and the Captain felt it would be best to just get out of the way. It almost cost the lives of three of our crew. I was one of the three.

We left our berth at 0700 hours on Monday, May 26 and set course straight out of Chesapeake Bay to get outside of the storms reach. As soon as we cleared the southern tip of the Virginia landmass, I knew we were in for a rough go. The rain was not profuse but the sea was ugly. I explained how low a submarine rides in the water. I mentioned that we were maybe fifteen feet above the sea in our lookout ports. The Officer of the Deck has the blessings of a plexiglas bubble to break the blast of waves riding over our bow, but the lookouts are exposed to the wall of water from the waist up.

The sea was coming from the southeast and the waves were a continuous mass of rolling billows. Visibility was reduced to less than 800 yards. The

Runner was off our starboard after beam and barely visible. There were times we could not even see her. The waves were increasing in height.

A ship has a choice in heavy water. It either heads directly into the sea or directly away from the sea. If the waves get too high and you get caught broadside, your boat can capsize. Remember now, a submarine has a round bottom and tends to roll much more than a ship with a sharp keel.

The waves increased in height to over thirty feet. I was starboard lookout and John Crist was port lookout. The OD was Mr. Wiseman.

Things got very stressful by the end of the day. We could not make any real head way. We had to slow to 5 knots to keep from hitting the waves so hard that we were breaking stuff in the boat. We had already rigged the ship for surface, but had sealed all hatches. This meant that we would always pop back up when a wave washed over us. But we were locked out of the boat. The water would raise our bow as the wave passed under us. When the wave reached our midship, the bow would dive into the trough, the screws would come out of the water and our Torsk would vibrate violently. This was on every wave for hours on end. The submarine would then dive under the next wave and we would hold our breath. We were going so deep that it hurt my ears. I feel safe in saying we probably were at least 40 feet deep or maybe more. Our lungs would be screaming for air when we surfaced.

We had come on watch at noon, but the sea got so bad that we couldn't take time to swap watch at 1600. We were now strapped in our lookout ports to keep from being swept overboard. The noise was so great that Mr. Wiseman had to put his ear to the speaker to hear what was being said from the control room.

Mr. Wiseman received word that the Runner had lost their starboard lookout. I felt a tremendous rush of compassion for the Runner and our lost mate. Our Captain and the Captain of the Runner were close friends. The Runner was out here because we were out here.

The fury of the sea was impossible to describe. It was all the Torsk could do to maintain headway against the power of the advancing waves. The wall of water would come at us as if it was angry. It had been dark all day with rain clouds obscuring any sunshine. The rain had subsided. Luckily we were in the Gulf Stream and the water was very warm considering it was the later part of May.

The power of the sea is immeasurable. As the Torsk would rise and then plummet into a wave, she would tremble as if dreading the impact. As darkness grew we turned our running lights on full bright. When we rose from the water we would flip our binoculars to clear water from the lens and strain to make a quick search around us for any imminent ships that were on collision course. As the next wall of water approached the bright running lights would reflect off the oncoming wave and it would look like a stone wall, half green and half red. We would look up to see how high the wall was. They were growing with each onslaught. The impact of the waves was taking its toll on all of us.

Crist and I were in our lookout ports, strapped in by a safety belt. Our bodies were exposed from the waist up and we were taking the full impact of the waves as we crashed through them. We were being dashed against the sail and had to hold our heads forward to keep from being knocked unconscious.

A new danger now presented itself. The Torsk would crash into the approaching wall of water as if we were diving the boat. The wave would wash over us and at the same time the sea was filling the void under the deck of the boat. Our deck is comprised of strips of teakwood decking that has spaces of around an inch between them to allow the passage of water on diving and surfacing. The sea was creating such a force in our super structure, that the water would shoot up between the decking and lift us off our feet. We now had water pressure from the front and from the bottom. We were being battered to death.

The OD had a steel plate near the front of the bridge that stopped the force of the water as it gushed up. He would cling to his hand hold and stand on the plate to keep from being thrown upward. None of this did anything to stop the agonizing time we had to hold our breath as we were submerged before rising to begin the brutal onslaught again.

I don't know how a human can stand that much punishment for the close to nine hours that we had been topside.

Mr. Wiseman made a decision. He knew that one of us was going to be injured sooner or later. The only thing he could do was remove as much of the battering as possible. His only choice was for us to move from our lookout ports to the doghouse. The doghouse is the enclosure that is in front of the bridge and about three feet further down. It is where the superstructure of the sail begins; it gets quite narrow, but would shield us from the force of the oncoming wall of water. The doghouse has a hatch on one side that allows access to the deck of the boat about one foot down. There is a little shelf at the very front for writing when the topside watch used the doghouse in rainy weather. There are four plexiglas windows, two on each side of the sail that we could observe for approaching ships.

We had to time our move precisely. If we were not in our new position before the next wave, we would be swept overboard. Somehow we managed the move. I felt a brief sense of relief knowing that the blow of the oncoming water was no longer a threat.

I was not prepared for what happened. The decking under the doghouse has openings as well as the bridge. When the water rushed into the superstructure under us, the force of the water drove us into the overhead of the doghouse. Crist and I were both dazed from the impact. It was a wonder we didn't drown while submerged under that dazed condition. Luckily we were not swept overboard as there was no place to safety our belts.

We collected our senses and found that the leading edge of the doghouse deck had a metal plate that was about 18 inch long. We both would stand on that plate and hold onto the little writing shelf with arms around each other. This would shield us from the upward blast of water and at least we were not being dashed against the overhead.

Mr. Wiseman told us to watch dead ahead, he would keep lookout to the beams and aft. We would crowd as tightly as we could into that small vee space as we watched the walls of red and green water approach. We noticed that the waves had lost their angle look and now looked as if they were straight up. We would strain our eyes to see the black outline of the sky at the top of the wave. It was easy to see as the sky would not reflect the red and green running lights. It was evident that the waves were well over 50 feet now.

I began to pray, I was not afraid and once again thought I was going to feel what it was like to die. I was keenly aware of the hatch to our right. It had only a lift handle to open it. Then sea was right outside. I really thought this was going to be our death.

When the weather is really bad, a submarine must ride it out on the surface. There are a number of reasons for this. A submarine must always power into the sea or away from the sea, in rough weather. A broadside sea will role a submarine over and there is no recovery from this on a sub. The batteries will dump acid and will fall out of their racks, remember they weigh one ton each and there are 222 of them. Also, the ballast tanks and fuel tanks are open to the sea on the bottom. The torpedoes will fall from their sleds and – well! -- You get the point.

When submerged and the sea is as bad as it is now, there would be no way to tell where the sea is coming from. A tropical storm in the Atlantic will give you the wind and sea in different directions during its passing. In order to tell the sea direction, we must come to periscope depth. In heavy seas the top of the sub would be exposed to the waves when a trough comes by and that could be disastrous. We simply ride it out on the surface. The sub was safe as long as we took the water head on, but the three of us on the bridge were getting weak.

The night dragged on and the onslaught worsened. I prayed while underwater. The desire for oxygen lessened as we became used to holding our breath. The knowledge that we would broach again helped our nerves.

We would open our eyes under water and gaze through the Plexiglas windows. The millions of tiny bubbles from under our superstructure would distort the red and green glare from our running lights and the sea would dance with multi colored hues as the light rays mixed in the tiny bubble spheres. We could hear our Torsk groaning in her fight against the mighty waves as they tossed us about. The "THUMPA – THUMP" of the screws was deafening. We could hear the clanging of broken steel braces under our deck. The vibrations were shaking us apart.

We could feel the rising sensation as our positive buoyancy would overpower the sea and our bow would rise rapidly. It was like going up in a fast elevator.

Our bow pierced the surface and we quickly cleared our eyes to make a visual pass ahead. As the bow continued to rise the sea disappeared. The rising sensation became more noticeable. Our bow was riding up the front side of a giant swell and the angle of vision was in the sky. As the swell reached our midship the bow plunged to the sea.

There was no wave ahead of us. Our vision was limited to maybe 800 feet. All we could see was the back side of this huge swell. We could feel the acceleration as our Torsk plunge down this mountain of water. I wondered if we had reached the edge of the world.

Suddenly, there it was, a wall of water coming at us, it looked solid, it was red on the left and green on the right. There was no top in sight. This one was different.

Mr. Wiseman exclaimed. "Oh! – My God!" I heard him sound the collision alarm. Our Torsk slide down that wave as a surfer would slide down a perfect wave. It was if it was in slow motion. The water came directly at us. I forced Crist into the front of the pocket where we stood and reached around him with both arms and held the little shelf with a death grip.

We struck the water and all went black. I vaguely remember my nose burning as my brain was telling my body to breath. My subconscious must have stopped it. I was half consciously aware that the hatch to the deck was banging open. I felt Crist's limp body pass over me as the water was forcing us out of the hatch to sea. "Dear Lord – Please - Accept my spirit!"

Suddenly I felt rope. Yes it was rope, a lot of rope. The line locker under the bridge had sprung open. I grabbed the rope with my left hand and blackness set in again, I told my hand not to let go, whatever happened. The blackness deepened.

I heard Lessor's voice. "Dammit! – Wardy! – Let go! – Shit! - He won't turn loose! I felt someone smacking my left hand. "Wardy – Let go! - We got him! – Man! – Turn loose!"

Someone was prying my fingers from the rope. Blackness over powered me again.

The stainless steel was cold as my cheek brushed against the side of the conning tower hatch. I was on someone's shoulders as they lowered me down the ladder. Ahh! The blackness again.

The brightness was overpowering. I had difficulty opening my eyes; I could hear some activity to my right and turned my head to see Crist lying on the chow hall table, with Doc working on his head. A couple of guys were holding Crist arms as he would attempt to flail the air in his semi- conscious state. I was on the table near the door to our sleeping quarters.

Doc would say. "Stitch one - pearl two!" He was sewing up a gaping wound on Crist head.

I began to reason that I was OK or hurt too bad to help. There was no one around me. I raised my hand to touch my face. I had no nose or jaw. The blackness swept over me again.

A soothing voice brought me back. It was Mac. "Man! - You'll do anything to take a nap won't you?" His nasal tone was comforting.

I know I smiled and was surprised that I felt no pain. My hand tingled as if it had been asleep. I raised my hand again and gingerly felt of my face. I wondered if I had dreamed all this.

My face was all there. I suppose, I had slapped my hand really hard on something and it was stunned or I had just imagined my face damaged.

I had been unconscious for about twenty minutes. Crist was still not totally with us as Doc was finishing up the dozen or so stitches on his head.

Something must have been in the water as we dove into that giant wave, because there was a hole in the port side of the sail that a man could crawl through. Somehow our officers managed to get the Torsk turned around and we were now headed with the sea and it was by far, a better ride. We had secured topside and sealed the hatch. We were navigating by periscope. We had been running the engines on snorkel mode with the snorkel mast as high as we felt it could handle the sea.

While we were fighting the storm topside, the crew below was having problems. The deep fat fryer flew from its base and strewed oil all over the galley. Bunk mattresses and crew gear was scattered everywhere, there were numerous head injuries as the men were thrown into the overhead by the sudden drop of our bow. We had many light fixtures and other fixtures that were broken due to the vibration from the exposed propellers.

The storm was supposed to make land fall between North Carolina and Virginia, but had changed course and was heading northeast. We had been sailing right into it. We all grieved the lost sailor from the Runner.

Lessor came back and told me he was sorry he cussed me so bad, but I wouldn't let go, so he had to pry my fingers.

I told him he would hold on to a rope too, if that was all he had between him and the deep blue sea.

Lessor looked at me and asked. "What rope?"

"The rope from the line locker -- Man! – I didn't want to fall over board!" I exclaimed.

"You thought you had hold of a rope?" He asked in amazement.

"UH! – Yeh!" I answered. "I remember you telling me to turn it loose!"

Lessor looked stunned. He sat down with a thud and muttered. "I'll be damned! – Wardy! -- You didn't have a hold on any rope -- you had a hold on the collar of Crist's foul weather jacket! -- You may have saved his life - Damn! – That's weird!" He stood up and walked away.

I looked over at Crist, he was still in a stupor and his eyes were glazed. I never mentioned what Lessor told me. God had a plan. That plan didn't call for Crist or me to die that night.

We put in to Yorktown, Virginia and stayed for about four hours to access our damages, then proceeded to Norfolk for four days of repairs. Our Torsk was a tough old girl and did all she was asked to do.

I have never seen a wilder sea before or since. This subtropical depression produced a wilder sea than Hurricane Becky, Daisey, Fifi or Helene. We experienced them all in 1958. We didn't deliberately sail into them but we had to encounter them at some point anyway.

We spent the most part of the summer on weekly exercises out of Norfolk. It was routine drills with our sister subs in Subron Six.

Our new cook, Kettlehut was doing quite well at his chosen profession. He was not a big guy and very good natured, however, we found out he had a breaking point. One of the older guys said something about his manhood one day. We were off loading some fresh beef from a cooler truck on the pier when the remark was made.

The old hand flew out of the back of the truck, hollering. "I was joking Kettlehut - honest I was just joking!" Kettlehut was right behind him brandishing a meat clever. It took some of the crew to calm Kettlehut down. He was really pissed at the sailor. I never found out what was said, but this incident stayed in my mind for quite a while.

I picked up a little spare money playing checkers from time to time. I didn't have to look for people to play. They would seek me out. I guess it was that old gunfighter syndrome that made them want to try me.

I went home for a weekend that summer and brought my bullwhip back. We would draw a crowd when I would go topside and crack it around a bit. It would sound like gunshots across Chesapeake Bay and sailors from other ships would line the rails to watch. I would stick pieces of rolled up paper about six inches long in the top of the post that held our life cables that ran around the deck. The cables were about mid-thigh height. I would pop the paper and it would fly in little pieces.

Mac volunteered to hold the paper one day and I popped several pieces from his hand.

"Red" Neale was from Texas and his prize possession was a genuine Bowie knife. It was quite large and he was telling everyone how well balanced it was and how accurate it was to throw. He began to tease me about how a man with a Bowie knife could easily take on a man with a measly little bullwhip. Neale was a really nice guy, but was defensive about Texas. He knew I was from Louisiana and began to tease me about why would I choose a Texas bullwhip over a Louisiana Bowie knife. He kept at me. I knew he was edging for a knife throwing contest. I knew he would ace me on that. It was his knife and he was used to it and I wouldn't stand a chance. He kept on and wouldn't hush.

I looked over on the pier and spotted a set of three creosoted post that were cabled together to form a bollard for tying up ships. There was a triangular brand burnt in the side of the center post facing us.

This is one of those wild things that men sometimes do on impulse. I asked to examine the Bowie knife. I was surprised at the weight of it. It was a beauty. I flipped it over in my hand a couple of times hoping that I looked like I knew what I was doing. As a kid, I had thrown knives and tomahawks at trees when playing and at scouting camps, but this was a different weapon. The feel of it was ominous.

"Red – See that diamond on that post there?" He looked and nodded. I was holding the knife by the handle and threw it at the post, without the slightest idea that it would even hit in the vicinity of the diamond brand, much less stick in the wood. I missed the diamond but it was close enough to be impressive. The knife sunk in the wood a good three inches.

"I just like a whip better - Red!" I coiled my whip and went below deck. It was a one in a million throw!

In a few minutes Mac came to my bunk. "You're one lucky "son of a gun" you know that?" He quirped.

"How you know I ain't just that good - Mac?" I wised back.

"Cause you woulda told me if you was that good and you ain't so good with that damn whip either!" He held up his hand and there was a nasty slice across the back of it. He had never said a word to the crowd. He was a true good friend. I wanted to cry.

It was a wild summer in Norfolk. Steinbeiser and Maynard both got in trouble and got restricted. My cooking mentor and friend "Catfish" Woodson had some domestic problems and got restricted.

We would spend long weekends in port and then hit our op areas with a vengeance. The Captain was dead set on having the best crew and best diving record in the fleet. The Nautilus and Seawolf were our nuclear boats. They were the most esteemed, but of the old diesel boats, the Torsk was the epitome of respect.

Mr. Bibby asked me to the ward room on Friday, June 6th, 1958. We had been to sea for the week. He asked me how I felt about going to the Naval Academy. I told him about my appointment out of high school and how fate had stopped me, not once, but twice. He told me that Subron Six was going to request a fleet appointment for me for the class in September. I was overwhelmed. He told me to keep it quiet, it was best not to say anything until the appointment was approved.

One weekend during that summer the fab five piled into Johnny North's 56 Chevy and headed for Virginia Beach. We had our summer civvies on and blended in with the beach crowd. We were cruising down the main drag and past a club named "The Top Hat." The marque spotlighted "Duane Eddy" as the nightly performer. I told the guys of the top notch performance I had witnessed at the Brass Rail at Tybee Island, last summer. We decided to pay Duane a visit that night.

We had an early dinner of burgers and fries at a little drive inn on the beach and made it to the club early in order to get a good table. We were right on the dance floor at least an hour before the "Rebels" were scheduled to go on. When the group started arriving, I had trouble picking Duane out of the group. Finally the best looking guy in the group picked up a guitar and played that familiar "TWANG – TWANG," that I knew so well.

I walked over and called. "Duane! – I know you don't remember me -- but I was at the Brass Rail last summer at Tybee when you first played "Rebel Rouser!"

He looked at me and grinned, I immediately knew why I had trouble recognizing him. He had his teeth fixed. Phyllis had remarked that he needed to make that improvement. I made a mental note to tell her about it.

"No Buddy! – I don't remember you but I sure remember that night! -- The response to that ditty was what convinced us to record it – say -- you guys gonna stay a while?"

"I suppose so – Duane -- if the music is as good now as it was then and some women show up!" I smiled and stuck out my hand.

"What brings you up this way -- Buddy?" He asked.

"The Navy -- I'm on a submarine and I'm here with some of my buddies! -- I told them how great you are and we came to take in your show!"

He grinned again with that new dazzling smile and leaned over close to my ear. "Stick around-- we gotta special treat for you guys tonight-- OK?"

"Yeh! – Sure- Duane – Break a leg -- ya heah!" I hoped he recognized that stage pun. I went back to the table and told the guys about the special treat that was promised.

It was a wonderful night, we found a good crowd attended the club and no one wanted to fight. Some other sailors and some marines from Quantico showed after a while, but there was no problem. The show was great and the staged fight by the band members was even better than the first time I saw it.

At near midnight, the band did a drumroll and Duane took the mic and began to speak. He asked for quiet and after some difficulty the crowd settled down to hear him.

"About a year ago -- we played "Rebel Rouser" for the first time in public -- it was at a club on Tybee Island, Georgia. -- We have a guest here tonight who was there that night and it's only fitting that we recognize him!" He motioned for me to stand.

There was some polite applause. "I'm telling you this because he was there the first time we played "Rebel Rouser" in public and he's here tonight."

Duane paused and boldly stated; " Ladies and Gentlemen; REBEL ROUSER just made the "Top Ten" on the "Pop Chart!"

The crowd went crazy and the band played a short blast of pompous music. Duane called for quiet again. "Mr. Manager -- please lock the doors! -- This is now a private party and you are all invited!" The band burst into the most memorable version of "Rebel Rouser" I ever heard.

It was a magnificent party and even the basket of fiddler crabs some drunk dumped on the dance floor didn't spoil it. Duane Eddy was off to stardom, and I was there to witness the blastoff.

July 3rd, 1958. The Captain's buddy, the commander of the Runner was being transferred. We held the ceremony in dress whites. I felt sorry for our Captain. I knew the feeling of having to leave a friend. It didn't mean that they would lose touch but they wouldn't be next door neighbors anymore and now, who would they play with?

We spent July operating as a sound boat and spent weekends in Norfolk. Catfish was put on the wheel as maneuvering watch helmsman to give him some practice, in case something was to happen to me.

We were at sea on July 22, 1958 at midnight when the sky lit up as if by a flash bulb. I had just come on watch as port lookout and relieved Mac. The other look outs were still topside when the flash occurred. We looked up to see a large meteor burning through the sky in the east. It then broke into two smaller pieces and finally burst into many smaller fragments as they fell into the sea. It was quite a show and we felt privileged to witness it. I wondered how much damage a meteor of any size would do if it struck earth. Mr. Sheehan told us that they could destroy entire cities if they were as large as a bus.

We operated with the destroyers, USS Waldron DD 699, USS Weeks DD 701 and USS Ault DD 698. We killed them and they hunted us, numerous times.

We took some marines from Little Creek, Virginia on a night raid to Camp Lejeune, North Carolina. We enjoyed them telling of sneaking on the base, and putting a note in the base commanders desk drawer that read BOOM – YOU'RE

DEAD. They taped the toilet lids down on the johns in the Officer's Club and numerous other hi-jinxes to show they had been there, unobserved.

Mr. Bibby called me to the ward room late on Friday afternoon, August 8th, 1958. He explained that the Bureau of Naval Personnel had turned me down due to my age for a fleet appointment. Subron Six had requested a waiver on my age restriction and it was granted. The Academy had now denied my appointment. There was a list of hundreds of candidates that met all requirements, and did not get accepted, so my exception was out of the question. I was really disappointed, but when God has a plan, you must take your time to recognize it. I knew, now, the Academy was not part of his plan for me.

Mr. Bibby told me when my reserve tour was up next year, that I was already qualified for OCS [Officers Candidate School] and all I would have to do was accept it and ship over to regular Navy. I told him I would think on it.

CHAPTER XI

THE GREAT FIGHT

On August 11th, 1958 we left port for San Juan again. We porpoised the boat, for four straight days. We chalked up dive after dive. We also fought the remnants of Hurricane Becky. We had a new officer on our boat. Mr. C.R. Bell, a Lieutenant. He was our new navigation officer.

We were snorkeling in rough weather when our emergency vacuum engine shutdown system failed. Our Torsk had two systems on board that would shut down the engines when snorkeling if the induction valve stayed shut too long. When snorkeling, the sub is submerged, but a long tube is extended to the sea surface to draw air for the diesels. If the waves get high enough to allow water into the tube, sensors will shut the valve and the engines will draw air from inside the submarine. If the vacuum, in the boat gets too great, it will rupture eardrums and cause other damage to the human body, including death.

Our main vacuum shut down system was under repair from damage suffered during the storm last May. The backup system failed and a vacuum was drawn in the boat that damaged over half the crews eardrums. I thought I was lucky, having only a little pain and seemingly no damage. Three days later I began to have hearing problems and Doc Johansen told me I had dried blood in my ears. He cleaned my ears and began to minister some drops to aid the healing.

Doc informed me that when eardrums are ruptured, the drops are important to allow the drums to heal properly.   Doc said, I may have hearing problems, later in life, as a result of the three days delay. This was one of the first symptoms of a neurological problem I had. It was no big deal, but my nervous system did not relay pain signals as most normal systems do. It simply meant I didn't feel pain as much as most folks. It was as much a hindrance as a blessing. There were numerous times, I thought I was sweating only to find I was bleeding from a cut or scratch.

San Juan was never more beautiful. The fab five, minus one, rented a car for the weekend and decided to tour the inland. We left early Saturday morning in our island civvies, which consisted of calf length old work dungarees, tee shirt and sandals.

The Volkswagen was not brand new but ran great. I drove as we made our way toward the inland. Our plans were to visit a straw hat factory inland and then head east to drive up EL Yunque, the tallest mountain on the island. We then were going to the northeast coast for dinner and back to San Juan by late evening.

We had been indoctrinated on the politics of Puerto Rico, and told to stay away from the southeastern part of the island due to the Nationalist Movement that was prevalent there. We remembered this is where the attempt on Truman's life was sparked.

We found the factory with no problem and each of us bought a nice dress hat made of straw. These were not your typical straw hats. Mine was a dark brown version, the type that Frank Sinatra wore. We really felt uptown. The factory was not used to tourist, so we were as much a show for them as they were for us.

We drove east and the mountains began to rise. El Yunque loomed ahead, the mist looked ominous. It was unusual to see such a profusion of greenery and flowers on a mountain. El Yunque is only about 3500 feet in elevation, but the road, even though paved was very narrow and had a lot of steep grades.

There were sections of the road that were almost dark as night due to the thick foliage of the tropical trees that spread overhead. We would round a turn and come across a water fall that would take your breath away.

We contemplated a swim in one of the many pools at the base of the water falls. We decided against it, however, being aware of how vulnerable we would be, away from the car and undressed. The road was winding up higher and higher. We rounded a curve and looked out at a scene of breathtaking beauty. Off to the southeast was a valley surrounded by mountains and numerous waterfalls cascading from the forest.

The mist moved in patches and formed little cloud banks that would magically disappear, only to reappear again a short distance away. It was cool and the air was thick with oxygen from the profuse forest. We would take long giant breaths and feel the gentle rush of rich oxygen in our bloodstreams. It made us giddy and we got a little silly. Johnny North was not with the group, but Mac, Dave Cummings and Jim Givens were really enjoying themselves. We had not passed a single vehicle on our trip, nor had we even met one.

We continued on our adventure and were on the downward side of El Yunque, when we came through a valley. We had just topped the northeastern side of the valley when I heard a "clip –clip – clip" sound from the left front tire. I pulled over to the side of the road but still kept the left side of the little Volkswagen on the pavement. We got out and examined the tire. On the very edge of the tire was the top of a tin can, stuck flat to the tire where the tread meets the sidewall. There was a nail driven through the can lid and sticking in our tire.

"Damn! –Look! – They're all over the road!" Growled Jim.

"Oh! – Shit!" We've been sabotaged!" Muttered Dave.

"Let's fix the tire and get outa here!" advised Mac.

We opened the deck on the front of the "Bug" and luckily found a fully inflated spare and a jack, but not a sign of a lug wrench. We searched all over the car and there was no lug wrench.

We were stuck. I told the guys, all was not lost; we could drive on the flat. It was not the best thing to do. The tire would shred in short order and then we would be on a steel rim and could not go very fast, but we could, at least, get away from there.

A brief examination of the road disclosed numerous devices of similar construction. We picked up over twenty of the booby traps, and put them in the car deck. It was a simple device. Cut the top from a tin can and drive a nail through the lid and place it on the road, nail up and wait for your victim. It was well after 1500 hours or mid- afternoon and El Yunque was on our western side. It gave our location the effect of sunset. The giant trees completely engulfed the road and it was hard to see very far down the road. It was as if it was dusk.

We heard the ominous "Ka-Chink!" of Mac's knife. Mac carried a knife that had a spring loaded blade in the handle. When you pressed the latch that kept it in the handle, the blade would spring forth with a very profound "Ka-Chink!"

We turned to see Mac at the rear of the car crouched in a defensive stance. He was looking at a figure approaching us out of the misty darkness from back down the hill where we had picked up the nail.

The figure made my blood turn cold. It was well over seven feet tall and had a head ten times the size of a normal head. It seemed to be rubbing its head in a manner of confusion. Our thoughts went wild. Was it a visitor from outer space, or a creature that was seeking humans by waylaying them on the highway. The creature stopped a short distance from us and slowly removed its head and sat it on the ground. We were dumbfounded.

A youthful voice called out meekly. "Que paso! – Amigos!"

I thought I was going to pass out. I had been holding my breath. The scene began to focus. It was a young boy of maybe fifteen or sixteen. He was carrying a huge jug of something on his shoulder. The jug was covered in a wicker wrapper with a top that resembled a hat. This was our monster. We relaxed with uncontrollable laughter and Dave had to take a leak.

I spoke with the youth in my broken Spanish and he was very attentive. He told us there was a little store back down the road at the base of the valley we had just come through. I told him we didn't remember seeing a store. He was very convincing that it was, indeed, there. The old man there, had some junk cars in the back and maybe he had a wrench. We decided to give it a try.

As we were about to help the youth pick up his jug we heard a commotion on the mountainside to our left. The road was actually cut out of this mountainside, and was much too steep to climb. Something was definitely coming down this mountainside and directly at us. The clanging and cursing in Spanish gave it away. The crescendo of noise gave the impression of a dozen men brandishing swords and shields. We were being attacked by Nationalist. They were crashing down this mountainside with our annihilation in mind.

"Ka-Chink! Mac was in his stance. I picked up the jack, ready to do whatever I had to do. I think Dave and Jim planned to roll the car over on our attackers as they went to the far side of the Volkswagen and crouched down.

To our amazement a body rolled out of the brush and onto the roadway. The Spanish profanity continued. The boy ran to the figure crying. "El Tio - Alonzo! – El Tio - Estas bien? – Estas bien?"

It was the boy's uncle, he was drunk as a skunk and was walking down a trail up on the mountainside and had lost his footing. The boy explained; his uncle was "loco en cabeza "and was somewhat of a recluse. He had everything he owned tied to his body. He had knives, forks, pans, pens, plates, old pistols, shovels, hammers, you name it and he had it on him somewhere. He had at least, a half dozen layers of clothes on his body, and smelled like last week's road kill. I wondered if he planted the booby traps.

We bid the youth "Hasta luego!" and proceeded back down the mountain. Sure enough, as we reached the base of the valley the outline of a light around a building door directed us to a little store. It was unusual to see a Royal Crown Cola sign in Spanish, but there it was, over the door. It was still late afternoon, but it was dark. We could look up and see that it was daylight. But there was nothing to reflect the sunshine here on the dark side of El Yunque. This adventure is far from over.

"Halo mi amigo!" I greeted the old man inside. The store was simple. There was a counter on the left with tobacco and wine behind it on wall shelves. The old man sat on a high stool at one end. There was a set of shelves across the back wall with breads and canned items in sparse display. On the right was a drink box. It was an old Coke box that opened from the top. Above the drink box were numerous Puerto Rican beer signs.

"Cerveza! - Por Favor?" I called out.

"Si! – Si! – Por ahi! – Senior! – Cerveza – Por ahi!" He pointed at the Coke box. It was full of iced beer. I guess the old man had an ice truck visit him every day, because there was no electricity in the store. There were two gas lamps burning that gave plenty of light. We drank our Coronas and I explained our dilemma to the old gentleman. He listened patiently and then informed me that he had no tools, but about a mile back in the jungle was a farm that had a barn with all kinds of tools. I could see us driving through thick jungle to a strange farm just to find a lug wrench.

The old fellow suggested we pay his nephew to go find the tool. That suited us just fine and he went to the back door and called his nephew. The boy was about ten years old and seemed eager to make a couple of bucks.

I took him outside and explained what we needed as I showed him the flat and the lug nuts. He seemed to completely understand and was off in a flash. I went back inside to try and enjoy my beer. Corona was no better than Bud, Miller, Schlitz, Falstaff, Jax or Pabst's Blue Ribbon. I think this Corona beer was from Jamaica. I drank it just the same. We just relaxed and made small talk as we waited. We were careful of what we said. The old man gave no indication that he understood English, but you never know.

Jim Givens walked over to the door to take a look at the car. He immediately shut the door and whispered. "Wardy! –Eh! - You need to take a look at this!"

"What! – Jim - the Nationals are coming?" I whispered back.

"No! - They're already here!" He whispered.

I opened the door and there stood a semi-circle of eight men between us and the car. Mac's hand went to his pocket; he was fingering the weapon gingerly as he moved to my side. The men were all in black trousers and white shirts. The shirts had a red bandana tied above the elbow on the left arm. They all carried a black book at their sides. Not a word was said as they looked us over. There were no smiles or frowns, just intense looks. Some of the men were barefoot and some had sandals. One old man had on a nice pair of black dress shoes. My blood ran cold.

Surely these were the men that set the booby traps. Apparently they tracked us to the store. Maybe it was all a ploy to lure us to our doom.

Mac softly said. "Looks like it's two apiece! - I'll handle mine and help you if I'm able!"

I focused on the older man with the nice shoes. I noticed his book and a sudden recognition flashed in my mind. There was a red ribbon hanging from the pages of his book and it had a gold edge on the pages. The men were carrying Bibles.

"Easy - Mac! – I think we may be OK!"

I looked at the older man and softly said. "Su Dios es mi Dios." I was trying to say. "Your God is my God!"

He understood and flashed a half toothless grin and exclaimed. "Alaba a Dios!" I think that meant "Praise God!"

All was well; we bought a round of Coronas for the local men's Bible Study group. We talked and were really enjoying ourselves when the nephew arrived with a lug wrench. It was a single socket handle and as I looked at it, I thought. "What chance did we have of a single socket lug wrench fitting a German made car in the mountains of Puerto Rico." The answer was one hundred percent. It fit perfectly.

We proceeded to position the jack when the whole Bible study group came out and began to protest. They removed the jack and stepped around the little car and completely lifted it clear of the ground and held it up as we changed the tire. It was amazing and we bought another round of Coronas. We found that the nails were probably from a service station on down the road that made a profit from flat repairs of unwary tourist.

Within an hour we were in the restaurant for our pre-arranged authentic Puerto Rican dinner. The restaurant was a thatched roof pavilion on the side of a low mountain. We could look west and marvel at the beautiful sunset as it played over the rolling western side of Puerto Rico. To the north was the vast expanse of the Caribbean that would merge with the Atlantic. It had been quite a day and the food was extremely well prepared. I had a seafood stew over rice with a salad that was as crisp as any I had ever had. The stew was deeply flavored with bits of fish, crab, shrimp and fleshy morsels called calamari. I found calamari was actually squid. It was delicious and ample. I had a tea that was really strong but was not acidic. It was, all in all, quite a dining experience.

We made it back to our Torsk and hit the sack at close to midnight. We had some good times recounting the day's adventure to the crew members that would listen.

We hit the Caribbean at 0700 hours on Monday and spent the week operating around the deep water north of Puerto Rico. We drilled intently that week and were really worn out the following weekend when we moored back in San Juan.

There was a fairly large group of us that descended on the Riviera Club that Saturday night. I forgot who's birthday it was, but we were celebrating, nevertheless. As Ron Rico began to share himself, our spirits began to soar as we made toasts to the birthday boy.

The Riviera Club was on the second floor of a building near the bay. We had a table in the center of the room. It was fairly early on that Saturday and the club was not yet crowded. There were a least twenty of our guys around the long table as we toasted our celebrity.

I think the same thought came into most everyone's mind at the same time. We all recalled a movie we had seen recently. I think maybe "The Count of Monte Cristo," the movie brought to mind, the French aristocracy threw their goblets into a fireplace to conclude a toast. We had no fireplace, but the juke box against the wall had tubes on the front that had little bubbles of oil rising from bottom to top and red to yellow lights cascading through the tubes. Close enough. Ron Rico said it was a fireplace. A barrage of glasses went at the juke box, followed by a crescendo of cheering drunken sailors as they saluted the birthday boy.

The bartender rushed to the window calling for the mass of Puerto Ricans on the street to come to his aid. I looked at Mac and he made a motion with his thumb that we should leave, and leave quickly. As we made our way down the stairs a mass of locals came storming up. Mac and I stepped aside and let them pass. The two groups merged like charging armies from medieval times. A chair flew through the window as Mac and I hit the street.

We felt honored to have survived the battle of the Riviera Club. I saw no point in fighting over throwing glasses at a juke box. I hadn't thrown a glass and I guess I wasn't as drunk as most of the guys. The next morning the shore patrol brought most of the guys back. They looked like a group of men returning from a work day on the River Kwai. I could almost hear the whistling of "Colonel Bogy."

Mac and I met up with Johnny North, Tom Nichol and Jay Neale. We were all feeling really good and had been partying with our friend Ron Rico all evening. As we made our way down the old banana piers we noticed that the piers, over time, had begun to sink and the fire hydrants were unusually high. We decided to leap frog over the hydrants. It was a strenuous job because some were at waist height. I have never been one to deliberately damaged property; I don't think that Ron Rico could even talk me into a deliberate act of vandalism.

I vaulted over a fire hydrant and I felt it move. I stopped and looked back at it. It was no longer standing straight as before. It had a weird slant to it. I went back and looked at it. It seemed OK, but it was not straight. In my rummy mind I figured I had made it crooked, so it was up to me to straighten it. I placed my foot against it and pushed it back up-right.

"Ahh! – That's much better!" I thought as the fire hydrant rocketed straight up followed by a stream of water that went higher than I thought possible. I don't know where the hydrant went, but I and the other guys left so fast that we hardly got wet. I felt bad about the accident and wanted to report it. The guys said Ron Rico would handle it and that seemed to make sense. We went back to the Torsk and the faceless lady soothed my shattered nerves.

The Torsk operated with the USS Argonaut SS 475 for the week. It was not pleasant as Hurricane Daisy was actually forming in our op area. We returned to San Juan for one night on August 28th. We left Friday, the next day, and made the five hour trip to St Thomas for the weekend.

We borrowed some trucks from the UDT complex and journeyed across the Island to a secluded bay. There was a party shack and some Bar-B - Q pits. We had a grand day and spent some of the bounty money from the torpedo we had recovered earlier in the year. It was a great day of fun and fellowship. Everyone got dunked in the ocean that day. The guys that didn't bring swim suits got their dungarees wet. There was no mercy shown.

We had a great football game. You haven't felt the intensity of physical violence until you've played semi-nude tackle football, in the sand, with a bunch of drunks. I didn't feel the pain, but my brain couldn't handle the concussions. I would tackle a ball carrier and then wake up with a mouthful of sand and the team would be 40 yards down field, coming back my way. Jonesy would run over me like I wasn't there. I quit when the ball went flat. It was a most remarkable day.

We made it back and some of the guys went on Liberty to St Thomas. I don't think it was a good idea. After all, we had partied all, day. Most of us were exhausted and still half drunk. Vandergrift and Wilson each got in separate fights and were restricted. Vandergrift got a nasty cut from a bottle on his head. Sunday was Derricot's turn as he also got returned by the shore patrol.

Monday found us operating with the Runner and her new skipper. We had an ORI [Operation Readiness Inspection] Team on board to evaluate our effectiveness. The new Runner team was impressive and I could feel a bond growing between the skippers.

They made a week of trying to outdo each other. Most of the crew thought that the new sound dome installed under our brow would slow us down considerably. Apparently, that was not the case, as we could still handily outrun the Runner. This pleased Captain King immensely.

These late summer Caribbean training missions were gruesome. Hurricane Ella passed to the south of the Virgin Islands, then FiFi swept north followed by Gerda to the south.

We were at battle stations, submerged at 150 feet and making about four knots. The ORI team had put us through our paces and we were feeling pretty good about our performances. I was at the wheel and tuned in to the proceedings in the control room below. The ocean bottom in our operating area was sandy and flat, but we were near the sudden drop off that is the beginning of the Puerto Rico Trench and is super deep. The trench separates the Atlantic Ocean on the north side from the Caribbean on the south side. The Captain had requested a fathometer reading every minute. I had heard a series of fathometer reports at 50 feet beneath the keel. We were submerged at 150 feet, so the ocean was 200 feet deep at this point. That had been the case for quite a while. Once again I heard Tighe, my New York City friend, give the fathometer reading as "fathometer reading 50 feet beneath the keel, Sir"

The Captain answered. "Very well!" I heard someone say "Water depth at 200 feet!" I noted that whoever said this was simply doing the math, we were at 150 feet and 50 feet beneath the keel put the ocean depth at 200 feet.

"Take her down to 250 feet Mr. Brink!" Exclaimed the Captain.

I couldn't believe my ears. I mentally did the math again. Had I missed something, had the Captain looked at the fathometer scope and seen something I didn't know about. He never did that, he always listened to the readings from the operator. The operator always read depths immediately upon a change. I heard no change. My mind raced.

Mr. Brink ordered a two degree down bubble and a command to make our depth 250 feet. I was convinced that a mistake was made. The impulse was to call out, "Belay that depth - we have insufficient water to achieve desired depth - Sir!" The ORI Team was observing, no one said a word. I must be wrong. I was distraught as to what to do.

I stepped back from the wheel and looked down. The Captain was directly below the ladder looking at the plotting board in the center of the control room.

In a low but forceful voice, I called. "Cap'n!" He didn't look up but held up a "hold on" finger. I called again. "But - Cap'n!" His head snapped up and his look was one that could kill. He was pissed that I had disturbed him.

It didn't matter; the impact threw him against the plotting table as our bow crashed into the sea bed. I was no longer in the Captain's thoughts. I was thrown against the wheel, but calmly reached up and sounded the collision alarm. I turned my attention to my helm to control the careening submarine as she developed a slight upward motion.

The boat went through the routine emergency procedures that accompany a collision drill. The glancing blow against the soft sandy bottom caused no internal damage at all. The crew suffered a few mild cuts and bumps, but the most damage was to our new sound dome that was on the lower bow of the Torsk. It was not completely out of order but it's effectiveness was seriously hampered. There were a considerable number of X's placed on the ORI Teams score sheet.

We spent a long weekend in San Juan to assess our damages and were back in fighting trim on Monday, September 8th, 1958. We set sail at 0803 hours to operate with the USS Escape ARS 6. The Escape was another rescue vessel and we looked forward to operating with her. We liked to take liberty with the crew of a rescue vessel and treat them in the clubs. It built a bond, if ever a rescue was required.   No one thought how close we were about to come to actually needing a rescue instead of a drill.

"Clear the bridge! – AHUUUUGA! – AHUUUUGA! – DIVE! – DIVE!"   The lookouts plummeted down the ladder from the bridge followed by Mr. Hoffman. He came halfway down the ladder, reached up and grabbed the lanyard attached to the upper hatch and swung free of the ladder. His entire 200 plus pounds was now on the lanyard that was designed to release the upper latch and pull the hatch closed. The hatch made an unfamiliar metallic clink. I left my wheel position and grabbed the handle to turn the dogging wheel and lock it in the closed position.

The handle didn't move. I looked up as the air whooshing from the ballast vents changed from an air sound to a monstrous gurgling sound. The sea was on the way and the hatch was jammed open. I could see at least three inches of daylight around the jammed open hatch.   Somehow the dog legs that were designed to come under the lip of the hatch base had extended enough that they had jammed against the inside of the hatch seat.

I called frantically.   "Hatch Jammed! -Shut the lower hatch! – SHUT THE LOWER HATCH!" The lower hatch slammed shut and I saw the dogging wheel spin it tight. I stepped away from the upper hatch and sounded the collision alarm. Mr. Hoffman raised himself from his position and grabbed the dogging handle in an attempt to free it.

The water blast tore him loose and sent him plunging into me and we were both driven to the rear of the conning tower.   It is unbelievable how much power is in the water rushing through a 3 inch gap that is 113 inches around. We were at the mercy of the torrent. The conning tower was flooding and we could not even get back to the hatch to try and get it shut.

The control room knew something was wrong. Of course, they reacted to the command "Shut the lower hatch!" They heard the collision alarm. It was probably evident that we were flooding. Our fate was in the hands of the men in the control room. I could not get back to the wheel to steer as the deluge of water was filing the conning tower rapidly.

Mr. Hoffman, Lessor and I stood in the rear of the tower as the water began to rise around us. We did not speak. I prayed again. "Lord – Please accept my spirit!" I felt no fear. No one screamed. No one panicked. We simply stood side by side, realizing that there was nothing we could do about the situation.

I had always heard that drowning was painless, I was about to find out. The lights went out as the air became charged with ozone as a result of the salt water getting to electrical circuits. The water proof emergency lights came on casting a red glow on everything. The water pressure was working on our ears even though the water was less than waist deep. The pressure was compressing the air. Our ears began to pulse as the air would leave the jammed hatch in slugs. We realized we were doomed and now had no chance of survival.

The boat had the customary down angle that is common in a diving condition. The air will rise to the top of a water level. We were in the back of the tower and that was where the remaining air was. When the boat began to surface the bow would rise and the trapped air would race to the front of the hatch to escape and the tower would completely flood. Even when we reached the surface and the top of the hatch is out of the water. We could not unjam the hatch. That would have to be done with a long lever from outside. The submarine would have to blow high enough out of the water to open a deck hatch, get the necessary tools and unjam the upper conning tower hatch before we could reach air. We couldn't survive that long.

I always heard that your life flashes before your eyes when you face death. Mine didn't. I thought of what it would be like on the other side. The thought of it being over never entered my mind. I never felt like it was the end of anything just that it was going to be different. We stood in calm resolve as we waited for the angel of death. I looked at Lessor, my hero, and Mr. Hoffman our new engineering officer since February. Mr. Hoffman had replaced Mr. Donahue when we left Philly. I wondered how they felt.

The water continued to rise. Our eyes began to burn from the electrolysis. I prayed again.

The tower was getting brighter, it was not red light. We could see the light coming through the water from under the jammed hatch. It was getting a brighter bluish-green. The pressure on our ears was getting better. We were coming up and we still had a down angle. The chief of the boat had informed the officers in the control room that if the tower flooded, the only air would be in the back of the conning tower and if we had any hope at all, the air must stay there. They had flooded the forward trim tank enough to maintain a down bubble on surfacing. Pappy Wright probably saved our lives that day.

A crew unjammed the upper hatch and we found the source of our problem. The locking device that held the hatch open had been re-installed on the wrong side of its bracket. Everything worked as it should, but the difference in spacing allowed the dogging wheel a quarter turn of free play. This quarter turn allowed the dogging arms to extend far enough to jam against the insides of the hatch seat. Mr. Hoffman's falling weight had forced the dogs into a jammed configuration that was too tight for human hands alone to unjam. It required a long pry-bar and considerable effort from the rescue team to free the hatch.

As we left the tower, Lessor looked at me and softly said, "You're some kinda son of a bitch -- boy!" I knew he wasn't angry, but never have understood why he made that comment, he transferred soon after that. God had a plan. It didn't call for us to die that day.

We returned to San Juan and moored at the Naval Base for repairs. We moved our gear from the boat to a nice two story barracks on the base and took our meals at the base chow hall as the tower was dried out and the hatch was repaired. My battle with that hatch was still not over.

It had rained for two days and Saturday, September 20th, 1958 was overcast. We had worked side by side with Naval Base personnel to get our Torsk repaired.

While working in the superstructure, Hoskinson, a fireman apprentice accidently stuck a paint scrapper in his leg and Mac and I had to help him out. It was quite a job working our way through the maze of supports, but we finally got him topside.

Saturday, we had all slept late and had a nice lunch. It seemed like no one wanted to go ashore and a big blackjack game got started. We had an enlisted crew of at least 70 men and I think most all of them were there that afternoon.

Somewhere around midafternoon, our friend, Ron Rico showed up. He was in fine form. 180 proof in fifth size bottles. He had no favorites. He freely shared himself with all who would partake. "WooWeee!" Were we feeling good or what?

I'm ashamed to say that I liked Ron a lot, but I didn't love him like some of the guys. Ron will whisper things in your ear that will get you in trouble. He will distort things and make the idlest comment seem the greatest of insults. He can make an innocent smile seem like a spit in the face. He will convince you that you can fly. He will tell a lie. He will convince you to do things that you would never consider doing without his whispering in your ear.

There were a half dozen of the Torsk's finest sailors playing Black Jack around a table in the back of our second floor dorm.

Ron was hiding in a locker and every time the swinging doors would open, all the rum and coke in cups would get guzzled and a fresh half cup of coke was poured in. Cokes were sitting everywhere. If an Officer or stranger were to come in, we were just playing cards, Ron was out of site and all that was in the cups was Coke. We were a fine example of the U.S. Navy Submarine Service. "Take er down, Buddy! – Hic!"

I don't remember exactly what was said that got this whole mess started, but the story I'm telling is absolutely true. Remember Jonesy, well he called me chickenshit a lot. I never knew why and just let it go. Jonesy was a rather quiet guy and never seemed to barhop and look for women like the rest of the guys. I heard he was planning to marry a school teacher from South Carolina. This man was one tough hombre though. His reputation was that he took care of business in a hurry and didn't put up with much gruff.

Jonesy was winning. His run of luck had about sapped the other guys at the table and he was having a hard time getting the pot big enough to suit him. He was also three sheets to the wind. His words were slurred and he had lost his quiet demeanor.

"Damn ya'll – ain't nobody got any balls? – This pot ain't even big enough to hit on! -- Hell it's ain't no bigger than my pecker and nobody's got a pecker littler than mine!" He slurred his words with conviction.

I'll never understand how grown, responsible men, that operate one of the most sophisticated war machines in the US Navy, can let Ron Rico talk them into such stupid juvenile actions.

Jonesy was a big man.

Ron whispered in my ear. "Look at the size of that man – Lynn - there's no way his pecker is smaller than yours!"

Somehow it made sense, here was my chance to embarrass Jonesy and get even for some of his chickenshit, name calling.

"Jonesy -- no man your size can have a pecker that small!" I exclaimed.

He snapped his attention to me and his attitude changed. "Tell you what -- Mr. Chickenshit -- I'll bet you five bucks my pecker is smaller than yours!"

The crew went wild, guys that had been ignoring the game came running. The table was cleared and preparations were being made for the "Littlest Pecker Contest!"

"Sound the trumpets! – Send in the clowns! – Oh! – The clowns are already here!" Ron Rico cheered the loudest. I stood in amazement at what was developing. The rules were laid out, the judges were selected.

I wanted to run, but I knew, if I backed down now, everyone would start calling me chickenshit.

Ron whispered in my ear. "You can do this – Lynn -- you da man!"

I looked at Jonesy. He was huge, there was that chest hair again, sticking out from the top of his tee shirt. The sleeves of the tee shirt had moved up over his biceps and made them very noticeable; they looked like grapefruits under his skin. My knees grew weak.

The crowd crescendo grew and the curtain came up on the show. Out came the peckers. They were laid out on the edge of the table and the body pressed against the table to extend the pecker as much as possible. Rules said that they could not be touched in any form.

"Damn – How could a man -- that size -- have a pecker that small?" I thought.

His pecker was, indeed, smaller than mine. The crowd went wild and Jonesy grinned in triumph. The crew patted him on the back and he strutted in victory. This normally, quiet man was a direct opposite of what I knew. That's the influence of Ron Rico.

I threw a five dollar bill on the table and said. "The world ain't gonna believe that the man with the biggest pecker loses!"

The men cracked up again as I turned and walked to my locker. It was getting dark and I wanted to go to town and find Nelly. I removed my dungarees and had put on my white pants when I noticed a hush had fallen over the dorm. I sensed someone behind me. I felt a tap on the shoulder and instinctively stepped to the side instead of turning straight around.

It was Jonesy. His eyes were bright with Ron's encouragement.

Ron had quit talking to me and my head was much clearer now.

Jones spoke as if possessed. "You're still chickenshit -- Wardlaw! - I'm gonna prove you're chickenshit! – I'm gonna whip your cracker ass this very night!" The entire crew was in a huge semi- circle behind him. I was in a spot.

I almost wheedled. "Jonesy -- we'll be court marshaled for fightin in the barracks and ---------- !" He cut me off.

"Oh! – Mr. Chickenshit -- we ain't gonna fight here! – No! – We gonna fight out in the field by the storage tanks!" He gritted his teeth in anticipation.

"You really mean this Jonesy?" I hoped for some laughter and him saying it was all a joke. No such luck.

"I can't stand a chickenshit -- especially a chickenshit from Georgia – now -- you coming or I gotta carry you?" He was dead serious. The chickenshit thing was not Ron Rico talking. Jonesy had called me that name when Ron was nowhere around. It was inevitable.

"Lemme change into my dungarees and I'll be right with you!" My mind was made up. If I was going out, I was going out in style.

"Put on your worst -- Chickenshit! -- Cause I'm gonna mess em up good!" Jonesy was planning on enjoying this.

As we opened the swinging doors to exit down the stairs, the entire crew was following.

Jonesy stopped and turned around. His voice was guttural. "This is for me and chickenshit only! – No one else allowed!"

Not a soul followed.

Jonesy knew he was in complete control. I wondered why he felt the way he did about me. I knew I was an outgoing person and appeared to be a showoff, but when people get to know me, well, they find out I'm really not like that. Jonesy simply didn't like me and Ron had talked him into whipping my ass.

All of Dad's advice came back, but I could not bring myself to sucker punch this monster of a man. Somehow I felt he was honorable, and even with his taunting, I think he felt justified. I thought how Dad would say. "Well - you got whupped with honor!"

God had a plan, but I don't think he had anything to do with what followed.

We exited the building and Jonesy turned around and stuck his hand out. He had his left hand in his back pocket. "Let's shake before I whip yo ass -- Chicken shit!"

"Jonesy! -- Take your hand out of your pocket!" I eased around and stepped out of the direct light under the building overhang.   I stepped back into a pile of rocks.

"Don't worry about my hand -- Chickenshit. -- Maybe I'm gonna whip your ass with one hand!"

I reached down and picked up a rock, just large enough to fit in the palm of my hand. Hopefully it would help to deliver some power in my blows.

We continued walking across the street into a large lot next to a fence that separates the Navy Base from a fuel depot and some gigantic storage tanks. The field had knee high grass on Friday, but had been fresh cut that morning when the rain stopped. It was still wet with water standing under the mat of fresh cut grass. Our feet squished as we walked through the mire.

The field looked ominous under the glare of floodlights mounted on the sides of the storage tanks. The light was not bright but adequate to see by. We stood and faced each other in the middle of the field.

Jonesy still had his hand in his pocket.

I suddenly got the impression he was simply trying to frighten me. Well! He was succeeding.

"Jonesy -- we don't have to do this! - You can beat my ass! - You know that! -- So you won't prove anything!" I was wheedling again.

"Come on! - Shake my hand – Wardy! - Let's get it on!" He was getting impatient.

We were about ten feet apart and his hand was still in his pocket.

I spoke again. "Jonesy - I don't know what you have in your pocket - but I've got this rock and---!"

He charged me with a cry. "Well -- throw the son of a bitch!"

I did. I threw the rock with all my strength and my aim had never been better. The missile struck him in the middle of his forehead with aloud "THOCK". I thought I had killed him. It didn't even slow him down. He plowed into me like a freight train. His fist were like sledge hammers.

I didn't fall down, and I didn't seem to feel the blows. Maybe his aim was seriously affected by Ron's influence or the rock may have addled him. It could have been my adrenaline, simply blocking the pain.

I was landing blows about his head and face that sounded like whacking a side of beef. You really don't have time to think and plan a strategy once the action starts in a fight. You simply go on instinct and experience.

I, somehow, was holding my own. His blows about my face didn't seem to have a lot of force. The ground was getting to be an awful mess where we fought and soon we lost our footing and began to wrestle along with the pummeling. The water had turned to mud and any kind of hold was useless.

As a fight progresses, a man's energy is spent in rushes and we would lock up in grips that would allow a breath or two. In one of these embraces I felt a sharp pain on the back side of my left bicep. The brute was biting me.

I had never been bitten in a fight before. Hell, I had never fought a grown man before and actually I was fighting Jonesy and Ron Rico.

I bit him on his left shoulder, I bit him hard. I think had he not had on a shirt I could have taken a plug out. I was continually working on his face. I knew my body strength was not enough to penetrate the muscle mass of his torso.

Somewhere in the grunting, cussing and pummeling, I felt a stinging sensation in my head and suddenly realized the man had a finger in my left eyeball socket. The finger was actually inserted into my head between the left eye ball and the bridge of my nose. I threw all my energy into removing the hand. I hoped I wouldn't lose the eye.

Somehow I managed to get up first and jumped straddle his back. I began to punch him as hard as I could on the back of the neck. He didn't get up, I continued to hit. I felt the impact of my blows as they shook through his body.

The sound of a fist against human flesh has a sound all its own. Hollywood does a pretty good job with their fight scenes, but it's nothing compared to the real thing. It was sickening. The thought struck me. I could kill this guy. He wasn't moving.

"Jonesy -- are you alright?" I didn't want to kill him. I didn't even want to fight him.

He answered. "Wardlaw -- is that all you've got?"

I thought the man had lost his mind. I stepped from his back and stood in front of him. He was on all fours with his head hung down. I was about to reach down to help him up when in a flash he grabbed both my feet and pulled them from under me. I hit the ground, flat on my back and he was astride my stomach in an instant. He pinned both my arms to the ground. I couldn't move under that iron grip.

His face was directly over me. The blood was steadily dripping on my face. I could taste the warm, salty pungency of it. It was not just a little drip either.

"Wardy! - You feel that! - That's me bleeding on you! – You've hurt me bad! – Boy -- you shoulda killed me when you had the chance – cause -- I'm gonna kill you now!"

I felt him turn my left hand loose and could see his right arm rise like a giant mallet. I tried to block the blow, but the block did little. I turned my head to the right and it was a glancing blow. It didn't matter.

People say that you see lights when you get knocked unconscious. Well! It's true, you see many lights and rockets and sparkly swirly things.

There is sound also. The sound was something like "SKRUUNCH!" Yeh! – "SKRUUNCH!! – That's pretty close.

I don't know if he hit me anymore or not. Eventually I began to come around. I vaguely remember Ron Rico telling me to get up and fight and the faceless lady telling me to lie really still and not make things worse.

I became aware of a gurgling and wheezing sound. I blinked my eyes open and saw ten thousand tiny red lights. I blinked again and the lights went to ten thousand plus and moved around a little. The gurgling and wheezing got more pronounced. I tried to rise up but an iron grip held me down.

Jonesy was still astride me, but had fallen over my right arm. I raised my left arm and rolled as much as I could, to see him. His face was in the water on the left side. His nose had the left nostril in the water and the right nostril was out of the water. His labored breathing had mixed the blood and water and he had blown the thousands of little red, bloody bubbles that now surrounded both our heads.

I was spent. "Jonesy - We gonna have to give this up! - I think it may kill me!" - I suddenly remembered when I was, maybe, four years old, I was playing with Johnny, my dog and suddenly got nauseous. My Momma told me I had an enlarged spleen and that's what made me sick. I never had another problem, but now I needed something.

"Jonesy -- I got an enlarged spleen and I may die!" I was pleading.

"Well! – At least you ain't chickenshit!" He rolled off me and moaned. The fight was a done deal and I was still alive. We helped each other up and staggered across the soggy field. We leaned on each other as we slogged along.

Suddenly something happened. We felt the shock of that damn fence that surrounded the fuel tanks. It was electrified. It was not a lethal charge but it got our attention. I tasted metal in my mouth and my feet felt like tiny little hot needles were pricking them. We focused on the lights from our barracks and staggered back up the stairs.

We threw the swinging doors open as we stepped into the dorm. The crew was in a semi-circle just inside the door. Their mouths dropped open as they viewed the spectacle we displayed. We were wet and muddy beyond recognition. Straw from the knee high grass was all sticking out all over us and the blood from the wounds was a matted brownish red.

Jonesy spoke these words only. "HE AIN'T CHICKENSHIT!" Kettlehut's eyes rolled back in his head as he fainted and slumped to the floor.

I went straight to the shower and washed with my clothes on. When I felt like they were clean enough, I undressed and bathed thoroughly. I began to feel pretty good. I looked at myself in the mirror and the left eyeball was turning red. Other than that I couldn't see a mark. I checked the back of my arm at the bite and sure enough, the shirt kept me from losing a plug. It looked pretty nasty. I didn't show it to anyone.

I didn't know where Jonesy was. He was a mess as well and needed to get cleaned up. I came out of the shower to find him. There was quite a gathering in the back of the dorm where the tables were. As I was making my way back, Mac found me.

"Lynn -- you need to be scarce for a while!" I could hear Jonesy groaning and saw Doc working on his face.

Mac continued. "We are sure Jonesy took a pretty bad fall somewhere - but if the wrong guy sees him and then sees you – well - things may add up and we don't want that!"

I loved em all, even the one who wanted to kill me. I went ashore, found Nelly and was back by midnight.

I never discussed the fight with anyone but Mac and Johnny North. I didn't dress it up. I told them the truth. I couldn't do much with the hunk of man that came at me.

The only outward signs that I had from the fight was my ruptured left eyeball. I showed no cuts, bruises or scratches.

The truth, however, was my nose cartilage was separated from the nose bone. I had a nasty wound on my left arm. My left jaw was shattered at the socket. My upper left jaw teeth were chipped, my left eyeball was ruptured and I had bit my tongue. I was sore, all over.

Jonesy had numerous stitches taken in his face. His forehead had taken the full brunt of the rock I threw. His lower lip was stitched down the left side and across to half way between the lower lip and chin. We never spoke of the fight and I felt guilty every time I looked at him. I wore a ring emblazoned with the Puerto Rican flag on my right hand and my high school ring on my left. I suppose they did a number on Jonesy's face.

Mac told me not to tell anyone else that story. "You walk in here - not a mark on you - take a shower - go to town - get laid - come back and hit the sack! - Jonesy face looks like a patchwork quilt! - Right now - everyone thinks you're the toughest thing since Rocky Marciano!"

He gave that nasal smirk and whispered. "I know the truth – you're just a pussy!"

"OK! – Mr. Ex Golden Gloves – Let's step outside and dance!" I jokingly challenged.

"Fine – Bring your bullwhip and I'll bring my knife!" He joked back. That's the last time we ever discussed the fight.

Jonesy transferred shortly after that. The day he left the boat I asked him why the "Chickenshit" thing.

He answered. "I just thought you were chickenshit - I really did!" – "I remember the big colored sailor in LeHarve that threatened you – You never said a word. - I saw you skip out on the big fight at the Rivera Club - I was there when you beat it out of that pub in Weymouth. - Hell! - You never stuck up for yourself! - I was wrong!" We shook hands and I wished him happiness with his South Carolina schoolteacher.

The conning tower repairs came at a good time. While the repairs were being made, Hurricane Helene blasted the Islands and all the way up our east coast. It was the worst storm of 1958, thank God we missed it. I think Captain King was disappointed.

We dived at 1407 hours on September 29, 1958. We held our breath, all seemed to be in good shape. Everything that was affected by the flooding, had been dried and cleaned. We were back in fighting trim. We engaged in a joint operation with the U.S. Air Force. Old Borinquen Field had been renamed Ramey Air Force Base and had a squadron of ace jets that had a good record on submarine kills. Our job was to log as many hours on the surface as possible without being theoretically sunk. The game was to operate without radar.

It was a game of hide and seek. We could tell immediately if an aircraft cheated. It was OK to listen for radar and we would hear the electronic signals long before they located us. We would simply dive and disappear. The jets at

Ramey Air Force Base took great delight in coming at us just above wave height and passing directly overhead at 500 plus miles per hour.

If you don't see them coming, you will not hear them as they are leading their sound blast. The blast will hit you with a concussion and deafening roar that will knock you hat off, jolt your coffee cup from your hand, and make you poop your pants. Your ears will ring for hours. They will sweep away and wag their wings in a laughing salute.

The operation was nearly completed and we had dodged about four contacts. We were back to our old stealthy selves. I was starboard lookout. It was late afternoon and the sun was a bright orange ball as it began to set on the western horizon. It was pretty easy to spot a jet up high, so I was focusing just above the horizon. All seemed to be clear as I quickly passed the sun to avoid sun blindness. I saw a black dot right in the middle of the sun. There is no way you see anything looking directly into the sun, so I made another quick pass and the dot was larger.

"Aircraft! - Dead astern! - Sir! - Coming out of the sun – Sir!" I called.

The OD spun around and leaned over the port side with his glasses to his eyes. He exclaimed. "I don't see him! – Wardlaw! Are you sure?"

"He's there - Sir and we're probably too late now!" I said.

He did not hesitate. "Clear the bridge! – AHUUUGA! – AHUUUGA! – DIVE! – DIVE!" I was first down the ladder, as I turned my hand loose from my grip on the upper hatch, the dogging lock slid under my loose watch band. My body had already started down the ladder and the band couldn't stand the strain and snapped. I hit the ladder and down we went, minus my watch.

I was gun-shy by now and wondered what else would mess up on this dive. We were on the way down, the boat was under, I knew the aircraft saw us, the only thing out of the water was the top of the sail. There are numerous openings in the top of the sail. We have two periscopes and a snorkel opening.

The attacking jet dropped one of those plaster depth charges with the phosphorescence paint to mark his prey. Normally these low charge explosives are harmless and only leave their traces for a judge to determine damage. However, everyone knows what happens when you put a little firecracker in a tin can.

This Air Force Ace placed that charge directly down our snorkel opening and the resulting blast knocked us off our feet. The periscope seals began to pour water and the snorkel valve mechanism jammed. We were sunk again.

We immediately surfaced and the jet buzzed us twice wagging his wings in exuberant exhilaration. I could almost hear him cackling, or was that my ears ringing. We saluted the Air Force jet as he buzzed the last time and sweep straight up over us with a series of spirals and was gone.

We had two Air Force Officers on board for the exercise and they were two scared guys, but were now very proud of the results of the exercise.

We limped back to San Juan and back to the Navy Base to make repairs again. They had saved our place. We had been to sea only two days. I wondered if our charmed luck was running out.

It only took two days to repack the scopes and repair the plumbing to the snorkel valve. The paint was so confined that the pressure washer peeled it right off.

CHAPTER XII

NORFOLK AND PHILLY '58

October 2, 1958, we bid San Juan, "Adios," as we made a straight shot to Norfolk. No drills, no exercises, just porpoising to chalk up dives. We docked October 7th at 2137 hours.

October 9th was on a Thursday and I was summoned to the ward room on the Orion. I was a witness in the hearing concerning our bottom collision last month. The room stretched the entire width of the upper deck. The officers sat behind a long mahogany table, the deck was green carpet with a single chair in the middle for the witness to sit in.   The entire affair was formal and intimidating. I told my story just as it happened. I hated to give evidence that indicated a mistake on the part of Captain King, but I told the truth. I had not discussed the incident with anyone and apparently everyone told the truth. We never heard of any reprimand or punitive action and Captain King stayed on as our skipper. I was glad. He still treated me with that same aloof reserve, as always.

We were back operating in our backyard. Area 19 is divided into separate segments and covers a vast area, east of Cape Hatteras. We defended this area against the enemy. One of the enemy was the USS Grampus, remember her, she was our other east coast missile boat. We sank the USS Seneca AT91, the USS Greene DDR711 and the USS Borie DD704.   We tracked and plotted firing resolutions on the USS Intrepid CV11, another of our finest WWII aircraft carriers, but never completed the drill. For some reason the exercise did not call for us to attack the Intrepid. It was an intense two months. During this time the Runner was nowhere around. She was still operating in the Caribbean. We thought how lucky these guys were.

In the middle of October we heard the first of our mystery noises. We were submerged at 250 feet and listening on our sound gear. Remember now, we have some pretty sophisticated sound equipment. The glancing blow off the bottom a few months earlier had decreased its efficiency somewhat, but it still functioned.

We heard a strange droning sound that approached us from our starboard side. Our sound men were aces at drawing a mental picture of the position of a sound source. They just had a sense of where it was. They could isolate the hydrophones and tell which ones were picking up the most noise and from this information and their instincts; they could be pretty accurate in positioning a noise source.

The noise was off the starboard side and maybe 20 feet deeper than we were. The sonar man felt it was about a hundred yards away. It was definitely aware of us. It would move slowly around as if checking us out. Finally the Captain could not stand it any longer. He wanted to see if it was metallic.

"Sonar! – Give me one ping! – One ping only!" Came the Captains measured order. The mystery noise disappeared with the ping. Sonar said they heard it leave with a hi-pitch drone and was gone.

"Give me a sweep - Sonar!" commanded the Captain.

Nothin Cap'n –there's nothing out there!" Sonar reported.

"Did you see anything on the single ping?" He asked sonar.

We think so – Sir! - It all happened so fast! - We didn't have repeat [scope recording] on - so we can't check!"

The Captain didn't like the report.

"If the phantom returns - turn the repeat on straight away, Sonar." The Captain was clearly concerned about this.

We all were. It's not a good feeling to be in the dark and not even have a clue as to what you are up against. The talk around the boat centered on this encounter, for weeks. It wasn't over either. We hoped it wasn't the Russkies.

Our operations were back on a weekly basis out of Norfolk and it was turning cold. By the first week in November it was downright frigid. We looked forward to operating, because our area was in the Gulf Stream and the weather was measurably warmer.

November 6th. Our area was 19E and we were operating with a destroyer, when our mystery noise showed up again. It really perplexed the Captain as he didn't want to ping for fear of giving our position away to the destroyer. The destroyer was some distance away and the Captain asked Sonar for a single ping and make sure the recorder was on the screen.

"She's gone Captain -- One ping and she's gone! We got a picture too! – It's something solid - that's all we know." Sonar reported.

The destroyer heard the ping and was charging our way. The Captain turned our stern to the destroyer and went to 300 feet and ultra quiet.   We hovered and soon the destroyer was gone.

November 11th. We were engaged in another stage of Operation Slamex and hovering at 200 feet. The mystery sound came again. This time we listened at length and determined the sound was higher pitched than before. It was more of a whine than a drone. We followed the sound around and drew profiles as to how it moved.

The Captain finally said. "Ping on it and see what it is! - Not just a single ping - but point at it and let's see how big and how far away it is!"

It disappeared at the first ping. The high pitched sound simply went away and the sonar showed one blip. This sonar search was not a circle sweep, it was a tight swinging sweep and it disappeared at the first ping. We were speechless and at a loss. We felt powerless against a mysterious vessel that observed us and left at our first sign of recognition. We hoped it wasn't Russian.

We had many a brainstorming session. It seemed inconceivable that any type of vessel could move so quickly underwater that it could outrun sonar signals. Sonar under water is nearly four times the speed of sound in the air. It seems impossible for a craft or possibly a mammal to move that fast.

An interesting theory was presented. What if it was a huge school of very small fish or shrimp and the sound was an audible collection of their communication. As the first ping was sensed, they instantly disbursed. The mass would diminish and the sonar would lose its image. That was the only plausible explanation we could conceive. We never found out for sure what the mystery noise was.

The rest of this 2nd week in November, 1958 was spent operating with the USS Ellison DD 864. We set our missile guidance detail and simulated a missile launch. The destroyers were on us in short order, but our Captain used every ploy he knew and after hours of depth charge attacks the exercise ended. We surfaced, not knowing how much yellow paint would show after our ordeal.

I was first up to the bridge. I took starboard lookout and there was not a speck of yellow to be seen. I held my breath as David Daniels checked the port side. We were clean. We had our "Mojo" back.

November 17th, 1958 and I celebrated my 22nd birthday on the Torsk. We were tied up at pier 21 berth 213. We were berthed next to the USS Sea Lion and the USS Piper was on our port side. Catfish baked me a cake. It was the best cake I ever ate.

That weekend, Johnny North and I drove over to Portsmouth, Virginia. Portsmouth was actually just across the river from Norfolk, but wasn't as anti-navy as Norfolk.

Johnny pulled into a drive-in just as the sun was setting. Johnny's 56 Chevy was a classic example of what was hot. It was a blue and white, two door hard-top with dual exhaust and a four barrel carburetor.

We pulled next to two girls sitting in a 53 Dodge. They looked over and smiled. Johnny and I were both in civies. The girls had not seen the Illinois tag on Johnny's Chevy so we figured we might get lucky.

Johnny deliberately lowered his head and muttered. "Be cool -- Dude!"

"Let's play hard to get!" I whispered. "Let's try something! – Just look and give a quick smile then don't look at them again! - OK !"

"OK! – whatever!" Mumbled Johnny. "You gonna screw it up – Lynn!"

"That's the idea – right?" I snapped back.

Johnny gave me that sly grin and a chin wave.

We looked the girls up and down in an obvious fashion and then we both looked away as if they were forgotten.

It was hard not to glance back, but we stuck it out. I rolled my window down, hoping it was not too obvious, because it really was getting cold. We made small talk and tried to be impressive with our discussion on the Berlin tension and Fidel Castro's success in Cuba. Recent headlines had told of federal troops deserting and joining the revolution and it was looking bad for Batista.

A horn blew a quick tap. We ignored it. The horn sounded again.

Johnny looked over his shoulder and said, "Lynn -- They're honking at us!"

I turned and looked at the girls, they had rolled their window down and the girl in the front passenger seat was leaning over the girl driving.

"Hey! - Did you guys borrow Dave's car?" The girl leaning over asked.

"Hold on! – I'll ask!" I turned to Johnny. "Johnny! – does Dave know you have his car?"

Johnny played right along. "It's not Dave's car –it's mine -- Dave just drives it sometimes!"

The girls looked flabbergasted. It was obvious that they had simply come up with a line to open a conversation.

Johnny was quick on the uptake. "Are you the two good looking girls - Dave said lived in his neighborhood?"

The girl in the passenger seat moved back to her side and put her hands over her mouth in astonishment. We couldn't believe how well this was going. We began a discussion through the car windows and quickly left Dave behind before he messed things up.

Thank you Dave, whoever you are. The girls were soon in the car with us, so we did not have to shout anymore.

Johnny and I didn't care which girl got in the front with him or in the back with me. They were both good looking and shapely. They appeared to be in their early twenties. We got along well and soon were getting familiar. Johnny's girl was Maxine and the cut little number in back with me was Vickie.

Johnny asked the girls if they could take us on a nice little nighttime country drive. Just leave their car in the back of the drive-in and we would bring them back. The girls seemed really interested but began to fret about Vickie's niece.

It seems that her sister went to work at eight o'clock and Vickie was supposed to baby sit. We were disappointed that the evening was going to end so soon. Maxine and Vickie had already moved conveniently close to both of us. Suddenly Maxine suggested we simply get the baby and bring him with us. We could follow them and they would leave their car at Vickie's sister's house and we could go for a nice drive.

Wow! – We could hardly believe our luck. As the girls went into the modest little bungalow, Johnny and I talked about our plans. We agreed that a baby could hamper things a bit but it appeared that my date had the responsibility for the child so he didn't have to worry. I mentioned this to him and he gave me that little hand under the chin, Italian, finger wave.

Soon the girls emerged and Vickie climbed into the back and sat a basket with a baby, maybe four months, old in the seat near the window. The child was wide eyed and alert, but never uttered a sound. Matter of fact the child never uttered a sound the whole time and I don't even know if he slept. He was no problem. He would take a bottle and play with a set of little noisy trinkets on a ring.

Vickie slide over close to me and turned to the baby and said. "Ronny, say hello to Uncle Lynn and Uncle Johnny!"

Johnny cranked the Chevy and eased off with that beautiful throaty sound of his dual Smittys.

Soon Vickie and I were locked in young loves sweet embrace. She was a little different than girls in the past. There is always a little game that is played where the boy moves his hands about in an ever so light fashion to explore his limits and get the feel of how things should progress. That was not necessary with Vickie. She was a willing, skillfull and somewhat aggressive participant. I was in a state of ecstasy when Johnny called me back to reality.

"What the hell is this -- Lynn?" I looked up to find ourselves on a narrow paved road approaching an equally narrow steel bridge. The bridge had a rail blocking the road. We could see the moon reflecting on the dark waters of a small creek. A sign read. "Toll $1.00."

Johnny said. "I'm not paying any toll - just to go for a drive! – Screw it! – I'll just turn around!" The road was too narrow and the sides fell away to a steep embankment. Johnny could not turn around.

Can you believe a little old lady stepped out of a shack built on the side of the bridge and folded her hands and waited. Johnny eased up to her and asked her why the toll.

"My land! – My bridge! –My toll!" She spat the words out along with a splat of tobacco juice.

I asked as politely as I could. "Where's this road go - Ma'am?"

She leaned and looked at me through the window. "Ask the guy driving - he's the one what brung you here!" She spat again.

"Where can we turn around?" Johnny asked.

"Bout three miles back up the road where you turned in!" The old girl was curt.

"I'll pay the dollar!" I told Johnny as I handed the old girl the money.

She spat again and stuck the money in her dress pocket. She walked over and lifted the crossing rail by hand. As we drove through, she said. "See ya!"

"Fat chance!" Johnny retorted as he drove us away.

We started laughing at the racket this old girl had going. We wondered how many suckers she got in a day with that deal. I began to pay close attention to the road.

"Johnny -- look at this road!" I was a little concerned. "The woods grow right up to the edge and it's cracked all over and the weeds have grown through the cracks!" It was obvious that Johnny was just driving and had turned into a side road, looking for a quiet place to park for a while.

Suddenly the head light caught the reflection of a sign. "DEAD END." We couldn't believe our eyes. We had not even been a mile and the road ended. Thank goodness, there was ample room to turn around.

Soon the lady stepped back out of the shack with a tobacco stained smirk and said. "Told ya - I'd see ya!"

This time there was a double barreled shotgun on the shelf by her hand. "That'll be another buck – if'n you please!"

We paid the toll and Johnny was well down the road before he rolled his window down to hurl an old lady slur at the woman.

I was soon back in "La La land" with Vickie. I won't go onto any great details, but her breathing began to quicken. I looked at her, her eyes were shut and her mouth was pursed as if in agony. Suddenly her head arched back. She moaned and went into a series of short convulsions. This time, I knew what it was.

"Deja Vu" It had been well over a year. My mind raced back to a Friday afternoon in an anti-room in Connecticut.

"My God" – How dumb could a guy get, and I had gone and got her mother. I was flushed with embarrassment. What on earth did those fine people think of me?

Vickie reached up and pulled me close. She whispered in my ear. "No Man has ever made me feel like that!" I was in a mental state like never before. I filed everything I had done away in mental notes. Vickie and I had not been fully intimate, just heavy foreplay.

We were soon back in the lights of the city and reached the home of Vickie's sister. We went inside and the girls excused themselves.

Johnny and I talked lowly and he stated we needed to get back to the boat.

The girls came back in and invited us to stay the night. I asked about the sister and Vickie told us her sister would not be back until noon tomorrow. She said she was doubling over at the hospital and would rest there.

We couldn't stay. Johnny had duty at 0800. Vickie said she would take me to the base tomorrow if I would stay. I gave it some serious thought, but declined. I told her we were getting ready for the Naval yard in Philly and I had a lot to do.

"I can't believe it!" She almost screeched. My home is in North Philly and I'm going back in two weeks!" She jumped into my arms as if her whole world had suddenly come alive. "I'll contact you when you get there! - Is that OK?"

"Sure - that's fine - but why can't I just call you?" I asked.

"Uh! – My – Uh! – phone is disconnected right now -- but I know how to reach personnel at the Naval Yard. -- I have friends that work there and they will get me the number! -- I promise - I'll call you!"

I thought this was all quite odd, but didn't press my luck any more. Johnny and I were quite proud of our night in Portsmouth, but never went back.

November 22nd, 1958. The Torsk had spent the week operating with the fleet and was tracking the USS Neosho AO 143. She was a new Navy oiler about 5 years old. She was fast and we simply couldn't close on her for a reasonable torpedo shot. The Captain finally fired a MK 14 - 3A expendable torpedo and hoped for the best. We would have to wait for the exercise report to see if we were successful.

The Captain's spirits were down. Suddenly we got word from sonar. Something big was coming. The Captain brought us to periscope depth and he was in his Hollywood style again as he met the scope with hat turned around.

"UHMMMM! – Boy!" – His body English told me he liked what he saw. "It's the Intrepid -- Gentlemen! – Mr. Bibby stand by for my mark! – Bearing! – Mark! - Range! –Mark!"

We were grooving again, the USS Intrepid CV 11 was doomed. The Intrepid was built during WWII and was one of our big carriers.

When the green flares reached the surface the chase was on. The Captain was at his best. We spent the rest of the afternoon and early evening evading the numerous attacks by the escorting destroyers. We went to 350 feet and let the Gulf Stream take us north east.

The operation ended and when we surfaced, a quick look confirmed once again, no yellow paint, our luck was holding.

We moored in Norfolk at 0750 on Tuesday morning, November 25th. "Sheesh Somolee!" It was cold. I had never seen it this cold in November before. The weather began to turn nasty. The temperature began to drop and it started to sleet and snow.

By Friday the bay had slush ice about a foot thick. We had banks of ice and snow over two feet deep on the sub. It was bitter cold. The humidity was cutting through almost any clothing were wore.

Friday noon the call came for the line party to report topside. We had a boat coming alongside. I was not on the line party but went topside all the same. We always enjoyed having one of our sister boats tie up next to us.

It was the Runner back from an extended stay in the Caribbean. As the lines were being thrown over to us and we were making the Runner secure to our port side, Mac and I spotted, Whitey, one of our Runner buddies.

Whitey was a pure albino. His eyes were pink and his skin was silky, milk white, almost matching his hair. He was very slim, and a heck of a swell buddy. He was in every way a regular guy. Whitey joined the Navy and volunteered for submarines, so he could keep out of the sun. The sun really wreaked havoc on his skin.

The weather was bitter. The skies were over cast and the wind bore ice crystals as it whipped about.

"Hey! – Mac! – Wardy!" Whitey called. He was facing us and cast a quick look around to see if anyone else was watching. He flashed his foul weather jacket open and there was our old friend "Ron Rico" stuck in Whitey's belt. "I got another bottle down below -- let's party!"

We motioned him over.

I commandeered a large can of fruit cocktail from the dry food locker. Catfish would miss it and have a fit, but I would explain to him before he found the discrepancy.

Mac, Jim Givens, Dave Cummings, Johnny North and I took roost on the fantail of the Torsk. Whitey and Childress came over from the Runner with Ron Rico and his twin.

The fantail was about the only place we could be out of sight of both crews and not be in two feet of snow and ice.   For some reason the snow and ice did not collect on the narrow protrusion that extended past the screw mounts. The super-structure ends here and we had maybe 12 feet of unfrozen area with the screw guards on each side.

We sat cross legged and would pass the can of fruit cocktail around, as well as the first bottle. Ron Rico was glad he made the trip and soon we were warm all over. It doesn't take Ron long, to ease your tensions and start lying to you about everything from your politics, to your manhood.

The large can of fruit cocktail was difficult to hold and turn up for a mouthful of fruit. We would then wash it down with a swig of Ron's best. It wasn't really difficult but was time consuming.

"We need a punchbowl! – Hic!" stuttered Givens.

"Wacha talkin bout? – Dum-ass! We don't got cups so we's wont 'trac no suspicions! – Hell! -- what wouda Ocifer shay if he saw a punchbowl? – Hic!" Dum-ass!" Childress was caustic drunk.

I grabbed the can of cocktail and dumped it into the soft-patch in the middle of the fantail. The soft-patch was a bowl like depression that bolted into the top of the fantail that allowed personnel to enter the after trim tank.

"Good idea!" slurred Mac and began to pour Ron and his brother into the patch as well.

"Der youse go! - Ready- made punch bowl! – Mighty Mac to de rescue!" Mac was proud of his mixture as he dipped his finger into the mixture and stirred. "Stirred -- not shaken!" He cackled and we all fell out, laughing that rum induced silly laughter that made no sense at all.

"How de hell we gonna drink it now! — Boy! -- You are all a bunch of dum-asses!" Childress was really upset about the possible loss of our concoction.

"Watch and learn my fine friend!" I answered as I lay on my side and placed my lips at the top of the liquid. I extended my tongue and cupped a cherry. I took my time, being proud of my dexterous tongue, and slowly brought the cherry into my mouth. I pursed my lips and sucked a long swig of the mixture. I then rolled it around in my mouth and looked at Childress.

He looked dumbfounded as the rest of the crew laughed hysterically with that rum rich attitude of invincibility.

We all took turns, tonguing fruit and sucking up the rum. We made drunken cracks about everything that you could do with your tongue and other things that I'm too ashamed to write about. Ron Rico was in rare form and picked no favorite. Whitey went to sleep. We lifted him up to the superstructure deck so he wouldn't roll into the bay. The fantail is not flat and is only about five feet wide at the widest point.

The screw guards are six inch round pipes that form a barrier and protect the propellers from bumping into the dock or pier. It is a big thing for a submariner to walk the screw guards. I never had the desire to do it, but Mac had said that one day he was walking both of them. Ron was telling him that this was the day. We cheered him on.

Mac stood and started on the forward end of the starboard screw guard. The water was very calm and had at least two feet of dirty slush ice on top. The bay looked like a giant coke float. Mac was planning to go home during December when we got to Philly. He had his advance leave pay check in his shirt pocket under his foul weather jacket.

Mac and Ron Rico had bonded quite well this evening and Ron was definitely in charge. Mac had that dazed look in his eyes. He made about four easy steps out on the guard before an icy spot caused him to slip. He didn't fall out into the water; instead he fell down and attempted to hold onto the guard. He gasped as the icy water penetrated his clothing and his arms went ridged. He was slowly sinking into the bay. I could see his check protruding from his pocket under his jacket.

"I'll save yor check – Buddy -- you sho don't wanna get it wet!" I said as I stretched out on a guard support and slipped the check from his pocket.

Mac continued to sink into the frigid water with his mouth agape and wheezing for breath against the icy grasp on his body. I was too far gone with Ron Rico to realize that Mac had no control over his body. In a moment his grip on the guard relaxed and he began to slip away in the icy slush.

Luckily Johnny and Dave realized the gravity of the situation and grabbed Mac with a grapple hook and we pulled him aboard. He was unresponsive. We took Mac below and put him in a hot shower.

To make a long story short, Mac wound up in sick bay for three days recovering from his encounter.

I had experienced water in the fifties before and it took help for me to get out. This water was obviously below freezing, because of the presence of ice. It was not frozen solid due to the high salinity from its close proximity to the ocean.

The next day, I went to visit Mac on the Orion and we had a long talk. We both agreed that drinking to the point where your reason is affected is just plain stupid. He said he no longer had any desire to walk the screw guards. I lost all taste for alcohol and have not drunk since. I can't handle it and made my mind up, I don't want anything to do with something that keeps me from recognizing danger. I almost lost my best friend and didn't know it.

God looks out for "Dum-asses!"

We made Philly 0732 on Saturday morning December 13, 1958. Mac and I spent the week getting the boat ready for dry dock and moving our gear onto a dormitory barge provided for the crew. It was not as nice as the barracks we had last year but was more economical and convenient. It was a two story floating building with crew's quarters, galley, mess hall and lounge on the upper deck and a work shop, machine shop and storage on the lower deck. The crew started a cash money, "Big Business Game," in the lounge that went on for two months. I bought into the game for a couple of days but was losing my "patootee!" I sold out to Torch Tortorigi, a new seaman that joined us recently.

Mac and I made arrangements for basket leave and caught the train Thursday night for Savannah. We were going to get my car for our stay in Philly. Basket leave was papers that gave permission to be over fifty miles from your base for a specific period of time. It was seldom for more than a long weekend. When you arrived back aboard your boat with no mishaps, the leave papers were thrown in the waste basket, thus the name "Basket Leave."

We arrived home Friday morning and caught a taxi to my home. Momma was up and welcomed Mac as if he were a long lost relative. Dad was working. Gray and Poco were both in school. I talked with Momma and it was quite obvious she was not in favor of me taking the car. She had every argument in the world against it.

"You stay within walking distance of your ship! - You have your meals right next to where you sleep! You have subways that take you all over that city! - What on earth do you need a car for?" Actually she was correct and she reminded me that we had made it just fine the year before. I hit a good point when I suggested that since I didn't have the car, maybe she should make the payments until I got out of the Navy.

I didn't mention Daddy had made a lot of extra payments since Momma was driving it to work. I knew Daddy hadn't told her and wasn't going to. I felt a little guilty but not enough to make me change my mind.

Mac and I spent the rest of Friday driving around Savannah. We went by Manger's on Broughton Street where Phyllis worked and she was tickled when two dashing sailors came to her office.

"Oh-- Lynn!" She exclaimed. "Ya'll haven't made planes for tomorrow night have you?" Mac and I had planned to leave early Sunday morning. It would take us all day and we would take turns driving. We had plans to get back in Philly around midnight Sunday night.

Mac shrugged his shoulders and his demeanor told me he was up to anything Phyllis suggested.

"What'cha got in mind -- Phyllis?" I asked.

"I'll call Claire Colson for a date with Mac and we can go to the Brass Rail at the beach -- just like old times! – Whatta you say - Honey?" She knew exactly what to say to make a guy look good in front of a friend.

Mac gave that nasal snicker and said. "Ok with me!"

"Hey! - how bout tonight, - Phyllis?" I asked.

"Can't do it on such quick notice - Mom can't be left alone anymore and I can't get anyone this late - Mike [her brother] has just married and moved to Jacksonville - It's just me and Mom now – Sorry-- Lynn!" She mimicked a frown.

"Hey -- it's OK – Honey! - I mean - you're great to treat us so nice - when we just drop in out of the blue like this!" I was truly grateful.

"Don't be silly!" She gave me a quick peck on the lips and said. I gotta get back to work now – see ya'll at seven - OK?"

We left and went home. Momma made dinner and Mac had his first genuine southern cooked fried chicken with rice and chicken gravy. Momma had butterbeans, squash and cornbread with genuine sweet ice tea. I've never seen a skinny Yankee boy eat so much in my life.

Gray was fifteen now and had joined the civil air patrol. He was in uniform for a Friday night meeting and really looked good. I was amazed at how much difference a year had made in both boys. Daddy was overjoyed and I had to tell him all about my adventures over the last nine months. He said that God was indeed looking out for us when he heard of our close calls.

Poco [James] was in awe of Mac. He kept saying he saw him in a movie. I had often caught a glimpse of Mac and he did remind me of someone I'd seen quite often in films. He always played a tough hood that was in the background. I never knew the actors name. Mac was quiet and did very little talking, but he was a good listener and you never felt as if he wasn't interested in what you were saying.

Mac was impressed with Claire. Her family was also old Savannah Elite. She was an attractive blonde, not quite as tall as Phyllis, but well built. These girl's social etiquettes were superb. Mac and I knew we were out of our class, but the girls treated us as if we were the most important guys in the world.

The Brass Rail was rocking and it was good to get back in the groove. Mac ordered a Hurricane and nursed it all night. Phyllis and Claire drank a lot of Tom Collins. I drank half coke and half ginger ale, with twist of lime and a swizzle stick. It gave just enough color that all my friends that dropped around didn't suspicion me a teetotaler. The brass Rail had not lost any of its charm and was a rockin place. We witnessed the choreographed moves of a colored group.

I told Phyllis of our night with Duane Eddy, at Virginia Beach.. She was flabbergasted that I remembered about his teeth.

Phyllis told me her brother, Mike, had married Glenda Bevill, one of my old girlfriends and sister to Donald Bevill, one of my best buddies.

We had the girls home by 2 AM.

We dropped Claire off first and Mac waited in the car as I walked Phyllis to her door. She turned to me at the door and placed both hands on my chest. It was a gentle move, but never the less I knew it meant no passion.

"Lynn-- I think you better not drop in on me anymore-- you see I'm met a guy and I'm really beginning to care about him. -- I've always cared for you Lynn and I'm happy when we're together but that confuses me -- and --- do you see what I mean?"

"Sure Phyllis -- I hope this date doesn't present a problem - I mean --!" She stopped me.

"Lynn - this guy and I are only dating -- I don't even know how he really feels -- but I know how I feel and I don't want any doubts until I'm sure – does that make sense to you?"

Actually it did and I told her so. I got a quick kiss and she quickly went in. I walked slowly back to the car and decided not to mention this to Mac.

It was snowing when we entered Philadelphia. I had made arrangements for a parking spot at a service station outside the main gate of the Naval Yard. The ground was covered with a fine powdery snow. It wasn't wet and slushy, I was thankful of that.

This snow crunched as we walked on it. I found that rather funny and Mac said that's the only kind he ever knew of, till he got south. We were in our bunks by 0100 hours. Mac told me that this was his first long driving experience with a Ford and he was impressed.

Words can't express how hard the work is on a submarine when you have a limited budget. The Officers handled all that, but we were constantly reminded that we must get the most for our dollar and we did a lot of the repair work ourselves. I buffed the bubble again along with repacking every valve in the conning tower. The wheel did not require re-lashing, but I did apply a new coat of green shellac. We sent the upper conning tower hatch to a machine shop for repairs and re-machining.

The fabulous five was relaxing in the lounge and listening to the Big Business players insulting each other when Vandergrift called me to the phone. My heart was in my throat.   I said a quick prayer that it wasn't a death at home or something.

"Hey -- Sailor Boy -- I told you I'd find you – It's Vickie –Where have you been lover?"

I couldn't believe that the girl had actually called me. "Vickie! – Are you here in Philly?" I asked.

"Sure – I told you I live here – I've been calling two weeks now -- where have you been?" She sounded upset.

"Hey – Girl – I've been right here -- I haven't even been to town yet! – I did go home last weekend to get my car – otherwise I've been right here!" I felt like she was expecting something more, but I didn't have to explain anything.

"Well – If you have no plans for tomorrow night -- I'm free and we could go out!" Vickie sounded excited.

"Sure give me your address and I'll pick you up!" I offered.

"Its way to hard to find my place – I'll meet you at the corner of North Pennsylvania Ave and Wingohocking Street. There is a little open lot on the right corner and I'll be waiting there." She sounded as if she were in a rush.

"Look – Vickie – The weather is awful – I'll find your house – Give me the address! - girl!" I was adamant. It didn't matter, she was insistent.

"Lynn – Just say you'll be there at six o'clock – Please!" She was pleading.

"Ok! – Sure! - 6 o'clock – At the corner of North Pennsylvania Ave and Wingohocking Street. You'll be on the right corner by a vacant lot – Right?" I repeated.

"You got it – lover -- I can't wait to see you -- please don't stand me up – Please!" She was really pleading. This was a sure thing, I was definitely gonna be there!

"OK- Vickie – Dress warm now – Ya hear! " She giggled as she hung up.

I rushed to tell Johnny North about the call. He couldn't believe it either. She had really called.

"Man – If you don't get some of that -- you are one sorry sailor – Hell! – Man! -- You were all over it in the car that night!" Johnny remembered the night as well as I did. We spent the rest of the evening talking over the event and laughed at recalling the old lady and her toll bridge.

The weather was terrible. I was not used to driving in this snow and slush. I drove as if I was in mud at home and it worked pretty well. The streets were not iced over so it wasn't all that slick.   I drove very slow as I looked for Wingohocking Street. I actually saw Vickie before I saw the street sign. She was bundled in a grey overcoat and seemed heavier than I remembered. She recognized the car from the description I gave her over the phone and began to wave. The snow had turned to sleet and the wind was beginning to whip about. I pulled into the empty lot. Apparently a building of some type had been there, as the lot was paved.

I intended to stop and get out and open the door for Vickie, but she rushed to the passenger door and opened it herself. She slid into the seat and directly to my side. She threw her arms around me and gave me a long passionate kiss. Yep, this was gonna be a night to remember.

"Well -- where to -- Vickie my dear?" I tried to give a Clark Gable impression. She missed it completely.

"Anywhere we can be alone!" She shivered in an effort to shake away the cold. "Also - make sure it's warm."

I seriously thought of suggesting a motel room, but decided against it. Every indication was that she was willing, but a motel puts a different slant on love.

"How about a drive- in movie - they have heaters I hear." I instantly thought how foolish the suggestion was, considering the weather.

"That's fine – Lynn -- I just want you to love me -- I don't care where!"

Well, that left no doubt as to how the night was going to go. My heart was beating like a school kid's but, I paid close attention to my driving. It gave me time to think. I wanted to be as mature about this as I could and not disappoint this girl.

We actually found a drive –in movie that was open and they did have in-car heaters. We settled down in the front seat and soon the windows were not just fogged but frozen. The little electric heater did an outstanding job as it blew the warmed air on our feet in the floorboard.

Vickie quickly went into a subconscious trance as she welcomed my caresses. It was a relief to be able to move my hands about freely on this woman's body and instantly feel the welcome response. This didn't occur on most dates as there is always that preventative attitude that most woman have. Women that make love professionally don't seem to require foreplay, they are in a hurry to finish with you, so they can move on to the next customer.

Vickie was a willing participant, and I was in no hurry. I felt the need to talk to her. I wanted to romance her. There was no way that anyone could see what was going on in the car. The windows were completely frosted over.

I began to tell Vickie how I felt. I told her how good she felt and how she made me feel warm inside. I told her she tasted good and was so soft. I mentioned how good it was to have an honest relationship without a set of rules and boundaries that could not be crossed.

She suddenly froze and began to cry. I thought maybe I had hurt her and whispered. "Vickie I'm sorry – Baby - Are my hands too rough, did I hurt you!"

"Noooo! – Noooo!" -- She sobbed – She was really sobbing now.

"Vickie! – What's wrong – Honey! – What did I do – Is it something I said?" I was concerned that I was going to miss this piece. I didn't feel I was using her. She was going to benefit as well.

"Yes! – It's what you said – You said this was an honest relationship! – Well it's noooot!" She sobbed again.

"What the Sam Hill are you talking about girl - I haven't lied to you about anything- as a matter of fact you haven't even asked me about anything – What's wrong?" I was pleading.

"Noooo! – There's nothing wrong with you – Lynn – It's me – Dammit! - It's me – I'm the one that's not honest!" She sat up in the seat and turned her head away from me.

"Lynn – I'm married – Ronny -- the baby is mine!"

My head reeled and I felt faint.

She continued. "My husband is in the Navy also and is in the Mediterranean – Lynn – I'm over three months pregnant again!" She really went to sobbing now.

I just sat there; I was in a mental stupor. I thought about what my Daddy would say. "Talk to yourself about what is right – Son -- and you will always do the right thing!"

I talked to myself. Vickie continued to sob.

I asked myself if I wanted to make love to another man's wife. My answer was no.

I asked myself if I wanted to betray a fellow sailor. My answer was no.

I asked myself if I wanted to make love to a pregnant woman. My answer, again, was no.

I asked myself what I was going to do. My answer was. "Take her home!" I cranked the car. I put the heater out in the rack, and eased out of the drive-in as the defroster began to clear the windshield.

Vickie continued to cry. We did not talk. She let me take her to the corner of Wingohocking and North 13th Street. I told her I would take her to her house, but she insisted this was close enough. I never saw or heard from her again. I drove back to the Navy Yard in a daze and in the icy sleet.

As I slept, the faceless lady told me I did the right thing!

The next morning, Mac and Johnny roused me out of the sack early with the "How did it go questions." I told them to get a table away from everyone else and I'd tell them at breakfast.

This was one of those things that was not going to be a secret. It seems every guy on the boat knew I was gonna get some guaranteed snatch.

Johnny, bless his heart, had bragged about my success on our night in Portsmouth and told the crew that the girl had come to Philly to find me. How can that not be a sure thing?

I told the story just as it happened and the crew couldn't believe I didn't go ahead and pop it to her. I looked at them in disbelief and then asked them the same questions I had asked myself.

The crew gave their comments, advice and criticism.

Hell! – Man – Her husband is probably laying some Italian broad right now in Naples!" One quipped.

Another chimed in. "What he don't know can't hurt you -- dumb-ass!"

Someone shouted. "Pregnant pussy is free pussy - you wiener!"

One "old salt" commented. "Damn! - Man! – I remember hiding behind my Momma's liver to keep Daddy from punching my eyes out!"

I simply took the abuse and let em rage on. Johnny and Mac both told me I did the right thing.

We dressed up, in our suits, that Saturday night and went to a dance we heard about, in a school gym in Philly. We checked to make sure that it was for adults also. We knew that high school girls were always trouble, especially if high school boys are around.

It was a swinging affair and I danced my fill. I made no attempt to pick up a date and it was nice to just play the field and simply dance.

I never went to town during the week. Some of the guys went ashore every night. I was content to stay at the barge and rest.

Johnny, Mac and I decided we would take the Quartermaster test in January. I had enough time in grade to test for any job, Mac and Johnny had just turned time. We studied together and helped each other with flashing light drills and semaphore [flag communication] drills. We would all work together and the study was quite interesting.

The third weekend in Philly, I took Mac with me to the YWCA, just off Independence Hall, in downtown Philly. It was where I had met Deloris a year before. She was quite a girl and I thought she was probably married by now.

It was difficult to find a parking space, but I remembered a vacant lot, just a few blocks away. As luck would have it the lot was still vacant. I parked my Ford and Mac and I walked the three blocks back to the Y. We had suits on. I had brought two suits from home and had chosen the dark blue for this night. I wore a pink shirt with white color and white French Cuffs. My dark blue tie was a woven straight bottom that was the style at the time.

Mac and I did that little brisk step that mission orientated men do as we climbed the short flight of stone steps that led to the lobby of that giant old building that housed the Y. We swung the elaborate doors open and there, under the chandelier, stood Deloris in that beautiful green dress she wore the first time I ever saw her. It had been a year and she was still here.

She smiled and walked over to me, took my hand and without a word led me to the dance floor. The band was playing "Begin the Beguine."

I started to speak. "Del I'm sorry --------!" She stopped me.

She placed her fingers over my lips and softly said. "It doesn't matter – You're here now – that's all that matters!" That's all that was ever said about the year that had passed between us. It was as if I had never left. All was well in Philadelphia.

Mac tied up with Nan and we had a very nice time. I asked Nan about the Marine and she said he transferred away and she never heard from the SOB again. I started to say what a dirty scoundrel he was, when I realized I had done the very same thing. Obviously Deloris didn't hate me though.

We took the girls home and Deloris asked me if I would have Christmas dinner with her and her family. I agreed and suggested I provide a Christmas Ham. We had a number of huge canned hams compliments of Hormel and I knew I could count on Catfish to get one for me.

I had hoped that Mac and Nan would hit it off. It would be nice for my best buddy to date my girl's sister, but that was not the case. Mac just did not care for Nan.

I discussed it with Mac and told him that Nan seemed to be a lot of fun. Mac agreed, but said he thought she had too much fun with too many guys. Mac never went out with us again.

Christmas came and we had a fine dinner. Del's Mom and older sister prepared the ham with a pineapple glaze and sweet potatoes. It was really tasty.

Deloris said her entire family was together for the first time in over five years. Her older brother was divorced, but her older sister was there with her fiancé. Nan had her present beau in tow, but Del's younger brother was gone as soon as Christmas dinner was done. Del's Mom and Dad was a nice quiet couple that stayed to themselves.

I had loaned my Ford to Mac. He had driven to Syracuse, New York for a short visit. He wanted to see his family. I hoped he could mend his problem with his girlfriend.

I was staying at Del's older brother's home in North Philly. Del would come and spend the day. I could never talk her into staying the night. Things were progressing very well between Del and me, but "dog gone it" – Nan got it in her head she was gonna vamp me.

Nan had always flirted with me. As we sat on the sofa one evening, enjoying a nice fire in the fireplace, Del got up to fix coffee. The instant she left the room Nan slipped next to me on the sofa and began to rub herself on me. She started kissing my ear and was actually embarrassing me. Del must have suspicioned her intentions, because in a flash Del had a handful of the hair on the back of Nan's head and pulled her from the sofa.

Not a word was uttered as Del escorted Nan to the front door, opened it and pushed the girl out. She reached for Nan's coat and threw it at her as she shut the door. Del proceeded back to the kitchen and presently came back with our coffee.

She set the coffee down on the little table and softly asked. "Black with two sugars – right?" I nodded. Nothing else was said. She stayed very late that night.

Deloris and her friends were all set for their annual skiing trip again at New Years. Deloris begged me to go, once again offering to pay all expenses. I couldn't bring myself to accept. There was no real reason I couldn't, I just wouldn't. She was very disappointed.

The fab five caught another Mummers Parade and it was as fabulous as I remembered. The Club 13 was out of the question.

We drove to Camden, New Jersey for a New Year's party at the Bamboo Club. We had to park about two blocks away and as we turned the corner, a group of local boys stepped from an alley and confronted us.

There were probably eight boys, all in their late teens or early twenties. "Youse guys think youse can just come on our turf any time youse want?" The littlest guy in the group spoke.

Mac stepped around me and took a short step forward. The knife was in his hand but tucked behind his trouser leg. He spoke with a typical Yankee big city brogue. "Hey! - Youse guys ain't got nutting to worry bout! - We're sailors from the Naval yard over in Philly and we got some Southern boys here that have never seen one of your fine Jersey clubs! – We're not bringing any grief -- Ka-peesh?" The boys looked at each other and seemed to relax a bit.

I couldn't stand it. My Scots – Indian blood was about to boil and I was planning something. I was going to nice em and if that didn't work, I was gonna bluff em and if that didn't work, I figured I could out run em to the car.

"Hey! – Why don't ya'll join us for a round in the club - we can get to know one nother!" I put on my best cracker drawl.

The Jersey boys cracked up. "Ya'll! – Ya'll!"

"Yeh!" - I said. "Ya'll – Come on – we'll have you saying – Youse'all in no time!" They really cracked up, now.

The little guy stated through his laughter. "Mr. Petrone would have our balls if we went into his club!"

Mac exclaimed. "Hey! – Ain't that the guy that told us about the club?"

Johnny picked up on the que and said. "Yeh! Some guy named Tom Petrone - that's the guy!"

Johnny had hit on something that got the boys attention. We suggested we could get some beer and slip it out to them. They were indignant about having to have beer slipped out to them,"Hell," they could do just as they pleased on their turf in Camden. They did take us up on the beer and we brought each one a brew.

The club was swank and had a lot of women. We got to dance some, but I really felt out of place. I had to dodge the guys that had one too many. The instant you make eye contact, they take it personal and start talking trash.

It was still a nice party and we got a lot of hugs and kisses at the stroke of midnight.

Sunday afternoon and Mac and I were relaxing in the lounge on the second deck of our barge. We were alone. I had a hot cup of coffee and a sweet roll that Lambert had baked. Deloris was due back that evening. I was thinking of calling her.

"Say! – Mac! – Tell me about your trip home!" I asked.

"Not much to say – Lynn -- My family is doing well -- I came up on a wreck -- just south of Syracuse and took some injured motorist to the Hospital -- other than that -- everything's OK." Mac was not going to enlighten me on his status with his girl.

"How did your weekend go with Deloris?" He asked, because I had told him about the skiing trip and I didn't go.

"It was OK – Mac!" I began to explain. "Nan put a move on me and Del put her out of the house -- I thought I was going to catch the devil -- but Del never said a word to me. -- Matter of fact -- she never spoke to Nan! -- She just grabbed her by the hair and pushed her out the door!"

Mac gave that nasal snicker and turned to look me straight in the eye. "What's your plans with Del -- Lynn?" The question took me by surprise.

"Uh! – Mac – I donno – I guess we'll just date till we go back to sea and - Sheesh – Somolee! – Mac - whatta you gettin at?" I was really caught off guard.

"Look – Buddy – Don't get me wrong – You're my best friend and you are really a nice guy -- You're honest and there ain't an ounch o bastard in ya -- but when it comes to women -- you're a first class prick!"

"What the hell you talkin about - Mac?" I was hurt. "I don't run around on Del! – Hell -- you were with me at the Bamboo Club! – I quit drinkin -- and I didn't even try to pick up a gal last night! - How the hell is that being a prick – now -- tell me that?" I was almost stammering.

"Cool it man! – I'm just telling you what I see! – Listen Lynn -- Del loves the hell outta you -- Man! - I can see that – It's obvious to everyone -- She waited a year for you to come back - She didn't bitch a bit - She comes at your beck and call – She offered to pay for a skiing trip for you for the second year in a row and you say you'll just date her till you go back to sea! -- That's prick talk!" Mac was serious. I had never seen him like this.

"Mac! – Look – I love the girl and --------!" Mac cut me off.

"Love -- my ass – Lynn -- you'er true dating! –This woman wants to spend the rest of her life with you and you're just enjoying the fringe benefits – You're gonna break her heart -- Buddy! - She doesn't deserve that and you don't deserve her! She's a fine woman and you don't realize how a situation like this can affect a person!" Mac sat back in his chair and lit a cigarette.

"Hell – I need a drink!" He was off in a flash.

I sat dumfounded by what Mac had said. I could tell he wasn't mad at me, but he was definitely concerned. I felt a deep sense of worldly wisdom in what Mac had said. I thought the situation over.

Was I ready to get married? – No!

Could I afford to get married? – No!

Did I want to spend the rest of my life with Deloris? – I hadn't thought about it 'till now, and now, I didn't want to think about it! - I guess that answered that! I realized she was a heck of a find! - She had a good job! – She was a looker! – She was not a flirt! – I was just using her! – Mac was right! – I was a first class prick.

I didn't call Deloris that night, as a matter of fact, I never called her again. I really proved what a prick I was.

The faceless lady would not even speak to me that night.

The Torsk came out of drydock at 1642 hours on Feburary 13, 1959. Our tanks had been sandblasted and repainted. The superstructure damaged during our venture into the tropical storm was repaired.

As I was laying tile in the chow hall, one of the yard birds working in the superstructure came in and showed me a crusty piece of dangly metal.

"I think it's a watch! – I found it in the superstructure around the front of the conning tower! - Maybe you can find who it belongs to and give it a proper burial!" He grinned and lay the crusted dangly mess on the table.

I finished laying the piece of tile I had in my hand, then sat at the table and looked at the clump of crud. It was dry but crusty. It still had the outline of a watch with a broken metal band. I picked the clump up and began to rub the crust and dry slime from the face, being careful.

The crystal had a thousand cracks in it even though it was still intact. Son – of – a – gun! - Through the fractured crystal I could plainly see the words "Aquacade." It was my watch I had lost when it caught on the upper hatch and fell to what I thought, was oblivion. That happened near the end of September. We had been to 300 feet numerous times since.

I carefully wiped and cleaned the watch until, aside from the broken band and fractured crystal, it looked pretty good. You could look directly at the crystal and see the face pretty clearly. If you put any angle on the watch, the thousands of tiny cracks blocked the face so it was not readable.

Mac walked in and I showed him the watch. He looked at it and gave that nasal smirk and simply wound the stem a couple of turns.

His eyes widened as he looked in astonishment. "The thing's running! – Lynn! - I can't believe it! - Look! – the thing's running!"

I took the watch and sure enough the sweep second hand was ticking around in that predictable one second fashion, characteristic of a wrist watch. I wound the watch fully and it ran from then on. A new band and I had my Aquacade back again.

I stayed away from the 'Y', not wanting to further my association with Deloris. I missed her, but I didn't want to get any more involved. My ears and thoughts still burned with Mac's searing advice.

I began to go to a little private dance club in North Philly. Mac went with me one Friday night and we teamed up with two sisters. I don't think there is an ugly girl in Philly. These sisters were lookers and fast. We asked them out to a drive-in movie on Saturday night.

Mac brought Ron Rico with us. I stuck to Coke, but the girls fell in love with Ron. Soon the night was in full swing. Ron brought out the street talk in the sisters. Mac didn't seem to mind, but it put a shadow on my mood. A good looking woman that begins to mouth vulgarities is simply not in keeping with what I call a romantic mood.

Mac and his date were desperately in need of some privacy, so I suggested my date and I go for a walk. My date was already slurring her words and insisted she wanted to stay and watch Mac and her sister.

"No way -- Jose!" I said and took her by the hand and dragged her away from the car. She began to put up a fuss and made such a ruckus that horns began to sound in protest. I tried to reason with her, but the profanities began to worsen. I was extremely embarrassed. I suppose that if I had let Ron influence me, I would not have cared.

The girl started cursing quite loudly and I tried placing my hand over her mouth to quieten her. I should not have done that. She turned on me with a vengeance. People began to turn on their headlights and sound their horns. Some guys even got out of their cars.

Amid the chaos she began to accuse me of slapping her. I am cold sober and could see where this was going. I began to plead with her to come back to the car with me and I would take her home. She would have no part of it and began to encourage someone to whip my ass. I was really getting concerned.

Her sister came to my aid. I guess she heard the turmoil and knowing her sister, she felt a responsibility. She managed to quieten her sister down, but there was no way she would get back in the car.

A rather large crowd had gathered and I saw my Ford easing up the row behind me. I looked and saw Mac at the wheel. He gave a sly "come on" wave and I eased away and dashed into the passenger side. He slowly drove out of the movie and stopped at the corner.

Mac jumped out and said. "Slide over and drive!" He ran behind the car and jumped in the passenger side. "Drive away real easy now and we'll be OK!" I did just that.

"Mac - what will the girls do -- we can't just leave em like that?" I was concerned.

"Women like that will always make out! – Don't let it bother you – Buddy -- they're probably already popping some guys back there right now!" Mac snickered. He was a good friend.

"Mac -- what if they call the cops and tell a bunch of lies on me?" I was worried.

"Not much chance of that - Man! – Hell! – They probably don't even remember how they got there! – Besides cops ain't fools and there were dozens of witnesses that saw everything. Those witnesses will get their stories so mixed up the cops may just run the whole theater in!" We both laughed at that thought.

Suddenly my blood ran cold! "Mac – What if someone got my tag number? – It's a Georgia tag and stands out like a sore thumb!" I was really upset with this thought.

"Mac gave that nasal snicker and held up a torn popcorn box. "Not to worry – Buddy -- I covered the tag before I pulled out of the movie! – I took it off when we switched at the corner!" He was one street wise guy and I was glad he was my best buddy.

Ray Tortorigi was a second generation Italian from Little Italy in New York City. We called him "Torch". He was a swell guy, but somewhat of a loner. He took to Mac and me, right off the bat.

"Youse guys ever been to an Italian dance before?" Torch asked us one night after chow. I certainly had not and Mac just shrugged his shoulders as if maybe he had or maybe not.

"Deys one comin up dis Saturday in my neighborhood and I'll sees if I can bring some buddies - if youse guys wanna?"

Mac and I agreed and asked Johnny North if he wanted to go. Johnny had a number of Italian friends in his hometown of Chillacothee, Ohio and said it would be a blast.

Torch called home and his brother checked with the Italian neighborhood powers and they said it would be OK, so Friday, February 6, 1959 we left Philly for a trip of less than a hundred miles to New York City.

The four of us were cruising along on the Pennsylvania turnpike on a bitter cold, overcast day. We had just been paid a few days before. We were really feeling free and had a good feelings, knowing that Torch was going to see his family. Torch said that arrangements had been made for us to stay at a neighboring boarding house that had a vacancy. It was going to cost each of us ten bucks each for two nights. It was not a bad deal.

The red light caught my attention immediately as I glanced in the rear view mirror. "Cops coming fast boys!" I said as I glanced at the speedometer. I was at close to 65 MPH. The limit was 60MPH. I didn't feel that the five miles over would arouse any attention. I held my speed hoping the approaching Chrysler 300 would scream by in pursuit of someone else.

No such luck. The black and white State Police car drew abreast of me on the left side and the officer in the passenger seat motioned me to pull over.

The driver stepped out, to approach me. I decided to be nice and got out of my Ford. The wind whipped across the flat grassy plain that was to the east of the turnpike and I jammed my hands into my coat pockets. The approaching officer immediately crouched and in a flash his revolver was in his hand.

"FREEZE! – BOY! – SLOWLY! - NOW! – Take your hands out of your pockets and come back to the patrol car!" He was on high alert. I suppose he perceived the hands in my pocket as a threat.

The other officer stepped from the passenger side of the cruiser and approached my Ford shouting. "Everyone in the car - remain still - put your hands where they can be seen!" His tone was demanding.

The officer confronting me ordered me to put my hands on the top of the police car and he briskly frisked me.

"Sir – I don't think I was going that fast! -- See! – My buddies and I were just talking and ----------! He held up his hand and said. "Lemme see your license and registration!"

"The registration's in the glove box -- Sir!" I replied as I drew my license and ID from my wallet. I also handed him my military driver's license.

He looked up as he viewed the licenses and asked. "All you guys in the Navy?"

I nodded in the affirmative. He sat in his cruiser and called in on his radio. I could see the other officer checking the registration from the glove box. Mac had heard me tell where it was and had obtained it for the officer. The officer walked back to the car and handed the driver the registration. A short discussion ensued on the radio.

The driving officer had holstered his pistol by this time. He got out of the patrol car and handed me my licenses and registration back.

"Sorry for the scare -- Son! - But we had a report of a stolen car from down south and you guys fit the bill pretty close! -- When you put your hands in your coat pockets I thought we were gonna have a shootout! -- You gave me quite a start!" He smiled.

Little did he know how bad I needed to go to the bathroom.

We came to the exit booth and handed the attendant the ticket, he stamped it and I paid the toll.

"You guys musta drove straight through – Eh!" The attendant asked.

I started to tell about the police stop but for some reason, simply nodded.

"Good thing – cause if you guys hadda been a few minutes sooner I coulda give ya a ticket!" He laughed as he waved us through.

The guys then told me that the ticket we got as we entered the Turnpike had a time stamped on it. When you exited the Turnpike the time again was stamped. If the time expired indicated you averaged faster than the speed limit, the attendant was authorized to issue a speeding ticket. The police stop actually did me a favor and added enough time to the ticket to avoid a fine.

Torch's family was genuine Italian. His Dad spoke fairly good English with a thick accent, but his Mother didn't even try. She was a doter; she smothered Torch with kisses and proceeded to kiss us all. She had a large wooden spoon in her hand. It was stained deep red from years of stirring tomato sauces. She took great delight in prodding Mac and Johnny's skinny rib cages with the spoon. She kept commenting something about "scheletros" and "poveno bambinos!"

Mrs. Tortorigi prepared an Italian meal that was out of this world that night. There were pastas and sauces and green salads and breads. I do not remember how many relatives I met that night, but they kept coming and going. I really think she simply fed the neighborhood. The people were very cordial, but we were all aware that we were accepted only because of Torch. We were not Italian. I was wondering how the dance would go Saturday night. I would find out.

By midnight I had heart burn that was killing me. Luckily there was a corner drugstore that stayed open late and I downed a bottle of Pepto-Bismol. The pink stuff helped, but it was mid-afternoon before the pooping stopped and I was able to venture far from the room.

Torch took us on a drive through Little Italy and neighboring Chinatown. We were just south of Lower Manhattan and very near the Bowery. It was an interesting drive and I was stopped again by the police. It seems that somehow the traffic light at intersections have control over traffic entering from nearby side streets that have no traffic lights. I simply stopped at the corner of a side street that had no traffic light. As soon as traffic cleared I pulled out onto the street.

"WooWee!" You woulda thought I spit on the officers shoes. Man! – was he pissed. I didn't see him standing on the corner and he blew his whistle so loud that I couldn't miss hearing it. He motioned me over as I made the turn and began to recite to me the entire book of rules regarding how traffic lights control traffic on adjacent side streets. He walked back and looked at the Georgia tag on the car and raised his hands to Heaven in a gesture of hopelessness.

"How much longer are ya gonna be in our fair city - me boy?" He spat the words in facetious good will.

"We're leaving in the morning!" I replied.

"May the saints be praised?" He muttered, and he waved me away. The guys really laughed this one up. I asked Torch why he didn't tell me all the crazy traffic light stuff.

"Whatsa matta you! - Sheesh! – I don't own a car! – Man! – Dey's got tubes for Joes like me! – Kapeech?" We all laughed.

The dance was on the second floor of the neighborhood Italian club and was quite large. We were in the middle of Little Italy and it was a world unto itself. Mac had dark hair and blended in with the crowd pretty good, but Johnny and I were strictly Northern European blondes with blue eyes. We stuck out even in the subdued light of the dance floor. The girls seemed to eye us a lot, but did not approach us at first.

Torch told us that if a girl asked us to dance, do not refuse, even if she was uglier than your pet dog. If you hurt a girls feelings, she's got a Brother, Daddy, Uncle or some guy that will make you respect her, also don't ask a girl to dance until you ask Torch and he'll make sure she's not some toughy's squeeze.

We didn't have to worry about dancing. There were plenty of girls that did the asking and they were not all that bad looking either. I enjoyed myself but really couldn't let myself go. The neighborhood boys watched the dancing closely to make sure that not too much touchy – touchy went on.

I still enjoyed the dance; however it was hard to find a drink that wouldn't make you start speaking Italian. There was an awful lot of wine and I did sample some. It is pleasing at first sip, but the aftertaste is like all the rest of the liquors. I missed my rum, but still did not fall off the wagon.

We made it back to our Torsk on Sunday afternoon and had left over meatloaf for dinner. It was nice to take a bite of something and not still taste it after an hour. The movie that night was "The Man from Planet X." I found a different dance club for the next weekend and went alone.

I met "Kosh". She was the prettiest girl there and was a good dancer. Her parents were immigrants from Poland. They had fled the Nazis when Poland was invaded.

She asked me to call her "Kosh." It was a Polish nickname and her father called her that. She was a typical young woman who liked to dance. We got along well. I met her on a Friday night and Saturday we had a nice dinner and took in a downtown movie.

I pulled my Ford into a dark spot across the street from her parent's home. She eagerly slid closer to me and as she lifted her face I gently kissed her lips. She responded immediately. I was now very proficient in playing the casual hand game. It was obvious this girl was going to be a willing participant. I knew just what to do and soon her quickened breathing told me I was doing something right. I thought of Vickie, she had been a quick disastrous romance. I thought of Yvonne, how she cried when I left and fate simply would not let me get back. I actually had chest pains when I had to leave England and Leslie.

I almost laughed when I thought of Nelly, she was a hooker and took me to meet her family, and here I was, on the brink of taking the step that would bond a man and woman in that invisible web of obligation.

I relaxed and suppressed my desires. Kosh soon stirred and asked if anything was wrong.

"No – Kosh! - Everything is fine!" I answered. "I really like you! -- You're that sweet sort of girl that every guy is looking for -- I can't believe you're still available -- I just feel like we should talk a bit and maybe get to know each other."

She sat up in the seat and placed her hands in her lap in a proper fashion and began to introduce herself. She jokingly took me through a brief tour of her adolescent years, then her teen and school years and her present job situation, ending with her being in the front seat of a Ford with a guy from Georgia that had her on cloud nine and then simply stopped to talk. I felt kind of foolish.

"Kosh! - I really care about you -- but I don't want us to get all messed up -- I don't want to cause any problems!" I really didn't know what I wanted. I was leaving Philly very shortly and I guess I just didn't want a one night stand.

"Hey! – Lynn! – Don't worry! -- My fiancé will be home in a couple of weeks and I'd probably stop seeing you anyway -- so let's just let the good times roll and don't worry about it!" I had that stunned body buzz again.

"Damn" – I thought. Women could be just as big a jerk as a man could be.

The good times did not roll that night and I never saw Kosh again. I wasn't going to be the guy her fiancé never knew about.

The faceless Lady returned to me that night and comforted me. She told me. "I done good - again!"

I drove my Ford home in mid February, 1959. I caught the bus back to Philly and slept the whole way back. I was really rested when we went to sea. I didn't have any heart aches. I had learned a lot this time and I felt like a grown man for the first time in my life. Little did I know how the Lord was about to try me.

CHAPTER XIII

SHORT TIMER

We departed Philly in late February and made a short checkout cruise with some yard birds aboard. These guys are good at what they do. After an extensive yard period, some supervisors from the crews that worked on the boat will make a shakedown cruise to see how their staff did the work. I was still not happy with the way our upper conning tower hatch worked. It seemed to operate OK, but something just felt different. I thought maybe it was just my imagination.

We made a short trip to New London for some training on the new sound gear. I don't even think I went topside the whole time.

Mac, Johnny and I got rated. We were all three rated as Quartermaster Third Class. I spent the whole weekend sewing my new Eagle Chevrons on my uniforms. I had turned four years in the reserves in May of 1958, but had never sewn my hash mark on my uniform's sleeve. I suppose I was ashamed of having four years in service and not being rated. I also sewed the new embroidered Dolphins on my jumpers, so I could stow my silver Dolphin pin away.

I'll never forget how proud I felt the first time I stood inspection in dress blues with the red chevron, white eagle and white Quartermaster emblem on my left sleeve. The long red hash mark slashed across my left forearm telling the world I was no newcomer to this man's Navy. My Momma had bought me a pair of expensive black cordovan leather Navy cut shoes at Belk – Griffith in Savannah while I was home. Man, did I look spiffy.

The Captain came by and gave me a once over, I think I saw a little smile.

Mr. Bibby stopped in front of me and softly whispered. "You oughta be on a recruiting poster!" I felt ten feet tall.

It was a different world when at sea now. I didn't scrub the decks or clean the heads anymore. I still took my turns at topside watch and was still the choice at the wheel for maneuvering watch, but the work day was at the charts or on the Lorain. Mr. Mobley was beginning to give me instructions on taking star shots. Johnny and Mac were already hitting the flashing light. Flashing light was giving me problems. The trick, to read flashing light is to see the flashes as the letter it represents. I still counted short and long flashes and then interpreted them. That takes too much time. If a good quartermaster sees a short and a long flash, he sees an "A". I counted the flashes and then went through my memory file and matched it to an "A". I was really lagging behind the other guys. I worked at the lights every chance I got.

Being a quartermaster has its perks. I could now go topside and just go about my business. It was exhilarating to just enjoy the majesty of the sea without having to be constantly aware of all that was around you. It was quite obvious when we reached deep water; I mean water over 1000 feet deep. The sea takes on a thick look and the water is almost like grape juice.

I had seldom been able to stand in the middle of the quarterdeck and watch the boat as she cut through the thick sea with a power that is comforting. I had seen this power quail at the full impact of the sea. The Torsk looked really slick with her new paint job. I thought the lines were a bit too distinct and high. The paint job was done by yard birds and was right on Navy specs. I made a note that perhaps I need to adjust my scheme next time I repaint. It didn't occur to me that my two years would be up in less than two months.

Keeping the navigation books up to date was my main job. It was not just an every once in a while thing. The pages and line changes were a constant chore. I made it a point to post all our books. A lot of guys would file the corrections away on the books that were unlikely to be used. I would spend my spare time making corrections in all the books. I remember adding a line to a book covering a seldom sailed section of the South Pacific. It was not a precise location, but a report of a mountain that came within five hundred feet of the surface. I seriously thought of omitting such an addition. I posted it anyway.

We were back in Captain King's world now. We drilled over and over. The Caribbean was calling.

The Torsk moored at the U.S. Army Depot at 1605 hours May 20, 1959. We spent one night in Old San Juan. It was not the same without Ron Rico! – Oh – He was there! – We just didn't speak! It was OK. I really enjoyed the scenery and old world luster. I sat in the square and watched the old men play checkers and the young men play with the girls. There was a constant breeze and there is always a rustling sound as the gentle wind moves through the palms. The Island Spanish is like a melody and I knew this was probably the last time I would savor it.

"Hey! – Lynn – still on the wagon?" It was Mac. He had that pretty little Chiquita he had met last fall. I think she really liked Mac. We sat and talked for a while and I asked if she knew Nelly. She frowned at the name and I realized that she probably never heard her called Nelly.

"Nelwaya es la nombre – Nelwaya - comprende?" I hoped she understood.

"Si! – Si!" Nelwaya – Ella se enfermo malo!" I thought she was telling me Nelwaya was bad sick. I was never able to find out any more.

We departed San Juan the next morning and operated for the day. We moored back at the same pier for one more night before we sailed for St Thomas. I didn't go ashore.

We spent Saturday, May 23 sailing to St Thomas. The water in the Caribbean is not deep until you hit the Puerto Rican Trench to the north of the Islands. It has that beautiful clear aqua green look that is so appealing to the eye. The water has inspired a paint color that is so prevalent throughout the Islands and South Florida. It is a magnificent view to cruise through the peaceful sea and watch the sea life around you.

We reached St Thomas at 1605 hours for one day. I made my last pass through town and once again relished the old world atmosphere. No one seemed to have a care in the world. I didn't either.

The Torsk departed the Caribbean on May 25th, 1959. We sailed for three days and operated with the USS Requin SS 481. When not operating, we porpoised and chalked up over forty dives to add to our record. It was amazing to see the Torsk as Captain King would trim her bow high in the water and her stern low to give the screws a lot of water to pull. We could clip along at twenty-six knots. I had old diesel sailors call me a liar when I would brag about our speed, but it doesn't matter, I was there and could watch the other boats fade away in the distance. We made Norfolk on May 29th, 1959 at 1425 hours. I slept the whole weekend.

The Torsk rested for a week in Norfolk. I spent my time practicing flashing light. Mac and Johnny were like pros by now and would practice at length to help me improve. I paid them back by handling the updates to the navigation logs. I didn't mind, as I would read the updates and let my imagination run wild as I would try to imagine what transpired to cause such a change.

There were considerable changes and corrections to the navigation books covering the Malaysian Islands and New Zealand. The corrections give no reason for the changes. I gathered that due to the numerous depth changes and coastal terrain changes, that volcanos and earth quakes were very prominent in that part of the world.

That upper hatch on the conning tower struck again. We were at sea on Tuesday June 9, 1959 when Mac relieved me at watch. As I stepped toward the hatch to go below deck, the spring that holds the hatch up, broke with a loud snap. The resulting shock caused the retaining latch to jump enough for the hatch to move and the slight port roll of the Torsk caused the hatch to slam down on my left foot.

Words cannot express the pain as the massive steel dome struck the instep of my left foot. It took two men to lift the hatch from my foot. The hatch had claimed another victim. We were not due to moor in Norfolk until Friday. The foot was a massive bruise. The hatch had landed directly on the left cuneiform bone of the big toe. The massive weight had flattened this bone and transferred the bruising to all four of the cuneiform bones of the remaining toes. Walking was out of the question. I spent the rest of the day sitting in the chow hall updating navigation books.

Doc Johanson gave me a multitude of shots of something new called antibiotics. He said it was the answer to infections. I got so many shots, I don't think even love could have infected me.

When we docked in Norfolk late that Friday, I was immediately transferred to sick bay on our tender, the USS Orion. The medical staff on the tender could handle anything. Within an hour I was feeling no pain, as a matter of fact, I don't even remember anything for a couple of days. I spent over a week in the Orion sick bay.

I woke up on Friday to hear Tom Nichol whining. He was in the bunk next to me. It was comical, because his condition was uncommon for a grown man. Tom had recently married his high school sweetheart. Tom had never been circumcised and had developed an infection. The Navy was pleased to provide this service to one of their finest sailors. Circumcision is not for the whimpy adult, especially for a newly married guy.

The sailors in sick bay would talk of nothing else but sexy stuff and kept Nichols pleading for pain killers and relief. It was particularly bad in the wee hours of early morning when it is natural for a male to grow along with his need to urinate. We were a cruel lot to have such a laugh at Nichols expense.

Sunday morning saw me much improved and I was released from sick bay. I walked back to my Torsk and felt an eerie sense of depression as I looked at her long sleek shape in the early morning mist. She was quiet and serene.

Al Lowerre was topside watch. "Welcome back – Wardy -- we missed ya Buddy!" He smiled and I felt good. It is amazing how one's attitude can change with just a few words. I went below and had my last breakfast on my Torsk.

Our new Chief of the Boat, Cunningham, came into the chow hall and informed me the new Executive Officer Mr. Bade was back.   Mr Bibby had transferred.   Mr. Bade was a fine officer, but I felt a loss with Mr. Bibby gone.

"The Exec wants to see you immediately – Wardy -- better hurry- we don't have a lot of time!"   Chief Cunningham seemed unusually distant.

"Chief -- come on -- I've been in sick bay for a week! -- how can I get in trouble this quick?" I was really concerned.

"No trouble -- Wardy – just go to the ward room – Son -- Mr. Bade will explain!" The chief was dead serious. I sopped the last of my baked beans with a piece of cornbread, deposited my plate in the sink and made my way to the ward room.

Mr. Bade was seated at the end of the table and motioned me to take the seat at the far end of the table. It was early Sunday morning and there was nowhere near a full crew on board our Torsk.   I noticed Mr. Bade had my military folder in front of him.

He looked at me and with a serious smile, he said. "There hasn't been a dull moment since you've been here – Wardlaw -- and you know what? – That ain't bad!"

Looking for sympathy, I childishly pleaded. "Mr. Bade – I've been in sick bay!"

Mr. Bade laughed and stated. "Easy sailor! – no trouble here - but we are on a tight schedule!"

He then explained; my time as a reservist on active duty was done. I now had to make a decision. The Torsk was leaving tomorrow for a short sea exercise and then on to the grand opening of the St. Lawrence Seaway and a cruise to the Great Lakes. This was a first for American Warships. Only the best of the Atlantic fleet was to be a part of this epic adventure.

Wardy -- when this cruise is over -- there is an OCS class waiting on you in September! – But you can't do it as a reserve -- son! – You gotta ship over! – I've got the papers right here!" Mr. Bade looked at me with expectation.

I was in shock. I had not realized that the time would come so soon. I had never wanted to go home, I was happy here on my Torsk. I didn't think of tomorrow, I didn't want to think of tomorrow. My nightmare was only beginning. I was trembling. I was not in a position to think rationally. God's plan was at work.

"Mr. Bade! – I need to call home and ------------!

"Oh! – That reminds me - Wardy -- I almost forgot! – Here is a telegram that came for you!" He picked up the folder and took the sealed envelope from under it and handed it to me. I instantly thought, this is one area the Navy could improve on. This was the second time the Navy had neglected to inform me of something in a timely manner.

I opened the envelope and it was from my Daddy. The Telephone Company had contacted them and wanted a response from me regarding holding my job. I could not believe the timing of this occurrence. My decision was made.

"Mr. Bade! -- What happens now -- if I say I want to go home?" I asked reluctantly.

"Simple – Wardy -- I just fill out some papers and you go pack your gear. – Catch the bus and you will be at Norfolk Separation Center in time for dinner!"

"I'll miss you guys!" I said, as I rose and turned my head. I didn't want Mr. Bade to see the tears. It wouldn't be right for a man just offered a commission in the U.S. Navy to be seen crying."

I made my way to my bunk and began packing. It is not a time consuming affair for a sailor to pack his sea bag. Most everything is stowed in a condition to be placed straight in the bag. The most extensive effort is to role the uniforms that you had stretched out. I was done in twenty minutes, luckily my laundry had been returned and Mac had stowed them for me.

I went in search of my buddies of the Fabulous Five and only found Dave Cummings. I told him goodby and please tell the other guys I would miss em.

On the way topside, Catfish told me he was privileged to know me. He then said something I never fully understood. He told me I was a "Plain White Man." I knew it wasn't anything bad, so I thanked him and left my Torsk.

At the head of the pier was that familiar grey bus with the Naval Base destination name above the front windshield. I turned to look at my Torsk as she lay serenely in the waters of Chesapeake Bay. She was alone. Tied up next to pier 21. She was proud as I admired her seamless paint lines that blended so well. She was lean, mean and a most beautiful machine and I loved her. I shouldered my sea bag, turned my back, it's not good to see a Submarine Qualified, Third Class Quartermaster cry.

CHAPTER XIV

DEATH

The chow was lousy. I suppose it was due to a Sunday afternoon and most everybody was on liberty. I made sure I was checked in correctly and in the right barracks. The Norfolk Naval Base had not been kind to me, in the past. It was not going to change now. God's plan shifted into high gear.

I found another Wardlaw that night. He was a second class gunners mate and was getting out after a four year hitch. I was really pleased to meet a distant cousin, but he didn't seem to be interested in passing any time with me. He was my age and from around Orangeburg, S.C. He had not enjoyed his tour at all and was eager to muster out. I didn't understand his attitude at all. He was young and made second class in his first tour, so he had to be on the ball, but that was his attitude. He felt the three days it took to muster out was too long.

Monday dawned bright and pleasant. About twenty of us mustered on the side of the barracks and listened as our names were called and we were told the schedule for our medical exams that were necessary for discharge. I really didn't understand why I was in with the dischargees, as I was simply going back to another four years as a reserve. I was told as far as the regular Navy was concerned I was treated the same way as a dischargee.

The medical exams went as usual with the Navy. They drew some blood, looked in all my orifices, bent me over and made me cough. "Piece - o - Cake."

I couldn't help but think of my Torsk. I knew she was submerged by now. I wondered if Catfish took her out. I felt jealous, thinking of someone else at the wheel when we went to battle stations. I wondered how long it would take for the new setup to become as smooth as when I was there. I could feel the tears well in my eyes. Had I made a mistake? Is this what I really wanted, to go home, and not be a part of the Torsk anymore. I put the thoughts out of my mind as I made my way back to the barracks.

The Petty Officer in charge assigned me to the laundry room. Like I said before, you will never just set around in the Navy during working hours. It was a pie job. I had access to big machines and washed the sheets and pillow cases. The sailors used the coin machines and took care of their own laundry. I just kept the laundry room clean. I didn't bother with any of my personal laundry as I was supposed to leave in two days.

The breakfast served on Tuesday was decent. I had three fried eggs, hash brown potatoes, biscuits and gravy. The coffee was not nearly as good as the Torsk coffee. I wondered why? I went to the galley to see if by some chance, Smoke was still there. I knew there was not much chance, sure enough, no one even remembered him. I walked around the base, remembering my previous experience and felt a deep sense of depression. I went back to my barracks and threw myself into my work in the laundry room.

The PO noticed my work intensity and rewarded me by not scheduling me for any watches. In the U.S. Navy, someone is always on watch.

I wondered if anyone on the Torsk had asked where I was. I felt the tears again. I threw on another load of sheets.

Late Tuesday afternoon, I saw a familiar face pass by the laundry room door. I couldn't place the face right off and went to the door to watch where he went. The sailor was bunking in a wing of the dorm for permanent personal. Sudden recognition flashed in my mind, it was Carlos Mobley, the magnificent quarterback on our high school football team.

Carlos had taken our high school team to the state championship game and had signed to play professional baseball straight out of high school.

We talked for a while and he told me things just had not worked out with the New York team and he was now playing service ball in the Navy. He was heading for practice and we had no more time to talk.

Wednesday morning, as soon as breakfast was done, I returned to the barracks and packed my gear. We mustered outside at 0900 hours and the PO began reading off the names of those that were leaving that day. My name, as usual, was at the end of the list.

Wardlaw! – You must report back to medical! – The PO's voice was matter of fact in tone.

I was shocked and asked why.

"Don't know – Buddy -- just says to report back! – It does say IMMEDIATELY!" He stressed the immediately.

I made my way back into the barracks and retrieved my gear from the staging area for departure. I threw my bag and duffle on my bunk and started across the two blocks to the hospital. It was a brilliant day with a slight breeze blowing across the bay.

I took the steps up the entrance to the Hospital Administration Office two at a time. The PO at the check- in took my name and looked me over as he went down a list on a clip board. He buzzed a male attendant to direct me to the Medical Commanding Officer's Office.

The attendant was a tall, colored, third class corpsman. As we proceeded down the hall the corpsman turned to me and whispered lowly. "You're one sick f__ker -- boy! – You know that? -- Yassuh! – You're one sick white boy! You got the syph! –Boy -- A whopping big case of the syph!" He was leering as I looked at him in disbelief.

I went numb as the words sank in. I had heard the term syph before and knew it was short for syphilis. I knew syphilis was a venereal disease and was much worse than gonorrhea. It never occurred to me that I would have any disease like that. I never questioned the corpsman, but followed him to the Commanding Officers office. He announced me at the door. As I entered, I looked into the face of the young colored corpsman and saw an expression that clearly expressed an attitude of "It serves you right!" I was still in a state of shock as I sat down at the desk of the Medical Officer.

I don't remember the rank or the name of the Base Medical Commanding Officer, but his tan coat and cap hung on a rack at the corner of his office and they had enough scrambled egg on them to provide breakfast to the base.

He calmly took a folder from in front of him and I could see my name typed on the front of the document. He sat a moment and scrutinized the contents. He pulled a handkerchief from his pocket and began to wipe his face and brow. He kept the handkerchief in his hand the entire time he talked to me and was continually wiping his face.

As he spoke he looked intently at my face and truly had a look of concern. "Have you been feeling well -- Son?" He asked with a tone of expectancy.

I answered with a subconscious reply. I told him I was feeling fine and then asked why the corpsman said I had the syph.

"He shouldn't have told you anything -- Son! – That's why you are in my office! – You see -- you've got the highest concentration of syphilis I – personally -- have ever seen in anyone's blood! – Your blood stream is teaming with this disease!" He grew silent.

My world collapsed. A darkness came over me that the brightness of day coming through the window could not penetrate. My surroundings became surreal. The Commanding Officer's voice seemed to be in a barrel, and even the chair I sat in seemed to be suspended. There was an echo to everything that was said. The Commanding Officer had to repeat himself numerous times in talking to me.

"Have you had many sores and lesions? -- How is your vision?" He asked hundreds of questions. He explained. He was trying to establish how advanced the disease was in my system.

My head was spinning. No man is prepared for this kind of news. My mind was suddenly shocked with a vision of the front page of the newspaper with headlines reading of the death of Al Capone. Capone had been dead about ten years when a front page story was written of his death in Miami. I remembered the sordid details of how his body was ravaged with syphilis. I read of how the disease ate away at the brain and caused blindness and deafness, not to mention the sores and eating away at the flesh. I suddenly felt dirty and corrupt. I knew now, why the Commanding Officer felt the need to wipe his face with the handkerchief.

The questions kept coming, not just about my health, but about my association with the people of the past months. The Commanding Officer explained that the syphilis germ does not just go away. It will hide in your body and lie in wait for your body to weaken. The germ can be transmitted to any one you are intimate with. I really tried to give all the information I could, but the shame of people being tested because of their association with me was overwhelming. I felt as if I was a pestilence to the world. The Commanding Officer voiced an opinion that my excellent physical condition and strong immune system had probably kept the disease from spreading quickly over my body, but the disease would not just go away.

"Son -- the United States Navy has a duty to perform and that requires me to take your liberty card and require you to be quarantined to the restricted wing of your barracks! -- You will not be allowed to leave the base or to take your meals with the general forces! --We are going to take some more blood from you now and map out a treatment program!"

He paused and looked at me with pity. "I'm not trying to give you any hope – Son -- from all indications - the concentration of the germ in your blood stream is far too great for that -- I'm just saying that your future will not be pleasant! Son -- there is no recovery from this disease when it is this advanced!"

The next few hours were a blur, as test were administered and I was examined by a bevy of medical people. The atmosphere was intimidating, as all wore mask and gloves and treated me as if I were a specimen rather than a human being. It didn't bother me, as I felt I didn't have the right to be a human being. The shame and guilt was overwhelming and I withdrew into a state of depression.   As I moved about the facility for various test and examinations, I began to feel that all efforts were unnecessary, I moved as a zombie. I was unable to focus on anything and was guided by attendants everywhere I went. No one recovered from this disease when it had such a hold on you. I realized that all the procedures being performed on me were an effort to gain knowledge to help others.

I made my way back to the barracks and moved to the second floor restricted wing. I was the only one in the whole wing. I guess, I was, indeed, the sickest white boy in the U.S. Navy.

Self-pity set in with the darkness. I lay in my rack and wondered if the guy that lay here before me was still alive. It suddenly hit me. I was dead. A truism came into my mind; the human body has too distinct states. You are alive or dead. There are many variables of each, but ultimately it is only one or the other. There was no need to sleep, I was going to die! There was no need to eat, I was going to die. There was no need to bathe, I was going to die. There was no need to speak; no one listens to a dead man.

The world seemed hollow and my thoughts seemed to echo in my mind. I had not felt any tears yet as the numbness was overpowering.   I suddenly realized I had not been to Church in over two years. My mind turned to God.

I rose from my bunk and clumsily pulled on my shoes. I remembered Brother Blackwell's words as he would tell us the importance of prayer.   Brother Blackwell was our Pastor at Clayton P. Miller Methodist Church where I had been an active member. I knew I could pray right by my bunk, but I had a burning desire to be in God's house.

I stumbled through the darkness, the watch at the barracks door, reminded me not to leave the base. I made my way two blocks to the Chapel and entered the dark Sanctuary. The only light came through the stained glass windows and fell on the modest Alter that stretched across the front of the small Sanctuary.

I fell on my knees at the Alter and all the self-pity that had built in me came forth in a torrent of tears.

"WHY DID YOU DO THIS TO ME - GOD?" I screamed in desperation. I heard nothing except the silence that seemed to be a crescendo of echoes.

"WHAT DID I DO TO DESERVE THIS?" My tears and sobs were uncontrollable.

Still the silence was overpowering. I heard nothing. I suddenly realized that God did not hear me. I was talking to oblivion. I was dead. Dead men don't talk. The realization hit me that whatever you do after death does not count, it's what you do while alive that counts, in the eyes of the Lord. I had not been to Church my entire time in the Navy. I had not even attended a Bible study session that Ferrand conducted every Sunday on my Torsk. I felt I was unworthy to even try to pray.

The self-pity faded away, but the emptiness of death still remained. I began to think of suicide. It would be easy to walk down to the bay and simply sink, but what was the use, I was already dead. I was simply waiting for my journey to hell to begin. I felt, I was in hell already.

The tears had stopped and as I knelt, my mind began to form thoughts I had never even considered. People never really think they will die. We talk about it and we see friends and relatives pass away, but somehow we never really think we will die. I was dead, spiritually. My body still breathed and the blood flowed in my veins and I moved about, but that part of me that was going to eternity was dead and I was not going to heaven.

The words of the many atheists I knew came back to me. "That heaven crap is for the birds - Man! – When you're dead - you're dead and there is nothing after that!"

My mind asked me if I ever remembered not being here, did I ever remember not being alive. In reality, none of us can remember not being here, but we never question the fact that there was a time when we weren't here. But that may not be true.

Science has proven that you can't make something out of nothing. Everything that exists is made up of other stuff. Every person is made of basically, two parts. One part is the egg from the mother and the other part the fertilization from the father. These components existed in the parents of these parents and so on, right on back to the creation of man.

My mind suddenly exploded with the thought that God did, indeed, create every one that ever lived, lives now and ever will live, when he created that first man and woman. My mind was filled with a barrage of weird thoughts that I did not fully understand.

I realized that I had been here since the beginning of man. God created me when he created the first man. I was two different parts existing over the milleniums in my ancestors. I didn't have any recollection of that, but it accounts for the feeling that I had always been here.

Another question formed in my mind: what was the purpose of life. God's plan calls for a carefully balanced universe in order to exist and be functional. The most advanced life form in the universe is man. Science has proven that. Nothing is ever fully destroyed. A giant rock can be crushed and lose its form, but it still exists, just in a different form and mass. A forest can be burned in a mighty blaze, but the gases and ashes still represent the trees in a different form. Water can be transformed from a liquid to a solid and then to a gas and then be condensed back to water a thousand miles away. God's nature was full of examples of things continuing to exist in different forms. How could man be any different?

The sudden truth hit me. We are not any different. This short span of time we exist here on this earth is the time we condition our soul to exist in the kingdom of Heaven. Our earthly death is the moment we give up our soul and commit it to eternity. That is the only theory that fits into what we all know as life. Heaven is being in the company of God. God is as the body of man. We are in his image. There is no room in the body of God for the sins of man.

God had not done anything to me; I had done it to myself. The close calls with death, while on my Torsk, flashed through my mind. We almost sank in the North Atlantic after leaving England. I had almost died in the storm that crunched the sail on my Torsk. I had slowly watched the water rise, as the conning tower flooded in the Carribean. Three strikes; I was out.

"He shall come as a thief in the night!" This prediction of Jesus' return, rang in my head. God gave his word to the ancient people and gave intricate detail on how to live. We couldn't do it. God then sent his son to show us how to live. We still couldn't get it right.

I was still on my knees as the realization of my plight finally set in. I was doomed to hell. It was not that God didn't love me; it was I loved the things of the world more than God.

I knew God wasn't listening to me. I simply asked Jesus to talk to God for me and I would do whatever he asked for the rest of my life, however short that may be.

I slept fitfully that night. The faceless lady came, but stood off in the distance and turned her back on me. I felt desperately alone. I thought of my Momma and Daddy. I hoped that they would never find out what I died from. The shame and blackness was overpowering.

The days that followed simply melted into each other. The PO assigned me the job of distributing sleeping gear and making out the watch detail. I heard every story in the book about why a sailor needed one more night in Norfolk. I tried to accommodate as many as possible. I didn't want anyone to be unhappy. It was something new for me. I walked in a daze for two weeks.

I was summoned back to the Hospital numerous times for more blood and tissue samples. On Thursday morning June 18, 1959, I was returning from breakfast, as I crossed the street in front of my barracks, I heard my name called from the base wide speaker system. It was probably the first time in the past weeks that I was truly aware of an occurrence. I was totally focused on the fact that I was alive and heard my name called on the base PA system. It had an effect on me that sent me into a deeper depression.

What was next? Was an announcement being made that I was a risk to the base, apprehend me at all cost and was my secret going to be made public to the whole innocent world. Again my name was being called and I was to report to the base hospital immediately.

This was it. The Base Hospital Commander was going to make arrangements for my funeral. I wanted my parents there, but was filled with shame, thinking of them looking down at me with shame and pity. I wondered if the Navy could just lie and say I was lost at sea.

As I approached the doors to the Hospital I could see two attendants waiting, they began to motion for me to hurry. I felt no eagerness to comply and this drew some agitation from them. I didn't care. I was not being mean or belligerent, but they had to understand, dead people simply don't get in a hurry.

I was abruptly rushed into the quarantined wing of the Hospital and the masks and gloves went to work on me immediately. It was a semiconscious blur. I didn't mind the blood that was drawn and they didn't seem to care how much they took. But the long needles that went deep into my abdomen were painful. The needles were fairly large and had a tiny scoop type end; they were by far the worst of the ordeal. I voiced no complaint. I knew they were following orders and had no desire to punish me. Still I felt like a specimen rather than a fellow human being. I guess that was some more of that self pity.

I was ushered back to Commanding Officer's office and his face was as cold and stern as chiseled marble. He looked intently into my face and then quickly lifted my arms and felt under my arm pits. He ordered me to sit down and I fully expected him to say for me not make plans for lunch as I would not be around that long. I wondered if the Navy provided flowers at their funerals.

"Son – I'm Sorry if we upset you but we're afraid the disease has gone into remission and we need to find where it is hiding! – You see - this is most unusual at this stage and were going to send some cultures to Walter Reed for an in-depth analysis. We may be dealing with a new strain of syphilis and need to identify it immediately!"

He had a deep look of concern on his face. I didn't know what he was thinking, maybe a new plague or something. "By the way! – How have you been feeling?" He asked.

"Sir! – I have not been sick if that's what you're asking!" The sound of my voice was alien to me. I realized that I had not spoken in days. The last time I could remember hearing my own voice was in the dark lonesome hours I spent in the Base Chapel. The blackness and isolation of that night was burnt deep in my memory. I had sought God, but my guilt and sin was far too great for me to be allowed to speak to God.

The Commanding Officer allowed me to go back to my barracks and as I was catching up on my work I began to feel that sense of hopelessness set in again. I would absorb myself in work to keep my mind off my plight. The days dragged slowly by. The nights were worse, when I did manage to sleep the faceless lady refused to look at me.

Friday June 26, 1959. I woke early to find a note on my work desk to report to the Medical Commanding Officers Office at 0900. I realized that I had not been back to the hospital in over a week.

Time didn't seem to matter much to a dead man. I remembered not looking at people; I suppose I didn't want to see them look at me. I felt unclean and unfit to associate with my fellow man. I was existing in hell without fire, I felt sure that the fire was coming. Everything I did was out of reflex; I had no will to do anything.

I didn't bother to go to breakfast. I had to sit in a special area with a somewhat smaller serving section. I was not allowed to eat near the base forces. On occasions I was aware of the scrutiny from the other guys. They knew I was under quarantine but none knew to what extent my misery was.

0900 Hours found me walking up the steps to the base hospital. I walked through the hall directly to the Commanding Officer's Office. I had not seen the colored corpsman since that first day. His leering look of satisfaction plagued me in my mental agony and I really wondered what had I ever done to him. I suppose he drew satisfaction in knowing that a white guy was in misery. I couldn't understand that type of thinking.

The corpsman in the anti-room ushered me into the Commanding Officers Office and told me to wait. I sat in solitude and silence. I was not concerned about the meeting. I was complacent and resolved to my fate. The Commander came in and never looked at me. He reached into the center drawer of his desk and handed me a letter.

I reached for the paper and he pulled it back just enough to stop me. "Read this carefully and when you fully understand it -- we will talk about your alternatives! Do you understand me?" His voiced cracked a little.

I remember this as unusual, but in my mental state, I didn't care. I was already dead and nothing else mattered.

The letter was not in its envelope and folded the customary three ways. I had no interest in its content and simply went through the motions as requested. The top of the single page was emblazoned with a gold and maroon crest and in bold letters, it read; WALTER REED MILITARY HOSPITAL.

The letter was addressed to the Commander of the Norfolk Naval Hospital and began; DEAR SIR: IF YOU AND YOUR STAFF ARE SO INCOMPETENT AS TO

NOT BE ABLE TO DETECT THE DIFFERENCE BETWEEN A SYPHLIS GERM AND AN ANTIBIOTIC, THEN YOU SHOULD ALL BE COURT MARTIALED FOR THE MENTAL ANGUISH YOU HAVE INFLICTED UPON THIS YOUNG SAILOR! I was stunned and slowly read the lines again.

My mental focus had been dormant for over two weeks and I was thinking perhaps this was another dream. I looked out the window at the rear of the Commanding Officers office. It was another brilliant day and slowly the realization of what I had read began to sink in.

I focused and mentally convinced myself I was fully awake. I remembered I had a gum infection that had given me problems. I simply thought it was part of my condition. I placed my tongue against the upper left wisdom teeth and gave a slight sucking and the pain immediately convinced me I was truly awake. I re-read the top line of the letter. It did say, what the medical staff thought was the syphilis germ was simply an antibiotic.

I could begin to feel the elation of new life and hope returning. I glanced at the rest of the letter and it simply referred to some additional information that gave in-depth results of the test. God's plan was still at work.

I looked at the Commanding Officer and asked. "Does this mean - I'm cured?" I could feel the tears welling in my eyes.

The Commanding Officer smiled as he sat down and replied. "Young man - you were never sick to begin with -- you see --we thought we had a pretty thorough staff here and depended on our standard test and procedures to provide us with sufficient information to make intelligent diagnosis. - Your case has changed all that!"

He leaned forward in his chair and I could tell he was fully committed to setting the record straight. I was fully focused now and was really interested in what was transpiring. Who wouldn't be interested in coming back to life after being dead?

It seems that antibiotics had some peculiar properties. I have no medical training other than Navy Survival, Red Cross First Aid and emergency training at the telephone company, but I'll try to tell what the doctor explained to me.

It started when the upper hatch fell on my foot. The bone was badly bruised and since we were at sea, Doc Johanson gave me shots of a general antibiotic to prevent infection. When we arrived back in Norfolk, I was sent to sick bay on the Orion and they also gave me massive injections of antibiotics. I went from sick bay to my Torsk and then to the Norfolk Base and the Medical exam all within two days. My blood test contained a much higher concentration of the antibiotics than the Medical Staff was accustomed to seeing, so they had it tested.

Antibiotics are used to fool your body's immune system into thinking it has an infection or disease. The antibiotics are not real germs and are essentially dead. Your body's immune system only knows it has a threat and responds to fight the invader.

The lab technicians simply saw my blood teeming with a foreign body and the shape of the antibodies were very similar to the syphilis germ. The lab technicians were always on guard for any germ that might cause problems to the troops and the alarm went up.

The syphilis germ, although not rampant, is not an unusual occurrence in the Navy. It is treatable in very early stages, but still is a very dangerous germ. The concentration of the antibiotic in my blood stream indicated I was well advanced with the disease and thus my condemnation came about.

The Doctor seemed as relieved as I was. He apologized profusely and assured me that lab procedures would never be the same again after this fiasco.

"Well Doctor! – As far as I'm concerned -- it's a miracle! – I was sick and now I'm cured! – I was dead and now I'm alive! – That's a miracle in my book! – Praise the Lord!"

I was beginning to feel a little giddy as the now healthy blood surged through my veins. I was developing a vibrant inner rhythm that was hard to control. A whole new concept of life was being formed in my mentality. I was beginning to understand the feeling of being born again.

"You fully understand, it was all a mistake -- a result of a careless testing error, don't you -- Son?" He was looking for an assurance that I was not going to cause a problem with the situation. He had no worry. My new outlook on life would not allow me to knowingly inflict any anguish on anyone.

I looked at the Doctor and with obvious joy in my voice, I answered. "Error to you! - Miracle to me!"

He was stunned, but his body English told me he accepted my response with resolve.

"Alright - my Boy -- here are some options! – We've reviewed your records and we are reminding you that your OCS option is still available. If you ship over today there is some incentive money and we will give you your choice of duty immediately. We will even send you to meet your Boat at the first port of call.

You don't have enough time in grade to advance to Quartermaster 2nd class yet, but you have enough tenure, over all, to be 2nd class so we can arrange for you to take the test. How's that sound?" The Commanding Officer was obviously relieved to see I wasn't angry over the past few weeks.

I wanted out. The Norfolk Naval Base did not like me. That was obvious.

"Sir -- I want to go home!" I looked at him and made the statement with my head turned down and looking at him under my eyebrows. I wanted no further discussion.

He got the message. "Alright – Sailor - go pack your gear and I'll have a car pick you up and take you wherever you want to depart from! - Is that OK?"

I agreed and left the office. I really wanted to see the colored corpsman and tell him of my miracle, but God would not allow me that selfish satisfaction.

I took a breath of God's clean fresh air as I walked from the hospital. I felt so incredibly clean. I was reborn and my whole being buzzed with thanks to my GOD.

CHAPTER XV

BORN AGAIN

I had mentioned before, it doesn't take a sailor long to pack up. I was up and waiting when a '58 Plymouth painted in that familiar Navy grey drove up and a seaman got out. I introduced myself to him and he opened the back door for me and my gear. I threw my two seabags in the back seat. I had gained another bag in my two week stay at the discharge center. It was filled with things that I could use as a reserve that guys leaving were simply throwing away, even in my depressed state I couldn't bear to throw good stuff away. A sailor had to be careful though. If he ever got in trouble and clothing or belongings that had another man's name on it was found in his possession, he could be in big trouble. I carried my duffle in front with me.

"You gonna hafta sit in back – Bud -- passengers ain't allowed up front with drivers!" The young seaman was telling me what his instructions had been. I wasn't going to give him a hard time but I opened the front passenger door and got in just the same. He looked in the driver's door and repeated the backseat request.

"It doesn't matter – driver -- we can go by the Hospital and see what the Commanding Officer has to say about it. -- If he tells me to get in the back and gives me some pills to keep me from getting sick -- then I'll do it – OK?"

I was matter of fact as I could be. I knew from past experience how far confidence would take you in unusual circumstances. I had already surmised that the Navy wanted me out of Norfolk as soon as possible.

He got in and looked me over. "You somebody special?" He quizzed.

I couldn't help but laugh. "No – Believe me – I'm not special to anyone but God!"

I proceded to tell him my story, he didn't drive to the Hospital but took me straight to the bus station. As we pulled up in the parking lot he exited the car and his helpful mood was much improved. As we walked across the lot I voiced my dread of the long ride home on a bus.

"Hey Man! – You been through hell! – Look – I'll take you anywhere you want – You wanta go by train – Plane – You name it! – I'll take you there!" He was serious.

A thought suddenly struck me. I was gonna hitch home. I enjoyed hitchhiking and had only one bad experience. I asked him if he could go about fifty miles out of town without getting in trouble.

I explained that I had hitched home and back a few times in the last few years and the Shore Patrol never bothered me after I was over fifty miles from Norfolk.

He looked at his watch, it was close to 1100 hours. He did some quick figuring and said he didn't think it would be a problem.

I went into the Bus Station and checked my bags to Savannah and paid the charge. I hustled back to the car and we headed out of town on Highway 58. We reached a little town called Franklin and I felt comfortable.

I bid farewell to my driver and he headed back to Norfolk. I don't think I was anywhere near fifty miles yet but the town was small and I stood in front of a small café. It was close to lunch and there was quite a lot of traffic.

I saw a tow truck park at the café with an address on U.S. 301, Emporia, Virginia. I remembered U.S Highway 301 would take me south where I could cross over to U.S. 21 and then U.S. 17 and straight into Savannah. I waited for the driver to come out of the restaurant and approached him.

He seemed congenial and I asked him if I could ride with him as far as Emporia. He said he would appreciate the company, but he would have to let me off a couple of blocks shy of U.S. 301, so his boss wouldn't see me. That was fine and the ride went quick. He was really enthused about me being on a submarine. I had time to tell him the story of the jammed hatch and flooded conning tower. He couldn't believe a man would seal himself up to drown.

I tried to explain how training can prepare you for anything and it was not really a heroic action. I suppose the tow guy was in his early thirties and it appeared his total travels had been only as far as his tow truck had ever taken him. He really was sorry he had to put me out early and he actually took me to the corner at U.S.301 before he turned south to go to the service station.

I waited until he made his turn and watched as he pulled into the service station. I crossed the highway and sat my bag down to position myself for thumbing. I saw it was only about a block and a half to the station.

I decided to walk to the station and get a coke. I would then walk to the south side of town to begin hitching. My experience had taught me that thumbing on the entering side of town reduced your chances of a lengthy ride.

I walked into the service station and immediately the driver saw me. His eyes grew wide; he probably thought I was going to give him away. I went to the coke machine and reached into my pocket. I faked not having enough change and asked for some help. The owner opened the register and proceeded to change my dollar.

I asked both of them. "How about a coke on the U.S. Navy -- I got my muster out money and I'll treat!" The owner declined, but the driver was relieved and burst into a big smile as he accepted.

I stepped outside to enjoy the slight summer breeze and the cold coke. It was a little past noon and the afternoon was going to be hot on the highway.

A brand spanking new Oldsmobile 98 pulled in and stopped at the gas pump. This was a good looking car. It was two tone light blue on white, with white interior. The windows were up so I knew it had that new factory air conditioning. The tires were also that new thin white wall that was the latest rage. It had the high taillights with a little fin on top of each side. It was truly a fine machine.

The driver looked out of place. He looked in his sixties. He was tall and slim, wore glasses and was partially bald. His dress was business attire with the tie loose and his coat thrown over the passenger seat. He got out of the car and as the tow driver approached he ordered a fill up and asked the driver to check everything, especially the tires. He walked into the station and I could see him talking to the boss.

The boss pointed to the rest room and the man disappeared inside. I finished my coke and set the bottle in a rack near the gas island. I called to the driver and gave him a saluting wave and a nod of thanks. I proceeded out to the highway and started south on my last hitch-hike home.

It was a glorious day and my heart was light with a new feeling of happiness and freedom. I didn't bother to stick out my thumb for at least a block or two from the station. Emporia was not a large place, by any means, but I was going quite a way down the road so drivers just going a mile or two would not help much.

I didn't see the big Olds when he left the station but I recognized it as he slowly passed me by. I had never made eye contact with the man driving and really didn't know if he ever saw me at the station, but it was evident he was looking me over as he drove by. He went almost the whole block before he abruptly stopped and began to back up.

It is courtesy for a hitchhiker to hustle when a car stops for him, so I hustled. The driver saw me coming and began to move forward.

I stopped and thought. "Was this old guy playing that game where you make the hitcher chase you?" I was wrong. He was only pulling off the highway.

I approached the passenger door; I suddenly went cold with the thought. "God – Please don't let this guy be looking for a "good time!" I hesitated as I reached for the door handle. The door was locked. The man leaned across the seat and rolled the window down just enough to talk through.

"Son - I've never pick up a hitchhiker before and the only reason I'm stopping now is because that man at the service station said you were a hero and needed a ride home!" He was apprehensive.

I was dumbfounded, me a hero, I suddenly remembered how impressed the tow driver was with my story. I humbly laughed and leaned over to speak through the partially opened window. "I'm no hero, Sir. I was just doing what I was trained to do!"

The man unlocked the door and threw his jacket onto the back seat. There was a small green metal thermos box on the floor board of the car. The man told me just to move it aside. There was plenty of room for my feet and I sat on the cool white leather seat. It may have been some of that new Naugahyde stuff that was the rage in plush vehicles. I don't know what the seats were covered in, but they were nice. I turned and sat my duffle on the back seat. I also straighten his coat. I noticed, he looked at me when I moved his coat, but he didn't say anything.

He checked traffic and pulled out onto the highway. I thanked him for the ride and told him I was going to Savannah. He said he was heading for Florida and he would check his map to see how close he could get me to Savannah. He introduced himself as Mr. Hughes from Boston.

I told him that if he was going to stay on Highway 301, it would put me within about 40 miles and that would be fine. I asked the man where in Florida he was going.

He stated he didn't have any special plans; he just needed a vacation and was heading south. He planned to stop for the night somewhere down the road.

I explained that going through Savannah was really not out of the way to Florida at all. We could stay on 301 until near Walterboro, South Carolina and pick up U.S. 21 to Yemassee, South Carolina and then take U.S. 17 straight to Savannah over the new Talmadge Bridge. The new bridge dumped us right into the heart of old Savannah and that would be a good place for him to stay the night.

He drove for a while and I grew quiet, thinking of my new lease on life. It was shortly after 1300 hours and less than five hours ago I was a dead man. It suddenly struck me, I had not thanked God for this miracle.

The thought of how my God had delivered me was in my mind from the instant I read the letter from Walter Reed, but I had not made that conscientious contact with my Lord and thanked him. I closed my eyes to pray a prayer of thanksgiving.

"Hey -- Son! –You can't be sleepy this early in the day – Hell! – That's old man stuff! -- If any one's gonna sleep -- it's gonna be me! – Tell me about the hero thing-- if you don't mind!" He seemed to be genuinely interested, so I began my story.

We had a long ride ahead of us, so, I took my time and I suppose I dressed the story up a bit. There was no need to dramatize anything. A flooding conning tower is dramatic enough, but I fabricated some intrigue on the part of Lessor and Mr. Hoffman. I really didn't have a clue as to how intense the occurrence was for them, as we never discussed it at length, but I felt extremely self-conscious telling the story as if I was "the man."

We drove on and Mr. Hughes was silent. He never commented on my tale, but I could tell that he was beginning to develop an interest in the thermos chest on the floorboard. Presently we stopped at a station and he excused himself to the rest room.

I waited for him to finish and took my turn. As I came out I saw him in the car on my side and he had the thermos chest open. It was loaded with Ballantine Ale on ice and he had a pint of Jack Daniels. He motioned me to get in the driver's side. I slide under the wheel and he handed me the keys.

"Can you drive one of these automatics?" I nodded affirmative. He slammed his door, unscrewed the pint, took a swig and washed it down with a double guzzle of Ballantine. His eyes puddled with water and he shook his head. "Ahhhh! – I needed that!"

He slouched back in his seat and with his free hand, pointed south. He never uttered another word as he shut his eyes. I pulled out onto the highway and began to pilot that massive Olds 98 home to Savannah.

Mr. Hughes would rouse occasionally to pull on Jack Daniels and by dark the floorboard was covered in empty Ballantine cans. 2200 hours saw me climbing the South Carolina side of the Talmadge Bridge and the lights of old Savannah glistened off to my left.

I could see the lights atop the Desoto Hotel in the heart of Old Savannah. I had tried to wake Mr. Hughes for the last twenty miles, but it was no use. The man was awash in his make-shift boiler makers.

I pulled into the little drive- up at the Desoto Hotel. The doorman helped me get Mr. Hughes into the lobby. I got his two bags from the trunk and his coat. I left the thermos where it lay in the front floorboard. He didn't need anything that may have been left in it.

Mr. Hughes sat in a huge chair in the lobby. He would half walk when urged, but was completely unresponsive to any communication. I took his wallet from his pocket and walked to the desk. The man had over $800 cash in his wallet. I checked him in and had the desk clerk lock his wallet in the safe for the night. The desk clerk voiced his concern about these unusual circumstances. I left my name and phone number and told him if any problems arose I would take care of them. He checked the phone book to make sure my name, telephone number and address agreed with the information I gave him.

I took Mr. Hughes and placed him on his bed. I didn't attempt to undress him. But I did remove his shoes. I left him a note explaining everything and thanked him for giving me a ride home. I went down to the lobby and took a taxi home. I was walking up my stairs and calming Silly Willy by 2300 hours. Dad was asleep sitting in the chair in front of the T.V. Mom was at work on the night shift. The boys were in bed.   I didn't disturb anyone. I lay on the sofa with Silly Willy in my arms and Rex on the floor at my side.   I was home and Silly Willy's broken motor didn't bother me at all.

CHAPTER XVI

GOD'S PLAN

Dad woke me about 1:30 A.M. [I'm home now, so I'll use civilian time]. He welcomed me and went straight to bed. Mom came home a little past 8:00 A.M.

It was Saturday and sunny. Everything seemed surreal. It was only one day and I was home and the Navy, my Torsk and the nightmare in hell was behind me. I never told my parents about my ordeal.

The phone rang at around 10:00 A.M. It was Mr. Hughes. He wanted me to come to the hotel for lunch and discuss a business proposition. I told him I had a job waiting and I felt an obligation to return to the Telephone Company. He said the job would only last a few months, but he needed an assistant. He explained he needed someone to look after him. I got the impression he was troubled about something. He said I would not lack for anything, within reason, while with him and the work would never be more than being a companion and seeing to his needs. I politely thanked him and refused his offer. He told me he felt privileged meeting a hero and hung up. I never heard from Mr. Hughes again.

I spent Saturday afternoon hitting my old haunts. Savannah hadn't changed much but it seemed I didn't know anyone. All my gang was gone. I went to Candler to see how the nurses were doing. It was only a week or so from graduation for the class that Patty and the girls were in.

Patty was not in, but Hanna was there. She had been Billy Miltiades girl. Claire was already graduated and working in Brunswick. Patty was engaged to a lab technician named Dave. She was supposed to get married right after graduation. I asked Hanna about Billy and she told me he was doing well with the FBI and was in Washington. They didn't communicate much and that prompted me to ask her out that night. I was surprised when she eagerly accepted.

I went home and polished up my Ford. It was good to be back, but I was beginning to feel like a kid again. I liked the man up situations the Navy presented.

I was missing the "what's next atmosphere" that exist in the fleet service of the U.S. Navy.

I picked up Hanna and we had a most enjoyable evening. It is surprising how fast a relationship can develop when you've known someone for quite a while and suddenly they arouse your interest. It was short lived, however, I let my Navy attitude with women get the better of me and I forgot how delicate our homegrown flowers are. During the course of the evening I somehow insulted Hanna and she would never go out with me again. It had a profound effect on me and ever since I have been very cautious to not transgress into that shadowy realm of female libido that so few men understands.

Sunday was a great day when I walked into Clayton Miller Methodist Church. God's plan was at work. The High School Boys teacher was ill and they had no teacher. The Sunday School Superintendent asked me if I would speak to the boys and maybe tell them about the Navy. I did not want to do that.

The words I said to the emptiness that night in the Chapel in Norfolk echoed back to my ears. Apparently the emptiness I felt was only in my heart. God did, indeed, hear me. "I'll do anything you want Lord, just ask me!"

God was asking. How could I refuse?

The boys seemed to enjoy my stories. I didn't mention the time I spent in hell. The entire Church seemed glad to see me. Brother Blackwell was gone and the Church had joined the United Methodist Association and had an appointed minister. He seemed like a nice man but was very refined.

Most of the old gang was off in college or married and moved away. The Sheppards were still there and Layton had opened a used cars business. He seemed to be doing well.

Wiley Flanders had a good job as an air conditioning technician and Jimmy Sumner was working as an accountant with the city. Billy Redd was really glad to see me. Billy had married a good looking red head and was one proud fellow. A lot of the girls that had been pigtailed squirts were now very pleasant to be around. I looked at the situation and realized that the girls were still too young for a seasoned nearly twenty-two year old sailor to get interested in.

Hey! I must remember, I'm back to being a telephone man again.

We went to Uncle C.F. and Aunt Nelva's for dinner that day. It was like I had never left. The family listened intently as I briefly took them through the two years I was on my Torsk. I never mentioned the trying time I had at my separation in Norfolk.

Monday found me at the District Office of Southern Bell Telephone Company. The old District Level Management Team was completely gone. I knew no one at all. The District Plant Manager was C.K. Spiers. His two second level managers were Ike Lynn and J.L. Whitney. I sat in a meeting with the three of them and in short order I was told to report back to 708 E. Gwinnett Street plant department on Monday the 6th of July, 1959. I had a week off.

I checked into the Naval Reserve Training Center and found that Mr. Blackburn was doing well as an Officer. The center still had weekly drills, but that was going to change soon. The Navy had deployed the U.S.S. Robinson DD562 to Charleston as a reserve training ship and the Savannah Reserve unit was going to be assigned a weekend a month to be part of the reserve crew on the Robinson.

The Unit immediately assigned me as an instructor at the center and I was given the job of preparing the young recruits with: Rules of the Road – Basic Seamanship – Personal Hygiene – Ships Nomenclature - Naval Protocol and Naval History.

It was a daunting task and I dearly loved it. I can still remember the eager faces of the new recruits as they attentively listened to a seasoned veteran, fresh from the Submarine service, tell them of the glories of service in the mightiest armada in the world.

Little did I know that in less than two years these young men would be answering their nations call as the U.S.S. Robinson was activated for the Berlin Crisis.

The telephone company put me in a cut-over crew. Our first job was putting up rural wire in Carver Village in West Savannah. The work was grueling, Mr. Shuman was a wise old foreman and would pull me down from a pole and send me on a driving mission every hour or so. I didn't realize it, but, he was simply letting me get back in shape a little at a time. Soon I was humping poles with the best of them.

Patty's sister, Mary and her husband Ed Smith were really concerned with Patty marrying a Catholic boy. Mary insisted I ask Patty out on a date and she shamed Patty into accepting on the grounds that I had served my country and wasn't home to woo her and how could she be sure if Dave was the right one and I deserved an opportunity to talk with her.

We doubled with Theo Bass and his date. The Town Tavern was the "in place" in Savannah. Patty and I had not been there many times as a couple. It generally had a more mature attendance. We had a really good time. We danced and talked of times past. She was indeed interested in my Navy experiences. It was almost like old times. Patty told me, Bill, her brother had married Sue Stafford and had moved, I think, to Atlanta.

As we were leaving, I opened the rear door of Theo's Chevy and Patty slid in. She sat very close to my side and as I slid in, I was right next to her. I took it as a sign of affection and immediately kissed her.

I felt a slight response and then she abruptly pushed me away and broke into uncontrollable tears. She began to lambast me and her sister and everyone she could think of, that thought Dave was not right for her. She told me how unfair it was for me to come back after all this time and play on her emotions.

I suddenly realized that I was indeed back to playing my old game. I wasn't ready to get married. I wasn't ready to commit and settle down. This guy Dave had promised to devote the rest of his life to making a home and family with this woman and I was really just a jerk for taking advantage of the situation.

"Patty! - I'm Sorry! - I'm truly sorry!" I could feel the tears welling in my eyes. I stepped out of the car and softly shut the door.

Theo had opened the front door for his date and I stopped him as he was walking to the driver's side.

"Theo! – Please take Patty back to her dorm and then come back and pick me up! – I'll explain later! - Please!" I requested.

Theo looked at me with a questioned expression and agreed. It was only about fifteen minutes before I saw Theo's headlights flash as he pulled to the curb and I climbed into the back seat. Theo and his date said Patty cried all the way back and they asked, "What on earth did you do to that girl?"

I didn't try to make myself look innocent. I told them as bluntly as possible what the situation was. They said it was not my fault. Patty was a grown woman and if she was not curious and didn't have a little interest in me she would not have gone out with me.

I explained that her sister and brother in-law had raised her; she felt she owed them a lot and they wanted her to go out with me. I had never met Dave and felt maybe Mary and Ed were uneasy about the wedding. I wasn't going to be the jerk that broke them up.

I will mention here that Patty and Dave stayed happily married for many years until his untimely death in a drowning accident in the Bahamas. Mary and Ed adored their kids.

Man, the supply of girls was slim. The faceless lady found her way to Savannah and would frequently visit me at night. Mary Delegal was off in College – Ann Fraps had moved to Atlanta – Hazel Banks had married Harvey Thaxton – Carolyn Vanbrackle married Jimmy Hart – Charlotte Carter married Joe Buhler, Ann Rutland was engaged, and Phyllis had married Jack Brown. A lot of the girls I knew were still in their last year of college.

I would call, trying to reach an old girlfriend and talk to a younger sister that was now older. That's how I met Rose Mary Smith. She was a sweet girl but also off in college. It was hard to build a relationship when you only see someone once or twice a month. I didn't realize it at the time, but my biological clock was ticking and that, along with Gods plan, was giving me problems.

I made a down payment on a home and the family moved to 504 E. 66th Street, right next door to the District Plant Manager, Mr. Charlie Spiers. Momma and Daddy made the payments and I paid rent. It seemed to be working pretty good.

I had now moved to the Installation – Repair Department and was working in Garden City, Georgia. It was a prime location, and I really liked it. Mr. Shuman was my boss.

One day I ran across an old friend from my neighborhood in Twickingham. John Chapman lived in the next block up on Screven Avenue. His Dad owned a taxi franchise and had a magnetic taxi sign that he put on the roof of his Chevy. When John and I would double date he would take the sign off and it was a regular car. John and I had a lot of fun in that old Chevy.

I was lamenting about the girl situation to John when he asked how I felt about dating younger girls. I told him the only ones I knew were at Church and they were like seven years younger.

"How about a seventeen year old - Lynn?" John smiled as he asked this.

"Well that's only five years -- I guess it would be OK -- if she were out of school!" I reluctantly figured that the five year difference may not be too much.

"Look! – My fiancé and I just broke up and I'm sure she'll like you. Let's call her and I'll introduce you!" He was sincere in his intent, but I felt sure he was using me as a ploy to simply get back in touch with his ex -fiancé.

We stopped at a payphone at the intersection of "Bee" Road and Anderson Street. John even used his money to place the call.

His ex's name was Judy Bowen and after a brief explanation he handed me the phone.

She sounded pleasant and very intelligent on the phone and I asked her out. She was a totally honest person and made it quite clear that she wanted to see me first.

She gave me the address and it was only a few blocks away from our location. John wanted to go as well, but I told him of my suspicions and he got miffed at my accusation.

I apologized for revealing my feelings, but for him to introduce me and then go with me was a bit much. I'll bet he was looking around the corner when I drove up to Judy's home.

She was a looker. She was by far the best looking little gal I had ever attempted to date. She was five feet, one inch tall, 100 pounds with dark brown moderate length hair in a ponytail. She was as shapely as any girl can get without being too stacked. Her legs were gorgeous. Her eyes sparkled with that innocent fire of desire for life. Apparently she liked what she saw because she agreed to go with me for a coke.

We talked and she did indeed, "talk the ears off a brass donkey!" I quote the exact words that John used when he described her. She made it quite plain to me that her relationship with John, even though they were engaged was not a serious thing. Judy said she really didn't know why she accepted John's proposal. She said, maybe she just was caught up in the big girl thing.

It was not even dark when I took her home. We talked about going to Church the next morning. I declined, because I was now the high school boy's teacher at Clayton P. Miller. I think maybe this impressed her and we agreed on her Church for Sunday night.

I enjoyed the Service at Morningside Baptist Church that Sunday night. It was a short sermon and a lot of singing. Judy and I went to the Triple X for a coke and fries after the service.

Judy began to tell me of her life's plans. She had a job with the FBI and was to report to Washington in a few weeks. She was going up on the train with a girlfriend, Barbara Adams. Both had secured jobs and were going to be in the typing pool at the bureau.

"OH! – By the way!" Judy explained. "John is going to law school in Washington and is staying with his uncle that happens to be a prominent lawyer there. -- He's going to ride up with us on the train."

Her innocent plans clearly told me this romance was not over, her and the ex- fiancé on a lengthy train ride, in the same town for a prolonged period of time.

DUH! I no longer wondered why John didn't mind loaning his girl to me for a weekend. I never called Judy back.

I was at the Triple X a couple of weeks later and John drove up. I got out of my car and walked over to speak and sure enough, there sat Judy in the front seat with John.

Judy look at me and in a somewhat put out tone asked me. "Why haven't you called me?"

I was not prepared for this and simply replied. "I've been busy."

I spoke to John and wished them luck as they were leaving the next day.

I threw myself into my work and was really getting in shape. I bought a new car. I now was the proud owner of a magnificent, black and white 1960 Town Victoria with a 352 cubic inch police engine. It was a dream with red plush interior. Ford was proud of its new paint job that was called a "Diamond Luster Finish." It was nothing more than a controlled orange peel finish that provided a very small texture to reflect more light.

I sure was proud of that car. It was not fast though. Everything in town outran me. I had a buddy that drove a six cylinder Plymouth Station Wagon. He could even take me to about fifty. It was depressing, but I managed to live with it.

The dating scene was also still depressing. Summer had gone and fall was virtually over.

My Union, the CWA, had scheduled our annual Christmas dance at the Desoto Hotel on December 5th, 1959 and I had asked the little soda clerk at the West Side Soda Shop to go with me.

We Westside telephone men would eat our lunches at the Soda Shop and would dance a little when the boss wasn't looking. I was really looking forward to the bash because this little gal could really dance.

The dance was Saturday night and when I came into the soda shop for lunch on Thursday, I could tell by the look on her face that something was wrong.

"Lynn! – I'm so sorry! -- My boyfriend came around last night and we went back together. He asked me to marry him and I said yes! – Oh! -- Lynn! -- I'm so sorry!" She was about to cry.

I assured her it was alright and it really was. I was resigned not to ever cause any girl any romantic grief. I asked the guy's name and was shocked to hear it was Lynn Jeffers. I knew Lynn and had no idea he cared for this girl. Here I was, two days before the big dance and no date. God still had a plan.

The next morning, my first job was to go to a fairly new shopping plaza, across from Memorial Hospital. I had to run the drop wires for a PBX crew that was installing multi–key telephones in some new shops. One of the new businesses was the Stagg Shop. In the process of terminating the wires I saw Butch Miltiades.

I called to Butch and to my surprise found he and Billy were going into the men's clothing business. Butch informed me that Billy was home and had plans to leave the FBI Bureau. He told me Billy would be there shortly.

Billy and I went to lunch at the Wig Wam Restaurant on DeRenne Ave. There were a lot of telephone people there. We had a central office next door and a work center only a few blocks away. Billy and I sat at a booth and talked of old times.

I asked Billy if he knew Judy Bowen. I told him of the two brief dates I had and about John and fully expected him to say something to the effect he had heard she married some guy from Savannah.

Billy thought for a moment and then asked some question about how petite and pretty she was. It only took a few questions before we knew we were talking about the same girl.

Billy said she was the talk of the single guys at the Bureau. She was very aloof and did not party. She was reclusive and he was pretty sure she had quit and came home. It was something about her sick Mother.

God had a plan and Billy just played his part in it.

As soon as the hasty lunch was over I beat it to the work center at 4905 Paulsen Street and found a secluded office to call Judy. Sure enough, she answered the phone.

I re-introduced myself on the phone, hoping the three months that passed had not dimmed her memory of me. She didn't voice any great enthusiasm over my call, but she listen politely as I apologized for not calling her sooner about the big dance. I was careful not to give the impression she was second choice, after all, I thought she was still in Washington.

I told her of the chance encounter with Billy Miltiades and maybe fate was involved here. I was honest and then told her of my previous date. I immediately remembered Judy had said she liked to dance, so I began to concentrate on how big a deal this dance was and the prominent band that was playing and it was in the main ballroom of the Desoto Hotel. She bought it. Whew! I had a date.

I never knew red could look so good! She stepped into the light of her living room and did a demure little pose for me. It was an innocent childish gesture that simply asked. "How do I look?" I was speechless. The previous three occasions I had seen this beauty she was just dressed as an everyday teenager.

This time it was different. Her dark eyes sparkled in the lamp light from beside her Dad's easy chair. The long earrings flashed tongues of fire as they dangled from under her hair that was now down in a fashionable flurry of soft curls that barely covered her smooth satin neck. The red velvet dress was knee length and caressed her dainty waist with not even a hint of a wrinkle. The heels were just high enough to raise her five feet frame to my chin. She flashed a smile that told me she was excited about the dance.

I noticed her mouth. It was not the least bit pouty but had a delicate purse about it. I immediately wanted to kiss those lips that resembled perfect little ruby red, rose petals. She was beyond the wildest expectation of a young man's dream!

I was the envy of the bachelors at the dance. Judy and I tied in a dance contest with the reigning telephone company dance champions, Buddy Newton and his wife.

We won a fifth of liquor and took it to our table. Judy was thrilled to find that I didn't drink so the guys at our table all shared our prize.

It was a swell dance. I got to kiss those ruby red, rose petal lips, good-night. They tasted as good as they looked. As I lay in my bed that night, the faceless lady came to me. I had never noticed she had ruby red, rose petal lips.

God has a plan for everyone. You must simply follow His Plan.

Eighteen days later I gave Judy a ring. Fifty-four years later, I still kiss those ruby red, rose petal lips. I never saw the faceless lady again.

NOT THE END OF THIS STORY